S0-AVD-646

AutoCAD® 2000
Instant Reference

George Omura

B. Robert Callori

San Francisco • Paris • Düsseldorf • Soest • London

SYBEX®

Associate Publisher: Amy Romanoff
Contracts & Licensing Manager: Kristine O'Callaghan
Acquisitions & Developmental Editor: Melanie Spiller
Editor: Diane Lowery
Technical Editor: Michael Gunderloy
Book Designer: Patrick Dintino
Electronic Publishing Specialist: Maureen Forys, Happenstance Type-O-Rama
Production Coordinator: David Zielonka
Proofreader: Emily K. Wolman
Indexer: Nancy Guenther
Cover Designer: Design Site
Cover Illustrator: Sergie Loobkoff

Library of Congress Card Number: 99-61304
ISBN: 0-7821-2497-6

Manufactured in the United States of America

10 9 8 7 6 5 4 3 2 1

I wish to dedicate the book to Earl Halstead. His special friendship and caring in the last 20 years has helped me persevere during the execution of these projects by undertaking the greater share of responsibilities normally required for daily survival, so that I could meet deadlines and commitments.

Acknowledgments

It takes the expertise and perseverance of trained professionals to make this project successful. It started as a team effort among Sybex authors David Frey, Bill Hill, and George Omura, with guidance from Acquisitions and Development Editor Melanie Spiller and Associate Publisher Amy Romanoff. Next, it required the fortitude and delicate scrutiny of Editor Diane Lowery combined with the acquired AutoCAD knowledge of Technical Editor Mike Gunderloy. Finally, I would like to thank Electronic Publishing Specialist Maureen Forys, Production Coordinator David Zielonka, Proofreader Emily Wolman, and Indexer Nancy Guenther. Michael Gallup and Jim Stoffers also deserve mention, because they have also helped soften the impact of those difficult and demanding times in my life.

Introduction

As many times as I have enjoyed updating this Instant Reference, I always perceive the experience as an anticipated new change. The scope unquestionably demands countless hours of dedication, research, and hard work. However, I welcome the responsibility because I know that the contents of this book will facilitate and enrich your understanding of the AutoCAD 2000 program.

New Features with AutoCAD 2000

AutoCAD 2000 comes with some of the following new features, which will be discussed in this book:

- Multiple document environment
- AutoCAD DesignCenter
- Direct browser access
- Layouts for multiple Paper Spaces
- Polar tracking
- Partial open and partial load of AutoCAD drawings
- Plotter Manager and Plot Style Editor
- 3D visualization tools
- Lineweight with WYSIWYG screen display
- Visual LISP Editor
- VBA Manager
- IntelliMouse (Pan and Zoom) support
- Command-specific shortcut menus
- In-place block and reference editing
- Object Properties Manager
- Dbconnect Manager

How This Book Is Organized

This book presents commands and features in alphabetical order. Most entries adhere to the following structure:

1. The *name* of the command or feature appears as a heading.
2. A short paragraph or two follows the command heading, explaining the command's *purpose*.
3. Unless the procedure is completely obvious, *instructions* on using the command follow a head that takes the form *To Do Such and Such*. The

instructions take you through the prompts and/or dialog settings that AutoCAD displays. They also tell you what information AutoCAD requires to complete the command.

4. Many AutoCAD commands present choices or options. Short descriptions of these options and notes on how to select them are presented in the *Options* section.

5. *Notes, Tips*, and *Warnings* identify command restrictions and shortcuts as well as point out possible trouble spots.

6. *See Also* directs you to related entries for further information.

We have also used the following typographic conventions. Command prompts are generally displayed in numbered sequence in boldface. Command options are initial cap, and system variables are in italic. Prompts that appear after commands and filenames are in program font (e.g., acad.pgp).

Working from the Command Line

All AutoCAD commands can be started by typing the command at the command prompt. They can also be selected from a pull-down menu or picked from a toolbar or dialog. Not all commands are available from the pull-down menu or a toolbar. Most commands will either execute immediately or prompt you for further information in the floating (or docked) command window or in a dialog that pops open. If you prefer the command-line approach, you can use the *Filedia* system variable to turn off the dialog in most cases. Some commands, such as **Layer**, **Block**, and **Linetype,** display a dialog instead of prompts at the command line. If you wish to use one of these commands at the command line, enter it by typing a hyphen in front of the command, such as **-Layer**. All hyphenated commands have been included in this book. Commands that are associated with shortcut keys with their alias stored in the acad.pgp file or that can be entered at the command line with one or two keystrokes are identified for each AutoCAD command.

Working with AutoCAD Dialogs

Dialogs allow you to see all the options necessary for an operation at one time. Make sure that *Filedia* is set to On (1). If *Filedia* is Off and you only wish to override it for the current command, type a ~ (tilde) at any prompt asking for a filename. Some commands open dialogs that can be docked or are floating with cells that feature drop-down boxes and allow you to drop-and-drag components into multiple drawing files in a single session. When a dialog opens, the cursor changes from a crosshair to an arrow, which you position on the item you want by moving and clicking a mouse (or some other point-and-click device) or by pressing the Tab key on your keyboard. You can also press and hold the Alt key on your keyboard and type the letter that is underscored in the item you want to pick. For example, typing **Alt+P** will activate the *Pattern* edit box for keyboard entry. The following dialog operations are standard throughout the AutoCAD dialog system:

- To select an item with the cursor, click the arrow on the item you want to pick.

- To type information in an edit box, click the arrow inside the edit box to place the cursor where you want it.

- To move a slide bar, drag the arrow in the direction you want (hold the mouse button down while moving the mouse).

- To toggle a radio button or check box, simply click it.

- To select a specific tab in a dialog box, click the tabbed section name.

- To expand a pop-up or drop-down list, double-click it.

- To view an image tile, double-click it.

- To pick an icon button, click it.

- To stretch a column heading or drag division, press your cursor over the vertical line to the right of the column until an anchor symbol appears, and then drag to expand or shrink its size.

- To expand or restore dialog boxes containing a Details>> or Details<< button, click the button.

- To display a cursor menu inside a dialog, press your right mouse button. This feature is available for dialogs such as Layer and Linetype.

- To toggle a command at the status bar, click it.

Working with the Windows Toolbars

AutoCAD 2000 comes with a set of standard toolbars. Frequently used commands are grouped on the toolbars for easy access. Toolbars can be docked on any side of the AutoCAD window or left floating in the drawing workspace. To dock a toolbar, click the toolbar's title bar. Each command (or subgroup of commands) is represented by a distinctive "coolbar" icon or button. Coolbar icons, which appear seamless by default, become raised and display a *ToolTip* when you rest your pointing device over an icon. This setting can be turned off in the Toolbar dialog by unchecking Show ToolTips. At the same time, a short description of its function appears in the status line. To start a command, simply click the icon and follow the prompts or provide information as required in the dialog. When you click an icon with a arrow (▶) in the lower right corner, yet another nested toolbar (called a flyout) appears, offering more choices within the command group. Note that any flyout icon you choose becomes the "default" and will appear on top of the flyout in the future. This setting is controlled by checking Show This Button's Icon in the Flyout Properties subdialog. To display the Flyout Properties subdialog (in the Toolbar dialog), right-click any icon to display a shortcut menu, pick Customize…, and then right-click the specific flyout button.

INSTANT
REFERENCE

AutoCAD 2000

A-Z

About

About identifies your AutoCAD version serial numbers, copyright data, and personal information entered during installation.

To Access AutoCAD Information

Command line: **About** (or **'About**, to use transparently)

Menu: Help ➤ About AutoCAD

Toolbar: None

See Also   Stats, Status

Acad.lsp

Acad.lsp file is not included with your AutoCAD software. Users must create this file to store and load their AutoLISP routines on startup of an Auto-CAD session. Checking Load acad.lsp with Every Drawing in the System tab of the Options dialog lets you control the loading of acad.lsp into every drawing or just in the first drawing opened in your AutoCAD session.

See Also   AutoLISP; *System Variable:* Acadlspasdoc

Acad.pgp

Acad.pgp is the ProGram Parameters ASCII file that contains information needed to launch a DOS program from within AutoCAD; it is also the location for command alias definitions. For example, Notepad is included in the acad.pgp file as an external Windows command and can be entered at the AutoCAD command line to edit text files that do not require formatting.

To Add External Commands and Aliases

Each external command has a maximum of four parts, each separated by a comma. The following terms describe the entries for Notepad, which have already been assigned by AutoCAD to represent the DOS executable notepad.exe in the acad.pgp file.

    NOTEPAD, START NOTEPAD, 1, *File to edit:,

- The first item is the command name you wish to use at the AutoCAD command prompt—NOTEPAD in our example.

- The second item is the actual command as it would be entered at the operating system prompt. The command **Start** opens a second window for the application—START NOTEPAD in our example.

- The third item is the Bit flag field that specifies how the application should run:

  - Bit value 1: start application and don't wait for it to finish

  - Bit value 2: start application minimized

  - Bit value 4: run the application "hidden"

  - Bit value 8: put the argument string in

- You can add these bits to combine their meaning, similar to the examples shown:

  - Bit value 0: start application and wait for it to finish

  - Bit value 3: start application minimized and don't wait for it to finish

  - Bit value 5: run the application "hidden" and don't wait for it to finish

- Bit values 2 and 4 temporarily suspend access to AutoCAD until the application has completed. Bit value 8 has some limitations but can be useful with long filenames containing spaces. The fourth item specifies the prompt (if there is one) that appears after the command is issued. An asterisk (optional) preceding the prompts tells AutoCAD to accept spaces within the user's response. If there is no prompt, this item can be blank–*File to edit:, is the prompt in our example.

- The command alias format is simple.

  AR, *ARRAY

  The first item, AR, is the alias or command that you would enter at the command line. It is followed by a comma, a space, an asterisk, and the name of the command being aliased.

  Use **Reinit** or **Re-init** to reinitialize the acad.pgp file if you edit it and want to activate those changes in the current drawing session.

NOTE The acad.pgp file also contains a list of aliases of discontinued commands.

See Also   *Express Tool:* Aliasedit; *System Variable:* Re-init

Acisin/Acisout
*See **Import/Export***

Adcenter

Opens the AutoCAD DesignCenter as a docked window at the left side of the display screen, serving as a content manager for various file-management and drawing-insertion procedures. You can hide or float the dialog by right-clicking over the title bar and choosing an option from the menu. To Allow Docking or to Hide the dialog, right-click along the bottom edge of the title bar; otherwise, picking the title bar displays menu options to Move, Size, or Hide. You can also dock/undock by just double-clicking the title bar.

TIP If you toggle Allow Docking off, move the dialog into position by picking it along the bottom edge of the title bar with your pointing device.

To Display the AutoCAD DesignCenter

Command line: **Adcenter**, **Adc**, **Ctrl+2** (or **'Adcenter** to use transparently)

Menu: Tools ➤ AutoCAD DesignCenter

Standard Toolbar: 🔳 AutoCAD DesignCenter

AutoCAD DesignCenter

The DesignCenter dialog displays a window divided into two panes; a profile on the left and a palette on the right offering options to view folders and files, various object types in a drawing, content from third-party developers, and the Web.

Tree View Toggle Toggles display mode of the DesignCenter into single or multiple panes.

Desktop Depending on the view selected, displays drawing preview with associated description, file, folder, and drive letter information in the Explorer window format.

Open Drawing Lists all drawings open in the current session. Double-clicking a filename extends the list to display block names, dimension styles, layer names, layouts, linetypes, and text styles associated with each drawing.

History Tracks and saves the names of the last 20 drawings that were open between sessions.

Favorites Depending on the view selected, displays a shortcut to the Profiles\Favorites\Autodesk folder and its contents. You can right-click any object to add it to Favorites.

Load   Opens the Load DesignCenter Palette dialog offering the Standard File Selection features that load the palette with content from Windows desktop, AutoCAD Favorites, and Internet locations. See **File Selection Dialog Features**.

Find   Displays the Find dialog to locate specific drawing information. See **Find**.

Move   Moves the current path up one level. Each level or path may contain additional subfolders and/or files.

Preview   Displays a preview image window of files selected in the palette window at bottom portion of the DesignCenter dialog.

Description   Opens a text description, such as a file path, creation date, and time, at bottom of the palette window of item previewed.

Views   Toggles the way items are displayed in the DesignCenter. The adjacent arrow displays a menu with the same options, allowing selection of Large Icons, Small Icons, a List, or Details format with adjustable column headers.

Shortcut Menu   Right-clicking the Profile (left) windowpane displays the shortcut menu with operating-system commands for **Explore**, **Find**, **Add to Favorites**, and **Organize Favorites**. Right-clicking the Palette (right) windowpane displays the shortcut menu with the above choices as well as *Refresh,* which updates new listings in the window.

See Also   Adcclose

Adcclose

Adcclose closes the AutoCAD DesignCenter.

To Close the AutoCAD DesignCenter

Command line: **Adcclose**

Menu: none

Toolbar: none

See Also   Adcenter

Ai_box

See 3D

Ai_cone

See **3D**

Ai_dish

See **3D**

Ai_mesh

See **3D**

Ai_molc

Ai_molc sets the layer of the object you select as the current layer. Generally, **Ai_molc** is executed from the Object Properties toolbar.

To Set a Layer Current

Command line: **Ai_molc**

Object Properties Toolbar: 🔲 Make Object's Layer Current

Select object whose layer will become current: Select an object on a layer you wish to set as current.

Ai_pyramid

See **3D**

Ai_sphere

See **3D**

Ai_torus

See **3D**

Ai_wedge

See **3D**

Align

Align moves, rotates, and scales objects in 2D or 3D using source points on the original object and destination points on the references object.

To Align Objects

Command line: **Align, Al**

Menu: Modify ➤ 3D Operation ➤ Align

1. **Select objects:** Pick objects to move, rotate, and scale, and then respond to steps 2–5 to align an object in only 2D, or continue to step 7 to move, rotate, and scale objects in 3D space.

2. **Specify first source point:** Select first source point on object you wish to align.

3. **Specify first destination point:** Select new position of first destination point where object is to be realigned.

4. **Specify second source point:** Select second source point on object you wish to align.

5. **Specify second destination point:** Select second destination point where object is to be realigned.

6. **Specify third source point or <continue>:** To relocate the object in 3D, specify the next pair of points, or press Enter for 2D alignment options.

7. **Scale objects based on alignment points? [Yes/No] <No>:** Enter **No** to rotate the object from the source point to the destination point and **Yes** to rotate and scale the object directly from the source point to the destination point.

See Also   Mirror3d, Move, Rotate3d; *Express Tools:* Arctext

Ameconvert

*See **Solid Modeling***

Aperture

Aperture sets the size of the Osnap (object snap) target box to your preference. The equivalent dialog command is **Ddosnap**.

To Set the Size of the Osnap Target Box

Command line: **Aperture (**or **'Aperture**, to use transparently)

Object snap target height (1–50 pixels) <10>: Enter the desired size of Osnap target in pixels. Default settings may vary depending on your display.

See Also Ddselect, Options (Drafting Tab) Osnap; *System Variables:* Aperture, Pickbox

---

Appload

Appload displays a dialog for loading and unloading AutoCAD applications.

To Load Applications

Command line: **Appload, Ap** (or **'Appload**, to use transparently)

Menu: Tools ➤ Load Application…

Options

Lookin/Filename/Files of Type   The top portion of the dialog offers standard file selection features. See **Standard File Selection Dialog Box**.

Load   Loads or reloads one or more selected file(s) from the list box, based on the files of type listed in the drop-down box; apply this step by using <shift> or <ctrl> key combinations with the mouse pick button or by dragging and dropping to the Loaded Applications tab. If the *Add to History* box is checked, applications are also appended to the History List tab.

Unload/Remove   Toggle to Unload all applications, except LISP and ARX from the Load Applications tab, or Remove selected items from the History List tab. Right-clicking displays a shortcut menu in the History List tab with options to Load, Remove, and Add to Startup Suite.

Contents   Opens the Startup Suite dialog with buttons to Add and Remove selected applications at the start of each AutoCAD session. Applications, except those from the AutoCAD Web browser, can also be loaded by choosing Add to Startup Suite from the shortcut menu in the History list.

Status Line   Reports the success of applications being loaded and is located below the tabbed sections.

TIP You can drag application files from other sources that support dragging into the Loaded Applications tab.

Close   Exits the dialog.

See Also   Arx, Options (System Tab)

Arc

Arc allows you to draw an arc using a variety of methods. The system prompts shown below will vary with the options chosen.

To Draw an Arc

Command line: **Arc, A**

Menu: Draw ➤ Arc ➤ Preset Options

Draw Toolbar: Arc

1. **Specify start point of arc or [CEnter]:** Pick start point of the arc, or select **CE** for more options.

2. **Specify second point of arc or [CEnter/ENd]:** Pick second point of the arc, or select **CE** to Specify center of arc or **EN** to Specify end point of arc:.

    Depending on the option selected, prompt 3 or 4 will appear:

3. **Specify end point of arc or [Angle/chord Length]:** Pick the end point of the arc, or enter an option as described below.

4. **Specify center point of arc or [Angle/Direction/Radius]:** Pick the center of the arc, or specify a value for selected option.

Options

Angle   Enters an arc in terms of degrees or current angular units. The Specify included angle: prompt appears. You can enter an angle value or use the cursor to select angle points onscreen.

Center   Enters the location of an arc's center point. At the prompt Specify center point of arc:, enter a coordinate, or pick a point with your cursor.

Direction   Enters a tangent direction from the start point of an arc. At the prompt Specify tangent direction for the start point of arc:, enter a relative coordinate, or pick a point with your cursor.

End   Enters the end point of an arc. At the prompt Specify end point of arc:, enter a coordinate, or pick a point with your cursor.

Chord Length   Enters the length of an arc's chord. At the prompt Specify length of chord:, enter a length, or drag and pick a length with your cursor.

Radius   Enters an arc's radius. At the prompt Specify radius of arc:, enter a radius, or pick a point that defines a radius length.

Start Point   Enters the beginning point of an arc.

If you press ↵ at the first prompt of the **Arc** command, AutoCAD uses the most recent point entered for a line or arc as the first point of the new arc. It then prompts you for a new end point. An arc is drawn at a tangent to the last line or arc drawn.

If you select **Arc** from the pull-down menu, the Arc Cascading menu appears with preset arc options. For example, Start, End, and Direction allow you to select the start point, end point, and direction of the arc. Figure A.1 illustrates how these options draw arcs.

You can convert arcs to lightweight polyline arcs with the **Pedit** or **Bpoly** command. You can also lengthen existing arcs using the **Lengthen** command.

See Also   Bpoly, Circle, Change, Elev, Ellipse, Lengthen, Pedit, Polyline, UCS, Viewres

FIGURE A.1:   The Arc menu options and their meanings

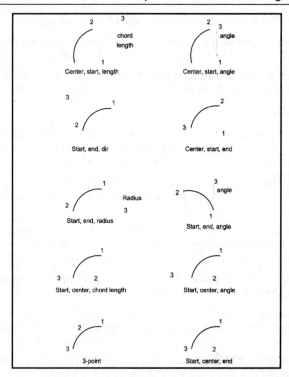

Area

Area carries out an area calculation based on dimensions that you specify by defining line segments, by selecting lines and polylines, or by doing both.

To Calculate an Area

Command line: **Area**, **A**

Menu: Tools ➤ Inquiry ➤ Area

Standard Toolbar: Distance Flyout Area

Inquiry Toolbar: Area

1. **Specify first corner point or [Object/Add/Subtract]:** Pick first point, or enter option.
2. **Specify next corner point or press ENTER for total:** Pick the next point. Continue picking points until you have defined the area, and then press ⏎ to display the calculated area and perimeter in the following format:

   ```
   Area = <Calculated area>, Perimeter = <Perimeter>
   ```

   The option for Object displays the calculated area and length in the following format:

   ```
   Area = <Calculated area>, Length = <Length>
   ```

Options

Next Corner Point   Continue selecting points until you have defined the area to be calculated. Once you have defined the area, press ⏎ at the Specify next corner point or press ENTER for total: prompt.

Object   Select a circle or polyline for area calculation. If you pick an open polyline, AutoCAD will calculate the area of the polyline as if its two end points were closed.

Add   Keeps a running count of areas. Normally, **Area** returns you to the command prompt as soon as an area has been calculated. If you enter **A** for the Add mode, you are returned to the **Area** command prompt once an area has been calculated, and you can continue to add area values to the current area.

Subtract   Enter **S** to toggle the subtract mode. Subtracts areas from a running count of areas.

Enter   Pressing Enter exits the command.

   Area does not calculate areas for arcs. To find the area of a shape that includes arcs, you must convert the arc areas into polylines (see **Pedit**) before you issue the **Area** command. Select the Object option, and pick the polyline—**Area** will calculate the area of the polyline. Add all the polyline areas to rectangular areas to arrive at the total area. You can also obtain areas for ellipses, splines, polygons, regions, or solids. Use **Bpoly** to create a closed polyline automatically. **Area** only calculates areas in a plane parallel to the current user coordinate system.

See Also Bhatch, Bpoly, Dblist, Dist, Id, List, Pedit; *System Variables:* Area, Perimeter

Array

Array makes multiple copies of an object or group of objects in a row- and-column matrix, a single row or column, or a circular array (to form such objects as teeth in a gear or the numbers on a circular clock).

To Create Object Arrays

Command line: **Array**, **Ar**

Menu: Modify ➤ Array

Modify Toolbar: 🔳 Array

1. **Select objects:** Pick objects to array.

2. **Enter the type of array [Rectangular or Polar] <R>/P):** Enter desired array type.

If you enter **R**, you are given the following series of prompts:

Specify center point of array: Pick the center of rotation.

Enter the number of rows (---) <1>: Enter the number of rows.

Enter the number of columns (|||) <1>: Enter the number of columns.

Enter the distance between rows or specify unit cell(---): Enter the numeric distance between rows or depth of cell (see Unit Cell option below).

Enter the distance between columns (|||): Enter the numeric distance between columns.

If you enter **P** for the Polar option at the Enter the type of array [Rectangular or Polar] <R>/P): prompt, you are asked for the following information:

Specify center point of array: Pick a center point for the polar array.

Enter the number of items in the array: Enter number of items in the array, including the originally selected objects.

Specify the angle to fill (+=ccw,-=cw) <360>: Enter the angle the array is to occupy. Use a negative value to indicate a clockwise array.

Rotate arrayed objects? [Yes/No] <Y>: Enter **N** if the arrayed objects are to maintain their current orientation or **Y** to rotate objects.

Options

Rectangular   Copies the selected objects in an array of rows and columns. You are then prompted for the number of rows and columns and the distance between them.

Polar   Copies the selected objects in a circular array. You are prompted first for the center point of the array and then for the number of items in the array. If you press ⏎ without entering a value at the Enter the number of items in the array: prompt, you will be prompted for the angle between items.

Unit Cell   Enter the size of the rectangular unit cell by picking two points dynamically or with an Osnap mode. After picking the first point, you are given the Specify opposite corner: prompt. Select an opposite diagonal corner for the unit cell.

Usually, row-and-column arrays are aligned with the X and Y axes of your current user-coordinate system. A positive distance number copies objects to the right and/or upward; a negative number copies object to the left and/or downward. To create an array at an angle, set the **Snap** command's Rotate option to the desired angle. Rectangular arrays will be rotated by the snap angle. The *Snapang* system variable also allows you to set the cursor rotation angle. The order in which you select the two points for the Unit Cell option determines the direction of the array.

See Also   Copy, Minsert, Select, Snap/Rotate, 3Darray; *System Variable:* Snapang

ARX

Loads, unloads, and furnishes information relating to **ARX** applications, such as third-party CAD software programs, or internal applications, such as Render or ASE.

To Load or Unload ARX Applications

Command line: **Arx**

Enter an option [?/Load/Unload/Commands/Options]: Specify an option as described below.

Options

?   Lists the **ARX** applications that are loaded in current drawing.

Load   Displays the Select ARX/DBX File dialog with the standard file-selection features to locate an **ARX** or **DBX** filename.

Unload   Displays prompt Enter an option [?/Load/Unload/Com-mands/Options]: Enter name of **ARX** or **DBX** file to unload.

Command   AutoCAD lists the commands registered by extension programs.

Options   Depending on the option selected, the Enter an option [Group/ Classes/Services] prompt appears. Group prompts for the Command Group Name:, Classes lists hierarchy for specific **ARX** applications, and Services displays the names of services entered into the arxService Dictionary.

ASE

ASE has been discontinued. AutoCAD has aliased the **ASE** command to **Dbconnect** in the acad.ppp file. See **Dbconnect**.

Attachurl

Attachurl attaches a URL to objects or areas in your drawing. A URL can be attached as Xdata (extended data) to one or more objects. Use the object method if geometry is scattered throughout the drawing. Attaching a URL by area places a rectangle around the specified area. Use area if there is no geometry.

To Attach a URL

Command line: **Attachurl**

Enter hyperlink insert option [Area/Object] <Object> : Specify an option.

Options

Area   Pick *First corner:* and *Other corner:* using window selection methods, and then specify a name at the Enter URL: prompt.

Object   First *Select objects:* to be attached, and then specify a name, such as <filename>.html, or press ↵ to accept the current drawing's name at the Enter hyperlink <current drawing>: prompt.

WARNING AutoCAD creates a layer named *urllayer* with the color red when selecting the Area option. Deleting, freezing, locking, or changing the visibility of the layer urllayer can destroy the hyperlink information in your drawing. Modifying the rectangles on urllayer or attaching URLs to them can create problematic results. If you turn the urllayer off, turn it on prior to using the **Dwfout** command.

See Also Detachurl, Dwfout, Gotourl, Inserturl, Listurl, Openurl, Selecturl; *Express Tools:* Browser

Attdef

Attdef opens the Attribute Definition dialog that lets you create attribute definitions that can store textual and numeric data with a block. The equivalent command-line prompt is **–Attdef**.

To Use the Attribute Definition Dialog

Command line: **Attdef**

Menu: Draw ➤ Block ➤ Define Attributes...

Provide information as needed in the dialog.

Options

Mode Sets Invisible, Constant, Verify, and Preset modes.

Attribute Sets Tag name, input Prompt, and default Value.

Insertion Point Allows you to Pick Point, or enter the XYZ coordinates.

Text Options Sets text Justification, Text Style, Height, or Rotation.

Align Below Previous Attribute Locates an attribute tag below a previously defined attribute.

NOTE Use **Change**, **Properties**, or **Ddedit** to edit the attribute definition. The Properties icon in the Object Properties Toolbar can also be used to edit attribute definitions. Attribute tags are always displayed in uppercase. AutoCAD replaces the tag name with the attribute value once the attribute definitions are inserted as a block.

See Also -Attdef, Attdisp, Attedit, -Attedit, Attext, -Attext, Attredef, Bmake, Change, Chprop, Ddedit, Insert, Mtext, Properties, Text; *System Variables:* Aflags, Attdia, Attmode, Attreq

-Attdef

-Attdef creates an attribute definition that allows you to store textual and numeric data with a block. When you insert a block containing an attribute definition into a drawing, you are prompted for the data that is to be stored with the block. Use **-Attdef** to work from the command line and **Attdef** to work from the Attribute Definition dialog. The **Attdef** command provides the added feature of aligning your new attribute definition below the previous one. Later you can use **Ddatte** to view the data and edit attributes. The **-Attext** and **Attext** commands extract attribute data into an ASCII text file. You can control the format of the extracted file for easy importation to a database manager, spreadsheet, or word-processing program.

To Create an Attribute Definition at the Command Line

Command line: **-Attdef**

1. **Current attribute modes:** Invisible=N Constant=N Verify=N Preset=N

   Enter an option to change [Invisible/Constant/Verify/ Preset] <done>: Enter **I**, **C**, **V**, or **P** to toggle an option on or off, or press ↵ to go to the next prompt.

2. **Enter attribute tag name:** Enter a unique name that can be used to identify and locate the occurrence of its existence in the drawing during extraction. *See* **Attext**.

3. **Enter attribute prompt:** Enter the prompt to be displayed for attribute input in the Edit Attributes dialog.

4. **Enter attribute default value:** Enter default value (if appropriate) for attribute input to automatically appear each time the Edit Attributes dialog opens.

5. **Current text style: "STANDARD"**

   Text height: 0.2000.

   Specify start point of text or [Justify/Style]: Enter coordinates or pick with the cursor to indicate the location of attribute text, or select an option to determine orientation or style of the attribute text.

6. **Specify height (0.2000):** Enter the attribute text height. This prompt appears only if the current text-style height is set to 0.

7. **Specify rotation angle of text <0.00>:** Enter the angle of the attribute text.

Options

Invisible Makes the attribute invisible when inserted. Use the On option of the **Attdisp** command to display invisible attribute values and the Normal option to restore invisibility.

Constant Gives the attribute a value that you cannot change during each insertion.

Verify Allows review of the attribute value after insertion by repeating the prompt and its default value when the *Attdia* system variable is set to 0.

Preset Automatically inputs the default attribute value on insertion. Unlike the Constant option, it lets you change the input value of a pre-set attribute by using the **Ddatte**, **-Attedit**, or **Attedit** commands. See **Text** for Attdef options related to location, style, and orientation of attributes. Use **Change**, **Properties**, or **Ddedit** to edit the attribute definition before making the attribute into a block.

TIP When inserting a block with attributes, the prompt sequence is determined by the order selected during creation of the block.

See Also Attdisp, Attedit, Attext, Attredef, Bmake, Change, Chprop, Ddatte, Ddedit, Insert, Mtext, Text; *System Variables:* Aflags, Attdia, Attmode, Attreq

Attdisp

Attdisp allows you to control the display and plotting of all attributes in a drawing. You can force attributes to be visible or invisible according to their display mode.

To Set Attribute Display Using Attdisp

Command line: **Attdisp** (or '**Attdisp**, to use transparently)

Menu: View ➤ Display ➤ Attribute Display ➤ Options

Enter attribute visibility setting [Normal/ON/OFF] <Normal>: Enter ON, OFF, or ↵ for your selection.

Options

Normal Hides attributes that are set to be invisible. All other attributes are displayed. See **-Attdef**.

ON Displays all attributes, including those set to be invisible.

OFF Hides all attributes, whether or not they are set to be invisible.

If automatic regeneration is on (see **Regenauto**), your drawing will regenerate when you complete the command, and the display of attributes will reflect the option you select. If automatic regeneration is off, the drawing will not regenerate until you issue **Regen**.

See Also   Attdef, Regen, Regenauto; *System Variables:* Aflags, Attmode

Attedit

Attedit and **Ddatte** display the Edit Attributes dialog that lets you view and edit the attribute values of a single block. The equivalent command-line prompt is -**Attedit**.

To Edit Attribute Values

Command line: **Attedit, Ate**

Menu: Modify ➤ Object ➤ Attribute ➤ Single

Modify II Toolbar: Edit Attribute

Select block reference: Pick the block containing the attribute(s) to edit. The Edit Attributes dialog appears containing the attribute prompts and values. Enter new attribute text or edit the existing attribute text by positioning the cursor at the appropriate location, deleting text, and typing your correction.

See Also   Attdef, -Attdef, -Attedit, Attext, -Attext, Attredef, Multiple

-Attedit

-**Attedit** edits attribute values at the command line after you have inserted them in a drawing. You can edit attributes individually or globally.

To Edit Attribute Values at the Command Line

Command line: -**Attedit**

Menu: Modify ➤ Object ➤ Attribute ➤ Global

1. **Edit attributes one at a time? [Yes/No] <Y>:** Enter **Y** for editing of individual attributes. If you enter **N** for global attribute editing, the prompt Performing global editing of attribute values. Edit only attributes visible on screen? [Yes/No] <Y>: appears. If you enter **Y** for global editing, only those attributes visible on the display screen are changed; otherwise, entering **N** toggles the text screen to display prompts 2, 3, and 4.

2. **Enter block name specification <*>:** Press ↵, or enter a block name to restrict the attribute edits to a specific block, or enter a wildcard filter list to limit it to a group of blocks.

3. **Enter attribute tag specification <*>:** Press ↵, or enter an attribute tag to restrict attribute edits to a specific attribute, or enter a wildcard filter list.

4. **Enter attribute value specification <*>:** Press ↵, or enter a value to restrict attribute edits to a specific attribute value, or enter a wildcard to filter a list.

5. **Select Attributes:** Pick the attributes you want to edit. If you elected in step 1 to edit the attributes one at a time, an *X* appears on the first attribute to be edited, and you will see the following prompt:

    Enter an option [Value/Position/Height/Angle/Style/ Layer/Color/Next]<N>: The options in this prompt are discussed below.

Options

Y (at first prompt)   Allows you to edit attribute values one at a time and change an attribute's position, height, angle, text style, layer, and color.

N (at first prompt)   Allows you to modify attribute values globally. If you select this option, you are asked whether you want to edit only visible attributes.

Y (at second prompt)   Allows you to edit attribute values globally appearing on the display screen.

N (at second prompt)   Allows you to edit attributes globally on the text screen by displaying prompts for string values:

-   Enter string to change:
-   Enter new string:

Value   Depending on the option selected, changes or replaces the value of the currently marked attribute(s) when prompted to Enter type of value modification [Change/Replace]<R>:.

Position   Moves selected attribute when prompted to Specify new text insertion point <no change>:.

Height   Changes the height of attribute text when prompted to Specify new height<12.0000>:, or using the attributes insertion point, picks a second point to set a new text height.

Angle   Changes the attribute angle when prompted to Specify new rotation angle<0>:.

Style   Changes the attribute text style when the prompt appears to `Enter new text style <STANDARD>:`.

Layer   Changes the layer that the attribute is on when prompted to `Enter new layer name <0>`.

Color   Changes the attribute color when prompted to `Enter new color name or value <BYLAYER>`. Colors are specified by numeric code or by name. See **Color**.

Next   Displays the next sequential attribute.

If you choose to edit attributes individually and answer all of the prompts (you select **Y** at the first prompt), you are prompted to select attributes. After you have made your selection, an **X** marks the first attribute to edit. The default option, Next, will move the marking **X** to the next attribute.

By entering **V** at the `Enter an option [Value/Position/Height/Angle/Style/Layer/Color/Next]<N>:` prompt, you can either change or replace the attribute value. If you choose Replace, the default option, you are prompted for a new attribute value. The new attribute value replaces the previous one, and you return to the `Value/Position/Height...` prompt. If you choose Change, you are prompted for a specific string of characters to change and for a new string to replace the old. This lets you change portions of an attribute's value without having to enter the entire attribute value. Clicking an attribute's grip also lets you change its position using the Stretch edit option.

If you choose to edit only visible attributes (after entering **N** at the first prompt), you are prompted to select attributes. You can then visually pick the attributes to edit. You are next prompted for the string to change the replacement string. Once you have answered the prompts, AutoCAD changes all the selected attributes. If you enter **N** at the prompt `Visible attribute:`, you won't be prompted to select attributes. Instead, AutoCAD assumes you want to edit all the attributes in the drawing, regardless of whether they are visible. The `Select Attribute:` prompt is skipped, and you are sent directly to the prompt `Change string:`.

When answering the attribute specification prompts, you can use wildcard characters (the question mark, the asterisk, etc.—see **Wildcard Characters**) to "filter" a group of attribute blocks, tags, or values. To restrict attribute edits to attributes that have a null value, enter \ (a backslash) at the `Attribute value specification <*>:` prompt. The **Ddatte** command dialog limits editing to attribute values only.

See Also   Attdef, Attdisp, Attedit, -Attedit, Attext, -Attext, Attredef, Ddatte, Ddedit, Select, Wildcards

Attext

Attext displays an Attribute Extraction dialog allowing you to convert attributes into external ASCII text files. These files can then be imported into database or spreadsheet programs.

To Convert Attributes to ASCII

Command line: **Attext**

Provide information in the dialog as needed.

Options

File Format Pick radio button Comma Deliminated File (CDF), Space Deliminated File (SDF), or DXFFormat Extract File (DXX) format for the extracted file. (See -**Attext** for descriptions of the file formats).

Select Objects< Click to temporarily exit the dialog, allowing you to select the attribute entities.

Template File... Opens the Output File subdialog, displaying a list box showing all cdf/txt extension files from which to make a selection for the corresponding edit box. A template file must have previously been created. A .txt file extension is automatically assigned to the filename in the edit box if you don't enter an extension. You may also enter the drive\path\filename in the edit box.

Output File... Opens the Output File subdialog, displaying a list box showing all .txt files from which to make a selection for the corresponding edit box. When an output filename is selected, the current drawing filename is automatically assigned to the filename in the edit box but with a .txt extension. You may also enter the drive\path\filename in the edit box.

NOTE The Template File... button is disabled when the DXF format is active.

See Also Attdef, Attedit, Multiple

-Attext

-**Attext** converts attribute information into external ASCII text files. You can then bring these files into database or spreadsheet programs for analysis. -**Attext** lets you choose from three standard database and spreadsheet file formats.

To Do an Attext Conversion at the Command Line

Command line: -**Attext**

1. **Enter extraction type or enable object selection [Cdf/Sdf/ Dxf/Objects] <C>:** Enter format of extracted file or **O** for objects to select specific attributes for extraction.

2. If the *Filedia* system variable is set to 1, the Select Template File dialog list box will appear to pick a template file, and the Create Extract File dialog list box will then open to name the extract file.

   If the *Filedia* system variable is set to 0, the command-line prompts are as follows:

   - **Enter template file name:** Enter path and name of the external template file.

   - **Enter extract file name <drawing name>:** Enter path and name of the file to hold the extracted information.

Options

CDF (comma-delimited file)   Creates an ASCII file using commas to delimit fields. Each attribute is treated as a field of a record, and all the attributes in a block are treated as one record. Character fields are enclosed in quotes. Some database can read this format without any alteration.

SDF (space-delimited format)   Creates an ASCII file using spaces to delimit fields. Each attribute is treated as a field of a record, and all attributes in a block are treated as one record. The field values are given a fixed width, and character fields are not given special treatment. If you open this file using a word processor, the attribute values appear as rows and columns. (The rows are the records, and the columns are the fields.)

DXF (data-exchange format)   Creates a subset of the AutoCAD DXX file that contains only the block reference, attribute, and end-of-sequence objects. Objects prompts you to select objects. You can then select specific attributes to extract. Once you are done with the selection, the Attribute extract: prompt reappears.

Both the comma- and space-delimited file formats require template files. Before you can extract attribute values with **Attext**, create a *template file* using an external ASCII text editor—such as Notepad or Wordpad—that contains a list of attribute tags you wish to extract. Template files, which have the extension .txt, also contain a code describing the characteristics of the attributes associated with each tag. The code denotes character and numeric values as well as the number of characters for string values or the number of placeholders for numeric values. For example, if you expect the maximum value entered for a numeric attribute, with the tag "cost," to be five characters long with two decimal places, include the following line in the template file:

```
cost              N005002
```

The *N* indicates that this attribute is a numeric value. The next three characters indicate the number of digits the value will hold. The last three characters indicate the number of decimal places the number will require. If you want to extract a character attribute, you might include the following line in the template file:

```
name          C030000
```

The *C* denotes a character value. The next three characters indicate the number of characters you expect for the attribute value. The last three characters are always zeros, because character values have no decimal places.

Follow the last line in the template file by a ↵, or you will receive an error message when you try to use the template file.

You can also extract information about the block that contains the attributes. Table A.1 shows the format you use in the template file to extract block information. A template file containing these codes must also contain at least one attribute tag, because AutoCAD must know which attribute it is extracting before it can tell which block the attribute is associated.

TABLE A.1: Template Tags and Codes for Extracting Information about Blocks

Tag	Code	Description
BL:LEVEL	N*xxx*000	Level of nesting for block
BL:NAME	C*xxx*000	Block name
BL:X	N*xxxxxx*	X value for block insertion point
BL:Y	N*xxxxxx*	Y value for block insertion point
BL:Z	N*xxxxxx*	Z value for block insertion point
BL:NUMBER	N*xxx*000	Block counter
BL:HANDLE	C*xxx*000	Block handle
BL:LAYER	C*xxx*000	Name of layer block is on
BL:ORIENT	N*xxxxxx*	Block rotation angle
BL:XSCALE	N*xxxxxx*	Block X scale
BL:YSCALE	N*xxxxxx*	Block Y scale
BL:ZSCALE	N*xxxxxx*	Block Z scale
BL:XEXTRUDE	N*xxxxxx*	X value for block extrusion direction
BL:YEXTRUDE	N*xxxxxx*	Y value for block extrusion direction
BL:ZEXTRUDE	N*xxxxxx*	Z value for block extrusion direction

Note: Italicized "x" indicate adjustable numeric variables.

See Also Attdef, -Attdef, Attedit, -Attedit, -Attext, Attredef; *System Variables:* Attdia, Attmode, Attreq, Filedia

Attredef

Attredef allows you to redefine an existing block and delete and/or update the associated attributes.

To Redefine Block Attributes

Command line: **Attredef** (or, **'Attredef** to use transparently)

1. **Enter name of Block you wish to redefine:** Enter the block name.

2. **Select objects for new block:** Select objects and attribute definition(s).

3. **Specify insertion base point of new Block:** Pick a new insertion point for the block. (You will probably want to select the same insertion point as the original block.)

   When you assign new attributes to an existing block reference, they are given default values; existing attributes keep their old values. If an old attribute is not included in the new block definition, it will be deleted from the block reference.

   TIP To avoid unpredictable results, it is important to redefine the attribute using the same insertion point. Drawing a small circle and then inserting the attribute as an exploded object at the circle's center point provides you with the block's same insertion point when the prompt Specify insertion base point of new Block: appears.

See Also   Attedit, -Attedit, Ddate

Audit

Use **Audit** to check a drawing file for errors or corrupted data. If errors are detected, you can choose to have them corrected.

To Use Audit

Command line: **Audit**

Fix any errors detected? <N>: Select **Y** to correct any errors found. Selecting **N** reports errors but will not fix them. If no errors are detected, a screen display like the following will appear:

```
4 Blocks audited
Pass 1 4 objects audited
Pass 2 4 objects audited
total errors found 0 fixed 0
```

Audit creates an ASCII file that contains a report of the audit and any action taken. The file has the extension .adt. The information presented by the **Audit** command may not be important to most users. However, it may help your AutoCAD dealer or Autodesk's product-support department to diagnose a problem with a file.

See Also   Recover; *System Variable:* Auditctl

AutoLISP

AutoLISP is a programming language embedded in AutoCAD. It lets you automate repetitive tasks and add custom commands to AutoCAD. **AutoLISP** enables you to link applications written in C to AutoCAD. Several **AutoLISP** programs are provided with AutoCAD, and others can be obtained from the Autodesk Web site, http://www.autodesk.com.

To Use AutoLISP

1. Enter your AutoLISP program code directly through the command prompt, or write your code with a text editor, such as Notepad, and store it as an ASCII file with the filename extension .lsp.

2. If you save your program code as a file on disk, use the **AutoLISP** *Load* function to load your program while in the AutoCAD drawing editor, or issue the **Appload** command. The following example shows the syntax for the Load function at the command line:

   ```
   (load "drive/directory/file name") ↵
   ```

   You can leave off the drive and directory information if your path points to the directory that holds the AutoLISP programs.

3. You can also open the Load and Unload Applications dialog, save the LISP file in the Loaded Applications or History List tabs, and then activate it by selecting *Load*.

4. Once a program file is loaded, you can use it by entering its name through the keyboard, just like a standard AutoCAD program. You don't have to load the file again while in the current editing session.

Selecting the Contents button in the Startup Suites section will open a dialog where you can Add or Remove LISP files that will automatically load each time you begin an AutoCAD session.

You can combine your favorite AutoLISP programs into a single file, called acad.lsp. Place this file in your AutoCAD directory. It will be loaded automatically every time you open a drawing file. AutoCAD routines do not need reloading and now remain "persistent" throughout the duration of drawing file initialization. AutoLISP code can also be embedded in the AutoCAD menu system.

See Also   Acad.lsp, Appload

Background
*See **Render***

Base

Base sets the drawing's *base point,* a point of reference for insertion when you insert one drawing into another. Select the base point in relation to the world coordinate system (WCS). The default base point for all drawings is the WCS origin point at coordinate 0,0,0.

To Set a Base Point

Command line: **Base** (or **'Base**, to use transparently).

Menu: Draw ➤ Block ➤ Base

Enter base point <0.0000,0.0000,0.0000>: Enter coordinates or pick a point.

NOTE You can enter any valid Object Snap mode at the Enter base point prompt to redefine a drawing's base or insertion point.

See Also -Block, Bmake, Insert, Select, Wblock; *System Variable:* Insbase

Batchplt

Batchplt is a utility that opens the AutoCAD Batch Plot Utility dialog, allowing you to plot multiple AutoCAD drawings to single or multiple devices.

To Run Batch Plotting

On NT 4, this utility starts a new session of AutoCAD 2000 and then starts the batchplot utility.

Assuming you have installed AutoCAD 2000 in the default folder for Windows 95/98 or NT 4, go to the Start menu ➤ Programs ➤ AutoCAD 2000 ➤ Batch Plot Utility.

Options

The AutoCAD Batch Plot Utility dialog box contains a pull-down menu and icons that allow you to select drawing files and previously saved .bp3 plot configurations for batch plotting. The list-box division headings identify the Drawing File, Path, Layout, Page Setup, and Plot Device.

Add Drawing Menu: File ➤ Add Drawing... 🔲 Opens Add Drawing File dialog to search drives, directories, and files, allowing you to select drawing (.dwg) and template (.dwt) files using standard Windows methods for a batch list. Selected files are displayed in a list box.

Remove Menu: File ➤ Remove 🔳 Deletes selected files from the batch list box.

Open List Menu: File ➤ Open List... (or Ctrl+O) 🔳 Displays the Open Batch Plot List File dialog to select a drive and path to load .bp3 files, replacing the contents of the current list box.

Save List Menu: File ➤ Save List... (or Ctrl+S) 🔳 Opens the Save Batch Plot List File dialog to select a drive and path for saving current batch list and associated configurations as a Batch Plot List (.bp3) file.

Plot Menu: File ➤ Plot 🔳 Plots all drawings displayed in list box.

Plot Test Menu: File ➤ Plot Test 🔳 Opens the Plot Test Results dialog to view, edit, and save the list of drawings that will be batch plotted.

Logging Menu: File ➤ Logging... 🔳 Opens the Logging dialog, offering options to track information about your plotting.

Layouts Menu: Options ➤ Layouts... 🔳 Opens the Layouts dialog, displaying a list box of layouts for a selected drawing that allow you to Plot All Layouts or Plot Selected Layouts.

Page Setups Menu: Options ➤ Page Setups... 🔳 Opens the Page Setups dialog to display and load page setups from a drawing or template for plotting.

Plot Devices Menu: Options ➤ Plot Devices... 🔳 Opens the Plot Devices dialog, listing available plot devices to use when plotting. Click Show Plot Device Description to enable the Description box and display information about the default plot configuration for selected drawing(s).

Plot Settings Menu: Options ➤ Plot Settings... 🔳 Opens the Plot Settings dialog with the Plot Settings tab active to set controls for plot area, plot scale, and file to plot.

Layers Menu: Options ➤ Layers... 🔳 Opens the Plot Settings dialog with the Layers tab active to toggle layers on and off for a specified plotted drawing.

Append List Menu: File ➤ Append List... Opens the Append Batch Plot List File dialog to load a .bp3 file, appending its contents to the list box.

Exit Menu: File ➤ Exit... Exits the dialog box and does not retain the current list of drawings and configurations unless previously saved to a .bp3 file.

-BHATCH

Notes To terminate a batch plot in progress, click the "X" at the upper right corner of the AutoCAD Batch Plot Utility window, and click OK when the message box appears. All remaining plots will be cancelled. Otherwise, pick Cancel to discontinue plotting of the current drawing.

See Also Layout, Layout Wizard, Page Setup, Plot, Plottermanager, Plotstyle

---

-Bhatch

-Bhatch enables you to create a hatching pattern from prompts at the command line.

To Create Hatch Patterns at the Command Line

Command Line: **-Bhatch**

Menu: None

Toolbar: None

1. **Specify internal point or [Properties/Select/Remove islands/Advanced]:** Pick points or enter an option. A screen display reports the following information and then repeats the prompt.

   - Current hatch pattern: ANSI31

   - Specify internal point or [Properties/Select/Remove islands/Advanced]:

   - Selecting everything...

   - Selecting everything visible...

   - Analyzing the selected data...

   - Analyzing internal islands...

   - Current hatch pattern: ANSI31

2. Depending on the option you select, additional prompts will appear.

Options

Specify Internal Point Pick a point within the bounded area, including blocks. If Island Detection (below) is enabled, objects within the boundary are defined as "islands" and are not hatched. Text contained within the bounded area is considered an "island." An imaginary rectangle is created around it, and the text is not hatched.

Properties Entering **P** at Specify internal point or [Properties/ Select/Remove islands/Advanced]: displays a series of prompts to change the pattern scale, angle, and spacing.

• Enter a pattern name or [?/Solid/User defined] <ANSI31>:

• Specify a scale for the pattern <1.0000>:

• Specify an angle for the pattern <0>:

If you enter a **?** at the first prompt, the text screen displays available patterns stored in the acad.pat file. Entering **S** sets the current hatch pattern to Solid, allows you to pick points to create a solid hatch pattern, and then returns to step 1. Enter **U** to display the following prompts to draw the hatch pattern as a series of parallel lines. You many optionally double (cross-hatch) the pattern by entering a **Y** at the Double hatch area? [Yes/No] <N>: prompt or create the pattern as an exploded block by prefacing the **U** with an asterisk (*) so that AutoCAD draws the pattern as a series of individual lines.

• Specify angle for crosshatch lines <0>:

• Specify spacing between the lines <1.0000>:

• Double hatch area? [Yes/No] <N>:

• Current hatch pattern: U

Select Select objects or use Osnap modes to define the area to be hatched.

Remove Islands Displays the following prompts to remove "islands" from the boundary set. Enter **U** or **Undo** to cancel your selection.

• Select island to remove:

• <Select island to remove>/Undo:

Advanced Displays the prompt Enter an option [Boundary set/Retain boundary/Island detection/Style/Associativity]:, allowing you to control the method AutoCAD uses to define the hatch. You can enter **N** to create a new boundary set or **E** to select everything on the screen. You can also Retain boundary as a polyline or region; if you don't choose this option, it is erased after the hatch pattern is created. Island Detection allows you to specify whether objects within the outermost boundary are to be hatched or to be treated as "islands." Style prompts you to Enter hatching style [Ignore/Outer/Normal] <Normal>:, allowing you to set hatch boundary options. Associativity offers you the choice to make your hatch editable by entering **Y** at the prompt Do you want associativity? [Yes/No] <Y>:.

See Also Bhatch, Boundary, -Boundary, Hatch, Hatchedit, -Hatchedit

Bhatch

Bhatch opens a dialog with hatching options, enabling you to fill an enclosed boundary defined by lines, arcs, circles, and polylines with a predefined pattern, a simple hatch pattern, or solid fill by pointing to it. The pattern can also be previewed from an image box or a hatch pattern palette dialog before being applied. Use **-Bhatch** to display all the prompts at the command line.

Inherit Properties   Temporarily closes dialog prompting to Select associative hatch object:, allowing you to duplicate the pattern within another closed boundary. During selection of the original object, crosshairs appear with a paintbrush image along with command-line information regarding the Inherited Properties, such as Name, Scale, and Angle. You can either pick a point at the prompt Select internal point:, causing the boundary area to highlight, enter **U** or **Undo** to deselect the object and pick another point, or right-click to display a shortcut menu for similar options. Picking the **Preview** button in the dialog offers an advance image of the hatched area and then prompts to <Hit enter or right-click to return to the dialog>.

Pick Points   Temporarily exits dialog to specify a point inside the area you wish to hatch.

Select Objects   Temporarily closes dialog to pick one or more objects for hatching.

Remove Islands   Temporarily discharges dialog and prompts to Select island to remove/Undo, and removes that object within the defining boundary.

View Selections   Temporarily dismisses dialog to view your hatch selection.

Type   Allows you to set hatch patterns using Predefined stored patterns from the acad.pat and acadiso.pat files, User-defined single line patterns, or Custom patterns from the drop-down list. Pick the *Swatch* graphic image, and open the Hatch Pattern Palette dialog to view and select a hatch pattern from the ANSI, ISO, Other Predefined, or Custom tabbed sections. To draw a 90-degree crossing hatch pattern, set the type to User-defined, and check Double. AutoCAD uses the *Hpdouble* system variable to store this setting.

Pattern   Allows you to select from a list for a Predefined pattern type and displays it in the graphic preview area. Pick the adjacent Ellipsis button or the preview area if you wish to open the Hatch Pattern Palette dialog.

Custom Pattern   Allows you to pick a pattern stored in any custom .pat file, stored in your AutoCAD search path, from the list. Use the ellipsis to display the Custom tabbed section of the Hatch Pattern Palette dialog, and pick from the list.

Angle Allows you to pick from a list of preset angles or specify a new value in the drop-down box and stores it in the *Hpang* system variable.

Scale Ungrays when you set Type to Predefined or Custom; allows you to choose from a preset list to enter a new number and stores it in the *Hpscale* system variable.

Spacing Sets the spacing of lines for User-defined Type patterns only, and saves the value in the *Hpspace* system variable.

ISO Pen Width Allows you to scale an ISO predefined pattern when you specify a value in its edit box and when Type is set to Predefined for any ISO pattern.

Advanced Tab Section

Island Detection Style Controls the manner in which internal objects, such as test, Mtext, or closed objects, should be hatched within the selected boundary if they exist. Although Normal is usually applicable for most hatch operations, you can use the image boxes to help specify Outer or Ignore Style.

Object Type Checking Retain Boundaries activates the drop-down list and allows you to retain an outline of the boundary area as a polyline or region; otherwise, it is erased after the hatch pattern is created.

Boundary Set Lists the type of objects AutoCAD recognizes for the specified boundary area. Depending on its findings, the results may expedite the specified hatch operation.

New Temporarily exits dialog to create the boundary set.

Island Detection Method Controls the hatch method defined by the extreme boundary edge. Options include Flood and Ray Casting. Specify Flood if you wish to retain islands as boundary objects; otherwise, select Ray Casting.

Pick Points prompts you to pick a point within the bounded area, including blocks. If Island Detection is enabled, objects within the boundary are defined as "islands" and are not hatched. Text contained within the bounded area is considered an "island." An imaginary rectangle is created around it, and the text is not hatched. Select Objects let you select objects or use **Osnap** modes to define the area to be hatched. Remove Islands removes from the boundary set "islands." View Selections highlights boundaries and objects selected for the hatching area and then returns you to the dialog.

Composition Specify Associative to link the hatch pattern with the hatch boundary object, so that it will adjust its shape when the object boundary is changed, or specify Nonassociative to create individual objects.

See Also -Bhatch, Boundary, Convert, Hatch, Hatchedit, -Hatchedit, Psfill; *System Variables:* Delobj, Fillmode, Hpang, Hpbound, Hpdouble, Hpname, Hpscale, Hpspace, Pickstyle

Blipmode

When you draw with AutoCAD, tiny crosses, called *blips,* appear wherever you select points. These blips are not part of your drawing; they merely help you locate the points that you have selected. You can use **Blipmode** to suppress these blips if you don't want them. Use the **Redraw**, **Regen**, **Zoom**, or **Pan** commands to remove blips.

To Reset Blipmode

Command line: **Blipmode** (or **'Blipmode**, to use transparently).

Enter mode [ON/OFF] <OFF>: Enter ON or OFF.

Options

ON   Displays blips when you enter points.

OFF   Suppresses blips when you enter points.

See Also   System Variable: Blipmode

-Block

-Block groups a set of drawing objects together to act as a single object. You can then insert, copy, mirror, move, rotate, scale, or save the block as an external file. The dialog equivalents are **Bmake** and **Block**.

To Create a Block at the Command Line

Command line: -**Block, -B**

Toolbar: none

1. **Enter block name or [?]:** Enter the name for the block. Enter a question mark to list existing blocks.

2. **Specify insertion base point:** Enter a coordinate value or pick a point to set the base point of the block. A base point can be selected by clicking the Insertion Specify Base Point icon or, if specified, from X, Y, and Z edit boxes in the dialog.

3. **Select objects:** Pick objects to include in the block. The objects you select will disappear, but you can restore them as individual objects by using the **Oops** command. If your block includes attributes, select each one in the order you wish them to appear in the dialog.

Blocks exist only within the drawing in which they are created. However, you can convert them into drawing files with the **Wblock** command. Blocks can contain other nested blocks. You can include attributes in blocks to allow the input and storage of information with the block; see **Attdef**.

If you attempt to create a block that has the same name as an existing block, you will see the prompt:

```
Block <name> already exists.
Redefine it? <N>
```

To redefine the existing block, enter **Y**. The **-Block** command proceeds as usual and replaces the existing block with the new one. If the existing block has been inserted into the drawing, the new block appears in its place. If **Regenauto** has been turned off, the new block will not appear until you issue a **Regen** command.

If you make a block containing a nested block with the same name, AutoCAD displays the prompt:

```
Block <block name> references itself
```

To correct the problem, open the drawing, explode the block, and purge the duplicate nested block name. To insert an exploded block into a drawing, preface the path\block name with an asterisk.

See Also   Attdisp, Attedit, Attext, Attredef, Block, Bmake, Ddatte, Insert, Regen, Regenauto, Wblock, Wildcards, Xbind, Xref

---

Block

*See **Bmake***

Blockicon

Blockicon creates a preview image of blocks for pre-AutoCAD 2000 drawings.

To Create a Block Icon

Command line: **Blockicon**

Menu: none

Toolbar: none

Enter block names <*>: Pressing ↵ opens the Block icon generation dialog to create preview images (icons) of all blocks stored in your current pre-AutoCAD 2000 drawing. You can enter block names separated by commas or use wildcard characters.

See Also   -Block, Bmake, Wblock, Wildcard Characters

Bmake

Bmake and **Block** display the same Block Definition dialog. You can then insert, copy, mirror, move, rotate, scale, or save the block as an external file. To display prompts at the command line, use **-Block**.

To Create a Block Using a Dialog

Command line: **Bmake, Block, B**

Menu: Draw ➤ Block ➤ Make...

Draw Toolbar: 🔲 Make Block

Enter information in the dialog.

Options

Name   Enter a name for the block in the edit box, or select from the drop-down list.

Objects   You can specify the manner in which the objects you select are stored in your drawing. Picking Retain creates a separate block definition and retains the original objects. Selecting Convert to Block changes the selected object(s) to a block, and choosing Delete erases the original object(s) from your drawing during block creation. AutoCAD also displays the number of objects selected.

🔲 **Select Objects**   Clicking the icon temporarily closes the dialog to select objects in your drawing. Use any selection method at the Select objects: prompt to pick objects to include in the block. Pressing ↵ or right-clicking returns you to the dialog.

🔲 **QuickSelect**   Displays the Quick Select dialog to specify a filter for your selection set. See **Qselect**.

Base Point   Allows you to enter the XYZ coordinate values in the edit boxes.

🔲 **Pick Insertion Base Point**   Temporarily exits the dialog, allowing you to Specify insertion base point: by picking or entering coordinate values.

Preview Icon   Clicking Create Icon from Block Geometry makes and stores a preview image of the block and displays it in the dialog; otherwise, use Do Not Include an Icon to disable it. AutoCAD also displays the icon in the Preview image window in the Select File dialog for the **Open** command if Save a Thumbnail Preview Image is checked in the Open and Save tab of the Options dialog.

Block Units   Specify a scaled unit format, or use the default Unitless for each block creation when dragged from the AutoCAD DesignCenter.

Description   Use the edit box to apply comments to each block definition.

See Also   -Block, Block, Units, Wblock

BMPOUT
*See **Import/Export***

-Boundary

-Boundary creates a region or polyline boundary from overlapping objects. The equivalent dialog commands are **Boundary** and **Bpoly**.

To Create an Enclosed Polyline or Region at the Command Line

Command line: **-Boundary**, **-Bo**

1. **Specify internal point or [Advanced options]:** Pick a point within the area you wish to create an enclosed polyline or region, enter **U** or **Undo** to cancel a selection, enter **A** for Advanced options, or press ↵ to end your point selection.

2. If you entered **A**, the prompt Enter an option [Boundary set/ Island detection/Object type]: appears with additional options:

   - Entering **B** displays the Specify Candidate set for Boundary, New/<Everything>: prompt. If you enter **N**, you are prompted to Select objects to define the boundary set; otherwise, entering **E** or pressing ↵ reports Selecting Everything Visible... and returns you to step 1.

   - Entering **I** at the prompt Enter an option [Boundary set/ Island detection/Object type]: responds with Do you want island detection? [Yes/No] <Y>:. If you accept the default **Y**, AutoCAD treats objects within the outermost boundary as "islands" and returns to step 2. If you enter **N**, the prompt Enter type of ray casting [Nearest/+X/-X/+Y/-Y/Angle] <+X>: allows you to set controls for AutoCAD to define the boundary object.

   - Enter **O** and then **R** to create the boundary as a region or **P** to define the boundary as polyline at the prompt Enter type of boundary object [Region/Polyline] <Polyline>:. Pressing ↵ specifies the current default and returns you to step 1.

   - Press ↵ to exit the command after setting one or more of the above options.

See Also   Bhatch, Boundary, Bpoly, Hatch, Hatchedit, -Hatchedit; *System Variable:* Hpbound

Boundary

Boundary works like the **Pedit** command and makes a region or polyline from overlapping objects. It displays the Advanced tab section of the Boundary Hatch dialog. See **Bhatch**.

Box

*See **Solid Modeling***

Bpoly

*See **Boundary***

Break

Break erases a line, trace, circle, arc, or a 2D polyline between two points.

To Use Break

Command line: **Break, Br**

Menu: Modify ➤ Break

Modify Toolbar: [icon] Break

1. **Select object:** Pick an object to be broken, right-click to display the shortcut menu, and then select a option or continue to step 2.

2. **Specify second break point or [First point]:** Pick second point of break, or enter **F** to specify first and second points.

Options

1 Point/Select   Allows you to select the object first, and then specify the break point by picking a point near the object or using an Object Snap mode.

2 Points   Allows you to break an object in two places. The *first* break is at the point of selection.

2 Points/Select   Allows you select the object, and then specify the *first* break point.

If you use the cursor to pick the object, the "pick" point becomes the first point of the break. Pick the second point of the break, or enter **F** to specify a different first break point. If you selected the object using a window, crossing window, wpolygon, cpolygon, fence, or a last or previous option, you are automatically prompted for a first and second point.

Break does not work on blocks, solids, text, shapes, 3D faces, or 3D polylines. You can now break objects that do not lie in a plane parallel to the current user coordinate system (UCS). Also, if you are not viewing the current UCS in plan, you may get the wrong result. Use the **Plan** command to view the current UCS in plan. When breaking circles, you must use the proper break-point selection sequence:

- In the case of a circle, a counterclockwise pick sequence causes the break to occur between the two break points.

- A clockwise pick sequence causes the segment between the two points to remain and the rest of the circle to disappear.

You can break a line at a distance from a specified base point if you use tracking. After selecting the object, use the **F** for First Point option, and then Shift+click to open the cursor menu, and pick Temporary Track Point from the Object Snap toolbar or enter **tk** at the command line. Once tracking is started, you are prompted for First tracking point:. Specify an Object Snap point, enter a distance, and then press ↵ at the prompt Next point (Press ENTER to end tracking): to end tracking. When the Enter second point prompt appears, specify the break distance, or enter the @ sign to apply the first break-point coordinates.

See Also   Change, Dsettings, Osnap, Pedit, Trim, UCS

Browser

Launches your installed Web browser.

To Access the Internet

Command line: **Browser**

Web Toolbar: Browse the Web

Location < current>: Press ↵ or specify another location for your connection at the prompt Enter Web location (URL) <D:\Acad2000\ Home.htm>:.

To use the **Browser** command, you must have version 3 or later of Netscape Navigator or Microsoft Internet Explorer installed on your computer.

See Also   Hyperlink; *Express Tools:* Browser

Cal

Cal is an online calculator. It stores calculated values as variables that can be recalled any time during the current editing session. It can be used transparently to supply values in response to command prompts.

To Use the Calculator

Command Line: **Cal** (or **'Cal**, to use transparently).

Initializing...>> >>Expression: Enter the desired mathematical expression.

Cal evaluates vector (point), real, or integer expressions. The expressions can access existing geometry using the Object Snap functions, such as Cen, End, and Ins. You may insert AutoLISP variables into the arithmetic expression and assign the value of the expression back to an AutoLISP variable. Use these arithmetic and vector expressions in any AutoCAD command that expects points, vectors, or numbers.

See Also   AutoLISP

Camera

Camera allows you to specify camera position and target points to view objects in your drawing.

To Set Camera Position and Target

Command: **Camera**

Menu: None

View Toolbar: Camera

Default values are displayed at the command line, and then prompts appear to enter a value or pick a point for camera position and target:

```
Current camera position is: 9,5,23

Current camera target is: 9,5,0
```

- **Specify new camera position <9,5,23>:**
- **Specify new camera target <9,5,0>:**

NOTE To set the camera and target locations for a 3D orbit view, enter **Camera** to set your camera and target points, and then enter the **3Dorbit** command.

See Also   3Dorbit

Catalog/Dir

Catalog displays a list of files in a specified drive or directory.

To View a Catalog or Directory in a DOS Window

Command line: **Catalog**

Command line: **Dir**

File specification: Enter any drive letter, directory name, or wildcard character as you would in DOS. If you give no specifications, **Catalog** displays the list for the current drive.

Both commands are stored as legacy in the acad.pgp file and are less applicable in the current Windows operating systems. **Catalog** is assigned to the external operating-system command **dir/w** and displays the directory in a DOS window with the DOS switch for wide. **Dir** invokes the operating-system **dir** command and scrolls the directory in a DOS window as a list of filenames.

See Also Acad.pgp

Chamfer

Chamfer joins two nonparallel lines with an intermediate line or bevel or adds intermediate lines between the line segments of a 2D polyline. You can chamfer a spline, ellipse, 3D polyline, ray, xline, segments of polylines, and polyline arcs as well as Lines and Polylines.

To Use Chamfer

Command line: **Chamfer**, **Cha**

Menu: Modify ➤ Chamfer

Modify Toolbar: [icon] Chamfer

1. **(TRIM mode) Current chamfer Dist1 = 0.5000, Dist2 = 0.5000**

   Select first line or [Polyline/Distance/Angle/Trim/ Method]: Pick first line or enter an option.

2. **Select second line:** Pick second line.

If the object is a 3D solid, the following prompt appears for step 3:

3. **Enter surface selection option [Next/OK (current)] <OK>:** Enter **N** to select an adjacent surface, or press ↵ to accept the current surface as the base surface.

4. Specify the two edges of the base surface to chamfer.

> **Specify base surface chamfer distance <0.5000>:** Press ↵, or enter a distance value.

> **Specify other surface chamfer distance <0.5000>:** Press ↵, or enter another distance value.

5. Select individual or all edges to chamfer.

> **Select an edge or [Loop]:** Enter **L**, select an edge, or press ↵ to select all edges. Loop switches to loop mode and prompts to Select an edge or [Loop]:.

Options

Polyline Chamfers all line segments within a polyline. This option prompts you to select a 2D polyline. All the joining polyline segments are then chamfered. The prompt is

- Select 2D polyline:

Distance Specifies the length of the chamfer. This option prompts you for the first and second chamfer distance, sets the values as defaults, and then requires you to repeat the command. The distances measured are from the intersection point of the two lines to the beginning of the chamfer.

- Specify first chamfer distance <0.25000>:

- Specify second chamfer distance <0.2500>:

Angle Specifies the angle of the chamfer from a selected point on the line segment. The prompts are

- Specify chamfer length on the first line <1.0000>:

- Specify chamfer angle from the first line <0>:

Trim Toggles the trim option ON or OFF and set it as a default. Turning Trim OFF allows you to add a chamfer while retaining the original line segments. The prompt is

- Enter Trim mode option [Trim/No trim] <Trim>:

Method Establishes a default method of chamfering, either by two distances or a distance and an angle.

You can chamfer objects that do not lie on the current user coordinate system (UCS). The two lines meet when the chamfer distances are set to 0 (the default value). If selected objects are not on the same layer, the chamfer line assumes all the properties of the current layer. The prompt is

- Enter trim method [Distance/Angle] <Distance>:

See Also Extend, Fillet, Trim; *System Variables:* Chamfera, Chamferb, Chamferc, Chamferd, Chammode, Trimmode

Change

Change can alter several properties of an object. You can change all the properties of lines. Move line end points by selecting a point at the first prompt. If you select several lines, all of the end points closest to the selected point are moved to the new point. If the Ortho mode is on, the lines become parallel, and their end points align with the selected point.

You can change the color, elevation, layer, line type, line type scale, or thickness of arcs, circles, lines, and polylines. You can also change the rotation angle, insertion point, or layer assignment of a block.

To Change the Properties of an Object

Command line: **Change**, **-Ch**

1. **Select objects:** Select objects to be changed.

2. **Specify change point or [Properties]:** Enter **P** to change the property of the selected object(s), or select a line and change its end point.

3. **Enter property to change [Color/Elev/LAyer/LType/ ltScale/LWeight/Thickness]:** If you specified **P** in step 1, enter any option to display prompts that change an object's properties:

    Enter new color <BYLAYER>: Enter a color name, color number, Bylayer, or Byblock.

    Specify new elevation <12.0000>: Enter a new elevation value.

    Enter new layer name <0>: Enter a new layer name.

    Enter new linetype name <BYLAYER>: Enter a new line type name, Bylayer, or Byblock.

    Specify new linetype scale <1.0000>: Enter a new line type scale value.

    Enter new lineweight < BYLAYER >: Enter a new line weight value, Bylayer, or Byblock.

    Specify new thickness <0.0000>: Enter a new thickness value.

4. If you select an attribute definition, pressing ↵ after the prompt Specify new text insertion point <no change>: displays the following prompts:

    Enter new text style <STANDARD>: Enter a new style name.

    Specify new height <0.2000>: Enter a new height.

    Specify new rotation angle <0>: Enter a new rotation angle.

Enter new tag <TAG>: Enter new attribute tag name.

Enter new prompt <prompt>: Enter new attribute prompt.

Enter new default value <value>: Enter new attribute default value.

5. If you select text, pressing ⏎ after the prompt Specify new text insertion point <no change>: yields the following prompts:

Specify new text insertion point <no change>: Pick new location for text.

Enter new text style <STANDARD>: Enter new text style.

Specify new height <0.3200>: Enter new text height.

Specify new rotation angle <0>: Enter new rotation angle.

Enter new text <current value>: Enter new text.

Options

Properties   Changes the color, elevation, layer, line type, or thickness of an object.

Color   Prompts you for color to change selected objects to.

Elev   Prompts you for a new elevation in the object's Z axis.

Layer   Prompts you for a new layer.

LType   Prompts you for a new line type.

LtScale   Prompts you for a new ltScale value for the selected object(s).

LWeight   Prompts you for a new line weight based on available default values for the selected object(s).

Thickness   Prompts you for a new thickness in the object's Z axis.

The Thickness option will extrude a two-dimensional line, arc, circle, or polyline into the Z axis. This option does not work on blocks. Elev changes an object's location in the Z axis. This option does not work on objects that are not in a plane parallel to the current UCS.

When you change an object's color, the object no longer has the color of the layer on which it resides. To make an object the same color as its layer, enter **Bylayer** at the Color prompt.

See Also   Chprop, Color, Elev, Ltscale, Lweight, Properties, Select, Thickness, UCS; *System Variables:* Cecolor, Celtype, Clayer, Elevation, Ltscale, Textsize, Textstyle, Thickness

Chprop

Chprop works like the **Change** command except that **Chprop** allows you to change the properties of all object types regardless of their 3D orientation. The Elev option is not offered—use the **Move** command instead. The equivalent dialog command is **Properties**.

To Change an Object's Properties

Command line: **Chprop**

1. **Select objects:** Select objects whose properties you wish to modify.

2. **Enter property to change [Color/LAyer/LType/ltScale/ LWeight/Thickness]:** Enter the option.

Options

Color   Prompts you for a color to which selected objects will be changed.

Layer   Prompts you for a new layer.

LType   Prompts you for a new line type.

LtScale   Prompts you for a new ltScale value for the selected object(s).

LWeight   Prompts to set an object's line weight using AutoCAD standard defaults.

Thickness   Prompts you for new thickness in the object's Z axis.

See Also   Change, Color, Elev, Properties, Select, Thickness, UCS

Circle

Circle offers several methods for drawing circles, the default being to choose a center point and enter or pick a diameter or radius.

To Draw a Circle

Command line: **Circle**, **C**

Menu: Draw ➤ Circle ➤ Center, Radius/Center, Diameter/2 Points/3 Points/Tan, Tan, Radius/Tan, Tan, Tan

Draw Toolbar: Circle

1. **Specify center point for circle or [3P/2P/Ttr (tan tan radius)]:** Pick a center point or enter an option.

2. **Specify radius of circle or [Diameter]:** Provide a radius by dynamically dragging, entering a value, or pressing the letter **D** to display the prompt Specify diameter of circle <current default>: to set the circle's diameter.

When selecting **Ttr**, prompts appear to enter two tangent Osnap points and a radius.

1. **Specify point on object for first tangent of circle:** Pick first Osnap point.

2. **Specify point on object for second tangent of circle:** Pick second Osnap point.

3. **Specify radius of circle <current value>:** Specify a radius or pick two points to dynamically set the circle's size.

The Draw ➢ Circle ➢ Tan, Tan, Tan pull-down menu option offers a method similar to the 3 Point option, allowing you to draw a circle by specifying three tangent points and automatically displaying Deferred Tangent autosnap points. Prompts for Specify second point on circle:, Specify third point on circle:, and Specify third point on circle: appear to set the circle's size.

Options

3P (3 Point)   Allows you to define a circle based on three points. Once you select this option, you are prompted for a first, second, and third point. The circle will be drawn to pass through these points.

2P (2 Point)   Allows you to define a circle's diameter based on two points. Once you select this option, you are prompted to select the first and second point. The two points will be the opposite ends of the diameter.

Ttr (Tangent, Tangent, Radius)   Allows you to define a circle based on two tangent points and a radius. The tangent points can be on lines, arcs, or circles.

See Also   Arc, Donut, Ellipse; *System Variable:* Circlerad

Close

Close allows you to save and exit a drawing, without ending your current AutoCAD session open. The command is similar to **Exit**.

To Close a Drawing

Command: **Close**

Menu: File ➢ Close

See Also   Save, Saveas, Quit

Color

Color opens the Select Color dialog and allows you to set the color for new objects. Once you select a color, all objects will be given the selected color regardless of their layers, unless you specify Bylayer or Byblock as the color. Objects you drew before using the **Color** command are not affected. The equivalent command-line prompt is **-Color.**

To Set the Object Color

Command line: **Color**, **Col**

Menu: Format ➤ Color...

Object Properties Toolbar: `☐ ByLayer ▼` Color Control pop-up list, Other...

Options

Standard Colors   Displays the AutoCAD standard colors 1 through 9. You can enter a color name, the first letter of the color name, or a color number in the *Color* edit box.

Gray Shades   Displays gray shades ranging from color numbers 250 through 255.

Logical Colors   Contains pick boxes for Bylayer and Byblock as described below.

Bylayer   Gives objects the color of the layer on which they are placed. It is the default color setting.

Byblock   Works on objects used in blocks. If such an object is assigned the Byblock color, it will take on the color of the layer in which the block is placed.

Full Color Palette   Displays full palette of 255 colors available in the AutoCAD Color Index (ACI) colors.

See Also   Change, Chprop, -Color, Layer, -Layer, Properties; *System Variable:* Cecolor

-Color

-Color sets the color of objects being drawn. The dialog equivalent is **Color**.

To Set the Color of Objects at the Command Line

Command line: **-Color** (or **'-Color**, to use transparently).

Enter default object color <BYLAYER>: Specify a color name, color number, or option.

Options

Bylayer   Draws all objects in the color of the layer on which they are placed. It is the default color setting.

Byblock   Applies to objects created in blocks. Table C.1 shows the color names that AutoCAD recognizes, and their number codes. You can enter any of these names, their first letter, or numbers—in fact, you can enter any number from 1 to 255. The color that is displayed depends on your display adapter and monitor, but the first seven colors are the same for most display systems.

TABLE C.1:   Color Names Recognized by AutoCAD

Color Name	Color Letter	Color Number
Red	R	1
Yellow	Y	2
Green	G	3
Cyan	C	4
Blue	B	5
Magenta	M	6
White	W	7
Bylayer		Color of the layer on which the object is located
Byblock		Color of the layer on which the block is located

Assign colors carefully, especially if you use them to distinguish different layers. A Color Control pop-up list is accessible through the Object Properties toolbar. Choosing Other... opens the Select Color dialog.

See Also   Change, Chprop, Color, Layer, Properties; *System Variable*: Cecolor

Colour
See Color

Command-Line Editing

You can repeat previous command-line entries using the up and down arrow keys. AutoCAD has adapted standard Windows editing methods allowing the use of the insert, backspace, overwrite, end, home, delete, page-up, and page-down keys at the command line. If you highlight a previously entered command and right-click the mouse, a menu appears offering the Paste to Cmdline option. Selecting this option pastes the text at the command line. You can also select from a list of five previous executed commands, saved as Recent Commands, in the cascading section of the right-click cursor menu.

Right-clicking the mouse over the command line displays a cursor menu to select the **Paste to Cmdline**, **Copy**, **Copy History**, **Paste**, or **Options**... commands.

See Also   Copy, Copyclip, Copyhist, Options, Paste

Compile

You can create your own text fonts and shapes by compiling a shape/font description file. This file is an ASCII file that uses a special system of codes to describe your fonts or shapes. **Compile** displays a dialog listing ASCII files with .shp or .pfb extensions for converting into a form that lets Auto-CAD read the descriptions and include them in a drawing.

To Compile Your Own Text Fonts

Command line: **Compile**

- When the *Filedia* system variable is set to 1, **Compile** opens the Select Shape or Font File dialog, displaying .shp extensions for Shape files or .pfb extensions for PostScript files. Enter a Shape/Font filename into the *File:* box to compile into a .shx extension.

- When *Filedia* is set to 0 and **Compile** is entered at the command line, the following prompt appears:

Enter shape (.shp) or PostScript font (.pfb) filename: Enter the shape or font filename.

Load inserts compiled files into a drawing. Compiled PostScript font .pfb files load quicker in drawings.

See Also   Load, Shape, Style

Cone

*See **Solid Modeling***

Convert

This command converts 2D polylines and associative hatches, optimizing them as AutoCAD Release 14 objects.

Command line: **Convert**

1. **Enter type of objects to convert [Hatch/Polyline/All]**
   <All>: Press ↵ to specify both hatch and polyline objects; enter **H** for hatch or **P** for polylines.

2. **Enter object selection preference [Select/All] <All>:**
   Depending on what you enter for item 1, press ↵ to convert all hatches or polylines in the drawing, or enter an **S** to select specific objects. Click **Yes** or **No** when the message box appears with the prompt Hatch objects may change appearance when converted. Do you want to proceed?

NOTE Generally, polylines are converted automatically by the *Plinetype* system variable when drawings are saved in AutoCAD release 14 or later.

See Also   Bhatch, Hatch, Pedit, Pline; *System Variable:* Plinetype

Config

*See **Options** and **Command-Line Editing***

Copy

Copy copies a single object or a set of objects.

To Copy

Command line: **Copy**, **Co**, **Cp**

Menu: Modify ➤ Copy

Shortcut menu: Copy

Modify Toolbar: Copy Objects

1. **Select objects:** Select objects to be copied.

2. **Specify base point or displacement, or [Multiple]:** Pick the reference, or base point, for copy, or enter **M** for multiple copies. The **M** option instructs AutoCAD that you wish to make several copies and prompts you to Specify base point: again.

3. **Specify second point of displacement or <use first point as displacement>:** Pick the copy distance and direction in relation to the base point, or press ↵ to use the first point's displacement value.

Options

Multiple   Allows you to make several copies of the selected objects. The second point is repeated until you press ↵ or Esc.

AutoCAD assumes you want to make copies within the current user coordinate system (UCS). However, you can make copies in 3D space by entering **0,0,0** as the base point and the desired XYZ coordinates as the second point, or by using the **Osnap** overrides to pick objects in 3D space.

If you press ↵ at the Specify second point of displacement prompt without entering a point value, the selected objects may be copied to an area that is off your current drawing. To recover, use the **Undo** command or **Zoom** extents. For multiple copying using grips, see **Move**.

See Also   Array, Grips, Move, Multiple, Select

Copybase

Copybase enables you to set a base point for selected objects you wish to copy. Use **Pasteclip** to paste the copied objects to a designated location based on your assigned base point.

To Set a Base Point for Copied Objects

Command line: **Copybase**

Menu: Edit ➤ Copy with Base Point

Shortcut menu: Copy with Base Point

1. **Specify base point:** Pick a point.
2. **Select objects:** Select the object(s) you wish to copy.

See Also   Copy, Copyclip, Pasteclip

Copyclip

Copyclip uses the Windows Clipboard to copy objects from AutoCAD to other Windows applications.

To Copy Objects to Other Applications

Command line: **Copyclip**

Menu: Edit ➤ Copy

Shortcut menu: Copy

Standard Toolbar: 📋 Copy to Clipboard

Select objects: Select the object(s) you wish to copy.

Select one or more objects, and then right-click for the shortcut menu, and pick **Copy** or use Ctrl+C to copy highlighted text from the command line, AutoCAD text window, or selected objects in the graphics area to the Clipboard. When only text is selected, **Copyclip** stores it in ASCII format.

See Also   Copyhist, Copylink, Cutclip, Pasteclip, Pastespec

Copyhist

Copyhist copies all text from the command line or history window to the Clipboard. The text can then be placed into other Windows applications by choosing Paste from most standard Windows pull-down menus or pressing Ctrl+V.

To Copy the AutoCAD Command-Line History

Command line: **Copyhist**, **Ctrl+V**

All the text in the history window is copied to the Clipboard.

Press the F2 function key to display the AutoCAD text window, and then use your pick button to highlight the text you wish to copy. Once highlighted, click the right mouse button to display the cursor menu, and pick Copy or Copy History. You can control the number of lines copied by highlighting text in the history window, then right-clicking to display the shortcut menu, and picking the **Copy History** command.

See Also   Copyclip, Copylink, Command-Line Editing, Options

Cutclip

Cutclip lets you export vector and bitmap graphics from AutoCAD to other programs that accept graphics from the Clipboard. It also lets you exchange graphics between multiple AutoCAD sessions or import text to AutoCAD from a text-based application.

To Cut Objects

Command line: **Cutclip**

Menu: Edit ➤ Cut

Shortcut: Cut

Standard Toolbar: Cut to Clipboard

Select objects: Select the object(s) you wish to Cut.

Cutclip moves selected objects to the Windows Clipboard. Cutting deletes the selected objects from the current drawing and stores them on the Clipboard for pasting into another drawing or application. The **Cut** command can also be activated by using the control-key sequence Ctrl+X.

See Also   Copybase, Copyclip, Copyhist, Copylink, Pastclip, Pastespec

Copylink

Copylink copies the current graphics screen to the Windows Clipboard for linking to other OLE applications.

To Copylink Objects

Command line: **Copylink**

Menu: Edit ➤ Copylink

Once invoked, all objects displayed on the graphics screen are copied to the clipboard, and then the command prompt returns.

Pastespec allows you to paste and link the copied view into another document. Views of AutoCAD drawings in both Model Space and Paper Space can be linked to and updated in other OLE applications. AutoCAD uses the current view when a single viewport is selected.

See Also   Insertobj, Olelinks, Pastespec

Cylinder

*See **Solid Modeling***

Dbcclose

Dbclose closes the Dbconnect Manager window and removes it from the menu bar.

To Close the Dbconnect Manager

Command line: **Dbcclose**

Menu: none

Toolbar: none

See Also   Dbconnect

Dbconnect

Dbconnect provides an AutoCAD interface to external database tables.

To Display the Dbconnect Manager Window

Command line: **Dbconnect, Dbc, Ctrl+6**

Menu: Tools ➤ Dbconnect

D DBCONNECT

NOTE The Dbconnect menu is automatically placed in the menu bar between Modify and Window when the command is executed.

Standard Toolbar: Dbconnect

Entering the command or picking the icon from the standard toolbar docks the Dbconnect Manager dialog along the left side of your display screen, allowing you to link AutoCAD to external database files. You can modify database files from within AutoCAD and link AutoCAD objects to database records.

NOTE AutoCAD provides a sample drawing in the Sample folder named **db_samp.dwg**, which can be used for learning.

Data Sources

Configure Data Source… Opens the Configure a *Data Source* dialog when right-clicking Data Source in the Dbconnect Manager dialog. Enter a name in the edit box, or select from the *Data Sources:* list. Pick OK and the Data Link Properties dialog opens to specify a connection method.

Data Link Properties Dialog

Provider Tab Depending on the application, selects an OLE-DB provider from the list box for the type of data you wish to access. Picking Next>> advances to the Connecton tab.

Connection Tab Enter a database name in the edit box, or pick the ellipsis to locate an existing file by selecting a drive, path, and filename, and then provide *User Name:* and *Password*. Checkboxes offer options to specify a Blank Password or Allows Saving of Password. After you have located the appropriate file, pick Test Connection for validation of your connection to Microsoft Access data. These options apply only to Access data; different options appear if you connect to, for example, SQL Server data.

Advanced Tab Depending on your provider, offers options for *Impersonation Level:* (Anonymous, Identity, Impersonate, and Delegate) and *Protection Level:* (None, Connect, Call, Pkt, Pkt Integrity, and Pkt Privacy).

The Other section contains a *Connect timeout:* edit box to set the amount of time in seconds for the OLE-DB provider to make a connection. You can specify network-access permissions as Read, Read Write, Share Deny None, Share Deny Read, Share Deny Write, Share Exclusive, and Wire.

All Tab Lists all settings specified. If you wish to edit an initalization property, select the value and then pick the Edit Value… button, or double-click any value and provide new information.

Dbconnect Manager

View Table   Menu: Dbconnect ➤ View Data ➤ View External
Table/Edit External Table/View Linked Table/ Edit Linked Table/
Execute Query

  Opens the Data View window in Read Only mode, allowing you to
view, link, query, and print records from a database table and displaying
the information in a spreadsheet format. A right-click menu offers four
options: Link, Link and Label Settings, Find, and Copy.

Edit Table   Opens the Data View window, allowing you to view,
link, query, and print records from a database table and displaying
the information in a spreadsheet format. A right-click menu offers ten
options: View Linked Objects, Link, Link and Label Settings, Find, Replace,
Edit, Cut, Copy, Paste, and Clear.

Execute Query   Menu: Dbconnect ➤ Queries ➤ Execute Query...
  Performs a query based on information you select from the Data
View dialog.

New Query   Menu: Dbconnect ➤ Queries ➤ New Query on an
External Table/New Query on a Link Template.

  Allows you to specify a query name, and then opens the Query Editor
when you click Continue to build your query.

New Link Template   Menu: Dbconnect ➤ Templates ➤ New Link
Template

  Opens the New Link Template dialog where you can specify a New
Link Template Name or Start with Template. Picking Continue opens
the Link Template dialog to select a key field from those available in the
current table.

New Label Template   Menu: Dbconnect ➤ Templates ➤ New Label
Template

  Opens the New Label Template dialog to enter a New label template
name, or choose from the Start with Template drop-down list. Picking
Continue displays the Label Template dialog to add label fields and specify their parameters.

See Also   Dbcclose

Dblist

Dblist lists the properties of all objects in a drawing.

To Display Drawing Information
Command: **Dblist**

When you invoke **Dblist**, the screen switches to Text mode and the list of objects pauses at each screen of text. Press Escape to cancel the listing. **Dblist** is similar to the **List** command and can be used as a subset of the objects.

See Also Area, Dist, ID, List

Ddattdef
Ddattdef has been discontinued. AutoCAD has aliased the **Ddattdef** command to **Attdef** in the acad.pgp file. See **Attdef**.

Ddatte
*See **Attedit***

Ddattext
Ddattext has been discontinued. AutoCAD has aliased the **Ddattext** command to **Attext** in the acad.pgp file. See **Attedit**.

Ddchprop
Ddchprop has been discontinued. AutoCAD has aliased the **Ddchprop** command to **Properties** in the acad.pgp file. See **Properties**.

Ddcolor
Ddcolor has been discontinued. AutoCAD has aliased the **Ddcolor** command to **Color** in the acad.pgp file. See **Color**.

Ddedit
Ddedit changes annotation (text), multiline text, or attribute definitions. **Ddedit** displays a line of text in an edit box for modifying and viewing. You can position a cursor to delete single characters, make corrections, or add to the text. The equivalent command line prompt is **Change**.

To Edit Text Objects

Command line: **Ddedit**, **Ed**

Menu: Modify ➤ Text

Modify II Toolbar: Edit Text

Shortcut Menu: Right-click a text or Mtext object, and pick Mtext edit... or Text edit....

Select an annotation object or [Undo]: Pick the line of text, Mtext, or attribute definition to edit. Depending upon your object selection, the Edit Text dialog will open (with a *Text* edit box), the Multiline Text Editor dialog will open (with tabs to edit text properties), or the Edit Attribute Definition dialog will open (with the *Tag, Prompt,* and *Default* edit boxes).

NOTE If an attribute has not yet been made into a block, you can edit the tag name, attribute prompt, or default value.

Options

Undo   Undoes the last procedure.

Annotation   Edit box for revising text.

Tag   Edit box to change the tag name.

Prompt   Edit box to change the attribute prompt.

Default   Edit box to change the attribute value.

NOTE Every time you finish editing one line of text, AutoCAD prompts you to select another text or **Attdef** object rather than returning you to the command prompt. To exit the **Ddedit** command, press ↵ (do not enter any text at the last Text: or Attdef: prompt) or the Escape key.

See Also   Attdef, Attedit, Change, Ddattdef, Mtext, Properties, Text

Ddgrips

See **Grips** in the Selection tab of the Option dialog. See **Options**.

Ddim

See **Dimstyle**

Ddinsert

*See **Insert***

Ddlmodes

Ddlmodes has been discontinued. AutoCAD has aliased the **Ddmodes** command to **Layer** in the acad.pgp file. See **Layer**.

Ddmodify

Ddmodify has been discontinued. AutoCAD has aliased the **Ddmodify** command to **Properties** in the acad.pgp file. See **Properties**.

Ddosnap

Ddosnap has been discontinued. AutoCAD has aliased the **Ddosnap** command to **Osnap** in the acad.pgp file. See **Osnap** and **Dsettings (Object Snap tab)**.

Ddptype

Ddptype opens the Point Style dialog to select and control the appearances of points and to place point objects in your drawing, using the Node Osnap override. Points also appear as markers for the **Divide** and **Measure** commands.

To Set a Point Style

Command line: **Ddptype** (or **'Ddptype**, to use transparently).

Menu: Format ➤ Point Style...

Select a point style, and define the point size.

Options

The dialog offers 16-point mode image tiles. Pick the desired tile, and then use the *Point Size* edit box to adjust point size.

Point Size   Edit box for setting point size. Selecting an option button changes the size specifications from Relative to Absolute.

Set Size Relative to Screen   Option button to set point size as percentage of screen size.

Set Size in Absolute Units   Option button to set actual point size based on absolute units.

> **NOTE** Each point style has an associated integer value, or *Pdmode*. For example, the node number for a cross is 2, a circle is 33, and its combined shape is 34. Different node types can also be set at the command line with the *Pdmode* system variable by entering the sum of the active modes.

See Also   Divide, Measure, Point; *System Variables:* Pdmode, Pdsize

Ddrename

Ddrename has been discontinued. See **Rename**.

Ddrmodes

Opens Snap and Grid tab of Drafting Settings dialog.

Ddselect

Ddselect opens the Object Selection Settings dialog to define your method for selecting objects.

To Set Object Modes

Command line: **Ddselect** (or **'Ddselect**, to use transparently).

Menu: Tools ➤ Selection...

Provide information as needed in the dialog(s).

Options

Selection Modes   Multiple settings can be configured from this section. *Noun/Verb Selection:* adds a target box to the graphics cursor for selecting objects prior to issuing specific commands, thus permitting the cursor to function as a pick box or by picking two opposite corner points. Table D.1 shows the commands that support noun/verb selections.

TABLE D.1: Commands Allowing You to Use the Cursor as a Pick Box

Array	Dview	Move
Block	Erase	Rotate
Change	Explode	Scale
Chprop	Hatch	Stretch
Copy	List	Wblock
Ddchprop	Mirror	

The Selection Modes section also offers the following combinations for object selection methods: *Use Shift to Add:*, which allows you to select objects. Once a selection set is defined, you must hold down the Shift key to add more objects to the set. If Shift is not held down, the original selection set is discarded and a new one is started for *Noun/Verb Selection* sets; *Press and Drag:*, which permits you to hold down the pick button, drag, and then release, for creating a selection window; *Implied Windowing:*, which enables you to use a selection window by picking from left to right or use a crossing window by picking from right to left at the Select objects: prompt; *Object Grouping,* which toggles object grouping on or off; *Associative Hatch,* controls object selection for associative hatched objects; *Default:*, which returns the Selection Mode settings to their original *Noun/Verb Selection* and *Implied Windowing*.

Pickbox Size   This section furnishes a slider bar with an image tile to dynamically alter your pick-box size.

Object Sort Method   This section opens the Object Sort Method subdialog and lets you rearrange the following sort methods for entities in your database. In most cases, you will not want to edit the sort order for object snaps or regens. However, you may want to use Object Selection to control which of two overlapping lines are selected when you pick them. Plotting and PostScript allows you to determine the overlay of screened or hatched areas.

- Object Selection
- Object Snap
- Redraws
- Regens
- Plotting
- PostScript Output

See Also   Draworder, Grips, Plot, Select; *System Variables:* Implied Windowing-Pickauto; Noun/Verb Selection-Pickfirst; Object Grouping-Pickstyle; Pickbox Size-Pickbox; Press and Drag-Pickdrag; Use Shift to Add-Pickadd

Ddstyle

*See **Style***

Dducs

Dducs has been discontinued. AutoCAD has aliased the **Dducs** command to **UCS** in the acad.pgp file. See **UCS**.

Dducsp

*See **UCSman***

Ddunits

Ddunits has been discontinued. AutoCAD has aliased the **Ddunits** command to **Units** in the acad.pgp file. See **Units**.

Ddview

Ddview has been discontinued. AutoCAD has aliased the **Ddview** command to **View** in the acad.pgp file. See **View**.

Ddvpoint

Ddvpoint opens the Viewpoint Presets dialog for establishing a 3D view by dynamically picking an angle from the X axis in the XY plane and an angle from the XY plane. The equivalent command-line prompt is **Vpoint**.

To Set a 3D View

Command line: **Ddvpoint**

Menu: View ➤ 3D Views ➤ Viewpoint Presets...

Provide information as needed in the dialog.

Options

The Viewpoint Presets dialog provides pick buttons to Set Viewing Angles Absolute to WCS or Relative to UCS. An image-tile box rotates a white arm to preset viewing angles with your cursor when picking outside the circle and to specific angles when picking within the circle. The designated angle then appears in the edit box for X Axis and XY Plane.

The image on the left indicates the angle in the XY plane, while the image on the right indicates the angle above or below the XY plane. Picking Set to Plan View shifts the view to plan view relative to the selected coordinate system.

See Also   Plan, View, Vpoint

Delay

Delay lets you set a designated time period for viewing a slide in a script file.

To Delay a Slide

Command line: **Delay** (or **'Delay**, to use transparently)

Enter delay time (in milliseconds): Enter the desired number (maximum 32767 ms).

See Also   Mslide, Rscript, Script, Slidebb.exe, Vslide

Detachurl

Detachurl lets you detach the URL from an object in a drawing to remove the hyperlink to a Web site.

To Detach a URL

Command line: **Detachurl**

Select objects: Use any selection method to detach the URL from a drawing.

AutoCAD removes the object's Xdata or the rectangle and its Xdata that represents the area. The urllayer created during attachment of the URL can be purged from the drawing. To update the drawing and its associated .dwf file, save the drawing as a .dwg and a .dwf file.

See Also   Attachurl, Gotourl, Hyperlink, Hyperlink options, Inserturl, Openurl, Selecturl

Dimensioning Commands

In earlier releases of AutoCAD, dimensioning was accomplished by first using the **Dim** command to put the command line in Dimensioning mode (**Dim:Mode**) and then issuing a dimensioning subcommand. To maintain compatibility with previous versions of AutoCAD, all of the existing Dimensioning mode subcommands are still available and may be used in the same way.

AutoCAD generally uses the same types of dimensions and dimension label components as standard drafting. Figure D.1 gives examples of the five types of dimensions possible in AutoCAD drawings: linear, angular, diametric, radial, and ordinate. Dimension labels consist of the elements illustrated in Figure D.2.

FIGURE D.1: Types of dimensions

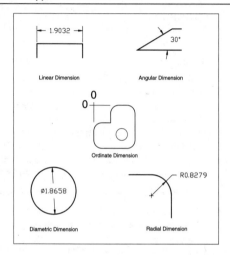

FIGURE D.2: Components of dimension labels

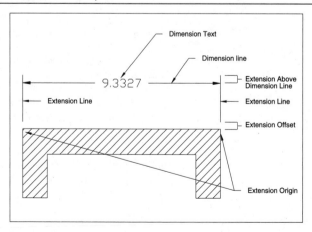

Variables for Controlling Dimensions

Table D.2 describes variables that control the way AutoCAD draws
dimensions. These variables control extension line and text location,
tolerance specifications, arrow styles and sizes, and much more.

TABLE D.2: The Dimension Variables

Variable	Description
Dimadec	Specifies the number of **dec**imal places for **a**ngular **dim**ension text: 1 = relies on current value of *Dimdec*; 0–8 = uses actual value specified. (Primary Units tab/Angular Dimensions section/Precision)
	Prompt: `Enter new value for DIMADEC <0>:`.
Dimalt	When on, **dim**ension texts for two measurement systems are inserted simultaneously (**alt**ernate). *Dimaltf* and *Dimaltd* must also be set appropriately. The alternate dimension is placed within brackets. Angular dimensions are not affected. This variable is commonly used when inches and metric units must be displayed at the same time in a dimension. The default setting is off. (Alternate Units tab/Display alternate units)
	Prompt: `Enter new value for DIMALT <OFF>:`.
Dimaltd	When *Dimalt* is on, *Dimaltd* controls the number of decimal places the alternate dimension will have (**alt**ernate **d**ecimal places). Values range from 0-8. The default value is 2. See **Dimaltz**. (Alternate Units tab/Alternate Units section/Precision)
	Prompt: `Enter new value for DIMALTD <2>:`.
Dimaltf	When *Dimalt* is on, *Dimaltf* controls the multiplication factor for the alternate dimension (**alt**ernate **f**actor). The value held by *Dimaltf* will be multiplied by the standard dimension value to determine the alternate dimension. The default value is 25.4, the number required to display metric units. (Alternate Units tab/Alternate Units section/Multiplier for alt units)
	Prompt: `Enter new value for DIMALTF <25.4000>:`.
Dimaltrnd	Controls the amount to which all dimensions for **alt**ernate units are **round**ed. The default is 0. (Alternate Units tab/Alternate Units section/Round distances to:)
	Prompt: `Enter new value for DIMALTRND <0.0000>:`.

TABLE D.2 (continued): The Dimension Variables

Variable	Description
Dimalttd	Sets the number of **alt**ernate unit tolerance **d**ecimal places. Values range from 0–8. (Tolerances tab/Alternate Unit Tolerance section/Precision)
	Prompt: `Enter new value for DIMALTTD <2>:`.
Dimalttz	When *Dimtol* is on, controls **alt**ernate **t**olerance value suppression of **z**eros. Values range from 0–15. See **Dimaltz**. (Tolerances tab/Zero Suppression/Leading and Trailing)
	Prompt: `Enter new value for DIMALTTZ <0>:`.
Dimaltu	Controls method for displaying dimension units format for all dimension styles expect angular for **alt**ernate **u**nits: 1 = Scientific; 2 = Decimal; 3 = Engineering; 4 = Architectural Stacked; 5 = Fractional Stacked; 6 = Architectural; 7 = Fractional; 8 = Windows Desktop. (Alternate Units tab/Alternate Units section/Unit format)
	Prompt: `Enter new value for DIMALTU <2>:`.
Dimaltz	When *Dimalt* is on, allows you to set the suppression zeros for alternate unit dimension values: 0 = Suppress zero feet/inches; 1 = Include zero feet/inches; 2 = Include zero feet/Suppress zero inches; 3 = Suppress zero feet/Include zero inches; 4 = Suppress leading zeroes for decimal dimensions; 8 = Suppress trailing zeros for decimal dimensions; 12 = Suppress leading and trialing zeroes. Values range from 0–15. See **Dimalttz**. (Alternate Units tab/Zero Suppression section/Leading and Trailing)
	Prompt: `Enter new value for DIMALTZ <0>:`.
Dimapost	When *Dimalt* is on, you can use *Dimapost* to append text to the alternate dimension (**a**lternate **post**). For example, if *Dimapost* is given the value "mm," the alternate dimension will appear as `valuemm` instead of just `value`. The default value is null. To change a previously set value to null, enter a period for the *Dimapost* new value. (Alternate Units tab/Alternate Units section/Prefix: and Suffix:)
	Prompt: `Enter new value for DIMAPOST, or . for none <" ">:`.
Dimaso	When on, dimensions will be associative (**asso**ciative). When off, dimensions will consist of separate drawing entities with none of the associative dimension properties. The default is on. (Set value at command line.)
	Prompt: `Enter new value for DIMASO <ON>:`.

TABLE D.2 (continued): The Dimension Variables

Variable	Description
Dimasz	Sets the size of dimension arrows or *Dimblks* (**a**rrow **si**ze). If set to 0, a tick is drawn in place of an arrow. See **Dimblk**. (Lines and Arrows tab/Arrowheads section/Arrow size:) Prompt: `Enter new value for DIMASZ <0.1800>:`.
Dimatfit	When *Dimalt* is on, sets a dimension style with **al**ter-nate **fit** options: 0 = Both text and arrows; 1 = Text; 2 = Arrows; 3 = Either the text or the arrows, which-ever fits best. (Fit tab/Fit Options section) Prompt: `Enter new value for DIMATFIT <3>:`.
Dimaunit	Sets **a**ngle format for angular **dim**ension **unit**s: 0 = Decimal degrees; 1 = Degrees/Minutes/Seconds; 2 = Gradians; 3 = Radians; 4 = Surveyor Units. (Pri-mary Units tab/Angular Dimensions section/Units format) (Set value for Surveyor at command line.) Prompt: `Enter new value for DIMAUNIT <0>:`.
Dimazin	Controls suppression of zeros for angular dimensions. See **Dimalttz**. (Primary Units tab/Angular Dimen-sions/Zero Suppression/Leading and Trailing) Values range from 0–3. Prompt: `Enter new value for DIMAZIN <0>:`.
Dimblk	You can replace the standard AutoCAD dimension arrow with one of your own design by creating a drawing of your symbol and making it a **bl**ock. You then give *Dim-blk* the name of your symbol block. This block must be drawn corresponding to a one-by-one unit area and must be oriented as the right side arrow. (Lines and Arrows tab/Arrowheads section/ 1st: and 2nd: User arrow...) Prompt: `Enter new value for DIMBLK, or . for default <" ">:`.
Dimblk1	With *Dimsah* set to On, you can replace the standard AutoCAD dimension arrows with two different arrows using *Dim**blk1*** and *Dimblk2*. *Dimblk1* holds the name of the block defining the first dimension arrow, while *Dim**blk2*** holds the name of the second dimension arrow **bl**ock. (Lines and Arrows tab/Arrowheads section/ 1st: and 2nd: User arrow...) Prompt: `Enter new value for DIMBLK1, or . for default <" ">:`.

TABLE D.2 (continued): The Dimension Variables

Variable	Description
Dimblk2	See **Dimblk1**.
Dimcen	Sets the size of **cen**ter marks used during the Center, Diameter, and Radius dimension subcommands. A negative value draws center lines instead of the center-mark cross, whereas a 0 value draws nothing. (Lines and Arrows tab/Center Marks for Circles section/Size)
	Prompt: `Enter new value for DIMCEN <0.0900>:`.
Dimclrd	Lets you specify **col**ors for **d**imensions lines, arrow-heads, and dimension leader lines. (Lines and Arrows tab/Dimension Lines/Color)
	Prompt: `Enter new value for DIMCLRD <0>:`.
Dimclre	Sets **col**or for dimension **e**xtension lines. The default is 0.(Lines and Arrows tab/Extension Lines/Color)
	Prompt: `Enter new value for DIMCLRE <0>:`.
Dimclrt	Sets **col**or for dimension **t**ext. (Text tab/Text Appearance/Text color)
	Prompt: `Enter new value for DIMCLRT <0>:`
Dimdec	Sets the precision from 0–8 for primary units dimensions **dec**imal place. (Primary Units/Linear Dimensions/Precision)
	Prompt: `Enter new value for DIMDEC <4>:`.
Dimdle	With *Dimtsz* given a value greater than 0, dimension lines can extend past the extension lines by the amount specified in *Dimdle* (**d**imension **l**ine **e**xtension). This amount is not adjusted by *Dimscale*. (Lines and Arrows tab/Extension Lines section/Extend beyond dim lines)
	Prompt: `Enter new value for DIMDLE <0.0000>:`.
Dimdli	Sets the distance at which dimension lines are offset when you use the *Baseline* or *Continue* dimension subcommands (**d**imension **l**ine **i**ncrement). (Lines and Arrows tab/Dimension Lines/Baseline spacing)
	Prompt: `Enter new value for DIMDLI <0.3800>:`.
Dimdsep	Provides you with options to **sep**arate linear dimensions for **d**ecimal unit format with a period, comma, or space. (Primary Units tab/Linear Dimensions section/Decimal separator)
	Prompt: `Enter new value for DIMDSEP <".">:`.

TABLE D.2 (continued): The Dimension Variables

Variable	Description
Dimexe	Sets the distance the extension lines are drawn past the dimension lines (**ex**tension line **e**xtension). (Lines and Arrows tab/Extension Lines section/Extend beyond dim lines)
	Prompt: `Enter new value for DIMEXE <0.1800>:`.
Dimexo	Sets the distance between the beginning of the dimensions extension line and the actual point selected at the `Extension line origin:` prompt (**ex**tension line **o**ffset). (Lines and Arrows tab/Extension Lines section/Offset from origin)
	Prompt: `Enter new value for DIMEXO <0.0625>:`.
Dimfit	When *Dimalt* is off, adjusts the dimension text and arrowheads so they **fit** inside and outside extension lines: 0 = Both text and arrows placed outside: 1 = Text supercedes, arrows placed outside extension lines; 2 = Arrows; 3 = Either the text or the arrows, whichever fits best; 4 = AutoCAD draws leader from dimension line to dimension text when text space is not available; 5 = Leader is eliminated. (Fit tab/Fit Options section)
	Prompt: `Enter new value for DIMFIT <3>:`.
Dimfrac	Provides options to set a dimensions **frac**tional format to Horizontal (0), Diagonal (1), or Not stacked (2) when *Dimlunit* is set to 4 (Architectural) or 5 (Fractional). (Primary Units tab/Linear Dimensions/Fraction format:)
	Prompt: `Enter new value for DIMFRAC <0>:`.
Dimgap	Sets the distance or **gap** between the text and the dimension line, and lets you enclose text within a box by assigning it a negative value. (Text tab/Text Placement section/Offset from Dim line)
	Prompt: `Enter new value for DIMGAP <0.0900>:`.
Dimjust	Controls the **just**ification of horizontal dimension text: 0 = centered between extension lines; 1 = adjacent to 1st extension line; 2 = adjacent to 2nd extension line; 3 = above and aligned with 1st extension line; 4 = above and aligned with 2nd extension line. (Set value at command line)
	Prompt: `Enter new value for DIMJUST <0>:`.
Dimldrblk	Sets arrow type for leaders. To disable arrow type, enter a dot (.).
	Prompt: `Enter new value for DIMLDRBLK, or . for default <"">:`.

TABLE D.2 (continued): The Dimension Variables

Variable	Description
Dimlfac	Sets the global scale factor for dimension values (**l**ength **fac**tor). Linear distances will be multiplied by the value held by *Dimlfac*. This multiple will be entered as the dimension text. This can be useful when drawings are not drawn to scale. (Primary Units tab/Measurement Scale section/Scale factor) Prompt: `Enter new value for DIMLFAC <1.0000>:`.
Dimlim	When set to on, dimension text is entered as two values representing a dimension range rather than a single value. This range or **lim**its is determined by the values given to *Dimtp* (**p**lus tolerance) and *Dimtm* (**m**inus **t**olerance). (Set value at command line) Prompt: `Enter new value for DIMLIM <OFF>:`.
Dimlunit	Sets the unit format for **l**inear dimensions primary **unit**s to: 1 (Scientific); 2 (Decimal); 3 (Engineering); 4 (Architectural); 5 (Fractional); 6 (Windows Desktop). (Primary Units tab/Linear Dimensions section/Unit format) Prompt: `Enter new value for DIMLUNIT <4>:`.
Dimlwd	Use the minus value of -2 to set **l**ine **wid**th of dimension lines Byblock and -1 for Bylayer; otherwise, enter a valid default value. (Lines and Arrows tab/Dimension Lines section/Lineweight) Prompt: `Enter new value for DIMLWD <-2>:`.
Dimlwe	Use the minus value of -2 to set a dimensions **l**ine **w**idth for **e**xtension lines Byblock and -1 for Bylayer; otherwise, enter a valid default value. (Lines and Arrows tab/Dimension Lines section/Lineweight) Prompt: `Enter new value for DIMLWE <-2>:`.
Dimpost	Automatically appends text strings to dimension text. For example, if *Dimpost* is given the value "inches," dimension text will appear as value inches instead of just value. To change a previously set value to null, enter a period for the *Dimpost* new value. If you use *Dimpost* in conjunction with appended dimension text, the *Dimpost* value is included as part of the default dimension text. (Primary Units tab/Linear Dimenions section/Prefix: and Suffix) Prompt: `Enter new value for DIMPOST, or .` `for none <"">:`.

TABLE D.2 (continued): The Dimension Variables

Variable	Description
Dimrnd	Sets the amount to which all dimensions are **round**ed. For example, if you set *Dimrnd* to 1, all dimensions will be integer values. The number of decimal places affected depends on the precision value set by the **Units** command. (Primary Units tab/Linear Dimensions section/Round off)
	Prompt: Enter new value for DIMRND <0.0000>:.
Dimsah	When set to on, allows the separate arrow blocks *Dimblk1* and *Dimblk2* to replace the standard AutoCAD arrows (**s**eparate **a**rrow **h**eads). If *Dimtsz* is set to a value greater than 0, *Dimsah* has no effect. (Set value at command line)
	Prompt: Enter new value for DIMSAH <OFF>:.
Dimscale	Sets the **scale** factor for dimension variables that control dimension lines and arrows and text size (unless current text style has a fixed height). If your drawing is not full scale, you should set this variable to reflect the drawing scale. For example, for a drawing whose scale is 1/4" equals 1', you should set *Dimscale* to 48. The default value is 1.0. (Fit tab/Scale for Dimension Features/Use overal scale of)
	Prompt: Enter new value for DIMSCALE <1.0000>:.
Dimsd1	When set on, the first dimension line is not drawn (**s**uppress **d**imension line **1**). (Lines and Arrows tab/Dimension Lines section/Suppress: Dim Line 1)
	Prompt: Enter new value for DIMSD1 <OFF>:.
Dimsd2	When set on, the second dimension line is not drawn (**s**uppress **d**imension line **2**). (Lines and Arrows tab/Dimension Lines section/Suppress: Dim Line 2)
	Prompt: Enter new value for DIMSD2 <OFF>:.
Dimse1	When set to on, the first dimension line extension is not drawn (**s**uppress **e**xtension **1**). (Lines and Arrows tab/Extension Lines section/Suppress: Ext Line 1)
	Prompt: Enter new value for DIMSE1 <OFF>:.
Dimse2	When set to on, the second dimension line extension is not drawn (**s**uppress **e**xtension **2**). (Lines and Arrows tab/Extension Lines section/Suppress: Ext Line 2)
	Prompt: Enter new value for DIMSE2 <OFF>:.

TABLE D.2 (continued): The Dimension Variables

Variable	Description
Dimsho	When set to on, dimension text in associative dimensions will dynamically change to reflect the location of a dimension point as it is being moved (**sho**w dimension). (Set value at command line)
	Prompt: `Enter new value for DIMSHO <ON>:`.
Dimsoxd	When set to on, dimension lines do not appear outside of the extension lines (**s**uppress **o**utside e**x**tension **d**imension lines). If *Dimtix* is also set to on and the space between the extension lines prohibits the display of a dimension line, no dimension line is drawn. (Set value at command line)
	Prompt: `Enter new value for DIMSOXD <OFF>:`.
Dimstyle	Read only. Opens the Dimension Style Manager dialog to identify and set the dimension **style** settings. (Enter as Setvar/Dimstyle)
Dimtad	When set to on and *Dimtih* is off, dimension text in linear dimensions will be placed above the dimension line (**t**ext **a**bove **d**imension line). When off, the dimension line will be split in two, and text will be placed in line with the dimension line. Available options: 0 = Centered; 1 = Above; 2 = Outside; 3 = JIS. (Text tab/Text Placement section/ Vertical)
	Prompt: `Enter new value for DIMTAD <0>:`.
Dimtdec	Controls **t**olerance value **dec**imal place for dimensions. (Tolerances tab/Tolerance Format section/Precision)
	Prompt: `Enter new value for DIMTDEC <4>:`.
Dimtfac	Sets **t**ext scale **fac**tor for text height of **t**olerance values based on *Dimtxt*, the dimension text height variable. Use *Dimtfac* to display the plus and minus characters when *Dimtol* is on and *Dimtm* does not equal *Dimtp*, or when *Dimlim* is on. (Tolerances tab/Tolerance Format section/ |Scaling for height)
	Prompt: `Enter new value for DIMTFAC <1.0000>:`.
Dimtih	When set to on, dimension text placed between extension lines will always be horizontal (**t**ext **i**nside **h**orizontal). When set to off, text will be aligned with the dimension line. (Text tab/Text Alignment section/Aligned with dimension line)
	Prompt: `Enter new value for DIMTIH <ON>:`.

TABLE D.2 (continued): The Dimension Variables

Variable	Description
Dimtix	When set to on, dimension text will always be placed between extension lines (**t**ext **i**nside e**x**tension). (Set value at command line)
	Prompt: `Enter new value for DIMTIX <ON>:`.
Dimtm	When *Dimtol* or *Dimlin* is on, *Dimtm* determines the minus tolerance value of the dimension text (**t**olerance **m**inus). (Tolerances tab/Tolerance Format/Lower value)
	Prompt: `Enter new value for DIMTM <0.0000>:`.
Dimtmove	Offers options for text placement when text is not in the default position: 0 = Beside the dimension line; 1 = Over the dimension line, with a leader; 3 = Over the dimension line, without a leader. (Fit tab/Text Placement section/options as listed)
	Prompt: `Enter new value for DIMTMOVE <0>:`.
Dimtofl	With *Dimtofl* on, a dimension line is always drawn between extension lines even when text is drawn outside (**t**ext **o**utside— **f**orced **l**ine). (Set value at command line)
	Prompt: `Enter new value for DIMTOFL <ON>:`.
Dimtoh	With *Dimtoh* on, dimension text placed outside extension lines will always be horizontal (**t**ext **o**utside—**h**orizontal). When set to off, text outside extension lines will be aligned with dimension line. (Set value at command line)
	Prompt: `Enter new value for DIMTOH <ON>:`.
Dimtol	With *Dimtol* on, tolerance values set by *Dimtp* and *Dimtm* are appended to the dimension text (**tol**erance). (Set value at command line)
	Prompt: `Enter new value for DIMTOL <OFF>:`.
Dimtolj	Provides control of vertical position of text for tolerance values: 0 = Bottom; 1 = Middle; 2 = Top. (Tolerances tab/Tolerance Format section/Vertical position)
	Prompt: `Enter new value for DIMTOLJ <1>:`.
Dimtp	When *Dimtol* or *Dimlim* is on, *Dimtp* determines the plus tolerance value of the dimension text (**t**olerance **p**lus). (Tolerances tab/Tolerance Format section/Upper value)
	Prompt: `Enter new value for DIMTP <0.0000>:`.

TABLE D.2 (continued): The Dimension Variables

Variable	Description
Dimtsz	Sets the size of tick marks drawn in place of the standard AutoCAD arrows (**t**ick **s**ize). When set to 0, the standard arrow is drawn. When greater than 0, tick marks are drawn and take precedence over *Dimblk1* and *Dimblk2*. (Lines and Arrows tab/Arrowheads section/Arrow size) Prompt: `Enter new value for DIMTSZ <0.0000>:.`
Dimtvp	When *Dimtad* is off, *Dimtvp* specifies the location of the dimension text in relation to the dimension line (**t**ext **v**ertical **p**osition). A positive value places the text above the dimension line, whereas a negative value places the text below the dimension line. The dimension line will split to accommodate the text unless the *Dimtvp* value is greater than 1. (Set value at command line) Prompt: `Enter new value for DIMTVP <0.0000>:.`
Dimtxsty	Selects a **t**ext **sty**le for your dimensions based on style names defined in your drawing. (Text tab/ Text Appearance section/ text style) Prompt: `Enter new value for DIMTXSTY <"STANDARD">:.`
Dimtxt	Sets the height of dimension **text** when the current text-style height is set to 0. (Text tab/Text Appearance section/Text height) Prompt: `Enter new value for DIMTXT <0.1800>:.`
Dimtzin	Sets the appearance for **t**olerance values for **z**ero suppression. See **Dimazin**. (Tolerances tab/Zero Suppression/options listed) Prompt: `Enter new value for DIMTZIN <0>:.`
Dimunit	When *Dimalt* is off, controls **unit** format for all dimension styles except angular. Values range from 0–8. See **Dimlunit**. (Primary Units tab/Linear Dimensions section/Unit format) Prompt: `Enter new value for DIMUNIT <3>:.`
Dimupt	If set to on, **up**dates **t**ext position during dimensioning. (Set value at command line) Prompt: `Enter new value for DIMUPT <ON>:.`
Dimzin	Determines the display of inches when Architectural units are used. When set to 0, zero feet or **z**ero **in**ches will not be displayed. When set to 1, zero feet and zero inches will be displayed. When set to 2, zero inches will not be displayed. When set to 3, zero feet will not be displayed. (Primary Units tab/Zero Suppression) Prompt: `Enter new value for DIMZIN <0>:.`

Dimensioning and Drawing Scales

Take care when dimensioning drawings at a scale other than one-to-one. If the *Dimscale* dimension variable is not set properly, arrows and text will appear too small or too large. In extreme cases, they may not appear at all. If you enter a dimension and arrows or text do not appear, check the *Dimscale* setting and make sure it is a value equal to the drawing scale. For instance, a drawing at one-to-one that is going to be plotted at 1/4″ =1′, the dimscale should be set to 48.

Starting the Dimensioning Process

Depending upon your system configuration or your preferences, you may access the dimensioning commands in a number of different ways.

Toolbar   From the Dimension toolbar, click the appropriate Dimensioning button.

Pull-down menu   From the Dimension menu, select the appropriate command on the menu.

Command line directly   Each Dimensioning Mode command has an equivalent AutoCAD command that can be invoked directly at the command prompt; for example, **Dimaligned**.

Command line with Dim/Dim1   All of the dimensioning subcommands from previous releases of AutoCAD are still available for compatibility purposes. To use them, enter **Dim** or **Dim1** at the command prompt. At this point, the prompt changes to Dim:, and you can enter any dimensioning subcommand. These and the transparent commands (see **Transparent**) are the only AutoCAD commands you can enter while in the Dimensioning mode. When you have finished entering dimensions under the **Dim** command, issue the **Exit** command, or press Escape to return to the standard command prompt. If you want to enter only a single dimension, use **Dim1**. The 1 tells AutoCAD to return you automatically to the command prompt after you complete one dimension. You can invoke any dimension command by entering just its shortcut key or alias. For example, you can enter **Dia** instead of **Diameter**. Alternative short command forms are shown with each subcommand as appropriate.

Dimaligned

Dimaligned aligns a dimension with two points or an object. The dimension text appears in the current style. Figure D.3 illustrates the difference between aligned and rotated dimensions. Dimension settings are modified with the Ddim dialog. The Dimensioning mode equivalent is **Dim ↵ Aligned/Al/Ali**.

FIGURE D.3: Aligned and rotated dimensions

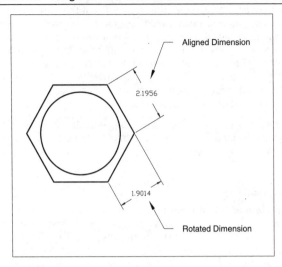

To Align a Dimension

Command line: **Dimaligned**, **Dal**, **Dimali**

Menu: Dimension ➤ Aligned

Dimension Toolbar: Aligned Dimension

1. **Specify first extension line origin or <select object>:** If you press enter, proceed to step 2 at the prompt Select object to dimension:. If you pick one end of object to be dimensioned or entered coordinates for an extension line, you will be prompted for the following:

   Specify second extension line origin: Pick the other end of the object.

2. **Specify dimension line location or [Mtext/Text/Angle]: Dimension text = measured length.** If you wish to modify the text or text angle, enter an option (**M**, **T**, **A**). To position the dimension line dynamically, drag your cursor and pick a point, or enter a coordinate for the location of the dimension line.

Options

Mtext Enter (**M**) to open the Multiline Text Editor dialog, and display the text as angle brackets <>. Accept the default and pick OK, or enter a new dimension text within the brackets. Additional text can be placed before or after the angle brackets as described in the Text option.

Text   This option (**T**) allows you to edit and customize the dimension. AutoCAD displays the dimension measurement at the command prompt. Enter **dimension text <measured length>:** allows you to modify the measurement. If you wish to enter a different value, enter it at the command prompt, and press ↵. If you wish to insert additional text before the dimension measurement or append text after it, place angle bracket signs (<>) to represent the default dimension value, and add the desired text before or after. For example, if you wish to add "inches" *after* the value, type <> **inches** at the Dimension text: prompt.

Angle   This option (**A**) allows you to change the default angle of the text. Text will be placed horizontally (0 degrees) unless you specify a dimension text orientation to the Specify angle of dimension text: prompt.

Dimangular

Dimangular creates a dimension label showing the angle described by an arc, circle, or two lines or by a set of three points. An arc with dimension arrows at each end is drawn, and the angle value is placed using current text style. Dimension settings can be modified with the Ddim dialog or by selecting each individual *Dim* variable. The Dimensioning mode equivalent is **Dim ↵ Angular/An**.

To Create an Angle Dimension Label

Command line: **Dimangular**, **Dan**, **Dimang**

Menu: Dimension ➤ Angular

Dimension Toolbar: Angular Dimension

1.   **Select arc, circle, line, or <specify vertex>:** Pick an object as indicated by the prompt, or press ↵ to indicate angles using your cursor.

   • If you selected an arc or a circle, continue with step 2.

   • If you selected a line, you will be prompted Select second line:. Select another line, and then continue with step 2.

   • If you pressed ↵, you may specify the desired angle by giving three points: the **Specify angle vertex:**, the **Specify first angle endpoint:**, and the **Specify second angle endpoint:**. Then continue with step 2.

2.   **Specify dimension arc line location or [Mtext/Text/Angle:]** If you wish to modify the text or text angle, enter an option (**M, T, A**). Otherwise, drag your cursor and pick a point, or enter a coordinate for the location of the dimension line as the extension line with text appears.

Options

For a description of the Mtext, Text, and Angle options, see the **Dimaligned** command.

Dimbaseline

Dimbaseline continues a dimension string using the first extension line of the most recently inserted dimension as its first extension line. You are prompted only for the second extension line origin. Each new dimension is offset by an increment set in the *Dimdli* system variable from the previous dimension line. Prompts vary depending on the type of dimension that was last created. The Dimensioning mode equivalent is **Dim ↵ Baseline/B**.

To Continue a Dimension from the Baseline

Command line: **Dimbaseline**, **Dba**, **Dimbase**

Menu: Dimension ➣ Baseline

Dimension Toolbar: [⊩⊩⊩] Baseline Dimension

1. **Specify a second extension line origin or [Undo/Select] <Select>:**. Pressing ↵ prompts to Select base dimension: if you wish to pick a new dimension for the start point. Otherwise, select as many points as you wish along the measured object. AutoCAD responds Dimension text = default dimension and draws a series of dimensions, each starting from the second point extension of the last dimension in the chain. To end the command, press ↵ or use the Escape key.

   • If no dimensions exist in the current session, the prompt appears: Select base dimension:, Linear, Ordinate, or Angular Associative Dimension Required.

   • If the previous dimension was linear, the prompt in step 1 appears. Otherwise, previous angular or ordinate dimensions display the prompt: Specify a second extension line origin or [Undo/Select] <Select>:. Pick a point, use an Object Snap mode option, or press ↵ to select a base dimension.

Option

Undo   Removes the last dimension string. AutoCAD allows you to repeat the **U** option until all dimension strings are undone and then displays the prompt to Select base dimension.

See Also   *Dimension Variable:* Dimdli

Dimcenter

Dimcenter places a cross at the center point of a selected arc or circle. To choose center lines instead of center marks, and to change the size of the center mark, use the *Dimcen* dimension variable or reset them in the Geometry dialog of the **Ddim** command. The Dimensioning mode equivalent is **Dim ⏎ Center/Ce**.

To Mark the Center of an Arc or Circle

Command line: **Dimcenter**, **Dce**

Menu: Dimension ➤ Center Mark

Dimension Toolbar: ⊕ Center Mark

Select arc or circle: Pick an arc or circle, and the mark will appear.

Dimcontinue

Dimcontinue draws a series, or "chain," of related dimensions by using the second extension line of the most recently inserted dimension as its first extension line. All of the "chained" dimension measurements add up to a total measurement of the object. You are prompted only for the second extension-line origin. If the original dimension is linear, the related dimensions are placed in line with and parallel to this dimension. The *Dimfit* system variable controls the positioning of the dimension lines and text between the selected points. The Dimensioning mode equivalent is **Dim ⏎ Continue/Co**.

To Continue a Dimension

Command line: **Dimcontinue**, **Dco**, **Dimcont**

Menu: Dimension ➤ Continue

Dimension Toolbar: ⊢┼┤ Continue Dimension

Specify a second extension line origin or [Undo/Select] <Select>: Select as many points as you wish along the measured object. AutoCAD responds with Dimension text = default dimension and draws a series of dimensions, each starting from the second extension line of the last dimension in the chain.

NOTE Pressing ⏎ displays the prompt Select continued dimension:. Pick a new dimension for the start point or ⏎ to exit **Dimcontinue**.

Option

Undo   Removes the last dimension string. AutoCAD allows you to repeat the U option until all dimension strings are undone and then displays the prompt to Specify a second extension line origin or (<select>/ Undo):.

Dimdiameter

Dimdiameter draws different types of diameter dimensions, depending upon the size of the arc or circle and upon the dimension settings created in the Dimstyle dialog. The Dimensioning mode equivalent is **Dim ⅃ Diameter/Di**.

To Dimension an Arc or Circle Diameter

Command line: **Dimdiameter**, **Ddi**, **Dimdia**

Menu: Dimension ➤ Diameter

Dimension Toolbar: 🔘 Diameter Dimension

1. **Select arc or circle:** Pick the arc or circle as appropriate.

2. **Specify dimension line location or [Mtext/Text/Angle]:** As the leader line extends in a dragging mode from the arc or circle, pick a point that indicates the location of the text, or enter an option (**M**, **T**, **A**). AutoCAD displays the value with **Dimension text = default dimension.** The direction of the leader is toward the center point. A center mark is also placed at the center of the arc or circle.

Options

For a description of the Mtext, Text, and Angle options, see the **Dimaligned** command.

> **NOTE**   Unless you modify the text, the dimension value will be preceded by a diameter symbol. The point at which you pick the arc or circle determines one end of the dimension arrow. If you want the dimension to be in a horizontal or vertical orientation, use the Quadrant Osnap override. Pick the left or right quadrant for a horizontal dimension; pick the top or bottom quadrant for a vertical dimension. If the *Dimtix* dimension variable is set to On, the dimension is placed inside the circle starting at your pick point. A center mark is also placed at the center of the arc or circle.

See Also   *Dimension Variables:* Dimcen, Dimtix.

Dimedit

Dimedit allows you to change and manipulate selected text and extension lines. **Dimedit** can be used to change the same elements on several dimension objects at once. Using this command, you can rotate text; shift it back to its original "home" position; and edit dimension text. The Oblique option allows you to skew existing dimension extension lines to an angle other than 90 degrees to the dimension line. This is used for isometrics. The **Dimedit** command combines the dimensioning subcommands **Dim: Hometext**; **Dim: Newtext**; **Dim: Trotate**; **and Dim: Oblique**.

To Edit Dimension Text

Command line: **Dimedit, Ded**

Menu: Dimension ➤ Oblique

Dimension Toolbar: ⊞ Dimension Edit

1. **Enter type of dimension editing [Home/New/Rotate/ Oblique] <Home>:** Select an option or press ↵.

2. **Select Objects:** Select dimensions and dimension text to edit.

Options

Home   Repositions all selected dimension text objects in their default positions. This has the same effect as the **Dim: Home** (or **Hom**) dimensioning subcommand.

New   Opens the Multiline Text Editor, replacing associative dimension text on several dimensions at once. Replace the angle brackets with new dimension text, pick OK, and then select the dimension text you wish to change. Entering text outside the brackets appends it to the existing dimension string. All associative dimensions selected will be changed to the new text. This has the same effect as the **Dim: Newtext** (or **N**) dimensioning subcommand.

Rotate   Allows you to rotate dimension text to a specified angle. At the prompt Enter text angle, enter the required angle. This has the same effect as the **Dim: Trotate** (or **Tr**) dimensioning subcommand.

Oblique   Allows you to change all selected extension lines to a specified angle. At the prompt: Enter obliquing angle (press ENTER for none):, enter the required angle. This has the same effect as the **Dim: Oblique** (or **Ob**) dimensioning subcommand.

Dimlinear

Creates a linear dimension. **Dimlinear** allows you to position linear dimensions in either a horizontal or a vertical direction as well as allows you to rotate the dimension line and text to a specified angle. This command combines the dimensioning subcommands **Dim: Horizontal** (or **Hor**), **Dim: Vertical** (or **Ver**), and **Dim: Rotate** (or **Ro**).

To Create Linear Dimensions

Command line: **Dimlinear, Dimed**

Menu: Dimension ➤ Linear

Dimension Toolbar: ⊢⊣ Linear Dimension

1. **Specify first extension line origin or <select object>:** Pick a point on the object to be dimensioned or press ↵.

2. **Specify second extension line origin:** Pick a second point on the object.

   - If you pressed ↵, you will be prompted to Select object to dimension:. When you select an object, AutoCAD automatically locates the origin points for the extension lines.

3. **Specify dimension line location or [Mtext/Text/Angle/ Horizontal/Vertical/Rotated]:** Enter an option, pick a location, or enter a coordinate for the location of the dimension line as the extension line with Mtext or text appears.

Options

For a description of the Mtext, Text, and Angle options, see the **Dimaligned** command.

Horizontal Allows you to specify a horizontal dimension at the Specify dimension line location or [Mtext/Text/Angle/Horizontal/Vertical/ Rotated]: prompt, or enter an option. You may also do this dynamically. If you drag your cursor up or down the screen, the horizontal dimension will appear.

Vertical Allows you to specify a vertical dimension at the Specify dimension line location or [Mtext/Text/Angle/Horizontal/Vertical/ Rotated]: prompt, or enter an option. You may also do this dynamically. If you drag your cursor to the left or right across the screen, the vertical dimension will appear.

Rotated Creates rotated dimensions. If you enter **R** to select the Rotated option, you will be prompted Specify angle of dimension line <0>: Enter an angle of rotation for the dimension line.

NOTE If you select a line or an arc, its end points are used as origins for the dimension lines; if you select a circle, the diameter end points are used as the origin points. Selecting polylines and other explodable objects only dimensions the individual line or arc segments. Objects mirrored or in a nonuniformly scaled block reference are not selectable.

Dimordinate

Dimordinate creates an ordinate dimension string based on a datum or origin point. The Dimensioning mode equivalent is **Dim ⊥ Ordinate/Or**. To set the origin point, use the **UCS** command, and specify an origin point for the part, e.g., the lower left corner of the part.

To Create Ordinate Dimensioning

Command line: **Dimordinate**, **Dor**, **Dimord**

Menu: Dimension ➤ Ordinate

Dimension Toolbar: Ordinate Dimension

1. **Specify feature location:** Pick the location of the feature to be dimensioned.

2. **Specify leader endpoint or [Xdatum/Ydatum/Mtext/ Text/Angle]:** Specify an end point for the leader. AutoCAD will determine automatically whether to measure the X or Y coordinate. Alternatively, you may enter **X** or **Y** to specify the axis along which the dimension is to be taken. Enter **T** or **M** if you wish to modify the dimension text. Then press ⊥ to display the value. The **Dimension text = default radius** value is displayed above the prompt.

Options

For a description of the Mtext, Text, and Angle options, see the **Dimaligned** command.

> **NOTE** If you pick a point at the `Specify leader endpoint:` prompt, then AutoCAD selects the dimension axis based on the angle defined by the points you pick during the `Select Feature:` and `Specify leader endpoint:` prompts.

See Also UCS

Dimoverride

Dimoverride changes an individual dimension's properties, such as its arrow style, colors, scale, text orientation, etc. It allows you to override current dimension variable settings for selected objects only, without changing the current Dimension style. The Dimensioning mode equivalent is **Dim ⊥ Override/Ove**.

To Override Dimension Variable Settings

Command line: **Dimoverride**, **Dov**, **Dimover**

Menu: Dimension ➤ Override

1. **Enter dimension variable name to override or [Clear overrides]:** Enter the name of a dimension variable, or type **C** to clear.

2. **Enter new value for dimension variable <(variables value)>:** Enter new value or setting for the dimension variable, pressing ↵ once to repeat the prompt or twice to exit the prompt.

3. **Select objects:** Select dimension object(s) to change.

Options

Clear Clears any dimension variable overrides. AutoCAD clears any overrides, and the dimension object reverts to the setting defined by its dimension style.

See Also Ddim, Dimstyle, Dim/Restore

Dimradius

Dimradius adds a radius dimension to arcs and circles in essentially the same way that **Dimdiameter** adds diameter dimensions. The Dimensioning mode equivalent is **Dim ↵ Radius/Ra**.

To Add a Radius Dimension

Command line: **Dimradius**, **Dra**, **Dimrad**

Menu: Dimension ➤ Radius

Dimension Toolbar: Radius Dimension

1. **Select arc or circle:** Pick the arc or circle. The point at which you pick the arc or circle determines one end of the dimension arrow.

2. **Specify dimension line location or [Mtext/Text/Angle]:** If you wish to modify the mtext, text, or text angle, enter an option (**M**, **T**, **A**), or drag the cursor to position the Mtext or text (and leader). The **Dimension text = default radius** value is displayed above the prompt.

Options

For a description of the Mtext, Text, and Angle options, see the **Dimaligned** command.

NOTE Unless you modify the Mtext or text, the dimension value will be preceded by the letter *R*. If a dimensioned circle or arc is large enough, the radius dimension will be positioned within it. Otherwise it is positioned outside the circle or arc, with a leader line pointing to the center. A center mark is also placed at the center of the arc or circle. To drag the dimension text outside the circle or arc, turn on **Dimupt**.

Dimstyle

Dimstyle opens the Dimension Style Manager dialog and allows you to set and visually control dimensions and extension-line settings, arrow type and size, text location and format, measurement units, dimension text appearance, and colors.

To Control and Modify Dimension Styles

Command line: **Dimstyle**, **Ddim**, **D**

Menu: Dimension ➤ Style...

Dimension Toolbar: Dimension Style

To activate a style, choose one from the *Styles* list, and pick Set Current. The *List:* drop-down box offers options to display All Styles or Styles in Use. If your drawing contains external reference files, remove the check mark for Don't List Files in Xref to display the xref filename and its saved dimensions' style names. Picking any name in the list provides a *Preview of:* <current dimension style> and a *Description* of the dimension style's settings. If you are not able to view all the comments about the dimension settings, place your cursor in the description area, and then use the arrow keys to maneuver down, up, left, or right.

The *Styles* list box contains the names of all the dimension styles that were created for the current drawing. Styles can be renamed by highlighting and then clicking the style name.

Set Current Highlight a dimension style name in the ***Style:*** list box, and then pick Set Current to make it current.

New... Displays New Dimension Style dialog with edit boxes to enter a *New Style Name:* by copying or Starting With an existing style, or to *Use For:* All dimensions, Linear dimensions, Angular dimensions, Radius dimensions, Diameter dimensions, Ordinate Dimensions, or Leaders and Tolerances. Continue exits the dialog and opens the New Dimension Style dialog to select settings for the new style.

Modify... Select a name from the ***Styles:*** list box, and then pick the button to open the Modify Dimension Style dialog to edit the settings for the selected dimension style.

Override... Select a name from the ***Styles:*** list box, and then pick the button to open the Override Current Style dialog to edit the settings for the selected dimension style.

Compare... Select a name from the ***Styles:*** list box, and then pick the button to open the Compare Dimension Styles dialog. Pick the style you wish to ***Compare:***, and then pick ***With:*** to display their differences in the list box below.

Print to Clipboard   Prints style comparison to the Windows Clipboard so you can paste it into another application, such as a word processing document.

Clicking **New...** opens the new Dimenstyle dialog to create a new dimension style. Clicking **Override...** or **Modify...** opens the Override Current Style dialog with six tabs: Lines and Arrows, Text, Fit, Primary Units, Alternate Units, and Tolerances.

Lines and Arrows   The Lines and Arrows tab controls the appearance of Dimension Lines, Extension Lines, Arrowheads, and Center Marks for Circles. You can set **Color** (*Dimclrd/Dimclre* variables) and **Lineweight** (*Dimlwd/Dimlwe* variables) of dimension and extension lines. When you are using Oblique strokes or Architectural ticks rather than arrows on the dimension line, the extension options specify the distance that the dimension line is to *Extend beyond Ticks:* (*Dimdle* variable). You can also specify a distance for the extension line to *Extend beyond Dim Lines:* (*Dimexe* variable). To **Suppress:** the display of dimension lines when they are outside the extension lines, use *Dim Line 1* for the first dimension line (*Dimsd1* variable) and *Dim Line 2* to suppress the second dimension line (*Dimesd2* variable). The **Suppress:** option suppresses the display of extension lines; *Ext Line 1* is used for the first extension line (*Dimse1* variable), and *Ext Line 2* is used for the second extension line (*Dimse2* variable). *Baseline spacing:* enters a distance for the spacing between the dimension lines of a baseline (*Dimdli* variable), and *Offset from Origin:* specifies a distance for the offset between the extension lines and the origin points (*Dimexo* variable).

Use the Arrowheads section to control the appearance of arrowheads. You can match the first and second arrowheads (*Dimblk* variable), or you may specify different arrowheads for dimensions by picking from the *1st:* and *2nd:* drop-down boxes (*Dimblk1/Dimblk2* variables) and for the *Leader:* (*Dimblk* variable). To change the **Arrow size:** (*Dimasz* variable), enter a value in the edit box. Selecting User Arrow... from the present options shown in the the *1st:* and *2nd:* dropdown boxes opens the Select Custom Arrow Block dialog to *Select from Drawing Blocks*. A non-zero *Arrow Size:* value draws oblique strokes instead of arrowheads based on the specified number multiplied by the **Dimscale** value and stores it in the *Dimtsz* variable.

The Preview window immediately shows changes to dimension values as they are made. The Center Marks for Circles section controls the appearance of center marks and lines for the diameter and radial dimensions used by the **Dimcenter**, **Dimdiameter**, and **Dimradius** commands. When you are using **Dimdiameter** or **Dimradius**, the center mark will be drawn only if you position the dimension line outside the circle or the arc. **Type:** uses the Mark option to create a center mark; the Line option to draw a center line; and the None option for no center mark or line. Pick the up or down arrow to specify the **Size:** of a center mark, or enter a value in the edit box. All of the values are stored in the *Dimcen* variable: a center mark is stored as a positive value; a center line is stored as a negative value; None is stored as a zero; and the size is stored as an actual value.

Text Tab   The Text tab is used to determine the appearance, placement, and alignment of dimension text inside and outside the extension lines. The Text Appearance section allows you to set the current style for dimension text by picking from available styles in the ***Text Style:*** (*Dimtxsty* variable) drop-down box. You can modify an existing style or create a new dimension text style by picking the adjacent ellipsis box and opening the Text Style dialog. The ***Text Color:*** edit box sets the color for dimension text (*Dimclrt* variable) by scrolling through and picking a color name from the list or by picking Other... to open the Select Color dialog and entering a color name or value in this dialog's **Color:** edit box. See **Color** for descriptions of the Byblock or Bylayer options. ***Text height:*** (*Dimtxt* variable) manipulates the height of the dimension text only if text style height is set to 0.

Fraction Scale Height sets the scale of fractions relative to dimension text. AutoCAD applies a multipler to the text height to set the height of dimension fractions relative to dimension text. AutoCAD stores the scale value in the *Dimtfac* system variable.

Pick the ***Draw Frame around Text*** checkbox if you wish to place a rectangle around dimension text.

The Text Placement section allows you to control ***Vertical:*** (*Dimtad* variable) orientation of text relative to the dimension line. Center centers the text between the extension lines; Above positions the text above or ***Offset from dim line:*** (*Dimgap* variable); Outside positions the text on the side of the dimension line farthest from the defining points; and JIS sets the text position to conform to Japanese Industrial Standards. To control ***Horizontal:*** (*Dimjust* variable) justification of text along dimension and extension lines, use the options available in the drop-down box. The Centered option centers the text between the extension lines; At Ext Line 1 left-justifies the text along the dimension line, near the first extension line; At Ext Line 2 right-justifies the text along the dimension line, near the second extension line; Over Ext Line 1 positions the text parallel to the first extension line; Over Ext Line 2 positions the text parallel to the second extension line.

Use the Text Alignment section to consistently manipulate the text ***Horizontal*** relative to the dimension line, ***Aligned with Dimension Line***, or per the ***ISO Standard***, in which case the text is aligned with the dimension line when placed inside the extension lines and horizontal when positioned outside the extension lines.

Fit Tab   The Fit Options sections offers several alternatives to place dimension text when insufficient space is available to fit both arrows and text between the extension lines. You can decide to relocate ***Either the Text or***

the Arrows, whichever Fits Best, the **Arrows**, the **Text**, or **Both Text and Arrows** (*Dimatfit* variable). Regardless of the option you choose, additional selections allow you to **Always Keep Text between Ext Lines,** which also centers the dimension text, and **Suppress Arrows If They Don't Fit inside Extension Lines** (*Dimtix* variable). If the *Dimtmove* system variable is set to 1, a leadered line is included when the default dimension text is displaced.

The Text Placement section controls the location of dimension text when it is not in the default position: Beside the dimension line; Over the dimension line, with a leader; Over the dimension line, without a leader.

The Scale for Dimension Features section allows you to manipulate the overall scale of the dimension. Pick **Use Overall Scale Of:** to set the overall scale factor of your drawing, and specify a value in the edit box, or use the up and down arrows. Picking **Scale Dimensions to Layout (PaperSpace)**, allows you to set a scale factor based on the scaling between the current ModelSpace viewport and PaperSpace.

Picking checkboxes in the Fine Tuning section allows you to **Place Text Manually when Dimensioning.** (*Dimupt* variable) so that you can determine placement of the dimension text as you draw the dimensions, or it allows you to **Always Draw Dim Lines between Ext Lines** for conditions when the arrowheads and the text will fit within the extension lines.

Primary Units Tab   The Linear Dimensions section controls the display of primary measurement units and also lets you add a text **Prefix:** or **Suffix:** to the default dimension text by entering labels in each edit box (*Dimpost* variable). For example, enter X.V.I.F. to display "V.I.F." below the dimension line. The **Unit Format:** drop-down allows you to set the unit format: for example, *Scientific, Decimal, Engineering, Architectural, Fractional, Windows Desktop* (*Dimunit* variable) as well as **Precision** (*Dimdec* variable), which gives the number of decimal places for units or for dimension text. When the unit format is set to Architectural or Fractional, the **Fraction Format:** (*Dimfrac* variable) edit box offers options to display fractional units as Diagonal, Horizontal, or Not Stacked. Use the **Decimal Separator** (*Dimdsep* value) edit box to show dimension text with a period (.), command (,), or space ( ) for all fractional formats except Windows Desktop. The Windows Desktop format is stored in the *Decimal Symbol* edit box in the Number tab of the Regional Settings Properties dialog, which is accessible from the Windows Control Panel. Use **Round Off:** (*Dimrnd* variable) to specify the value of dimensions that are rounded off. The maximum allowable is five decimal places with settings determined in conjunction with your precision value.

The Measurement Scale section allows you to control how AutoCAD displays dimensioned objects. Entering any nonzero positive value in the **Scale Factor:** (*Dimlfac* variable) edit box multiplies the actual value for linear, radius, diameter, ordinate, baseline, and continued dimensions by that value. A line, two units long, displays a dimension of six units when the scale factor is set to 3. Pick **Apply to Layout Dimensions Only** if you wish to manipulate your dimension text for layout scale in viewports.

The Angular Dimensions section offers a **Units format:** (*Dimaunit* variable) drop-down box to select the angle format, such as Decimal degrees, Degrees/Minutes/Seconds, Grads, Radians, and Surveyor. Use the **Precision:** (*Dimadec* variable) edit box to specify the number of decimal places to be used in measurements. Both Linear and Angular sections contain a Zero Suppression section with checkboxes for settings the appearance of feet and inches as well as suppressing **Leading** and **Trailing** zeros (*Dimazin* variable) in dimension text.

Alternate Units Tab Pick **Display alternate units** (*Dimalt* variable) in the Alternate Units tab section to set alternate unit dimensioning on, which will appear in square brackets [ ] adjacent to dimension text primary units. Many of the variables are identical to those in the Primary Units tab, including labels for **Unit Format:** (*Dimaltu* variable), **Precision** (*Dimalt* variable), **Prefix: and Suffix** (*Dimapost* variable), **Round Off:** or **Rounding distances to:** (*Dimaltrnd* variable), and **Zero Suppression** (*Dimaltz* variable). If you wish to display dimension *text* in imperial units as inches and in the metric system as millimeters then set the **Multiplier for Alt Units:** (*Dimaltf* variable) to a value of 25.4. Use the Placement section to control the alternate dimension text location: **After Primary Value** or **Below Primary Value**.

Tolerances Tab The Tolerance Format section allows you to append dimension tolerances. The **Method:** (*Dimtol* variable) choices include None (turns of tolerance display), Symmetrical (values are identical), Deviation (values are different), Limits (a limit expression with the maximum value over the minimum value), and Basic. The Basic option creates dimension text with a box drawn to its full extent, which may imply exact dimensions. You can also set **Precision** for Tolerance Format and Alternate Unit Tolerance as described for Primary Units. Depending upon the choices, you will need to specify **Upper Value:** (*Dimtp* variable) and/or **Lower Value:** (*Dimtm* variable) as well as **Vertical Position:** of the text (Top/Middle/Bottom) and **Scaling for Height** for the tolerance text. Pick checkboxes in the Zero Suppression sections (*Dimtzin* variable) for Tolerance Format and Alternate Unit Tolerance format to control **Leading** and **Trailing** zeros in dimension units and to suppress the display of **0 Feet** and **0 Inches**.

-Dimstyle

-Dimstyle creates and modifies dimension styles at the command line. **Dimstyle** or **Ddim** dialogs offer a more detailed and graphical approach to creating dimension styles, but **Dimstyle** allows a quick method of saving and creating dimension styles on the fly.

To Create/Modify a Dimension Style at the Command Line

Command line: **-Dimstyle**

Menu: none

Toolbar: none

1. **Current dimension style: STANDARD [Save/Restore/STatus/ Variables/Apply/?] <Restore>:** Enter a dimension style option. Type **?** to list the dimension styles in the current drawing, or select an option. AutoCAD also reports the current dimension style along the prompt.

2. Depending upon the option chosen, the prompts will vary. Enter the required information.

Options

Save Displays the prompt Enter name for new dimension style or [?]: when you type **S**. Enter a name to save the current dimension variable settings as a dimension style that can later be restored using the Restore option. You can save multiple dimension styles. You can also redefine an existing style by saving it back as the same name. This updates all the dims that have that style.

Restore Typing **R** returns the prompt Current dimension style: STANDARD Enter a dimension style name, [?] or <select dimension>: Select dimension: to the select dimension. Enter a name makes an existing dimension style the current default style. You can either name a specific style or select an object that uses the style. Restore immediately changes the current dimension style to reflect any differences.

Status Select this option by entering **St** to display the current dimension variable settings and descriptions. Once the dimension variables have been listed, **Dimstyle** ends.

Variables To list the dimension variable settings of a dimension style, enter **V** for the prompt Current dimension style: STANDARD Enter a dimension style name, [?] or <select dimension>:, and then press ⏎. You can either name a specific style or select an object that uses the style at the Select dimension: prompt. Once the dimension variables have been listed, **Dimstyle** ends.

Apply Typing **A** displays the Select objects: prompt allowing you to update selected dimension objects with the current dimension style, including any overrides.

? Lists the named dimension styles in the current drawing. Pressing ⏎ displays the Enter dimension style(s) to list <*>: prompt and reports the Named dimension styles: that are stored in the current drawing.

See Also Dim/Restore, Dim/Save, Ddim, Dimstyle

Dimtedit

Modifies the placement, justification, and rotation angle of a single dimension text object. The Dimensioning mode equivalent is **Dim ↵ Dimtedit**.

To Modify Dimension Text

Command line: **Dim ↵ Tedit/Te**, **Dimted**

Menu: Dimension ➤ Align Text ➤ Home/Angle/Center/Right

Dimension Toolbar: Dimension Text Edit

1. **Select Dimension:** Pick a single dimension.

2. **Specify new location for dimension text or [Left/Right/ Center/Home/Angle]:** Enter an option, or pick a new location for the dimension text. You can drag the text to the next location with the cursor. If you move the text to a position in line with the dimension line, the dimension will automatically join to become a continuous line.

Options

Left Justifies text to the left within the extension lines on linear, radius, and diameter dimensions.

Right Justifies text to the right within the extension lines on linear, radius, and diameter dimensions.

Center Justifies text to the midpoint centered within the extension lines on linear dimensions and to the outside for radius and diameter dimensions.

Home Places text in its default dimension. This has the same effect as the **Hometext** subcommand.

Angle Changes the angle for text. At the prompt Specify angle for dimension text:, enter an angle value, or indicate an angle by picking two points.

NOTE When **Dim/Tedit** is used on a dimension, the style is updated to the current dimension-style settings. If no style is associated with the dimension, then current dimension variable settings are used.

See Also Dim: Hometext; *System Variables:* Dimaso, Dimsho

Dimensioning Mode Subcommands

Most of the dimensioning commands are still available as subcommands in Dimensioning mode (**Dim: mode**). **Dim: mode** equivalents, where available, are identified with each command reviewed above. A number of dimensioning variables remain as **Dim:** subcommands only.

TABLE D.3: The DIM Subcommands and the Dimensioning Commands

DIM subcomand	Dimensioning Commands
Dim: Aligned/AL	DIMALIGNED
Dim: Angular/AN	DIMANGULAR
Dim: Baseline/B	DIMBASELINE
Dim: Center/CE	DIMCENTER
Dim: Continue/CO	DIMCONTINUE
Dim: Diameter/D	DIMDIAMETER
Dim: Hometext/HOM	DIMEDIT Home
Dim: Horizontal/HOR	DIMLINEAR Horizontal
Dim: Leader/L	LEADER
Dim: Newtext/N	DIMEDIT New
Dim: Oblique/OB	DIMEDIT Oblique
Dim: Ordinate/OR	DIMORDINATE
Dim: Override/OV	DIMOVERRIDE
Dim: Radius/RA	DIMRADIUS
Dim: Restore/RES	DIMSTYLE Restore
Dim: Rotated/RO	DIMLINEAR Rotated
Dim: Save/SA	DIMSTYLE Save
Dim: Status/STA	DIMSTYLE Status
Dim: Tedit/TE	DIMTEDIT
Dim: Trotate/TR	DIMEDIT Angle
Dim: Variables/VA	DIMSTYLE Variables
Dim: Tedit/TE	DIMTEDIT
Dim: Vertical/VE	DIMLINEAR Vertical
Remaining Subcommands	
Dim: Exit/E	Exits **Dim:** mode and returns to command mode
Dim: Redraw/RED	Redraws the display
Dim: Style/STY	Switches to a new text style
Dim: Undo/U	Erases the most recent dimension objects
Dim: Update/UP	Redraws dimensions to match the current settings

Dim: Exit

This command exits the **Dim** command and returns you to the standard command prompt.

To Exit Dim

Command line: **Dim** ↵ **Exit, E**

You can press the Escape key or type **E** in place of Exit. If you entered **Dim1** to begin dimensioning, Exit is not needed.

Dim: Leader

Dim: Leader adds leadered dimensions to drawings based on the current dimension style. You can replace the default dimension text with a single line of text.

To Add Dimensions/Text with Leaders

Command line: **Dim** ↵ **Leader, L.**

1. **Leader start:** Pick a point to start the leader. This is the point where the arrow will be placed.

2. **To point:** Pick the next point along the leader line, or continue to pick points as you would in drawing a line. When you are finished, press ↵. You can enter **U** to undo the last line segment drawn.

3. **Dimension text <default dimension>:** Press ↵ to accept the default, or enter new dimension text or a single line of text.

The distance between the Leader start point and the next point must be at least twice the length of the arrow; otherwise, an arrow will not be placed. If the last line segment of the leader is not horizontal, a horizontal line segment is added.

Leadered text does not take on the properties of associative dimensioning. You can append text to the default dimension value. The default value is usually the last dimension entered.

NOTE The gap or space between the end of the last horizontal line segment and the dimension text is set with the *Dimgap* system variable.

See Also Dimstyle, Leader, Mtext, Qleader, Spline, Tolerance; *Express Tools:* Qlattach, Qlattachset, Qldeattachset

Dim: Oblique

Dim: Oblique skews existing dimension extension lines to an angle other than 90 degrees to the dimension line.

To Skew Extension Lines

Command line: **Dim** ↵ **Oblique, Ob**

Menu: Dimension ➤ Oblique

1. **Select objects:** Pick the dimensions to be edited.

2. **Enter obliquing angle (press ENTER for none):** Enter the desired angle for extension lines.

If the dimension being edited has a dimension style setting, then this setting is maintained. If no style is associated with the dimension, the current dimension variable settings are used to update the obliqued dimension.

See Also Dimedit, Dimstyle

Dim: Redraw

Redraw behaves like a transparent command and allows you to refresh the screen in the current viewport.

To Refresh the Screen

Command line: **Dim** ↵ **Redraw, Red**

See Also Redraw

Dim: Restore

Makes an existing dimension style the current default style.

To Use Restore

Command line: **Dim** ↵ **Restore, Res**

Current dimension style: STANDARD. Enter a dimension style name, [?] or <select dimension>: Enter **?** to list available dimension styles, enter the name of a known dimension style (wildcard characters are accepted), or press ↵ to pick a dimension whose dimension style you want to make current.

To select a dimension style, either pick an associative dimension that is associated with the desired style, or enter the name of the style. The tilde (~) can also be used to compare styles. To find the differences between the current dimension style and another style, enter a dimension style name preceded by a tilde (~) at the prompt **Enter a dimension style name, [?] or <select dimension>:**. Differences are displayed in a list of dimension variable settings.

See Also Dimoverride, Dim/Save

DIMSTYLE

Dim/Save

Dim/Save saves the current dimension variable settings as a dimension
style that can later be restored using the Dim/Restore subcommand. You
can save multiple dimension styles.

To Save Dimension Settings

Command line: **Dim ↵ Save**, **Sa**

> **Enter name for new dimension style or [?]:** Enter a new
> dimension style name. If you enter **?**, the following prompt appears:
>
> > **Enter dimension style(s) to list <*>:** Press ↵, or enter a name
> > specification using wildcards.

NOTE The tilde (~) can also be used to compare styles. To find the
differences between the current dimension style and another style,
enter a dimension style name preceded by a tilde (~) at the prompt
`Enter a dimension style name, [?] or <select dimension>:`.
Differences are displayed in a list of dimension variable settings.

See Also Ddim, Dimoverride, Dim/Restore.

Dim: Status

Dim: Status displays the current dimension variable settings and
descriptions.

To Display Dimension Settings

Command line: **Dim ↵ Status**, **Sta.**

The text screen appears listing dimension settings, their status or values,
and a brief description.

Dim: Style

Dim: Style specifies a text style for the dimension text. Once the text
style is changed, any subsequent dimensions will contain text in the
new style. Existing dimension text is not affected.

To Specify a Text Style

Command line: **Dim: ↵ Style**, **Sty**

1. **New text style <current style name>:** Press ↵ to accept the
   current style, or enter another previously created style name to set
   as the current text style.

2. If you enter the name of a style that does not exist, you receive the
   message *No style found*.

See Also Style

Dim: Undo

Undo rescinds a dimension you decide you do not want, as long as you are still in the dimension mode.

To Undo a Dimension

Command line: **Dim** ⏎ **Undo**, **U**

> **NOTE** If you issue **Undo** during the **Leader** command, the last leader line segment drawn will be undone. (**Undo** does not work when drawing leader lines with **Dim/Leader**.)

Dim: Update

Update changes old dimensions to new dimension variable settings. **Update** works only on associative dimensions that have not been exploded.

Command line: **Dim** ⏎ **Update**, **Up**.

Menu: Dimension ➤ Update

Dimension Toobar: ![icon] Dimension Update

Select objects: Pick dimension string to update.

Dim: Variables

Variables lists the dimension variable settings of a dimension style.

To List the Dimension Variable Settings

Command line: **Dim** ⏎ **Variables**, **Va**.

Enter a dimension style name, [?] or <select dimension>: Enter **?** to view available dimension styles, enter the name of a known dimension style (wildcards are accepted), or press ⏎ at the prompt Select dimension: to pick a dimension whose dimension style you wish to list.

The tilde (~) can also be used to compare styles. To find the differences between the current dimension style and another style, enter a dimension style name preceded by a tilde (~) at the prompt Enter dimension style(s) to list <*>:. Differences are displayed in a list of dimension variable settings.

See Also Ddim, Dimstyle

Additional Dimensioning Options

The two processes described below can be used in conjunction with both dimensioning commands as well as in **Dim/Mode**.

At the Dimension text: prompt, you can append text to the default dimension text.

To Append Dimension Text

Start the required dimensioning command, then provide the following information:

> **Dimension text <default text>:** Using the <> signs to retain the dimension text default value, you can place text before and/or after the <> brackets.

To Use Automatic Dimensioning

Start the required dimensioning command, and then provide the following information:

1. **Specify first extension line origin or <select object>:** Press ↵.

2. **Select object to dimension:** Pick the object to be dimensioned.

> **NOTE** After selecting a line, circle, or arc, you may drag your cursor and the dimension text to a chosen location point.

Dim Style Control

Allows you to pick a style from the drop-down box in the Dimension Toolbar.

Command: none

Dimension Toolbar: | Standard | Dim Style Control

Quick Dimensioning

See **Qdim and Qleader**

Tolerance Dimensioning

See **Tolerance**

DIST

Dist gives the distance between two points in 2D or 3D space. It also gives the angle in the current XY plane, the angle *from* the current XY plane, and the distance in XYZ coordinate values. It also gives you the change in XYZ. This is the *Delta* XYZ information.

To Find the Distance between Two Points

Command line: **Dist, Di** (or **'Dist**, to use transparently)

Menu: Tools ➤ Inquiry ➤ Distance

Inquiry Toolbar Distance

1. **Specify first point:** Pick the beginning point of the distance.

2. **Specify second point:** Pick the end point of the distance.

See Also   Divide, Id, Measure; *System Variable:* Distance

Divide

Divide marks an object into equal divisions. You specify the number of divisions, and AutoCAD marks the object into equal parts.

To Divide an Object

Command line: **Divide**, **Div**

Menu: Draw ➤ Point ➤ Divide

1. **Select object to divide:** Pick a single object.

2. **Enter the number of segments or [Block]:** Enter the number of segments to be marked with a point, or enter **B** to use a block as the marker. If you enter **B,** the prompt Enter name of block to insert: appears first, followed by an option to align the block with an object, and then you are prompted to Enter the number of segments:.

Options

Number of Segments   A marker or point is located at specified intervals using the *Pdmode* and *Pdsize* variables for point size and type.

Block   Allows you to use an existing block as a marking device. You receive the prompt Enter name of block to insert: and are asked whether you want to align the block with the object. If you respond **Y** to the Align block with object? [Yes/No] <Y>: prompt, the block will be aligned either along the axis of a line or tangent to a selected polyline, circle, or arc. The Block option is useful for drawing a series of objects that are equally spaced along a curved path.

By default, **Divide** uses a point object as a marker. Often, a point is difficult to see when placed over a line or arc. You can set the *Pdmode* system variable using the '**Ddptype** command transparently to change the appearance of the points, or you can use the Block option. The point marker can be picked with the **Node** Object Snap mode.

See Also   Block, Bmake, Ddptype, Measure, Point; *System Variables:* Pdmode, Pdsize

Donut/Doughnut

Donut draws a circle whose line thickness you specify by entering its inside and outside diameters. To create a solid dot, enter **0** at the Inside diameter: prompt. The most recent diameters entered are the default values for the inside and outside diameter. Once you issue the **Donut** command and answer the prompts, you can place as many donuts as you like. Press ↵ to terminate the command.

To Create a Donut

Command line: **Donut** or **Doughnut**, **Do**

Menu: Draw ➤ Donut

Toolbar: None

1. **Specify inside diameter of donut <current value>:** Enter the inside diameter of the donut, or pick a point for which a prompt will specify a Second point:.

2. **Specify outside diameter of donut <current value>:** Enter the outside diameter of the donut, or pick two points.

3. **Specify center of donut or <exit>:** Pick a point for the center of the donut, and then press ↵ to exit the command or continue selecting center points.

NOTE Because donuts are actually polylines, you can edit them with the **Pedit** command.

See Also Fill; Pedit; *System Variable:* Fillmode

Dragmode

Dragmode controls when the Drag facility is used. The default, Auto, temporarily repositions selected objects by moving them with a cursor.

To Drag an Object

Command line: **Dragmode** (or **'Dragmode** to use transparently)

Enter new value [ON/OFF/Auto] <Auto>: Enter the setting.

Options

ON Enables the Drag mode, so that objects will be dragged whenever you issue the **Drag** command modifier.

OFF Disables the Drag mode, so that no dragging can occur.

Auto   Causes all commands that allow dragging to automatically drag objects, whether you issue the **Drag** command modifier or not.

When you are editing large sets of objects, the Drag function can slow you down. It takes time for AutoCAD to refresh a temporary image, especially a complex one. If you set Drag mode on, you can use the Drag function when appropriate by entering **Drag** as a subcommand while performing an operation, and dispense with it when editing large groups of objects.

See Also   *System Variable:* Dragmode

Draworder

Draworder prioritizes the display of objects and hard-copy output when two or more objects overlay each other.

To Set the Display of Objects

Command line: **Draworder**, **Dr**

Menu: Tools ➤ Display Order ➤ Bring to Front/Send to Back/Bring above Object/Send under Object

Toolbar:

1. **Select objects:** Select one or more objects to arrange their display and plotted output by picking or using any selection set method.

2. **Enter object ordering option [Above object/Under object/ Front/Back] <Back>:** Select an option.

Options

Above Object   Moves object above or on the top of other objects.

Under Object   Moves object below or under other objects.

Front   Selected object is reassigned to the top of the drawing order.

Back   Selected object is reassigned to the bottom of the drawing order.

The **Draworder** command toggles on all Object-Sort Method options. Sorting is enabled only for plotting and PostScript output. Specifying the appropriate value at the command line for the *sortents* system variable will also set an object sort method.

See Also   Options; *System Variable:* Sortents

Dsettings

Dsettings combines the setting for Snap and Grid, Polar Tracking, and Object Snap in a single dialog. **Ddrmodes** can also be used at the command line for **Ddsettings**.

To Open the Dsettings Dialog

Command: **Ddsettings**, **Ds**, **Rm**, **Ddrmodes**

Menu: Tools ➤ Drafting Settings...

Shortcut Menu: Right-click Snap, Grid, Polar, Osnap, or Otrack on status bar and Pick Settings....

Select the desired function from the dialog.

Options

Snap and Grid   Snap and Grid offers a method to change mode settings. These options can also be controlled from the status line with a single pick or from a right-click shortcut menu.

Snap On (F9)   Picking the box sets the Snap mode On.

Grid On (F7)   Picking the box sets the Grid mode On and displays a grid of reference dots on the screen.

Snap   The *Snap X spacing, Snap Y spacing,* and *Angle* edit boxes let you adjust the spacing and angle of the X and Y axis. *X base* and *Y base* edit boxes let you enter a snap basepoint's XY coordinates.

Grid   Edit boxes for *Grid X spacing* and *Grid Y spacing* allow you to set the same intervals for your Grid and Snap distances.

Snap style & type   Pick *Rectangular Snap* to set Snap settings for nonisometric or Standard mode. Picking *Isometric Snap* for Isometric mode. Pick *Polar Snap* to snap along polar alignment angles based on starting polar tracking point; pick *Grid Snap* to snap along the grid.

You can toggle Left, Top, and Right drawing planes using Ctrl+E when the isometric snap/grid is on.

Polar Tracking   When set on, Polar Tracking temporarily extends a dotted line with a tooltip that references polar increment distances and angles based on other points on the drawing.

Polar Tracking On (F10)   Picking the box sets Polar Tracking mode On.

Polar Angle Settings   Select from default values 45, 30, 22.5, 18, 15, 10, and 5 in the *Increment Angle:* list, or pick the *Additional Angle:* list in which you can store a maximum of 10 additional values for polar tracking. Pick *New* to append or *Delete* to remove values from the list.

Object Snap Tracking Settings   Pick *Track Orthogonally Only* to force Object Snap tracking paths horizontal and vertical, or pick *Track Using All Polar Angle Settings* to allow tracking based the default increment angle values and, if checked, to include those additional values entered in the *Additional Angles* list.

Polar Angle measurement Sets the method for polar angle to *Absolute* based on the current UCS or to *Relative to Last Segment,* which references the last object created.

Object Snap Displays the Object Snap tabbed section for running object snaps, which allow you to have multiple Object Snap modes active while picking specific geometric points on an object. To override a running Osnap, enter the specific object snap at the command prompt.

Object Snap On (F3) Picking the box turns on Object Snap mode, which lets you pick specific geometric points on an object.

Object Snap Tracking On (F11) Picking the box turns on Object Snap tracking, which lets you use the aid of a temporary dashed projected line to draw objects.

Object Snap modes Activating one or more pick boxes lets your pick location determine the Osnap modes applied. For example, if both the Endpoint and Midpoint boxes are checked, AutoCAD automatically selects the mode based on which point is closer to the target. Position your cursor over the object, and then use the Tab key to cycle through checked snap settings. Depending on the settings when an Object Snap box is checked, an associated marker and snap tip appears. Each mode can be overridden at the command line by entering the uppercase letters shown:

ENDpoint Picks the end point of objects.

MIDpoint Picks the midpoints of lines and arcs.

CENter Picks the center of circles and arcs.

NODe Picks a point object. (See **Ddptype**.)

QUAdrant Picks a main point on an arc or circle.

INTersection Picks the intersection of objects.

EXTension Picks a point based on an object's extended length.

INSertion Picks the insertion point of blocks and text.

PERpendicular Picks the point on an object perpendicular to the last point.

TANgent Picks a tanget point on a circle or arc.

NEArest Picks the point on an object nearest to the cursor.

APParent Intersection Picks the apparent intersection of two dimensionally separated lines.

QUIck Shortens the time it takes AutoCAD to find an Object Snap point by stopping as soon as it finds one object. Quick does not work in conjunction with INTersect.

PARallel Creates a series of parallel vectors after you select a point on another object.

Select All   Selects all Object Snap modes.

Clear All   Deselects all Object Snap modes.

Options

View, Options, and Help   Opens the Drafting tab section of the Options dialog to control AutoSnap, Auto Tacking, Alignment Point Acquisition, AutoSnap Marker, and Aperture size settings.

See Also   Grid, Isoplane, Ortho, Snap; *System Variables:* Apbox, Autosnap, Gridmode, Gridunit, Osmode, Snapang, Snapbase, Snapmode

Dsviewer

Dsviewer opens the Aerial View dialog as a navigation tool that lets you see an entire drawing in a separate window, locate the area you want, and move to it quickly. The dialog contains View, Options, and Help pull-down menus.

To Open the Aerial View Window

Command line: **Dsviewer**, **Av**

Menu: View ➤ Aeriel View

The entire drawing is displayed in the Aerial view window. Use the Minimize, Maximize, and System icons in title bar to manage the Aeriel View application.

Menus

View   Zoom In increases and Zoom Out decreases drawing magnification by a factor of 2. Global displays the entire drawing and the current view.

Options   Toggle Auto Viewport to automatically display the model space view of the active viewport, Dynamic Update to update the aerial view while the drawing is being edited, and Realtime Zoom to turn real-time zoom on or off.

Help   Aeriel View Help displays help for the **Dsviewer** command.

Dtext/Text

Dtext allows you to enter several lines of text at once. This command also displays the text on the drawing area as you type. At the first prompt, you can set the justification or set the current text style. Using either the Fit or Align options, you can tell AutoCAD to fit the text between two points.

To Enter Text

Command line: **Dtext**, **Dt**

Menu: Draw ➤ Text ➤ Single Line Text

Toolbar: None

1. **Current text style:** "STANDARD"

   - **Text height:** 0.2000

   - **Specify start point of text or [Justify/Style]:** Enter the desired options, pick a start point for your text, or enter a justification.

2. If you pick a point to indicate the beginning location of your text, you get the following prompts:

   - **Specify height <default height>:** Enter the desired text height, or press ↵ to accept the default. This prompt only appears if the current style has its height set to 0.

   - **Specify rotation angle of text <0>:** Enter a rotation angle, or press ↵ to accept the default.

   - **Enter text:** Enter the desired text.

   These prompts also appear after you have selected a style or set the justification option.

Options

Specify Start Point of Text   Lets you indicate the location of your text. The text is automatically left-justified.

Justify   Specifies the justification of text. The prompt is Enter an option [Align/Fit/Center/Middle/Right/TL/TC/TR/ML/MC/MR/BL/BC/BR]:.

The two-letter options in this prompt set the justification based on the combination of top, middle, or bottom and left, center, or right. For example, TL stands for "top left," and MC stands for "middle center." If you know the option, it can be entered directly at the Justify prompt.

Align   Forces proportional resizing of text to fit between two points. You are prompted to select the two points. The text height is scaled in proportion to its width in the current text style.

Center   Centers text on the start point, which also defines the baseline of the text.

Fit   Forces text to fit between two points. Unlike Align, Fit keeps the default height and either stretches or compresses the text to fit.

Middle   Centers text at the start point. The start point is in the middle of the text height.

Right   Right-justifies the text. The start point is on the right side of
the text.

Style   Allows a new text style. The style you enter becomes the current
style.

⌐   If no option has been selected at the first prompt, pressing ⌐ highlights the most recently entered line of text and displays the prompt
Enter text:, allowing you to continue to add text just below that line.
The current text style and angle are assumed, as is the justification setting of the most recently entered text.

A cursor mark appears showing the approximate size of the text. The
text appears on your drawing as you type, and the box moves along as a
cursor. When you press ⌐, the box moves down one line. You can also
pick a point anywhere on the screen for the next line of text and still
backspace all the way to the beginning line to make corrections. If you
choose a justification option other than Left, the effects will not be seen
until you finish entering the text.

Dtext does not work with script files. Control codes such as %%d can
be entered before or after your text to add diameter, underscores, tolerance symbols, and so on to your text.

See Also   AutoLISP: Chtext, Change, Color, Ddedit, Ddstyle, Mtext,
Qtext, Rename; *System Variables:* Texteval, Textsize, Textstyle; *Express
Tools:* Arctext, Rtedit, Rtext, Textfit, Textmask, Textunmask, Txtexp,
Txtzmtxt

Dview

Dview displays your drawing in perspective and enables you to clip a
portion of a view. Unlike the standard **Zoom** and **Pan** commands,
Dview allows you to perform zooms and pans on perspective views.

To Display a Drawing with DView

Command line: **Dview**, **Dv**

Menu: View ➤ 3D Dynamic View

Toolbar: None

1. **Select objects or <use DVIEWBLOCK>:** Pick the objects that
   will help set up your perspective view, or press ⌐ to use the default
   dviewblock.

2. **Enter option [CAmera/TArget/Distance/POints/PAn/
   Zoom/TWist/CLip/Hide/Off/Undo]** Pick a point or select an

option from the menu, or enter the capitalized letter(s) of the desired option.

- If you pick a point, you will be prompted to Enter direction and magnitude angles:. Before you select an option, enter the direction (+ or -) and the desired angle, separated by a comma.

The prompts you receive next depend on the option selected in the preceding step.

Options

CAmera Moves the camera location as if you were moving a camera around, while continually aiming at the target point. CAmera prompts you for the two angles of rotation: Specify camera location, or enter angle from XY plane, or [Toggle (angle in)] <current value>:. At each prompt, either enter a value or select the view by using the cursor. If you enter a value, it will be interpreted in relation to the current UCS. See Figure D.4.

FIGURE D.4: The CAmera option controls the camera location relative to the target.

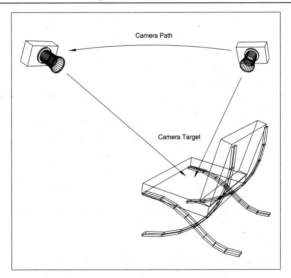

Camera Path

Camera Target

TArget Moves the target location, as if you were pointing a camera in different directions while keeping the camera location the same. TArget prompts you for two angles of rotation, Specify camera location, r enter angle from XY plane, or [Toggle (angle in)] <current value>:. At each prompt, either enter a value or select the view by using the cursor. See Figure D.5.

FIGURE D.5: The TArget option controls the target location relative to the camera.

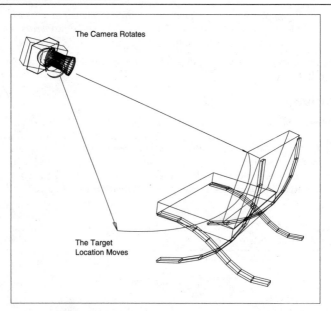

The Camera Rotates

The Target
Location Moves

Distance Turns on the Perspective mode and sets the distance from the target to the camera, as if you were moving a camera toward or away from the target point. At the prompt, `Specify new camera-target distance <1.0000>:`, enter a new distance, or move the slide bar at the top of the screen to drag the 3D image into the desired position.

POints Sets the target and camera points at the same time. The points you pick are in relation to the current UCS. At the prompt, `Specify target point <current x value, current y value, current z value>:`, pick a point for the target first, and then pick one for your camera location when prompted to `Specify camera point <<current x value, current y value, current z value >:`.

PAn Moves your camera and target point together, as if you were pointing a camera out the side window of a moving car. You cannot use the standard **Pan** command while viewing a drawing in perspective. Enter the option, and then pick `Specify displacement base point:` and `Specify second point:`. See **Pan** for more information.

Zoom Zooms in and out when you are viewing a drawing in parallel projection. Provides the lens focal length when you are viewing a drawing in perspective. You cannot use the standard **Zoom** command while viewing a drawing in perspective.

If your 3D view is a parallel projection, enter a new scale factor, or use the slide bar at the top of the screen to visually adjust the scale factor at the **Dview/Zoom** prompt. If your 3D view is a perspective, enter a new lens-length value at the prompt `Specify lens length <50.000mm>:`, or use the slide bar at the top of the screen to determine the new lens length at the **Dview/Zoom** prompt. If you use the slide bar to adjust the focal length, the coordinate readout on the status line will dynamically display the focal length value.

TWist   Rotates the camera about the camera's line of sight, as if you were rotating the view in a camera frame. At the `Specify view twist angle <0.00>:` prompt, enter an angle, or use the cursor to visually twist the camera view. If you use the cursor, the coordinate readout on the status line dynamically displays the camera-twist angle.

CLip   Hides portions of a 3D view. For example, it removes foreground objects that may interfere with a view of the background (see Figure D.6). **CLip** displays the prompt `Enter clipping option [Back/Front/Off] <Off>:`. Enter **B** to set Back Clip Plane, **F** to set Front Clip Plane, or **O** or ↵ to turn off the Clip Plane function. If you select Back or Front, a prompt allows you to either turn the selected clip plane on or off or to set a distance to the clip plane. You can use the slide bar at the top of the screen to visually determine the location of the clip plane or enter a distance value. A positive value places the clip plane in front of the target point; a negative number places it behind the target point.

Hide   Removes hidden lines from the objects displayed, turning a wireframe view into a planar view.

Undo   Resends the previous option.

FIGURE D.6:   The CLip option allows you to hide foreground or background portions of your drawing.

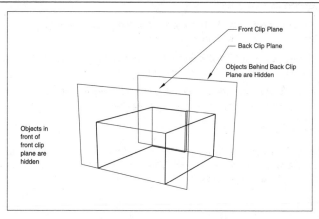

NOTE Because a large drawing slows down the drag function, you are prompted to select objects for dragging at the beginning of the **Dview** command. This limits the number of objects to be dragged. You should select objects that give the general outline of your drawing and sufficient detail to indicate the drawing's orientation. If you do not pick any objects, a default 3D house image appears to help you select a view. You can create your own block image and use that as the default. The block should be named *Dviewblock*.

See Also 3dorbit, Block, Dsviewer, Hide, Pan, Vpoint, Zoom; *System Variables:* Backz, Frontz, Lenslength, Target, Viewctr, Viewdir, Viewmode, Viewsize, Viewtwist

Dwfout

Dwfout displays the Create .dwf File dialog to create an external drawing Web format (.dwf) file. AutoCAD displays the message *NOTE: The DWFOUT command has been deprecated, and will not be supported in future versions of AutoCAD. It is provided here for limited backward compatability only. Please refer to the User's Guide for a complete discussion of the new, powerful features of DWF ePlot before displaying the prompt.*

To Export a .dwf Drawing

Command line: **Dwfout**

If the *Filedia* system variable is set to 0, the following prompts appear at the command line:

1. **Enter file name <current drawing name>:** Enter a name to export as a .dwf file.

2. **Enter precision (Low/High/<Medium>):** Set the level of decimal precision as low, medium, or high.

3. **Compress file? (No/<Yes>):** Specify whether the .dwf file should be exported using file compression.

If the *Filedia* system variable is set to 1, the Create .dwf File dialog opens to enter a drive/path and name for the .dwf file.

Options

Options Click the Options... button to set buttons for Low, Medium, or High precision. Check the *Use File Compress* box if you wish the file to be exported using compression.

NOTE Drawings created in Paper Space (Tilemode = 0) do not have drawing Web format support. Only the geometry in the current view is written to the `.dwf` file. Values set for the system variables *Viewres*, *Facetres*, *Dispsilh*, and *Hide* determine output quality of the `.dwf` file. Named views are saved with the `.dwf` file, and a view called *Initial* is automatically created from the Current Drawings view when the command is invoked. Clicking the right mouse button restores named views of `.dwf` files if you are using the WHIP! menu. The `.dwf` file contains the same background color as the AutoCAD graphics window. To reduce file size, use a black or white background.

Dwgprops

Dwgprops allows you to save information for each drawing that can be viewed by invoking the command from a dialog in the drawing or by right-clicking the filename in Windows Explorer.

To Save Drawing Information

Command: **Dwgprops**

View data or enter information as appropriate in the dialog.

General Tab   Provides file information in read-only mode and check-boxes for system-level file attributes.

Icon: Displays the associated window's file icon and filename.

Type: Identifies the file type, for example, AutoCAD Drawing.

Location: Indicates the files drive letter and folder names.

Size: Displays file size.

MS_DOS name: Shows the filename and extension.

Created: Identifies the day of the week, month, day, year, and time the file was created.

Modified: Identifies the day of the week, month, day, year, and time the file was edited last.

Accessed: Reports that the file is open by displaying the day of the week, month, day, and year.

Attributes: Displays operating-systems file attributes for Read Only, Archive, Hidden, and System in Read Only mode. Values can only be edited by picking their checkboxes from the Windows Explorer.

Summary Tab Contains edit boxes to save information about the drawing file that can later be retrieved by searching keywords from the Auto-CAD DesignCenter.

Title: Enter appropriate information, such as the drawing title.

Subject: Enter appropriate information, such as the drawing type.

Author: Enter appropriate information, such as the creator of the drawing.

Keywords: Enter words or phrases (up to 511 characters) that you can use to find the file.

Comments: Add remarks, limited to 511 characters, about the file for future searches.

Hyperlink Base: Identify an Internet location or a network path for links inserted in the drawing.

Statistics Tab Provides drawing file data in Read Only mode.

Created: Specifies day of the week, month, day, year, and time the file was created. (*Tdcreate* system variable)

Modified: Identifies day of the week, month, day, year, and time the file was modified. (*Tdupdate* system variable)

Last Saved By: Uses operating system login name to show name of the person who last edited the file.

Revision Number: Shows the files revision number.

Total Editing Time: Indicates total amount of time the drawing has been open for editing. (*Tdindwg* system variable)

NOTE AutoCAD will display a warning message in this dialog if the drawing was saved using another program.

Custom Tab Enter appropriate information in the edit boxes.

Name: Enter a reference item, such as Revision 1 or Version 2.

Value: Enter a comment, such as Issued for Construction, for the referenced item.

Dxbin

See Import/Export

Dxfin

See Import/Export

Dxfout

See **Import/Export**

Edge

Edge turns the visibility of 3D face edges on or off.

Command line: **Edge**

Menu: Draw ➤ Surfaces ➤ Edge

Surfaces Toolbar: 🖼️ Edge

To Change the Visibility of a 3D Edge

Specify edge of 3dface to toggle visibility or [Display]: Type **D** or select an edge to make invisible. The prompt is repeated, allowing you to select different edges until you press ⏎.

If you select the Display option by typing **D**, you will be prompted Enter selection method for display of hidden edges [Select/All] <All>:. Press ⏎, or type **A** to highlight all edges; otherwise, if you enter **S**, you are prompted to Select objects. Then select the edge(s) to unhide. Press ⏎ to complete the command.

Options

Select Edge Selects individual edges, and then hides the selected edges.

Display Highlights invisible edges, either selected edges, or all invisible edges.

See Also 3Dface, Edgesurf; *System Variables:* Splframe

Edgesurf

Edgesurf draws a 3D surface polygon mesh from four adjoining edges. These edges can be lines, arcs, polylines, or 3D polylines, but they must join exactly end-to-end.

To Create a 3D Surface Using Edgesurf

Command line: **Edgesurf**

Menu: Draw ➤ Surfaces ➤ Edge Surface

Surfaces Toolbar: 🖼️ Edge Surface

1. **Current wire frame density:** SURFTAB1=6 SURFTAB2=6.

2. **Select object 1 for surface edge:** Pick the first object defining an edge.

3. **Select object 2 for surface edge:** Pick the second object defining an edge.

4. **Select object 3 for surface edge:** Pick the third object defining an edge.

5. **Select object 4 for surface edge:** Pick the fourth object defining an edge.

The type of surface drawn by **Edgesurf** is called a *Coons surface patch* (see Figure E.1). The first edge selected defines the *M* direction of the mesh, and the edges adjoining the first define the *N* direction. The endpoint closest to the point selected becomes the origin of the *M* and *N* directions.

FIGURE E.1:   A Coons surface patch

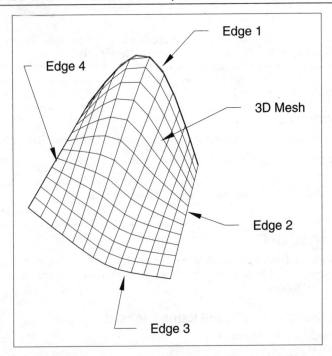

The *Surftab1* and *Surftab2* system variables control the number of facets in the *M* and *N* directions, respectively. Increasing the number of facets gives a smoother mesh but increases the file size of the drawing. This increases file-opening, redrawing, and regeneration times. Increasing the values of *Surftab1* and *Surftab2* after creating the edgesurf will not smooth the 3D surface. Only edgesurfs created after, with the new values, will reflect the changes. See **System Variables/Setvar**.

See Also   Pedit; Pface; 3Dface, 3Dmesh, Revsurf, Rulesurf, Tabsurf; *System Variables:* Surftab1, Surftab2

Elev

Elev allows you to set the default Zaxis elevation and thickness of objects being drawn. Normally, objects will be placed at a zero elevation. Once you enter an elevation or thickness with **Elev**, all objects drawn afterwards will be given the new Zaxis value; objects you drew before using the **Elev** command are not affected. You can also change the elevation of an existing object with the **Move** command.

To Set Elevation and Thickness

Command line: **Elev**

1. **Specify new default elevation <current default>:** Set a new default starting plane elevation in the Zaxis.

2. **Specify new default thickness<current default>:** Set a new default extrusion thickness in the Zaxis.

NOTE   3D polylines, faces, and meshes, as well as viewports and dimensions, ignore the **Elev** setting of thickness. They do so because these entities cannot have thickness. Text and attribute-definition entities are always given a zero thickness, regardless of the **Elev** values used during initial creation.

See Also   Change, Dducs, Elevation, Move, Properties, Thickness, UCS, UCSman, Vports; *System Variables:* Elevation, Thickness

Ellipse

Ellipse draws an ellipse for which you specify the major and minor axes, a center point, and two axis points, or it draws the center point and the radius or diameter of an isometric circle. It also lets you define a second projection of a 3D circle by using the Rotation option.

To Draw an Ellipse

Command line: **Ellipse**, **El**

Menu: Draw ➤ Ellipse ➤ Center/Axis, End/Arc

Draw Toolbar: ⬭ Ellipse

The following prompts vary depending upon the preset options selected and the Isometric Snap mode.

1. The Isometric option under **Snap** is On or Off.

   If your Isometric Snap mode is active, the following prompt appears:

   • **Specify axis endpoint of ellipse or [Arc/Center/Isocircle]:** Enter **I**, and then pick a point defining one end of the ellipse, or enter **A** for arc or **C** to enter a center point.

   If your Isometric Snap mode is not active, the following prompt appears:

   • **Specify axis endpoint of ellipse or [Arc/Center]:** Pick a point defining one end of the ellipse, enter **A** for arc, or type **C** to enter the center point.

2. For either of the above, the following prompts appear if you select the default option by picking a point:

   • **Specify other endpoint of axis:** Pick a point defining the opposite end of the ellipse.

   • **Specify distance to other axis or [Rotation]:** Pick a point defining the other axis of the ellipse, or enter **R** to enter a rotation value.

Options

Axis Endpoint   Allows you to enter the endpoint of one of the ellipse's axes (see Figure E.2).

Other Endpoint of Axis   Appears after you have already defined one of the ellipse's axes. Enter the distance from the center of the ellipse to the second axis endpoint.

Center   Allows you to pick the ellipse center point. If you enter **C** at the prompt Specify axis endpoint of elliptical arc or [Center]:, you can create an elliptical arc by picking a center point and then picking the first axis endpoint followed by the second point of the first axis.

   • Specify center of elliptical arc:

   • Specify endpoint of axis:

Arc   Creates an elliptical arc. The angle of the first axis determines the angle of the arc.

Isocircle   Appears when you set the Style option for the **Snap** command to Isometric or if you enter the **Dsettings** command and pick Isometric Snap in the Snap and Grid tab. This option creates an isometric circle in the current isometric drawing plane.

FIGURE E.2: Axis endpoints and other axis distance

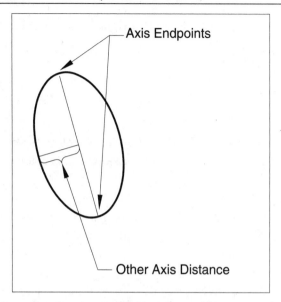

Axis Endpoints

Other Axis Distance

Rotation Allows you to enter an ellipse rotation value between 0 and 89.4 degrees or to pick a point if you enter **R** at the prompt Specify distance to other axis or [Rotation]:. Imagine the ellipse to be a 2D projection of a 3D circle rotated on an axis. As the circle is rotated, its projection turns into an ellipse. The rotation value determines the rotation angle of this circle. A 0 degree value displays a full circle; an 80 degree value displays a narrow ellipse.

- Specify rotation around major axis:

Perimeter Allows you to apply a parametric vector calculation when creating an elliptical arc. If you enter **P** at the prompt Specify start angle or [Parameter]:, you can pick a start point for the parameter and then pick an endpoint (parameter), or you can enter an Angle or use the Included Angle option for the endpoint.

- Specify start parameter or [Angle]:

- Specify end parameter or [Angle/Included angle]:

Set the *Pellipse* system variable to 1 for a polyline ellipse or 0 for a true ellipse. If you create an ellipse that is actually a polyline, you can edit it using **Pedit**.

See Also Dsettings, Isoplane, Snap/Style, Spline; *System Variables:* Pellipse, Snapisopair

Erase

Erase deletes one or several selected objects from a drawing.

To Erase Objects

Command line: **Erase**, **E**

Menu: Modify ➤ Erase

Modify Toolbar: Erase

Shortcut Menu: Right-click after selecting object and choose **Erase**.

Select objects: Select the objects to be erased by picking or using any selection method.

Options

The standard selection options, as well as the following options, are useful with the **Erase** command.

Single Lets you pick a single object only. From the keyboard you can also enter **Si** at the Select objects: prompt.

Last Lets you erase the last entity drawn. From the keyboard, you can enter **L** at the Select objects: prompt. You can also enter **Previous** or **P** from the keyboard to erase the previous selection set.

Oops Lets you unerase the last erase. (See **Oops**). (The **Undo** command will reverse the entire **Erase** sequence but not the last object erased.)

   To erase an object that is overlapped or superimposed by another, hold down the Ctrl key at the Select object: prompt. Pick a point where two or more objects overlap, where it is difficult to select the correct object. The prompt <Cycle on> appears at the command line. Continue clicking the same point until the object you want to erase is highlighted, and then press ↵.

See Also   Multiple, Oops, Select/Si, Undo

Exit

Exit has been discontinued. AutoCAD has aliased the **Exit** command to **Quit** in the acad.pgp file. See **Quit**.

Explode

Explode reduces a block, polyline, associative dimension, body, multiline, polyface, polygon mesh, region, group, or 3D mesh or solid to its component objects.

To Explode an Object

Command line: **Explode**, **X**

Menu: Modify ➤ Explode

Modify Toolbar: 🖉 Explode

1. **Select objects:** Select block, 2D, 3D, or wide polyline, multiline, 3D solid, region, polyface mesh, circle, or arc to be exploded by picking or specifying any window selection set, including window, wpolygon, cpolygon, and fence.

2. Depending on whether the object explodes, the results may differ:

   3D Solid   Planar surfaces turn into regions, and nonplanar surfaces become bodies.

   Blocks   If a block is nested, **Explode** only "unblocks" the outermost block. You can also explode nonuniformly scaled blocks, but the results may explode into unexpected objects.

   Region   A region explodes into lines, arcs, and splines.

   2D/wide polyline   Returns lines and arcs with width of 0, and discards tangent information.

   Body   Converts object into single surface body (nonplanar surfaces), regions, or curves.

   Polyface mesh   One-vertex mesh explodes into a point object, two-vertex meshes turn into a line, and three-vertex meshes become 3D faces.

   3D polyline   Exploding a 3D polyline turns it into line segments.

   Circle   Exploding a circle in a nonuniformly scaled block turns it into an ellipse.

   Multiline   Multilines explode into lines.

   Arc   Exploding an arc in a nonuniform block turns it into elliptical arcs.

   Blocks inserted with **Minsert** cannot be exploded. You can't explode Xrefs and their dependent blocks unless you bind them. Mirrored blocks cannot be exploded with the **Explode** command, but they may be exploded using the new **Xplode** command. Wide polylines lose their width properties when exploded.

See Also   Oops, Select, Undo, Xplode, Xref; *Express Tools:* Burst, Txtexp

Export
See Import/Export

Extend

Extend lengthens an object to meet another object. Objects that can be extended include arcs, elliptical arcs, lines, open polylines, and rays. You can extend objects to an "implied" as well as to an actual boundary.

To Extend an Object

Command line: **Extend**, **Ex**

Menu: Modify ➤ Extend

Modify Toolbar: [icon] Extend

1. **Current settings: Projection=UCS, Edge=None, Select boundary edges...**

   Select objects: Select the object, or use fence selection to designate the boundary objects. If you press ⏎ at the Select objects: prompt, AutoCAD selects all objects in your drawing and then displays the prompt shown in step 2.

2. **Select object to extend or [Project/Edge/Undo]:** Select objects to be extended by picking an object, using fence selection, or entering **U** to undo the last extend operation. You may also enter **P** or **E** to reset the Project or Edge settings.

   • If you type **P**, you will be prompted None/Ucs/View/<current value>:.

   • If you type **E**, you will be prompted Extend/No extend <current value>:.

Options

Project   Specifies the projection mode for AutoCAD to use when extending objects: with *None:*, only selected objects that actually intersect with the boundary are extended; *UCS:* specifies projection onto the XY plane of the current UCS; *View:* extends all selected objects that intersect with the boundary in the current view. This option is controlled by the system variable *Projmode*. *Projmode* settings are 0 = "None"; 1 = "UCS"; 2 = "View".

Edge   Extends objects to implied as well as actual boundaries; boundary edges do not have to be exactly in the path of the objects to be extended. This option is controlled by the system variable *Edgemode*: a setting of 0 = "No extend" will not extend objects to the implied boundary; a setting of 1 = "Extend" will let objects extend to an implied boundary.

Undo   Restores the previously executed option. You cannot extend objects within blocks or use blocks as boundary edges.

See Also   Change, Grips, Lengthen, Stretch, Trim; *Express Tools:* Bextend; *System Variables:* Edgemode, Projmode

Extensions

Table E.1 lists some AutoCAD file extensions and their meanings. When entering filenames, you must include the file extension. When deleting files, take care not to delete files AutoCAD needs for its internal operation. If you or someone on your network is currently editing a file, do not delete AutoCAD temporary files with the extension .$AC, .AC$, or .$A.

TABLE E.1: AutoCAD File Extensions and Their Meanings

Standard Extension	File Description
.arx	AutoCAD Run-Time Extension file
.avi	Internet file
.bak	Drawing Backup file
.bd	Display Font file
.bkn	Emergency Backup file where n = sequential number
.bmp	Bitmap file
.cfg	AutoCAD Configuration file
.cnt	Help content file
.cus	Custom Dictionary file
.dcl	Dialog Control Language Description file
.dct	Dictionary file
.dwt	Drawing Template file
.dll	Dynamically Linked Library file
.dwg	Drawing file
.dxb	Binary Data Exchange file
.dxf	Drawing Interchange file
.dxt	AutoCAD Dxfix Support
.dxx	Attribute data in DXF format
.fmp	Font Map file
.eps	Encapsulated PostScript file
.err	AutoCAD error report
.exe	Executable file
.gid	Help Index file
.gif	(CompuServe) Graphics Image Format file
.gsf	Ghostscript default font

TABLE E.1 (continued): AutoCAD File Extensions and Their Meanings

Standard Extension	File Description
.hdi	Heidi Device Interface File
.hlp	Windows Help file
.hdx	Help Index file
.ini	Initialization file
.isu	Uninstall Information File
.lin	Line Type Definition file
.lli	Render file
.mak	C++ Make file
.map	Map file
.mli	Render Materials file
.mln	Multiline Library file
.mnc	Compiled Menu file (Windows only)
.mnl	AutoLISP functions related with a Menu file
.mnr	Menu Source file
.mns	Menu Source file
.mnu	Menu Template file
.old	Backup of a file converted from an early version of AutoCAD
.pat	Hatch-Pattern Library file
.pcp	Plot Configuration Settings file
.pc2	Plot Configuration Settings file
.pc3	Plot Configuration Settings file
.pcx	PCX Raster-Image file
.pfb	PostScript Font file
.pfm	PostScript Font Metric file
.pif	Program Information File
.plt	Plot file
.ps	PostScript file
.psf	PostScript Support file
.plt	Plot file
.reg	Registry Merge File
.scr	Script file

TABLE E.1 (continued): AutoCAD File Extensions and Their Meanings

Standard Extension	File Description
.shp	Font file
.shx	Shape or Font file
.slb	Slide Library file
.sld	Slide files
.stl	Stereolithography file
.svf	Express Tools file
.tga	TrueVision Targa Image file
.tif	Tiff Raster-Image file
.tlb	Type library
.ttf	TrueType Font file
.txt	Attribute Extract or Template file (CDF/SDF format)
.unt	Units file
.wmf	Windows metafile
.xlg	External References Log file
.xmx	External Message file

Extrude

*See **Solid Modeling***

Fileopen

Fileopen allows you to open an AutoCAD drawing at the command line.

To Open a Drawing at the Command Line

Command line: **Fileopen**

Enter name of drawing to open: Enter the drive letter, path, and filename or a tilde (~) to display the Select File dialog.

NOTE Fileopen is often used in LISP programming files, a toolbar dialog, Diesel, and menu macro applications.

See Also Open, Save, Saveas

File Selection Dialog

File selection dialog features, common to most dialog boxes, assist you in locating directories and files to open.

File Selection Dialog Features

Command line: **Image**, **Import**, **Export**, **Open**, **Recover**, **Save**, **Xattach**

Options

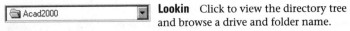

Lookin   Click to view the directory tree and browse a drive and folder name.

Up One Level   Click to move your current path back one level to the previous folder.

Create New Folder   Click to create a new folder or subfolder in the list box based on the current folder displayed in the *Look In* drop-down box.

List   Click to display files and folders in a list-view format.

Details   Click to display files and folders in a detailed view format with column headings for Name, Size, Type, Modifier, and Attributes in the list box.

Search the Web   Click to open the Browse the Web dialog to access and copy AutoCAD files on the Internet.

Look in Favorites   Click to set your path to a folder named Favorites, displaying subfolders and files in the list box.

Add to Favorites   Displays a shortcut menu with options to Add "< Folder Name>" to Favorites and Add Selected Item to Favorites.

Preview   Shows a preview image of a file selected from the list box.

File Name   Enter a filename and extension in the edit box, or use wildcards to filter names and display the files you select from the list box. Selecting multiple files will display them in quotation marks.

Files of Type   Click the drop-down box to filter the type of file extension you wish to display in the list box.

Open   Click to open one or more files selected in the list box.

Find File   Clicking opens the Browse and Search dialog containing Browse and Search tabs to browse using preview images of files or search through drives and folders based on criteria such as filter patterns, file size, date, time, and so forth.

Locate   Uses the AutoCAD search path you define in the Files tab of the Options dialog to locate files.

Options...   Opens the Options dialog to set controls for your AutoCAD sessions.

Open As Read Only   Open a drawing in Read Only mode to view its contents. Enter the **Saveas** command if you wish to edit the drawings and save changes.

Select Initial View   Opens a drawing, and restores a saved view you select from a list in the View Name dialog.

Partial Open   Clicking opens the Partial Open dialog to partially load and open based on a selected view and layers.

Fill

Fill turns on or off the solid fills of solids, traces, and polylines. When **Fill** is off, solid filled areas are only outlined, both on the screen and in prints. The dialog box option for solid fill is **Ddrmodes** (Tools ➤ Drawing Aids).

To Fill an Object

Command line: **Fill** (or '**Fill** to use transparently)

Enter mode [ON/OFF] <ON>: Enter On or Off, or press ↵.

See Also   Dsettings, Options, Pline, Solid, Trace; *System Variable:* Fillmode

---

Fillet

Fillet uses an intermediate arc to join two nonparallel lines, a line, and an arc or segments of a polyline.

To Use Fillet

Command line: **Fillet**, **F**

Menu: Modify ➤ Fillet

Modify Toolbar: ▛ Fillet

1. **Current settings:** Mode = TRIM, Radius = 0.5000

   Select first object or [Polyline/Radius/Trim]: Pick the first line to fillet.

   Select second line: Pick the second line.

2. In step 1, if you enter **P**, the prompt Select 2D polyline: appears; if you enter **R**, you are prompted to Specify fillet radius <current value>: If you enter **T**, you are prompted: Enter Trim mode option [Trim/No trim] <Trim>:.

- If you select multiple edges of a 3D solid, the following prompt appears: Enter fillet radius <0.5000>:. Type in a distance, or press Enter to display Select an edge or [Chain/Radius]: prompt. Select an edge, enter **C** to pick adjacent edges, or enter **R** to set a new radius.

Options

Polyline   Fillets all line segments within a polyline. You are prompted to select a 2D polyline. All joining polyline segments are then filleted.

Radius   Specifies the radius of the fillet arc.

Trim/No Trim   Toggles the Trim option On or Off, and sets it as a temporary default (using the system variable *Trimmode*). Turning trim Off adds an arc while retaining the original line segments.

Chain   Activates multiple adjacent edges selection.

Edge   Activates single edge selection.

NOTE **Fillet** joins the end points closest to the intersection. The location you use to pick objects determines which part of the object is retained. If the lines (or line and arc) already intersect, **Fillet** substitutes the specified arc for the existing corner. To connect two nonparallel lines with a corner rather than an arc, set the radius to 0. If you select two parallel lines, **Fillet** joins them with an arc segment. You can also fillet just a corner of a polyline by picking its adjacent segments. Both segments, however, must be part of the same polyline. Lines and polylines can be joined together with **Fillet**. The result produces a polyline. If you are not viewing the current UCS in plan, **Fillet** may give you the wrong result. Use the **Plan** command to view the current UCS in plan before issuing **Fillet**.

See Also   Chamfer; *System Variables:* Filletrad, Trimmode

Filter

Filter opens the Object Selection Filters dialog to generate a selection-set filter based on combinations of object properties and to save them to a filename.

To Filter Properties

Command line: **Filter**, **Fi** (or **'Filter** to use transparently)

Apply coordinates, object type, color, layer, line type, block name, text style, or thickness to a filter.

Options

List Box   Displays a list box (in the upper portion of the dialog) of the filtered objects in your current selection set.

Edit Item   Pick box used to transfer the highlighted filter shown in the list box (at the upper portion of the dialog) to the Select Filter area below. Pick **Edit Item** to transfer additional filters from the list box to the Select Filter area for editing. You can modify and substitute the filters and their values displayed in the edit boxes below the Select Filter area.

Delete   Pick box to remove the highlighted filter from the list box.

Clear List   Pick box to remove all the filters from the list box.

Named Filters   Area containing options to save, restore, and delete the current filter list.

Current   Pop-up list displaying names of saved filters.

Save As   Edit box for assigning a name and saving a filter list.

Delete Current Filter List   Pick box for removing the saved filtered names from the current pop-up list.

Apply   Exits dialog, and executes the filtering procedure.

Select Filter   Area containing XYZ coordinate edit boxes, and a Select subdialog box listing object types and relational operators as well as additional pick boxes. The Select subdialog box is specific to the entity type being filtered.

Add to List   Appends an object in the Select Filter area to the filter list in upper portion of the dialog.

Substitute   Pick box to replace highlighted filter criteria with the one in the Select Filter area.

Add Selected Object   Pick box temporarily exits the dialog allowing you to select objects from the drawing and add them to the filter list.

Entering **Filter** transparently (**'Filter**) at the command line allows you to apply the **P** (previous) selection set to access the filtered entities. The following operands must be paired and balanced for filters to operate correctly:

- Begin AND/End AND

- Begin OR/End OR

- Begin XOR/End XOR

- Begin NOT/End NOT

Find

Find allows you to search and replace selected text, dimensioned text, Mtext, attributed block values, and hyperlinks in your drawing.

Command line: **Find**

Menu: Edit ➤ Find

Standard Toolbar: 🔍 Find and Replace

To Find and Replace Text

Provide information as needed in the dialog.

Options

Find Text String   Enter a single word or text string to find in your drawing.

Replace With   Enter the new word or text string that you wish to replace. AutoCAD stores the six most recent text-string searches in both the *Find Text String:* and *Replace With:* edit boxes.

Search In   Specifies the Entire drawing or the Current selection as your search criteria. Pick the Select Objects icon button 🔲 to temporarily exit the dialog, and select specific textual objects in your drawing that you wish to include for the search-and-replace procedure.

Find/Find Next   Choose to begin search-and-replace operation. After the first occurrence is located, the search results appear in the Context area. Then Find changes to Find Next to locate additional text replacement instances.

Replace   Allows you to view and acknowledge each instance of replacement text for the specified search criteria.

Replace All   Performs a global text search-and-replace of text entered in *Find Text String:* with text in *Replace With:* lists.

Select All   Performs a search operation only of text entered in *Find Text String:,* and then locates and displays the result as highlighted text in your drawing.

Zoom To   Shows the portion of the drawing containing the text being searched-and-replaced in the current Model or Layout tab.

Options…   Check boxes to limit or expand your search to include Block Attribute Value, Dimension Annotation Text, Text (Mtext, Dtext, Text), Hyperlink Description, Hyperlink, Match Case, and Find Whole Words Only.

Status Area Reports results of the current operation.

See Also Spell; *Express Tools:* Bcount, Block?, Getsel, Sstools, Ssx, Xdlist

Fog
*See **Render***

Gotourl

Gotourl allows you to select an object with an attached URL and accesses the specified address assigned to the URL.

To Select an Object's Attached URL

Command line: **Gotourl**

Select objects: Select object with an attached URL, and AutoCAD will automatically open your default Internet browser and go to that URL.

> **NOTE** If you pick a URL to display its grips and place your pointing device near a grip, an icon appears with the name of the URL. Right-clicking a gripped URL displays a context-sensitive shortcut menu with hyperlink options.

See Also Attatchurl, Detachurl, Hyperlink, Hyperlinkoptions, Inserturl, Listurl, Openurl, Saveurl, Selecturl

Graphscr

Graphscr switches you from the text screen to the graphics screen when you are working on a single-screen system. Pressing the F2 function key has the same effect. Although **Graphscr** can be used at the command line, its intent is for use in Menu and Script files when a command, such as **List**, forces display of the text screen.

To Switch to the Graphics Screen

Command line: **Graphscr**

If the text screen is displayed, AutoCAD switches to the graphics screen.

See Also Textscr; *Express Tools:* Fullscreen

Grid

Grid turns on the grid and sets the grid spacing.

To Turn on the Grid

Command line: **Grid, Ctrl+F9** (or **'Grid** to use transparently)

Status Line: Grid

To Change the Grid Settings

Menu: Tools ➤ Drafting Settings...

Specify grid spacing(X) or [ON/OFF/Snap/Aspect] <0.5000>:
Enter the desired Grid spacing or other options.

Options

Grid Spacing(X)   Allows you to enter the desired Grid spacing in drawing units. Enter **0** to make the Grid spacing match the Snap setting.

ON   Turns on the Grid display. (The F7 key performs the same function).

OFF   Turns off the Grid display. (The F7 key performs the same function.)

Snap   Sets the Grid spacing to match the Snap spacing. Once set, Grid spacing will dynamically follow every change in the Snap spacing.

Aspect   Specifies a Grid spacing in the Y axis that is different from the spacing in the X axis.

NOTE If you follow the Grid spacing value with **X** at the prompt, AutoCAD interprets the value as a multiple of the Snap setting. For example, if you enter **2**, the Grid points will be spaced two units apart, but if you enter **2X**, the Grid points will be twice as far apart as the Snap settings.

NOTE At times, a Grid setting may obscure the view of your drawing. If this happens, AutoCAD automatically turns off the Grid mode and displays the message "Grid too dense to display." If you are using multiple viewports in Paper Space, you can set the grid differently for each viewport.

See Also   Dsettings, Snap; *System Variables:* Gridmode, Gridunit

Grips

Grips allows you to make quick changes to objects in a drawing. With this feature turned on (using the **Ddgrips** command), you can grab end points, center points, and midpoints of objects, as well as stretch, move, copy, rotate, mirror, or scale them. To reveal the Grip points, click on a single object, or select multiple objects at the command prompt. Click a single grip to edit it, or shift-click more than one grip to select several points. If you select multiple grips, you must click one of the selected grips to begin editing.

To Use Grips

Command: **Grips**

Menu: Tools ➤ Grips...

You may toggle grips on or off at the command line as well as checking the **EnableGrips** in the Selection tab of the Options dialog.

1. At the New value for GRIPS: prompt, type **0** to turn Grips off or **1** to turn Grips on.

   • When you click a grip, it becomes a solid color and is called a *hot grip*. The command prompt will change to tell you the current edit option. You can tell you are in a Grips edit option by the asterisks that surround the option name, as in ****STRETCH**** or ****MOVE****.

   • Pressing the Tab key while right-clicking the mouse button on a hot grip displays a pop-up menu for alternate selection of commands. In additon to the standard **Grip** command option, Auto-CAD includes commands such as **Properties**, **Go to URL**... (**Gotourl**), and **Exit** (to close the shortcut menu).

NOTE Once you select a grip, you see the Stretch prompt along with another prompt showing the options available under "Stretch." To switch to the Move, Rotate, Scale, and Mirror options, press ↵ (the options repeat after Mirror). The hot grip is assumed to be the base point of the edit for all of these options. To specify a new base point, enter **B** ↵ at any of the Grips options. You can also copy the selected objects by entering **C** ↵, or undo the last Grips option by entering **U**. To remove **Grips** from an entity, press the Esc key.

See Also Copy, Mirror, Move, Rotate, Scale, Stretch; *Express Tools:* Mocord

Group

Group opens the Object Grouping dialog that allows you to group objects for editing purposes.

To Select Object Groups

Command line: **Group**, **G**

Menu: Tools ➤ Object Group...

Enter information as appropriate in the dialog.

Options

Group Name   Displays the names of existing groups.

Selectable   Indicates whether a group is selectable. If a group is selectable, selecting just a single group member will select all group members, except those on locked layers. If a group is unselectable, selecting a single group member will select only that object.

Group Identification   The group name and optional description are shown in this area when a group is selected from the Group Name list.

Create Group   Allows you to create a New group and specify whether it is Selectable. Enter a name in the Group Identification text box, or use the Unnamed checkbox to create an unnamed group.

Change Group   Allows you to make changes to an existing group. You may Remove or Add Objects to the group, Rename or Reorder the group, change or add the Description and Selectable setting, or Explode the group.

> **NOTE**   Although a "group" has been created, you may edit individual objects within the group using **Grips**. Use Crtl+A to toggle grouping on or off.

See Also   Block, Bmake, Filter, Select, Wblock; *System Variable:* Pickstyle

-Group

-Group displays prompts at the command line to collect objects.

To Select Object Groups at the Command Line

Command line: -**Group**, -**G**

Enter a group option [?/Order/Add/Remove/Explode/REName/Selectable/Create] <Create>: Press ↵, and then Enter a group name or [?]: and Enter a group description:, or enter the appropriate uppercase letter (maximum of 31 characters) for options. Group names cannot have spaces.

Options

?   Press ↵ at the Enter group name(s) to list <*>: prompt to display a list of groups defined in your drawing with their selectable status and description, or enter a group name using any wildcard characters.

Order   If you know the group name, you can enter it at the command line; otherwise, enter a **?** at the prompt Enter a group name or [?]:, and then specify a new order number when prompted to Enter position number of the object to reorder (0 - 1) or [Reverse order]:, or type **R** to reverse the current order of the group.

Add   Specify a name or enter **?** to list groups, and then pick objects to add when prompted to Enter a group name or [?]: and Select objects to add to group....

Remove   Specify a name or enter **?** to list groups, and then pick objects to remove when prompted to Enter a group name or [?]: and Select objects to remove from group....

Explode   Prompts to Enter a group name or [?], or type **?** to display a list and then repeat prompt to reenter a name, which will ungroup and remove the name from the drawing.

Rename   Prompts to Enter a group name to rename or [?]: and then Enter a new name for group or [?]:, allowing you to assign a new name to a group.

Selectable   Toggles grouping On and Off by displaying the prompt This group is selectable, do you want to change it [Yes/No]? <Y>. If you enter **N**, only the individual objects in a group are selected, not the entire group of objects.

Hatch

Hatch fills an area defined by lines, arcs, circles, or polylines with either a predefined pattern, a user-defined pattern, or a solid or simple non-associative hatch pattern. The equivalent dialog command is **Bhatch**.

To Select a Hatch

Command line: **Hatch, -H**

1. **Enter pattern name or [?/Solid/User defined] <current pattern>:** Specify a pattern name, or enter an option.

2. After you enter a pattern name, the following prompts appear:

- **Specify a scale for the pattern <current default>:**
  Specify a new value, or press ↵.

- **Specify an angle for the pattern <current value>:**
  Specify a new value, or press ↵.

- **Select objects to define hatch boundary or <direct hatch>:** Select hatch boundaries, or press ↵ at the Select objects: prompt for the Direct Hatch option.

- **Select objects:** Pick objects that define the hatch boundary, or press ↵ for additional options. If you press ↵, the Retain polyline boundary? [Yes/No] <N>: prompt appears. Entering **Y** retains the boundary as a polyline; otherwise, **N** discards the boundary. Next, use the Specify start point: prompt and [Arc/Close/Length/Undo] options to create a boundary. Once the area is closed, the Specify start point for new boundary or <apply hatch>: prompt asks you to pick additional points or to press ↵ to apply the hatch pattern.

Options

Pattern Name You may enter any valid AutoCAD pattern name as defined in the acad.pat file. To list all of the patterns, use the **?** option. To fill the area with individual lines instead of a hatch block, you should precede the pattern name with an asterisk (*). In general, the pattern scale should be the same as the drawing scale. The following modifiers (**N, O, I**) control how the pattern is created. To use these modifiers, enter the pattern name at the Pattern prompt, followed by a comma and the modifier.

N Fills alternating areas (default option).

O Fills only the outermost area selected.

I Causes the entire area within the objects selected to be hatched, regardless of other enclosed areas within the selected area. Text is not hatched over.

? Lists the names of available hatch patterns.

Solid Specifies a solid fill.

Arc Allows you to draw an arc as the boundary edge with the **Arc** command options [Arc/Close/Length/Undo].

Close Closes the end points of a polyline.

Length Extend a line by dragging and picking with your cursor or entering a value at the Length of line: prompt.

Undo   Resends the previous option.

User Defined   This option allows you to define a simple user-defined hatch pattern, including **Specify angle for crosshatch lines <0>:** (hatch angle), **Specify spacing between the lines <1.0000>:**, and whether or not you want a single hatch or a **Double hatch area ?[Yes/No]<N>:** (cross-hatch). Cross-hatching occurs at 90 degrees to the first hatch lines. As with the predefined patterns, you may pre-cede the **U** with an asterisk (*) to fill the area with single lines rather than hatch block, and you may append the hatch style codes (**N**, **O**, **I**) to control how the hatching is applied.

ScaleXP   When entered at the Scale prompt (for example, 1/96xp), this modifier lets you specify a hatch scale relative to Paper Space. See **Zoom/XP**.

You can create your own hatch patterns by editing the acad.pat file. This file uses numeric codes to define the patterns.

Use the **List** command to identify the pattern name, spacing, and scale.

The objects that define the hatch area should be joined end-to-end and be closed. If you use lines and arcs, the end points of the objects must meet exactly end-to-end. Polylines should be closed. If you select two lines as bounding edges, AutoCAD will use the shortest line length as the limits for the hatch pattern.

To make the hatch pattern begin at a specific point, use the Rotate option under the **Snap** command to set the snap origin to the desired beginning point. Hatch uses the Snap origin (*Snapbase* system variable) to determine where to start the hatch pattern.

The *Fillmode* system variable can be used to toggle globally the display of solid fills and hatches. AutoCAD now stores the hatch-boundary information along with a pointer to the hatch definition instead of an unnamed block identifed as *X.

See Also   Bhatch, Boundary, -Boundary, Explode, Hatchedit, -Hatchedit, Snap/Rotate; *Express Tools:* Superhatch; *System Variables:* Fillmode, Hpang, Hpdouble, Hpname, Hpscale, Hpspace

Hatchedit

Hatchedit modifies an existing *associative* hatch block. The hatch pat-tern must have been associated with the hatched object via the **Bhatch** command. If the original object is altered, you may resize the hatching to follow the object. **Hatchedit** uses the same dialog as **Bhatch** but disables some options. Use -**Hatchedit** to display all the prompts at the command line.

To Edit a Hatch

Command line: **Hatchedit**, **He**

Menu: Modify ➤ Object ➤ Hatch

Modify II Toolbar: ▨ Edit Hatch

1. **Select associative hatch object:** Select the hatch object you wish to modify.

2. In the Hatch Edit dialog, make the required modifications to the hatch pattern from the available options.

Options

Quick Tab

Type   Select a pattern type by clicking the drop-down box to choose between predefined, user-defined, and custom hatch patterns.

Pattern   Select a predefined pattern from the drop-down box or pick the ellipsis button to open the Hatch Pattern Palette dialog to view and choose a pattern from one of the tabbed groups.

Swatch   Select a pattern from the drop-down box to display a sample or swatch in the image box. Clicking the image box opens the Hatch Pattern Palette dialog, which displays the four-tabbed pattern groups.

Custom   Choose Custom in the Pattern drop-down to select a custom pattern that you create and store in a .pat file in your AutoCAD search path.

Angle   Click the drop-down box to specify an angle for the hatch pattern.

Scale   Click the drop-down box to specify an scale for the hatch pattern.

Preview   Click Preview to temporarily exit the dialog to view the results of the hatch pattern you selected and display the prompt <Hit enter or right-click to return to the dialog>. You can also press the space-bar or Esc to restore the dialog.

▨**Inherit Properties**   Allows you to select a hatch object from your current drawing and apply its properties to the hatch object that you are currently editing.

Advanced Tab

Click a radio button to control the hatch pattern boundaries for Normal, Outer, and Ignore.

See Also   Bhatch, Boundary, -Boundary, Hatch, -Hatchedit; *Express Tools:* Superhatch; *System Variable:* Hpang, Hpdouble, Hpname, Hpscale, Hpspace, Snapbase

-Hatchedit

-Hatchedit displays prompts at the command line to edit an existing associated hatch.

To Edit an Associated Hatch

Command line: -**Hatchedit**

1. **Select hatch object:** Select the hatch you wish to edit.

2. **Disassociate/Style/<Properties>:** Enter an option or press ↵ for the following prompt:

    *   **Enter pattern name or [?/Solid/User defined] <ANSI31>:** Enter a pattern name, or type **?** to list names of available patterns, **S** for a solid fill pattern, or **U** for a user-defined pattern. The U option displays additional prompts for setting the Angle for Crosshatch Lines, Spacing between Lines, and Single or Double Hatch Area.

Options

Disassociate   Removes associativity from the hatch object.

Style   Press ↵ at the prompt Ignore/Outer/<Normal>: to fill alternating areas, or enter **I** fill entire area within objects selected, or **O** for outermost area selected.

See Also   Bhatch, Boundary, -Boundary, Hatch, Hatchedit

Help/?

Help or **?** opens up the Help Topics: AutoCAD Help dialog to provide a brief description of how to use a particular command. You can use it on the fly by entering '**Help** or '**?** at any prompt in the command. You may press F1 to get context-sensitive Help on the current command. Express Tools provides a separate Help menu: Express ➤ Help.

To Use Help

Command line: **Help, ?, F1** (or '**Help**, to use transparently).

Menu: Help ➤ AutoCAD Help Topics

Standard toolbar: [?] Help

Hide

Hide removes hidden lines on an orthogonal or 3D view when using Vpoint, Dview, or View.

To Hide Lines

Command line: **Hide**, **Hi**

Menu: View ➤ Hide

Render Toolbar: Hide

> **NOTE** For complex 3D views, you may want to use **Mslide** to save the view with hidden lines removed. In a perspective view, use the Hide option under **Dview**. You can also use **Shade** to get a quick rendering of a 3D model.

See Also Dview, Mview, Options, Shade, View

Hyperlink

Hyperlink opens the Insert Hyperlink dialog to attach a hyperlink to a graphic object, linking it to a file in another application or drawings, or to edit any existing hyperlink. Saving a drawing in the current release changes AutoCAD R14-attached URL's to hyperlinks but preserves them and restores the attached URL when saved back to R14 format.

To Attach or Edit a Hyperlink

Command line: **Hyperlink**

Provide information as needed in the dialog. You can specify an Internet location (URL) on the World Wide Web or a word or spreadsheet document on your local drive or your firm's network.

Select Object: Depending on the specific task being performed, the name of the dialog changes: the Insert Hyperlink dialog allows you to create a link to a file or URL, and the Edit Hyperlink dialog serves to edit the properties of a existing hyperlinks.

Options

Link to File or URL   Displays the dialog name Insert Hyperlink, which allows you to enter and store paths and filenames for hyperlinks, including local drive, network drive, Internet, or intranet. Information entered in the drop-down edit box appears in *Path* and *Base*. Check **Use Relative Path for Hyperlink** to store information on the relative path. The link is only sustained if both the drawings and the hyperlinked files are moved together. If you do not intend to move the hyperlinked files, this box can remain unchecked. If you exclude the path, AutoCAD uses the current path of your drawing and displays it in *Base*. You can also use the *Hyperlinkbase* system variable to set the default base path.

Remove Link   Selecting an object that has been linked displays the Remove Link button. This button appears only when a link is created, allowing you to detach the hyperlink.

Named Location in File (optional)   Specifying the name, such as a saved view name in an AutoCAD drawing file or a bookmark in a word-processing program will retrieve it when the hyperlink is open. Saving a ModelSpace view restores it in the Model tab. Creating a PaperSpace view will restore it from the last active Layout tab.

Hyperlink Description   Enter a brief comment for the hyperlink.

See Also   Attachurl, Detachurl, Inserturl, -Hyperlink, Hyperlinkoptions, Openurl, Selecturl

---

-Hyperlink

Hyperlink attaches a URL to objects or areas in your drawing. A URL can be attached as Xdata (extended data) to one or more objects. Use the object method if geometry is scattered throughout the drawing. Attaching a URL by area places a rectangle around the specified area on the layer Urllayer. Use area if there is no geometry.

To Create a Hyperlink at the Command Line

Command line: **-Hyperlink**

1. **Enter an option [Remove/Insert] <Insert>:** Press ⏎ if you wish to insert a hyperlink or **R** to remove the link. If you entered **R**, the Select objects: prompt appears to select the objects; if you entered **All** for a list of hyperlinks, another prompt appears to Enter number, hyperlink, or * for all:. Specify a number, a hyperlink name, or enter an asterisk (*) to remove all hyperlinks.

2. **Enter hyperlink insert option [Area/Object] <Object>:** If you pressed ⏎ in step 1, you can specify an option method.

3. **Select objects:** Use an object selection method.

4. **Enter hyperlink <current drawing>:** Specify a local path name, press ↵ to associate a hyperlink to a saved view name in your drawing, or enter the URL's location

5. **Enter named location <none>:** Press ↵ to create a hyperlink with a defined location; otherwise, enter the name of a view saved in your AutoCAD drawing.

6. **Enter description <none>:** Enter a brief description. Information you enter displays it as a tooltip when passing your cursor over the hyperlink.

Options

Area   Pick *First corner:* and *Other corner:* using window selection methods, and then specify a name at the Enter hyperlink <current drawing>: prompt.

Object   Select objects to be inserted, and then specify a name at the Enter hyperlink <current drawing>: prompt.

See Also   Attachurl, Detachurl, Hyperlink, Hyperlinkoptions, Inserturl, Openurl, Selecturl

---

Hyperlinkoptions

Hyperlinkoptions allows you to include hyperlink options as part of the cursor menu. Passing your cursor over objects displays a hyperlink icon and tooltip.

To Display Hyperlink Shortcut Menu

Command line: **Hyperlinkoptions**

1. **Display hyperlink cursor and shortcut menu? [Yes/No] <Yes>:** Pressing ↵ toggles Hyperlink on in the cursor menu, allowing it to appear as a cascading menu with options. You must first display the object's grips and then right-click to activate this feature. If you enter **N**, the hyperlink shortcut menu and hyperlink tooltips will be disabled.

2. **Display hyperlink tooltip? [Yes/No] <Yes>:** If you pressed ↵ in step 1, you can enter **Y** to display tooltips for hyperlinks; otherwise, **N** will turn hyperlink tooltips off.

See Also   Attachurl, Detachurl, Hyperlink, -Hyperlink, Inserturl, Openurl, Selecturl

Id

Id displays the XYZ coordinate values of a point.

To Display a Point's Coordinates

Command line: **Id** (or **'Id** to use transparently)

Menu: Tools ➤ Inquiry ➤ ID Point

Inquiry Toolbar: ▦ Locate Point

Specify point: Pick a point.

A point you select with **Id** becomes the last point in the current editing session (stored in the *Lastpoint* variable). This can be accessed by inserting the @ sign when you are asked to pick a point.

See Also Ddptype, Point; *System variable:* Lastpoint

Image

Image inserts images in different formats, such as .bmp, .tif, .rle, .jpg, .gif, and .tga into an AutoCAD drawing file. The equivalent command-line prompt is **-Image**.

To Insert an Image

Command line: **Image**, **Im**

Menu: Insert ➤ Image Manager

Insert Toolbar: ▦ Image

Reference Toolbar: ▦ Image

Draw Toolbar: ▦ Insert Flyout ▦ Image

Opens the Image Manager dialog for you to select a raster or bit-mapped bitonal, color-image file for insertion into the drawing. Images can be 8-bit gray, 8-bit color, or 24-bit image. Pick Attach... to display the Select Image File dialog, and locate the file. Next, pick the Open button to open the Image dialog to specify a method of insertion. If you choose to check all boxes, prompts appear at the command line; otherwise, provide information as needed in the dialog(s).

1. **Specify insertion point <0,0>:** Enter coordinate values, or pick a point.

   Base image size: Width: 1.000000, Height: 1.837500 Inches, Unitless

   Specify scale factor <1>: Enter a scale value.

2. **Specify rotation angle <0>:** Enter a rotation value.

Options

List View   The Image list box contains six drag division headings, including Image Name, Status, Size, Type, Data, and Saved Path that can be sorted alphabetically or numerically. The default sort order is alphabetical by image name. Change column widths by placing your cursor over the vertical divider line, until the heading changes to an anchor symbol, and then drag it. Double-click the vertical line to restore the heading default width, or close the dialog to save its size. Images can be renamed by clicking the name and then pressing the F2 key. Names are limited to 31 characters, including letters, digits, and the special characters, hyphen (-) and underscore (_). Although an image in the drawing can be renamed, the actual file remains unchanged. You cannot rename an image if it is inside an external reference file.

Tree View   Pressing F3 and F4 toggles the display of images as a list of individual names or a tree structure with reference to its source. Images inserted directly into the drawing are located at the top, followed by images nested in block, and then those nested in external reference files, which branch off from their Xref filename, are below. Their identification is similar to an Xref layer, with the file and image names separated by the pipe character (|). When individual names are displayed in tree view lists, you can select multiple files using standard windows Shift and Control key methods.

Attach   Opens the Select Image File dialog with standard file selection features to locate and insert a new image object and definition to the current drawing, and then displays the Image dialog. The image file Name, Path, Insertion Point, Scale, and Rotation can all be edited in this dialog by picking Specify Onscreen checkboxes or entering values in edit boxes. You can use the Browse... button to access the Select Image File dialog, check Retain Path to save the image's path, and pick the Details>> button to view the Image Information section. The **Imageattach** command opens the same dialog. See **Imageattach**.

Detach   Detaches the selected image definitions and removes all associated image objects from the drawing database and display screen.

Reload   Loads a new drawing or reloads an image that had been unloaded, placing its draworder on top.

Unload   Unloads an image, displaying it as a boundary and minimizing AutoCAD's memory requirement. It does not delete or permanently detach the image object from the drawing. Use Reload to restore the image.

Image Found At   Identifies actual drive letter, directory path, and filename for a selected image.

Browse   Opens the Attach Image File dialog with standard file-selection features, allowing you to preview as well as search and/or select an image from a list box, enter a filename, or choose a file type from the Files of Type drop-down box. Clicking Hide Preview prevents the image from being displayed and toggles the button to Show Preview.

Save Path Retains the new path information. If you press Escape while editing the image's path, the old path is restored. If AutoCAD cannot locate the image, an alert dialog appears with the message *Image file not found. Do you really want to use this path?* Clicking Yes reports Not Found in the Status column. If Save Path is not picked after the path is edited, the original image path is used the next time you load the drawing.

Details Selecting an image and clicking the button opens the Image File Details dialog, providing you with information, such as the image name, saved path, active path, file creation date and time, file size and type, color, color depth, width and height in pixels, resolution, default size in units, and a preview image.

See Also Draworder, Imageadjust, Imageattach, Imageclip, Image-frame, Imagequality, Transparency; *Express Tools:* Tframe; *System Variables:* Sortents

---

-Image

-Image inserts .bmp, .tif, .rle, and .jpg image files at the command line.

To Insert an Image from the Command Line

Command line: **-Image**, **-Im**

? / Detach / Path / Reload / Unload / <Attach>: Enter an option or press ⏎ to attach the image to your current drawing.

Options

? Alphabetically displays the image name, instances occurring, and the hard-coded path.

Images to list **<*>:** Press ⏎ or an image name.

Detach Removes the named image from your drawing.

Enter list of images to detach: Enter an image name.

Path Allows you to edit the filename and associated path of specified image.

Enter list of images for path modification: Enter the image name or an * for multiple images. If you entered an asterisk (*), the Old Path and Enter New Path prompts appear for entering the current and new paths for the image.

Reload Reloads image data into memory for display and plotting. AutoCAD displays these messages:

```
    Reloading...
Reload image <image name>: <hard-coded path name>
<image name> loaded and relinked.
Enter list of images to reload: Enter an image name
```

Unload   Removes image data from working memory to improve performance. Unloaded images are displayed as a frame, and their information remains stored with the drawing.

Enter list of images to unload: Enter a loaded image name.

See Also   Image, Imageadjust, Imageattach, Imageclip, Imageframe, Imagequality

Imageadjust

Imageadjust displays a dialog to set control for an image's brightness, contrast, and fade values. The equivalent command-line prompt is **-Imageadjust**.

To Adjust an Image

Command line: **Imageadjust**, **Iad**

Menu: Modify ➤ Object ➤ Image ➤ Adjust…

Reference Toolbar: Image Adjust

Opens the Image Adjust dialog, allowing you to use a slider button or corresponding edit boxes to adjust the Brightness, Contrast, and Fade of an image.

Brightness   Set to higher values if you wish to brighten the image; causes pixels to become whiter.

Contrast   Use a higher value to force pixels to their primary or secondary color.

Fade   Specify a higher value to merge image with its background color.

Image Preview   Thumbnail image used to dynamically display specified adjustments.

Reset   Resets image to default values: Brightness = 50, Contrast = 50, and Fade = 0.

NOTE   The command-line prompt is useful for adjusting multiple images at one time.

See Also   -Imageadjust

-Imageadjust

-Imageadjust lets you select one or more images at the command line to adjust the contrast, fade, and brightness.

To Adjust an Image

Command line: **-Imageadjust**

1. **Select image:** Pick an image you wish to adjust.

   Enter image option [Contrast/Fade/Brightness] <Brightness>: Press ↵, or enter an option. Contrast and Brightness default values are 50; Fade defaults to 0.

   Enter contrast value (0-100) <50>: Enter a value within the range indicated.

   Enter fade value (0-100) <0>: Enter a value within the range indicated.

   Enter brightness value (0-100) <50>: Enter a value within the range indicated.

See Also   Image, Imageadjust, Imageattach, Imageclip, Imageframe, Imagequality, Transparency

---

Imageattach

Imageattach loads an image object into memory while attaching its definition and displaying it in the current drawing.

To Attach an Image

Command line: **Imageattach**, **Iat**

Menu: Insert ➤ Raster Image

Reference Toolbar: 📷 Image Attach

Opens the Select Image File dialog directly, bypassing the Image Manager dialog and displaying options similar to the Select File dialog. Select a file from the list in the Select Image File dialog, and then pick the Open button to display the Image dialog. Provide information as needed in the Image dialog, and then respond to the prompts:

1. **Specify insertion point <0,0>:** Press ↵ or enter coordinate values.

   Base image size: Width: 1.000000, Height: 0.666667, Inches

2. **Specify scale factor <1>:** Press ↵ or enter a value.

Name   Click the Browse... button to open the Select Image File dialog to enter a filename in the *File Name* edit box, select from the list box, or locate drives using the Look In: drop-down box. Use the Hide Preview button to prevent the image from being displayed. Once the image is hidden, the button changes to Show Preview. The drop-down box lists all the images in the current drawing. Highlighting a name displays the Path: below. See **Open** for additional features.

Insertion Point   Use the checkbox to Specify Onscreen input of your image or the edit boxes to enter *X:, Y:,* and *Z:* values.

Scale   Enter a scale in the edit box, or pick the Specify Onscreen to enter the information at the command line.

Rotation   Pick the Specify Onscreen checkbox, or use the Angle: edit box to set the image's rotation angle.

Retain Path   Check this box if you wish to save the path of the image file with its definition, or uncheck the box to save the image name only. AutoCAD will peruse the Project Files Search Path, stored in the *Project-name* system variable, when the box is unchecked.

Details>>   Select this button to obtain more detailed information about the image, including horizontal and vertical resolution, width and height in pixels, as well as units. The units for some images, such as .tif files, are listed under Current AutoCAD Unit. The width and height of an image is automatically converted to AutoCAD units and displayed with a default size.

See Also   *System Variable:* Project Name

Imageclip

Imageclip lets you make a clipping boundary within an image object.

To Clip an Image

Command line: **Imageclip, Icl**

Menu: Modify ➤ Object ➤ Imageclip

Reference Toolbar: ▨ Image Clip

1. **Select image to clip:** Pick an image object you wish to clip.

2. **Enter image clipping option [ON/OFF/Delete/New boundary]** **<New>:** Specify an option, or press ↵ to create a new boundary.

3. **Enter clipping type [Polygonal/Rectangular] <Rectangular>:** Press ↵, and then pick opposite corners for a rectangular clipping boundary, or type **P** to draw any closed polygon shape you define.

4. **Delete old boundary? [No/Yes] <Yes>:** (This prompt appears if you select a clipped image to create a new boundary.) Press ↵ to restore the original image and then create a new boundary, or press **N** to exit the command.

Options

ON   Toggles clipping on and restores the images clipped area to show its previously defined boundary.

OFF Toggles clipping off to show the entire image and frame. AutoCAD automatically turns on any image selected for reclipping and gives the prompt Delete old boundary?

Delete Removes the clipped boundary, and restores original image.

See Also Imageadjust, Imageframe, Imagequality

Imageframe

Imageframe controls the visibility of all image frames in the current drawing at the command line.

To Turn an Image Frame Off

Command line: **Imageframe**

Menu: Modify ➤ Object ➤ Image ➤ Frame

Reference Toolbar: ▦ Image Frame

Enter image frame setting [ON/OFF] <ON>: Enter On or Off.

See Also Imageadjust, Imageclip, Imagequality; *Express Tools:* Tframe

Imagequality

Imagequality allows you to choose between two display image resolutions.

To Control Image Quality

Command line: **Imagequality**

Menu: Modify ➤ Object ➤ Image ➤ Quality

Reference Toolbar: ▦ Image Frame

Enter image quality setting [High/Draft] <High>: Specify an option.

Options

High Increases quality, and displays images slower.

Draft Decreases quality, and displays the images faster.

NOTE Setting image quality in the drawing does not affect the plotted output; images always plot with high quality.

See Also Imageadjust, Imageclip, Imageframe, Transparency

Import/Export

Import and **Export** commands offer several ways to transfer data to and from other applications and file formats.

Import Functions

You can bring drawings or images from other applications into the current AutoCAD drawing by using the Import functions in the Import File dialog. The program supports these file formats: .3ds, .sat, .eps, and .wmf.

To Import Files Created in Other File Formats

Command line: **Import**

Draw Toobar: 🔳 Insert Flyout 🔳 Import

Insert Toolbar: 🔳 Import

1. Opens the Import File dialog. Click the required file format in the Files of Type drop-down box, and then search Directories and/or Drives to find the file that you wish to import. A preview image displays selected images prior to importing them into your drawing. If you are unable to locate the file, click the Find File... button to open the Browse and Search dialog for further global investigation.

2. Click the Options button to open the WMF in Options subdialog box, and set .wmf in Toggles; Wire Frame (No Fills) offers the option to import objects as wire frames or filled objected, and Wide Lines maintains line and border width or imports the file with 0 width.

Although the above steps outline the basic procedures for importing other file formats, there are a number of variations and some additional prompts. Moreover, all of these file import options have equivalent command-line versions. Table I.1 lists the AutoCAD import options and their command equivalents, as well as any procedural variations.

TABLE I.1: AutoCAD File Import Functions

File Format	Command	Description/Comments
3D Studio Files		
.3ds	3DSIN	Imports selected 3D Studio geometry and rendering information. Prior to import, you must provide layer- and materials-handling information in the 3D Studio File Import Options dialog.

TABLE I.1 (continued):   AutoCAD File Import Functions

File Format	Command	Description/Comments
Solid Models		
.sat	ACISIN	Converts geometric objects stored in ASCII (.sat) format into AutoCAD bodies, solids, and regions.
PostScript		
.eps, .ps	PSIN	Inserts Encapsulated PostScript and Post-Script images into the current drawing as an anonymous block. You need to specify the insertion point and scale factor for the block.
Windows		
.wmf	WMFIN	Imports Windows Metafile format files. You need to specify an insertion point and scale factor, rotation, and scale when importing the file at the prompt Specify insertion point or [Scale/X/Y/Z/ Rotate/PScale/PX/PY/PZ/PRotate]:.

Export Functions

Using the AutoCAD export functions, you can convert AutoCAD drawings into several different formats. The formats can then be read by other applications: .dwf, .dwg, .dxf, .dxx, .3ds, .sat, .stl, .eps, .bmp, and .wmf.

To Create Other File Formats

Command line: **Export**

Menu: File ➤ Export Data

1. Opens the Export Data dialog. Highlight the required file format in the Save as Type drop-down box.

2. For some file formats, the Options button ungrays, letting you set specific controls for PostScript file types.

Table I.2 lists the AutoCAD export options, their command equivalents, and any variations in the general procedure described above.

TABLE I.2: AutoCAD File Export Functions

File Format	Command	Description/Comments
AutoCAD Drawing File		
.dwg	WBLOCK	Creates an AutoCAD drawing file. See **Wblock**.
3D Studio Files		
.3ds	3DSOUT	Converts selected AutoCAD geometry and rendering information into 3D Studio format. Prior to conversion, you must specify the division method and provide smoothing and welding information in the 3D Studio File Export Options dialog.
Solid Models		
.sat	ACISOUT	Converts AutoCAD objects, representing surfaces, solids, and regions to an **ACIS** file in ASCII format.
Stereolithography		
.stl	STLOUT	Outputs a single solid into an ASCII or binary format. The .stl format is compatible with Stereolithography Apparatus (SLA). The solid data is output as a triangulated mesh that represents the solid. After selecting the solid for output, you need to specify ASCII or binary format.
Windows Metafile and Bitmap Files		
.wmf	WMFOUT	Saves selected objects to Windows Metafile format, containing both vector and raster graphics.
.bmp	BMPOUT	Creates a bitmap image of selected objects in your drawing. There is no menu or dialog option for creating bitmaps.
PostScript file		
.eps	PSOUT	Makes an Encapsulated PostScript (.eps) file.

TABLE I.2 (continued):   AutoCAD File Export Functions

File Format	Command	Description/Comments
Attribute Extract File		
.dxx	Ddattext, DXF Output File Option	Used in the Ddattext dialog for drawing interchange file format (.dxf) to differentiate the output file from normal .dxf files.

Options

DWG   Uses **Wblock** command to open the Write Block dialog, letting you select objects and then write them out as an AutoCAD drawing file or block, similar to the **Bmake** and **Block** commands, which store the file's definitions inside the drawing database.

EPS   Opens an Export Options subdialog box with edit boxes and radio buttons to set controls for PostScript output. An optional *Prolog Section Name* edit box is used to read from the acad.psf file when using the **Psout** command. The What to Plot section contains radio buttons for selecting different area configurations: plotting your current Display screen and drawing Extents and Limits. You can also save a view or create a window to define the drawing area to plot. The View and Window... buttons allow you to retrieve saved images or pick points from the screen.

The Preview section allows you to specify an EPSI, Tiff, or None (no preview screen image). Use the Pixels section to set your screen preview image at 128, 256, or 512.

Use the *Scale Section* edit boxes to specify the number of Drawings Units equal to Output Units. Check Fit to Paper to maximize the image for the specified paper size.

The Paper Size section has an edit box to enter a Width and a Height as well as a drop-down menu to select predefined sizes.

NOTE   AutoCAD system variables and other options can be used to control the quality and precision of a number of these file conversions.

See Also   Cutclip, Image, Insertobj, Mslide, Olelinks, Paste

Insert

Insert opens the Insert dialog to insert a named block (or drawing) within the current file.

To Insert Blocks

Command line: **Insert**, **I**

Menu: Insert ➤ Block

Insert Toolbar: 🔲 Insert Block

Provide information as needed in the dialog.

Options

Name   Click the Browse... button to open the Select Drawing File dialog to search drives, path names, and filenames, or select from the *Name:* drop-down box. Blocks placed as a file into the drawing have their *Path:* displayed during initial insertion.

Insertion Point   Check the box *Specify Onscreen* to input your image, or enter XYZ coordinate values in the edit boxes. If the box is checked, the prompt appears; pick a point or enter coordinate values at the command line:

    Specify insertion point:

Scale   Check the box *Specify Onscreen* to enter the information at the command line, or enter values in the *X, Y,* and *Z* edit boxes. Checking the box displays prompts at the command line:

    Enter X scale factor or specify opposite corner <1>:
    Enter Y scale factor <use X scale factor>:

Unchecking *Specify Onscreen* and checking *Uniform Scale* boxes grays out the *Y- and Z-Scale Factor* edit boxes allowing you to place the block into your drawing based solely on the Z-scale factor.

Rotation   Checking the box *Specify Onscreen* allows you to enter the block's rotation angle at the command line; otherwise, enter a value in the *Angle:* edit box.

    Specify rotation angle <0>:

See Also   Attdef, Attredef, Base, Block, Bmake, Explode, -Insert, Files

---

-Insert

Insert places a named block (or drawing) within the current file. The equivalent dialog command is **Insert**.

To Insert Blocks

Command line: **-Insert**, **I**

1. **Enter block name or [?] <last block inserted>:** Enter the block or drawing name or a tilde (~) to display the Select Drawing File dialog.

2. **Specify insertion point or [Scale/X/Y/Z/Rotate/PScale/ PX/PY/PZ/PRotate]:** Enter a coordinate value, pick a point with the cursor, or enter a preset option (see "Preset Options" below).

3. **Enter X-scale factor, specify opposite corner, or [Corner/ XYZ] <1>:** Enter an X-scale factor; **C** for corner; **XYZ** to specify the individual X-, Y-, and Z-scale factors; or press ↵ to accept the default X-scale factor of 1.

4. **Enter Y-scale factor <use X-scale factor>:** (This prompt appears if you press ↵ without entering a value or option.) Enter a Y-scale factor, or press ↵ to use the scale factor for the Y-axis as well.

5. **Specify rotation angle <0>:** Enter the rotation angle for the block, or pick a point on the screen to indicate the angle. (This last prompt does not appear if you use the Rotate preset option.)

Options

Tilde (~) Entered at the Block name... prompt, causes the Select Drawing File dialog to appear. The dialog lets you select external files for insertion.

= Replaces a block with an external file. (See "Notes" below.)

* To insert the individual entities in a block (rather than the block as a single object), type an asterisk (*) before its drive letter, path, and name at the Block name: prompt.

X-Scale Factor Scales the block in the X axis. If you enter a value, you are then prompted for the Y-scale factor. The prompt is

- Enter X-scale factor, specify opposite corner, or [Corner/XYZ] <1>:

Corner Allows you to enter the X- and Y-scale factors simultaneously. To scale the block by a factor of 1 in the X axis and 2 in the Y axis, enter **C** at the Enter X-scale factor, specify opposite corner, or [Corner/XYZ] <1>: prompt, and then enter **@1,2**. Otherwise, enter a coordinate value, or pick a point at the X-scale factor... prompt to scale your block. The prompt is

- Specify opposite corner:

XYZ Gives individual X-, Y-, and Z-scale factors. You will be prompted for the factors. The prompts are

- Specify X-scale factor or [Corner] <1>:
- Enter Y-scale factor <use X-scale factor>:
- Specify Z-scale factor or <use X-scale factor>:

Preset Options The following options are available at the Insertion point: prompt. They are called Insert "presets" because they allow you to preset the scale and rotation angle of a block before you select an insertion point. Once you select a preset option, the dragged image will conform to the setting used; you will not be prompted for a scale factor after you select the insertion point.

Scale   Allows you to enter a single scale factor for the block at the prompt Specify scale factor for XYZ axes:. This factor governs X, Y, and Z axis scaling.

X   Displays prompt Specify X-scale factor: to set the X-scale factor.

Y   Displays prompt Specify Y-scale factor: to set the Y-scale factor.

Z   Displays prompt Specify Z-scale factor: to set the Z-scale factor.

Rotate   Displays prompt Specify rotation angle: to enter a rotation angle for the block.

PScale   The same as Scale, but is used only while positioning the block for insertion to "preview" the scaled block. Prompts Specify preview scale factor for XYZ axes:, and then prompts for a scale factor.

PX   The same as PScale but affects only the X-scale factor. The prompt is Specify preview X-scale factor:

PY   The same as PScale but affects only the Y-scale factor. The prompt is Specify preview Y-scale factor:

PZ   The same as PScale but affects only the Z-scale factor. The prompt is Specify preview Z-scale factor:

PRotate   The same as Rotate, prompting to Specify preview rotation angle:, but is used only while positioning the block for insertion. You are later prompted for a rotation factor.

If a block has previously been inserted, it becomes the default block for insertion (stored in the *Insname* system variable). Enter **?** to see a list of the blocks in the current file. Coordinate values are in relation to the current UCS.

To bring the contents of an external file in as individual entities, insert the file in the normal way, and use the **Explode** command to break it into its individual components. To insert a mirror image of a block, enter a negative value at either the X-scale factor... or Y-scale factor... prompt.

If the inserted block or file contains an attribute and the *Attreq* system variable is set to 1, you are prompted for the attribute information after you have entered the rotation angle. If the system variable *Attdia* is set to 1, a dialog with the attribute prompts appears. (The default setting for *Attreq* is 1; *Attdia* is normally set to 0.)

You can also use **Insert** to replace or update a block with an external drawing file. For example, to replace a block named Chair1 with an external file named Chair2, enter **Chair1=Chair2** at the Block name: prompt. If the block and the external filenames are the same (Chair1, for example), enter **Chair1=**. Note, however, that named objects in the current drawing have priority over those in an imported file.

When you attempt to replace blocks containing attributes, the old attributes will remain even though the block has been changed. To avoid them, you must delete the old block, insert the new (external) block, and reenter the attribute values or use the **Attredef** command to redefine an attributed block.

Finally, an external file will be inserted with its WCS (world coordinate system) aligned with the current UCS (user coordinate system). A block will be inserted with its UCS orientation aligned with the current UCS.

See Also   Attdef, Attredef, Base, Block, Explode, Files, Insert, Xplode, Xref; *System Variables:* Attdia, Attreq, Filedia, Insname

---

Insertobj

Insertobj inserts a range of graphic and multimedia objects into an existing AutoCAD drawing. Objects include other AutoCAD drawings, sound clips, music clips, media clips, clip art, paint files, word-processed documents, and presentation slides. **Insertobj** works with Windows' Object Linking and Embedding (OLE). It allows you to create objects for embedding into your current AutoCAD drawing.

To Insert an Object into a Drawing

Command line: **Insertobj**, **Io**

Menu: Insert ➤ OLE Object

Draw Toolbar: 🔲 Insert Flyout 🔲 OLE Object

Insert Toolbar: 🔲 OLE Object

Opens the Insert Object dialog with options: Create New and Create from File. Elements shared by both options include the Result section, providing a brief description of the procedure being implemented, and the Display as Icon checkbox, used to replicate the link or embedded object with its associated icon.

Options

Create New

1. When the Insert Object dialog opens, pick Create New, and then double-click the *Object Type:* that you wish to embed in your drawing.

AutoCAD starts the native Windows application associated with the type of object that you have selected. For example, if you click PowerPoint Slide, it will open PowerPoint and allow you to create a slide file (.ppt) for insertion into your drawing. If you click Microsoft Clip Gallery, it will load the Clip Art gallery and allow you to select the item you require.

The *Object Type:* list box contains all of the applications on your system that support Object Linking and Embedding. To delete an OLE object, right-click it to display a shortcut menu, and choose cut.

2. Once you have created a new application object, choose Files ➤ Exit & Return to AutoCAD to simultaneously exit the application and insert the new object into your drawing.

The new object is inserted at the upper left corner of the drawing. To reposition it, click the object, and drag it to a new position. When you click an object, a frame and handles appear. Use the handles to resize the object to the desired dimensions. If you need to edit an object that you have inserted, double-click the object. The native application will be loaded again. Make the required changes, choose File ➤ Update to update the changes to your drawing, and then pick Files ➤ Exit & Return to AutoCAD again.

Create from File

File   Enter a path and filename in the edit box, or pick Browse... to open the Browse dialog and find a file for embedding or linking.

Link   Checking the box sets a link to the file.

See Also   Copyembed, Copylink, Cut and Paste, Olelinks, Olescale, Pasteclip, Pastespec

Inserturl

See **Block**

Interfere

Interfere combines the common portions of two or more solid objects into a single 3D composite solid.

To Create an Interference Object

Command line: **Interfere**, **Inf**

Menu: Draw ➤ Solids ➤ Interference

Solids Toolbar: Interference

Select first set of solids: Pick one or more solid objects to include in the interference operation.

Select second set of solids: Pick one or more solid objects to perform the interference against. The results display the following:

```
Comparing 1 solid against 1 solid.
Interfering solids (first set): 1
                  (second set): 1
Interfering pairs           : 1
```

Create interference solids? [Yes/No] <N>: Entering **Y** forms and highlights the new volume on the current layer from the objects; otherwise, pressing ↵ cycles through the interfering objects with these prompts:

- **Highlight pairs of interfering solids? [Yes/No] <N>:** Enter **Y** to highlight the object, or press ↵.

- **Enter an option [Next pair/eXit] <Next>:** Enter **N** to highlight the next object or **X** to exit the command.

See Also   Intersect, Subtract, Union

Intersect

Intersect allows you to create a composite solid or region that contains only the common volume of two or more overlapping solid objects or regions. In effect, it joins the objects, leaving only the area or volume where the objects intersect.

To Create an Intersection Object

Command line: **Intersect**, **In**

Menu: Modify ➤ Solids Editing ➤ Intersect

Solids Editing Toolbar: Intersect

Select objects: Click the overlapping solids or regions for which you wish to derive the intersection.

AutoCAD removes all nonoverlapping sections of the selected objects, leaving only the intersection objects created by their common areas and/or volumes.

NOTE Intersect can be used only for regions or solids. You may select both regions and solids at the same time, and you may select objects from any number of planes. AutoCAD will group the selection set into subsets by region/solid and by plane before calculating the intersections and creating the intersection objects.

See Also   Interfere, Subtract, Union

Isoplane

Isoplane lets you switch the cursor orientation between the left, top, and right isometric planes when the Snap mode is set to the Isometric style.

To Change the Cursor Orientation

Command line: **Isoplane**, **Ctrl+E**, **F5** (or **'Isoplane**, to use transparently).

[Left/Top/Right]<Toggle>: Enter your choice or press ↵ to go to the next isoplane.

Current isometric: Lists the new isoplane.

> **NOTE** Ctrl+E is a toggle control key that selects the next iso-metric plane in a cycle of isometric planes.

See Also Dsettings, Snap; *System Variable:* Snapisopair

Layer

Layer opens the Layer Properties Manager dialog to create, set current, delete, rename, and manage layers, and control linetype, plot styles, and plotting.

To Manage Layers

Command line: **Layer**, **La** (or **'Layer** to use transparently)

Menu: Format ➢ Layer

Object Properties Toolbar: 🖾 Layers

Object Properties Toolbar: ⟨ ♀ ☼ 🗗🖾□ 0 ▼⟩ Layer Control

The resizable dialog offers features that provide ease of use over managing layers and plotting. Based on the columns function, clicking a heading sorts information in descending or ascending order. Column widths are drag divisions that can be resized by pressing the Pick button on your cursor over the vertical line, to the right of the column, until an anchor symbol appears. Drag the column heading to expand or shrink its size. Double-click the vertical line to restore the column's default width. Use the right-click menu to Select All, Clear All, and Select All but Current layers, or serve as an alternative method to access some of same functions appearing in checkboxes, drop-down lists, and buttons at the top of the dialog. You can also select single or groups of names by holding the Shift key or Control key. Highlight a name, and then click it after a box appears, so that you can move your cursor over any character to rename an existing layer.

Provide information as needed in the dialog.

Options

Named Layer Filters   Allows you to filter which layers are displayed in the layer list box. You can use the drop-down list to select Show All Layers, Show All Unused Layers, or Show All Xref Dependent Layers or pick the Ellipsis button to open the Named Layer Filters dialog and set layer groups or filters. If you enter a name, such as **Floor Plan**, in the *Filter Name* edit drop-down box, then specify one or more layers separated by commas and/or wildcards in the *Layer Name* edit box, you can set appropriate parameters in the remaining On/Off, Freeze/Thaw, Active Viewport, New Viewport, Lock/Unlock, and Plot drop-down boxes or the *Color, Lineweight, Linetype,* and *Plot Style* edit boxes. Pick Add to append the name to the *Filter Name* drop-down box. Names are saved in the Name Layer Filters list in the Layer Properties Manager dialog and in the *Filter Name* drop-down edit box. Click the Delete button to remove the filter name. Use Reset to quickly restore the default values. Click Invert Filter to view the reverse layering status in your drawing. If a filter is set, then check the Apply to Object Properties toolbar; you can pass your cursor over the right side of the Layer States combo box in the Object Properties toolbar and the tooltip Filter Applied appears.

Layer List Box   Contains the following nine drag-division headings: Name, On, Freeze in All VP (Viewports), Lock, Color, Linetype, Lineweight, Plot Style, and Plot. Depending on the particular layer icon, clicking the graphic image will set the layers status On or Off, Frozen or Thawed, Locked or Unlocked, Open the Select Color dialog, Open the Select Linetype dialog, Open the Select Lineweight dialog, Open the Select Plot Style dialog, or disable plotting of a layer.

New   Creates new, editable default layer names: Layer1, Layer2, and so forth. Once a new layer is created in the list box, press ↵ immediately or type a comma (,) if you wish to add default sequential layer names. If a layer in the list box is highlighted, new layers automatically inherit their properties. You can enter layer names in upper- or lowercase, up to 256 characters that contain spaces and other nonalphabetic characters. Invalid characters include brackets (<>), slashes (/ \), single quote (') double quote ("), colon (:), question mark (?), asterick (*), pipe or vertical bar (|), comma (,), and equal sign(=).

Current   Sets and identifies the current layer in the status area above the column heading. The current layer name is saved to the *Clayer* system variable. Double-click a layer name in the list box to make it current.

Delete   Purges any unused layers. If a layer is current, it cannot be purged.

Show Details or Hide Details   Expands the dialog providing an alternate method to create new layer names and set layer status. New or less experienced users can click Show Details to access the more conventional edit and the checkboxes to manage layers, and then click Hide Details to retract this feature. Highlighting an existing layer name or clicking New displays

the layer name in the *Name* edit box for renaming or editing its properties: Color, Lineweight, Line Type, and/or Plot Style. Checkboxes allow
you to set toggles: Off for Display, Lock for Editing, Do Not Plot, Freeze in
All Viewports, Freeze in Active Viewport, and Freeze in New Viewport.

Name   Click New for a default layer name, which can be renamed, or
highlight and click an existing layer name to rename. Use the right-click
menu to make a layer current or to create a new layer whose properties
you may wish to inherit. Double-click the Name heading to sort layers
in ascending or descending order.

On   Displays global On/Off status of layers. Double-click the On heading to create On and Off layer groups for visibility and plotting. Layers
that are Off are not plotted if their Plot status is On.

Freeze in All VP   Displays global Freeze/Thaw status of layers. Freezing
layers makes them unavailable for regeneration, hiding, rendering, and
plotting to improve speed during zooming and panning operations. Double-
click the heading to create Freeze and Thaw layer groups for visibility and
plotting. Layers that are Frozen are not plotted regardless of their Plot
status. Use the Active VP Freeze column to control plotting of layers in
floating (PaperSpace) viewports.

Active VP Freeze   Displays Freeze/Thaw status of layers for floating
viewports in active/current Layout tabs.

New VP Freeze   Presets status of Freeze/Thaw display of layers for floating viewports in New Layout tabs.

Lock   Displays Lock/Unlock status of layers. Locking retains layer visibility but prevents you from inadvertently selecting and editing objects
on those layers.

Color   Clicking a layer color name displays the Select Color dialog to
set a layers assigned color. See **Color**.

Linetype   Clicking a layer Linetype name displays the Select Linetype
dialog to select from preloaded linetypes. Sort column information in
ascending or descending order by clicking the Linetype and Description
headings. Pick Load... to open the Load or Reload Linetypes dialog to
view and select one or more predefined linetypes stored in the acad.lin
file. The right-click mouse menu allows you to Select All or Clear All
linetypes. Pick the File... button to open the Select Linetype File dialog
for user-defined linetypes stored in alternate .lin files.

Lineweight   Clicking a Lineweight name displays the Lineweight dialog
to choose a lineweight from a list of available defaults. The name "default"
appearing in the Layer Manager Properties dialog automatically assumes
a value of 0.01 or 0.25mm unless changed in the Lineweight dialog.
Default's value is stored in the *Lwdefault* system variable. The lower portion
of the dialog reports each New and Original assigned lineweight values as
they are selected.

Plot Style   Clicking a plot style name displays the Select Plot Style dialog. Select a plot style from the list box, the default is Normal. Click the Active Plot Style Table button to specify a plot style. The dialog reports the Original and New plot style and indicates which tab the style is Attached To.

Plot   Clicking the icon toggles the display of the standard international graphics of a circle intersected diagonally with a line to verify that plotting is set On or Off for that layer. If you toggle plotting Off, the layer can remain visible (On/Thawed) or invisible (Off/Frozen), but it will not plot.

Editor   Opens the Plot Style Table Editor dialog to edit plot styles in a spreadsheet format. You can attach a plot style table to a layout, Model tab, or viewport. Color-dependent plot style tables are saved with a .ctb file extension, and named plot styles are saved as a .stb file.

See Also   Color, -Color, -Layer, Layout, -Layout, Linetype, - Linetype, Mspace, Mview, Pagesetup, Pspace, Rename, Tilemode, Viewports, Vplayer; *System Variables:* Celscale, Psltscale, Visretain

---

-Layer

-Layer is used at the command line to create new layers, assign colors and linetypes to layers, set the current layer, repress editing of layers, define a linetype, specify a lineweight, and set a layer's Plot Status, allowing you to control which layers are displayed. The dialog box equivalent is **Layer**.

To Create and Modify Layers

Command line: **-Layer**, **-La** (or **-'Layer**, to use transparently)

Enter an option [**?/Make/Set/New/ON/OFF/Color/Ltype/ LWeight/Plot/Freeze/Thaw/LOck/Unlock**]:.

Options

?   Displays the prompt Enter layer name(s) to list <*>: to show the list of existing layers. Wildcards are accepted.

Make   Displays the prompt Enter name for new layer (becomes the current layer) <0>: to create a new layer and makes it current.

Set   Displays the prompt Enter layer name to make current <0>: to make an existing layer the current layer.

New   Displays the prompt Enter name list for new layer(s): to create a new layer.

On Displays the prompt `Enter name list of layer(s) to turn on:` to turn on layers.

Off Displays the prompt `Enter name list of layer(s) to turn off:` to turn off layers.

Color Displays the prompt `Enter color name or number (1-255):` to set color of a layer.

Ltype Displays the prompt `Enter loaded linetype name or [?]` `<CONTINUOUS>:` to set linetype of a layer.

Lweight Displays the prompt `Enter lineweight (0.0mm - 2.11mm):` to set lineweight of a layer. Specifying an invalid lineweight displays the prompt `Lineweight rounded to nearest valid value of ( default value):` and sets the lineweight to the nearest allowable value.

Plot Displays the prompt `Enter a plotting preference [Plot/No plot]` `<Plot>:` to control layers for plotting. Once a plot preference is determined, layers can be specified at the prompt `Enter layer name(s) for this plot preference <0>:`.

PStyle Displays the prompt `Enter Plot Style or [?]` `<Normal>:`, allowing you to enter a name, **?** to list existing plot styles, or apply the Normal default. Entering a plot-style name, such as Bylayer or Byblock, or accepting the default displays the applicable prompt: `Enter name list of layer(s) for plot style name ByLayer <Layer name>:`.

Freeze Displays the prompt `Enter name list of layer(s) to freeze:` to freeze one or more layers, making them invisible and unplottable.

Thaw Displays the prompt `Enter name list of layer(s) to thaw:` unfreezes one or more layers, making them visible and plottable.

Lock Displays the prompt `Enter name list of layer(s) to lock:` to prevent editing of visible layers.

Unlock Displays the prompt `Enter name list of layer(s) to` `unlock:` to release locked layers to allow editing.

NOTE All Layer options except Make, Set, and New allow you to enter wildcard characters (question marks and asterisks) for input. For example, if you want to turn off all layers whose names begin with *G,* enter **G*** at the prompt.

NOTE The option pairs Freeze/Thaw and On/Off both control whether or not a layer is displayed. However, unlike Off, Freeze makes AutoCAD ignore objects on frozen layers. This allows faster regenerations. Freeze also affects blocks differently than Off. Thawing layers requires a **Regen** if **Regenauto** is off.

NOTE Layer 0, the default layer when you open a new file, is white (number 7) and has the continuous linetype. Layer 0 also has some unique properties. If you include objects on Layer 0 in a block, they take on the color and linetype of the layer on which the block is inserted. The objects must be created with the Byblock option (see **Color**). The dimension layer Defpoints is also unique. When it is turned off, objects on this layer are still displayed and are not selectable, but they will not appear on prints or plots. Defpoints is unique in that objects assigned to this layer will not plan or accept a color setting; everything remains white. This makes the Defpoints layer suitable for layout lines.

See Also Color, Linetype, Regen, Regenauto, Vplayer, Wildcards; *System Variable:* Clayer

Layout

Layout allows you to create, rename, save, copy, or delete Layout tabs so that you can arrange multiple floating viewports in the same drawing file.

To Make a Layout

Command line: **Layout**

Menu: Insert ➤ Layout ➤ New Layout/Layout from Template

Layout Toolbar: ▦ New Layout

Layout Toolbar: ▦ Layout from Template

1. **Enter layout option [Copy/Delete/New/Template/Rename/SAveas/Set/?] <set>:** Press ↵ to retrieve an existing layout, or enter an option.

2. **Enter layout to make current <Layout name>:** Enter name of layout you wish to make current.

Right-clicking a Layout tab displays a shortcut menu with the following options: New Layout, From Template..., Delete, Rename, Move or Copy..., Select All Layouts, Page Setup..., and Plot....

Options

? Lists all layout names created in the drawing.

Set Allows you to make a layout current. Clicking a Layout tab with your pointing device also makes it current.

Copy Press ↵, or specify an existing layout name at the prompt Enter name of layout to copy <current>: and then enter a new name, or press ↵ to accept the default when prompted to Enter layout name for copy <default>:. If you pressed ⏎ for both prompts, the new Layout tab assumes the name of the active tab with a sequential number in parenthesis and is positioned to the right side.

Delete   Enter the name of the layout you wish to remove when prompted to Enter name of layout to delete <current>:. The default name is the active layout.

New   Adds a new Layout tab at the prompt Enter new Layout name <current>:.

Template   Opens the Select File dialog to choose a Template.dwt, Drawing.dwg, or Data Exchange File.dxf file from the template folder.

Rename   Displays the prompt Enter layout to rename <current>:, allowing you to rename a Layout tab. Press ⏎ and a prompt appears to Enter new layout name:. The current layout name becomes the default for the new Layout tab name similar to the Copy option.

Save As   Prompts to Enter layout to save to template <current>:, and then opens the Create Drawing File dialog to save the layout as a .dwt, .dwg or .dxf template file.

Move   Right-click a Layout tab, and then pick Move or Copy... to open the Move or Copy dialog containing the names of all the Layout tabs. Highlighting (move to end) and then picking OK relocates the current layout to the end. Highlighting a layout and clicking Create a Copy duplicates the current layout to the left or the Before layout: list box you specify.

Select All Layouts   Allows you to select all layouts, including the Model tab for plotting.

Page Setup   Opens the Page Setup dialog with two tabbed sections: Plot Device and Layout Settings. The Plot Device tab allows you to specify a Plotter Configuration from a drop-down list box. Clicking the Properties... button in the Plot Configuration section opens the Plotter Configuration Editor for your current output device and allows you to specify and access additional plot device parameters. Picking the Hints... button displays a plot driver Help file. The Plot Style Table (pen assignments) section offers a drop-down box with table names and pick boxes. You can create a New... .ctb file using a Wizard or Edit... existing tables in the Plot Style Table Editor. Toggle Display Plot Styles on to display and enable plotting for the plot styles and plot style names assigned to objects in your drawing.

Clicking Display When Creating a New Layout will open the dialog each time a new layout is created. This checkbox is controlled in the Display tab of the Options dialog by clicking Show Page Setup Dialog for New Layouts.

Plot   Opens the Plot dialog to specify plot device, paper size, scale factor, plot orientation, and area to plot for the current layout.

See Also   -Layout, Pagesetup, Plot, Options

-Layout

-Layout allows you to copy or delete an existing layout, create a new Layout tab, create a template from an existing Layout tab, rename a Layout tab, save an existing Layout tab with a new name, set a Layout tab current, or list Layout tabs.

To Manage Layouts

Command line: -**Layout**, **Lo**

Menu: none

Enter layout option [Copy/Delete/New/Template/Rename/SAveas/Set/?] <set>: Press ↵ or enter an option.

Options

Copy   Copies a layout.

Delete   Deletes a layout.

New   Creates new layout tab.

Template   Creates new template from existing layout in a template .dwt or drawing .dwg file.

Rename   Renames a layout.

Saveas   Saves a layout.

Set   Makes a layout current.

?   Lists layout names in drawing.

See Also   Layout, Pagesetup, Plot, Options

Layoutwizard

Layoutwizard opens the Create Layout Wizard to simplify page and plot setup procedures for a new layout.

To Use the Layout Wizard

Command line: **Layoutwizard**

Layout Toolbar: 📇 New Layoutwizard

Once your plotter is configured, use the **Layoutwizard** command to create multiple PaperSpace layouts in a drawing. Make selections as desired, and then pick Next> to proceed through the Wizard as described below:

Begin   Enter the name of your Layout tab in the edit box.

Printer   Highlight a configured plotter from the list for the new layout.

Paper Size   Click the drop-down box to specify a paper size. The Paper Size in Units section displays the results of your selection. Radio buttons allow you to choose Drawing Units for millimeters, inches, or pixels.

Orientation   Select the orientation for your drawing in the layout.

Titleblock   You can choose from predrawn titleblocks in the list box and place them into your layout tab at the lower left corner as an external reference file or as an inserted block. Highlighting files displays their path and filename with a Preview in an image box.

Define Viewports   Allows you to specify the Viewport setup types: None, Single, Std. 3D Engineering Views, and Array. Depending on your selection, *Spacing between Rows* and *Spacing Between Columns* edit boxes, in addition to Rows and Columns, become available.

Pick Location   Click the Select Location< button to temporarily exit the Wizard, and pick opposite corner points to place your viewport.

Finish   Completes the Wizard setup. Right-click the Layout tab to open the shortcut menu, and pick Page Setup... if you wish to edit your selections.

See Also   Layout, -Layout, Pagesetup, Plot, Options

Leader

Leader creates a line-connecting annotation to an object or feature. A leader line can be either a spline or made up of straight line segments. An arrowhead can be attached if desired. In some cases, a short horizontal line, called a hook line, connects the text or feature control frames to the leader line. An annotation placed at the end of a leader line becomes associated with the leader line. When you move, stretch, or copy the leader line, the annotation moves with it.

To Create a Leader Line

Command line: **Leader**, **Le**, **Lead**

1. **Specify leader start point:** Specify a point (or use Object Snap) to attach the leader to an object.

2. **Specify next point:** Specify another point.

3. **Specify next point or [Annotation/Format/Undo] <Annotation>:** Specify further point(s) as required, enter an option (A/F/U), or press ↵.

4. **Enter first line of annotation text or <options>:** Enter a line of text, and then press ↵ for repeated prompts of Enter next line of annotation text:. Exit the command by pressing Enter twice. If you press Enter, the following prompt appears:

> **Enter an annotation option [Tolerance/Copy/Block/ None/Mtext] <Mtext>:** Enter an option for the leader line.

Options

Format   Displays the prompt Spline/Straight/Arrow/None/<Exit>: and allows you to specify the format of the leader line. Selecting Spline draws the leader line as a spline. Straight draws the leader as straight line segments. Arrow draws an arrowhead at the start point of the leader. None temporarily resets the arrow default to draw a leader with no arrowhead. Exit returns you to the Specify next point or [Annotation/Format/ Undo] <Annotation>: prompt.

Annotation   Displays the prompt Enter an annotation option [Tolerance/Copy/Block/None/Mtext] <Mtext>: to insert annotation at the end of the leader line. The annotation may be text, a block, an Mtext object, or a feature control frame specifying geometric tolerances. If you wish to add text, enter it at this point. The Mtext option allows you to define a window in the drawing and then opens the Multiline Text Editor dialog. You may then enter the desired multiline text (Mtext) and/ or format strings. When you exit the editor, the text entered is inserted into the drawing as an Mtext object. The Tolerance option first opens the Symbol dialog and then opens the Geometric Tolerance dialog so you can create a feature control frame containing geometric tolerances. The feature control frame is attached to the end of the last vertex of the leader line. The Copy option copies any kind of annotation (text, block, feature control frame, or Mtext) to the leader you are drawing. The copied annotation is associated with the leader line. The Block option allows you to insert a block at the end of the last vertex of the leader line. None ends the command without adding any annotation to the leader line.

Undo   Deletes the last line segment drawn.

NOTE   The **Leader** command creates complex leader lines, unlike **Dimdiameter** and **Dimradius**, which create simple automatic leaders for circles and arcs. How Mtext is displayed is determined by the prevailing measurement units and current text style in the drawing. The Mtext is vertically centered and is aligned horizontally with the last two segments of the leader line. Text and Mtext are inserted at a location determined by the current text gap (*Dimgap* system variable).

NOTE Leader lines are 2D objects similar to dimension objects. Like dimensions, they cannot have elevation or thickness. Although leader lines are not actually dimensions, their appearance is controlled by the same *Ddim* dimension variables: *Dimclrd* controls the leader color; *Dimclrt* controls the color of the annotation; *Dimblk/Dimblk1* controls the arrowheads; *Dimasz* controls the size of arrowheads; *Dimgap* controls the text gap between annotation and the hook line.

See Also Ddim, Dimensioning Commands, Insert, Mtext, Spline, Tolerance; *System Variables:* Dimasz, Dimblk, Dimclrd, Dimclrt, Dimdiameter, Dimgap, Dimradius, Dimtad

Lengthen

Lengthen changes the length of selected objects and the included angle of arcs. Closed objects cannot be lengthened.

To Lengthen an Object

Command line: **Lengthen**, **Len**

Menu: Modify ➤ Lengthen

Modify Toolbar: ◢ Lengthen

`Select an object or [DElta/Percent/Total/DYnamic]:` Select an object to display current length or enter an option.

For most options, you are prompted to `Select an object to change or [Undo]:`.

Options

Delta Allows you to specify an incremental length or angle by which to lengthen a selected object. The length is incrementally increased from the endpoint closest to the pick point. If an arc is selected, the angle of the arc is changed by the specified increment. A positive value produces an extension; a negative value trims the object. The prompt is

`Enter delta length or [Angle] <0.0000>:`

Angle Changes the length of an arc by specifying a positive or negative angle value for the Delta and Total options.

Percent Allows you to specify a percentage. The selected object is lengthened by that percentage. If an arc is selected, the included angle is increased by the specified percentage.

Total   Allows you to specify an absolute value for the length (or included angle) for the selected object. The prompt is

```
Specify total length or [Angle] <1.0000)>:
```

Dynamic   Enters dynamic dragging mode. You may change the length or included angle by dragging one endpoint while the other remains fixed.

Undo   Allows you to undo the last specification at any point while using the command options.

See Also   Change, Extend, Grips, Trim

Light
*See **Render***

Limits

Limits determines the drawing boundaries. If you use a grid, it will appear only within the limits.

To Establish Drawing Boundaries

Command line: **Limits** (or **'Limits** to use transparently)

Menu: Format ➤ Drawing Limits

Toolbar: None

AutoCAD will indicate which limits are being set with one of these prompts: Reset Model space limits: or Reset paper space limits:.

1. **Specify lower left corner or [ON/OFF] <0.0000,0.0000>:**
    Enter the coordinate for the lower left corner or the On/Off option.

2. **Specify upper right corner <12.0000,9.0000>:** Enter the coordinate for the upper right corner.

Options

ON   Turns on the limit-checking function. This keeps your drawing activity within the drawing limits.

OFF   Turns off the limit-checking function. This allows you to draw objects without respect to the drawing limits.

<lower left corner>   Sets the drawing limits by entering the coordinates for the lower left corner of the desired limits.

<upper right corner>   Sets the drawing limits by entering the coordinates for the upper right corner of the desired limits.

NOTE To make the virtual screen conform to the limits of the drawing, turn on the limit-checking feature and then perform a Zoom/All operation. The **Mvsetup** command will set the limits of your drawing automatically according to the sheet size and draw-ing scale you select. The limits for Paper Space must be set inde-pendently of the Model Space limits.

See Also Mspace, Mview, Pagesetup, Pspace, Regen, Viewres, Zoom; *System Variables:* Limcheck, Limmin, Limmax

Line

Line draws simple lines—either a single line or a series of line segments end-to-end.

To Draw a Line

Command line: **Line, L**

Menu: Draw ➤ Line

Draw Toolbar: Line

1. **Specify first point:** Select a point to begin the line.

2. **Specify next point or [Undo]:** Select the line endpoint, or press **U** to remove the last line segment drawn.

3. **Specify next point or [Close/Undo]:** Continue to select points to draw consecutive lines, press ↵ to exit the command, or enter an option.

Options

C Closes a series of lines, connecting the last start point and the last end point with a line.

↵ At the From point: prompt, lets you continue a series of lines from a previously entered line, arc, point, or polyline. If the last object drawn is an arc, the line is drawn at a tangent from the end of the arc.

Undo At the Specify next point... prompt, deletes the last line segment.

NOTE You can convert lines to polylines using the **Pedit** command.

See Also Dsettings, Mline, Pedit, Pline, Ray, Xline

Linetype

Linetype opens the Linetype Manager dialog with buttons to load, delete, make current, and expand the dialog for displaying more information about a Linetype. **-Linetype** is the command line equivalent.

To Load a Linetype

Command line: **Linetype**, **Ltype**, **Lf**

Menu: Format ➤ Linetype

Object Properties Toolbar: | ───── ByLayer ▼ | Linetype Control

The Linetypes list box contains drag division headings: Linetype, Appearance, and Description. The Appearance column provides a graphic replica for each line type. Clicking the Linetype or Description heading sorts the information in ascending or descending order. Column widths are drag divisions that can be resized by pressing the pick button on your cursor over the vertical line to the right of the column, until an anchor symbol appears. Drag the column heading to expand or shrink its size. Double-clicking the vertical line maximizes the column to fit the largest item in the list. You can also select single or groups of names by holding the Shift key or Control key. Click a Linetype name in the list box and a box appears around it, allowing you to move your cursor over any character to rename an existing line type. Right-click to display a shortcut menu to Select All or Clear All linetypes.

Options

Linetype Filters   Click the drop-down list to select from Show All Linetypes, Show All Unused Linetypes, and Show All Xref Dependent Linetypes loaded in the drawing. Otherwise, pick Invert Filter to reverse the display of your Linetype filter.

Load...   Opens the Load or Reload Linetypes dialog to view and select predefined linetypes stored in the acad.lin file. The right-click mouse menu allows you to Select All or Clear All linetypes.

Delete   Purges any highlighted unused Linetypes.

Current   Sets and identifies the current Linetype, displaying it above the list box.

Show Details/Hide Details   Clicking Show Details expands the dialog, offering edit boxes, checkboxes, and drop-down boxes specific to Name or rename a Linetype, modify Description, change the Global Scale Factor: (*Ltscale* variable), Current Object Scale: (*Celtscale* variable), and ISO Pen Width: of Linetypes. When you select a pen width from the ISO Linetypes list, the Linetype scale is updated to conform to the ISO standard for that width. Clicking the Use Paper Space Units for Scaling toggles *Psltscale* system variable on and off. Pick Hide details to retract this expanded section.

See Also   Layer, -Layer, -Linetype, Preferences, Rename; *System variables:* Celscale, Celtype, Psltscale, Visretain, Vplayer

-Linetype

-Linetype is a command-line prompt that enables you to control the type of line you can draw. The default linetype is continuous **Bylayer**, but you can choose from several other types, such as a dotted or dashed line or a combination of the two. Predefined linetypes are stored in a file called acad.lin.

To Change the Linetype

Command line: **-Linetype**, **-Lt**, **-Ltype** (or '**-Linetype**, to use transparently)

Current line type: ByLayer

Enter an option [?/Create/Load/Set]: Enter the option name.

Options

?   Lists available linetypes in a specified external Linetype file.

Create   Creates a new linetype.

Load   Loads a linetype from a specified Linetype file.

Set   Sets the current default linetype.

The Create option first prompts you for a Linetype name. This name can be any alphanumeric string of 47 characters or less (although the status line will display only the first eight characters). You are then prompted for the name of the file in which to store your linetype. Next, you enter a description or graphic representation of the linetype. Finally, you enter the Linetype pattern on the next line, where you will see an A (for pattern alignment) followed by a comma and the cursor. A-type alignments force lines and arcs to start and end with a dash. Enter a string of numeric values separated by commas. These values should represent the lengths of lines as they will be plotted. Positive values represent the "drawn" portion of the line; negative values represent the "pen up," or blank, portion of the line; and a zero indicates a dot. The following below produces a Linetype segment with a dash .3 drawing units long and three dots spaced .05 drawing units apart:

```
.3,-.05,0,-.05,0,-.05,0,-.05
```

You can create complex linetypes by editing only the acad.lin file.

The size of the line segments for each ISO line is defined for use with a 1mm pen width. To use them with other ISO predefined pen widths, scale the line using the appropriate value. For a pen width of 0.5mm., use an **Ltscale** of 0.5.

You can assign linetypes to layers or to individual objects. Use the **Ltscale** command to make the scale of the linetypes correspond with the scale of your drawing.

A linetype may appear continuous even though it is a noncontinuous type. Several things can affect the appearance of linetypes. For example, if the drawing scale is not 1:1, the **Ltscale**, must be set to correspond with your drawing scale. If the drawing scale is 1/4″ equals 1′, the **Ltscale** must be set to 48. A low Viewres value can also affect appearance, making line-types appear continuous onscreen even though they plot as a noncontin-uous linetype. Regenerating exhibits the true appearance of linetypes. To display a list of linetypes currently loaded in your drawing, use **Linetype**.

Use the **Ltscale** command to set the Linetype Global-Scale Factor, **Celtscale** for individual linetype scaling per object, and **Psltscale** (with a value of 1) for viewport scaling. For global editing, it is best to define linetypes by layer and not by a property.

See Also   Change, Layer, Linetype, Ltscale, Preferences, Viewres; *System Variables:* Plinegen, Psltscale

Linetype Control Box

The **Linetype Control** or **Linetype Combo** box allows you to click and set a Linetype current from available loaded linetype.

To Set a Linetype

Object Properties Toolbar: | ——— ByLayer ▼ | Lineweight Control

See Also   Linetype, -Linetype

Lineweight

See *Lweight*

Lineweight Control Box

The **Lineweight Control** or **Lineweight Combo** drop-down box allows you to choose from available defaults to set a specific Lineweight current.

To Set a Lineweight

Object Properties Toolbar: [———— Default ▼] Lineweight Control

See Also Lineweight, -Lineweight, Preferences

List

List displays most of the properties of an object, including coordinate location, color, layer, and linetype. **List** informs you whether the object is a block or text. If the object is text, **List** gives its height, style, and width factor. If the object is a block, **List** gives its XYZ scale and insertion point. Attribute tags, defaults, and current values are also listed, if available. If the object is a polyline, the coordinate values for all its vertices are listed. You can also use **List** to identify hatch-pattern scale and angle.

To List Properties of an Object

Command line: **List**, **Li**, **Ls**

Menu: Tools ➤ Inquiry ➤ List

Inquiry Toolbar: [🔳] List

Standard Toolbar: [▦] Inquiry Flyout [🔳] List

Select objects: Pick the objects whose properties you wish to see.

NOTE Listing objects causes AutoCAD to flip the screen to Text mode and to pause when the response is lengthy. Pressing ↵ continues through successive screens and then returns to the command line and the Graphics mode.

See Also Dblist; *Express Tools:* Xlist

Load

Load imports a shape definition file (.shp file) into a drawing and converts it to an .shx file. Like text and blocks, shapes are single objects made up of lines and arcs.

To Load a Shape

Command line: **Load**

1. Opens the Select Shape File dialog box. If *Filedia* is set to zero, you will be prompted: Enter name of shape file to load or [?]:.

2. Enter the name of the shape file (.shp) at the prompt, or if you are using the dialog box, use the Files of Type box to select and load an .shp file.

TIP You can define shapes using Shape codes. You can include shape definitions in Linetype patterns in the new complex linetypes.

See Also   Linetype, Shape; *System Variable:* Shpname

Logfileon/Logfileoff

Logfileon instructs AutoCAD to record everything that appears in the text window (both keystrokes and system prompts and responses) and writes it to an ASCII file. It continues to record until you exit AutoCAD or use the **Logfileoff** command.

To Turn On and Off the Log File

Command line: **Logfileon**

Command line: **Logfileoff**

NOTE A new log session begins each time you open AutoCAD. The log file grows with each session, and should be periodically edited or deleted. The default log filename is **acad.log**. Use the Open and Save tab in the Options dialog box to create a log file and the Files tab to specify a location.

See Also   *System Variables:* Logfilemode, Logfilename, Loginname

Lsedit
See *Render*

Lslib
See *Render*

Lsnew
See *Render*

Ltscale

Ltscale controls the scale of line types. Normally, linetype definitions are created for a scale of 1:1. For larger scale drawings, such as 1:20, set **Ltscale** so that line types fit the drawing scale. **Ltscale** globally adjusts all linetype definitions to the value you give to **Ltscale**.

To Set the Scale of Linetypes

Command line: **Ltscale**, **Lts** (or **'Ltscale** to use transparently)

Enter new linetype scale factor <current default>: Enter the desired scale factor.

> **NOTE** **Ltscale** forces a drawing regeneration when **Regenauto** is on. If **Regenauto** is turned off, you won't see the effects of **Ltscale** until you issue **Regen**.

See Also   Change, Ltype, Linetype, -Linetype, Lineweight, -Lineweight; *System Variables:* Celtscale, Ltscale, Psltscale

Ltype
See *Linetype*

-Ltype
See *-Linetype*

Lweight

Lweight opens the Lineweight Settings dialog allows you to set the current Lineweight, as well as Lineweight properties for unit type, display in Model Space, default value, and scale.

To Set Controls for Lineweight

Command line: **Lweight**, **Lw**

Provided information as needed in the dialog.

Options

Lineweights   Use the scroll bar to select from available Lineweight default values (*Lwdefault* variable), including **ByBlock** and **Bylayer**.

AutoCAD displays 0.00mm as the minimum Lineweight width, which appears as one pixel wide in Model Space. Choosing a Lineweight from the list and clicking OK makes it current.

Units for Listing   Delineates Lineweights in millimeters or inches (*Lwunits variable*).

Display Lineweight in Model Space   Toggles the display of Lineweights in the Model tab. Click the drop-down box to set a default Lineweight for layers and objects.

Adjust Display Scale   Controls the display scale of Lineweights in Model Space.

See Also   Layer, Linetype, Lineweight Control Box

Make Object's Layer Current
See **Ai_molc**

Massprop
See **Solid Modeling**

Matchprop

Matchprop and **Painter** copy properties from a selected object to one or more objects.

To Match Properties

Command line: **Matchprop**, **Ma**

Command line: **Painter**

Menu: Modify ➤ Matchprop

Standard Toolbar: ▨ Match Properties

1. **Select Source Object:** Pick a single object.

   Current active settings: Color Layer Ltype Ltscale Lineweight Thickness PlotStyle Text Dim Hatch

2. **Select destination object(s) or [Settings]:** Enter **S** to open the Property Settings dialog to specify property settings, or press ↵ to display the painter cursor and select one or more objects to change properties.

> **NOTE** The Property Settings dialog contains a Basic Properties
> section allowing you to set toggles for Color, Layer, Linetype, Line-
> type Scale, Lineweight, or Thickness properties to be copied with
> the **Matchprop** or **Painter** command.

You can also click checkboxes in the Special Properties section for Dimension, Text, and Hatch. *Text* changes the text style of the destination object
to that of the source object and is available only for line-text and para-
graph-text objects. *Dimension* modifies the dimension style of the destination object to that of the source object and should be used for dimension,
leader, and tolerance objects. *Hatch* only applies to hatched objects and
should be used to edit the hatch pattern of the destination object to that
of the source object.

See Also   Change, Chprop, Properties

Matlib
*See **Render***

Measure

Measure marks an object into divisions of a specified length. Measurement begins at the end of the object closest to the pick point. If the
object does not divide evenly by the specified length, the remaining
portion will be located at the end farthest from the pick point.

To Measure an Object

Command line: **Measure**

Menu: Draw ➤ Point ➤ Measure

1. **Select object to measure:** Pick a single object.
2. **Specify length of segment or [Block]:** Enter the length of the
   segments to mark or the name of the block to use for marking.

Options

Block   Establishes an existing, user-defined block as a marking device.
You are prompted to Enter name of block to insert: and asked if you
want to align the block with the object. The prompts are

- Align block with object? [Yes/No] <Y>:
- Specify length of segment:

NOTE By default, **Measure** uses a point as a marker, but a point is often difficult to see when placed over a line or arc. Use **Ddptype** to set a point style or set the *Pdmode* and *Pdsize* system variables to change the appearance of the points, or select the Block option and use a block in place of the point.

TIP The Block option is useful if you need to draw a series of objects a specified distance apart along a curved path. For example, to draw identical parking stalls for vehicles, create a block consisting of a line (or stripe), and identify the block name in step 2 above.

See Also   Block, Bmake, Ddptype, Divide, Point, Wblock

Menu

Menu loads a custom menu file. Once you have loaded a menu into a drawing, that drawing file will include the menu filename. The next time you open the drawing file, AutoCAD will load the last menu used with the file.

To Load a Menu

Command line: **Menu**

If the *Filedia* system variable is set to 1, the Select Menu File dialog list box appears. Use this box to select the menu file you want to use. If *Filedia* is not set to 1, respond to the following prompt at the command line:

Enter menu file name or [. (for none)] <menu path and filename>: Enter the menu filename.

TIP You can customize the `acad.mnu` and `acad.mns` file using a text editor to make AutoCAD load a recompiled version of these same filenames. When you load a menu file, AutoCAD looks for a corresponding `.mnl` file to load. You may place any custom AutoLISP file routines specified in this `.mnl` file.

NOTE The `acad.mnu`, `acad.mnr`, `acad.mns`, and `acad.mnu` menu files serve different functions. The various sections found among these menus include pull-down menus, toolbars, cursor menu, Image Tile menus, screen menu, Pointing Device Button menu, accelerator keys, and Digitizer Tablet menus. If you created toolbars with custom icon buttons, the information is stored in the `.mns` file and recompiled into the `.mnc` file. Attempting to load the `acad.mnu` displays a message box to alert you that you are attempting to override (and consequently delete) any customization of the `acad.mns`.

See Also Menuload/Menuunload; *System Variables:* Menuctl, Menuecho, Menuname

Menuload/Menuunload

Menuload allows you to create custom menu groups or supplement existing menu groups with additional submenus. Both commands open the Menu Customization dialog so you can customize, load, and unload menu groups.

To Load a Menu Group

Command line: **Menuload**

Command line: **Menuunload**

1. If the *Filedia* system variable is set to 1, the Menu Customization dialog appears for selecting a menu group. If the *Filedia* system variable is set to 0, respond to the following prompt at the command line:

   • Enter name of menu file to load: Enter the menu file name.

2. To change an existing menu group or create a new group, click the Menu Bar tab. Then add or remove submenu groups as required from the selection presented.

3. Click the Load button to load the new menu into your drawing. Pick the Unload button in the Menu Group tab to remove a menu.

4. You can also use the **Menuunload** command to unload a previously loaded menu. When the Menu Customization dialog appears, select the Unload button. If the *Filedia* system variable is set to 0, a prompt appears to Enter the name of a MENUGROUP to unload:. Enter the path and menu filename, or if you do not recall the menu filename, type a tilde (~) to open the Menu Customization dialog, and locate the file.

Options

Menu Group Tab Displays list box of all existing menu files. You may enter a menu name in the *File Name* edit box or select a menu from the Browse... pick box. Menu groups can be individually loaded and unloaded from the list box. Check Replace All to remove all existing menu groups.

Menu Bar Tab Contains a pop-up list of current menu groups. When you highlight a specific menu group, the Menu area shows the submenus that make up the highlighted menu group. You may customize menu groups by using the Insert>> and Remove>> options to insert and remove submenus in the displayed group.

NOTE AutoCAD offers persistent partial menus that save and reload the partial menu the next time you start AutoCAD. If you do not want to load a menu, set the *Filedia* system variable to 0, enter **Menu** at the command line, and then type a period (.) at the `Menu file name or . for none <current menu>:` prompt.

See Also Menu

Minsert

Minsert simultaneously inserts a block and creates a rectangular array of that block. You can rotate the array by specifying an angle other than 0 at the prompt.

To Insert Multiple Objects

Command line: **Minsert**

The prompts for **Minsert** are similar to **Insert**, except for the following:

1. **Specify rotation Angle <0>:** Enter the array angle.

2. **Enter number of rows (---) <1>:** Enter the number of rows in the block array. If the number of rows is greater than 1, the following prompt appears:

   Enter distance between rows or specify unit cell (---): Enter the distance between rows. Selecting Unit Cell requires picking two points with your cursor; after picking the First Corner, you are prompted for the Other Corner.

3. **Enter number of columns (|||) <1>:** Enter the number of columns in the block array. If the number of columns is greater than 1, the following prompt appears:

   Specify distance between columns (|||): Enter the distance or select the distance using your cursor.

A row-and-column array of the block will then appear at the specified angle.

The entire array acts like one block. Unlike **Insert**, **Minsert** does not permit you to explode a block or use an asterisk option. Listing the **Minsert** entities will provide such information as the number of columns, number of rows, and their spacing. Inserting a block with **Minsert** groups the objects into a single object. See **Insert** for a description of the additional option prompts not described here.

See Also Array, Block, Bmake, Insert, 3Darray

Mirror/Mirror3D

Mirror makes a mirror-image copy of an object or a group of objects.

To Mirror Objects

Command line: **Mirror/Mirror3D**

Menu: Modify ➤ Mirror

Menu: Modify ➤ 3D Operaton ➤ Mirror 3D

Modify Toolbar: Mirror

1. **Select objects:** Pick the objects to be mirrored.

2. **Specify first point of mirror line:** Pick one end of the mirror axis.

3. **Specify second point of mirror line:** Pick the other end of the mirror axis.

4. **Delete source objects? [Yes/No] <N>:** Enter **Y** to delete the originally selected objects, or press ↵ to keep them.

If you selected Mirror 3D, in place of steps 2 and 3 above, the following prompts will appear to define a plane and axis for the mirror:

- Specify first point of mirror plane (3 points) or [Object/Last/Zaxis/View/XY/YZ/ZX/3points] <3points>:

- Specify second point on mirror plane:

- Specify third point on mirror plane:

Alternate: Grips   If you have enabled grips for mirroring, the sequence of steps is as follows:

1. Select the object(s) to be mirrored, and the grips will appear as the objects are highlighted.

2. Pick one of the grips as your "base" point. (A base, or selected, grip appears as a solid filled rectangle.) The Stretch mode prompt then appears at the command line.

3. Cycle through the Grip mode commands by pressing ↵ or the spacebar a sufficient number of times until the following prompt appears or by entering **mirror** or **mi**:

   MIRROR
   Specify second point or [Base point/Copy/Undo/eXit]:

> **TIP**   Enter **Ddgrips** and use the Select Settings area of the Grips dialog to enable grips.

4. To mirror the image *without* retaining the original object(s), using the selected grip as the base or first point of the mirror line, drag

your cursor, and pick the second point of the mirror-line axis. To mirror the image while *retaining* the original object(s), using the selected grip as the base point, enter **C** for Copy, and pick the second point of the mirror-line axis. (You can hold the Shift key and drag your cursor to pick the second point instead of entering **C**.) Then press ↵ to exit.

TIP To select a new base point, enter **B** before picking the second point or before entering **C**.

Options

B or Base point Disengages the cursor from the selected grip so you can assign a new base point for the first point of the mirror-line axis.

C, Copy, or Shift Makes a duplicate of original object(s).

U or Undo Allows you to undo the previous operation.

X, eXit, or ↵ Exits the command.

TIP Normally, text, attributes, and attribute-definition objects are mirrored. To prevent this, set the *Mirrtext* system variable to 0. Mirroring occurs in a plane parallel to the current UCS (user coordinate system). Use the **Mirror3D** command to duplicate selected objects about an arbitrary plane.

See Also Copy, Ddgrips, Grips, Move, Rotate, Scale, Stretch; *System Variable:* Mirrtext

Mledit

Mledit allows you to edit characteristics of a multiline object. Multilines consist of multiple parallel lines. **Mledit** allows you to control the way that multilines intersect in a drawing, to add and delete vertices, and to manipulate the display of corner joints.

To Edit a Multiline

Command line: **Mledit**

Menu: Modify ➤ Multiline...

Modify II Toolbar: Edit Multiline

1. When the Multiline Edit Tools dialog box appears, double-click the desired option in the icon menu.

2. **Select mline:** Select the multiline to be edited (or the vertex to be changed).

3. **Select mline or [Undo]:** Select the next multiline, enter **U** to restore multiline, or enter to exit the command.

Options

The icon menu in the Multiline Edit Tools dialog has four columns: the first column pertains to multilines that cross; the second to multilines that form a tee; the third to corner joints and vertices; and the fourth to cutting and welding multilines.

Cross   Offers three cross-intersection options: Closed Cross, Open Cross, and Merged Cross. At the Select first mline: prompt, select the foreground multiline. At the Select second mline: prompt, select the intersecting multiline.

Tee   Offers three options: Closed Tee, Open Tee, and Merged Tee. At the Select first time: prompt, select the multiline to trim or extend. At the Select second mline: prompt, select the intersecting multiline.

Corner Joint and Vertices   Corner Joint creates a corner joint between multilines. AutoCAD trims or extends the first Mline selected to its intersection with the second Mline selected. Add Vertex/Delete Vertex allows you to add a vertex to a multiline segment or delete an existing vertex.

Cut and Weld   The Cut Single and Cut All options allow you to cut selected (or all) elements of a multiline at specified points.

Weld All   Restores cut multiline segments. Select the break points on the multiline, and AutoCAD will weld the cut sections.

See Also   -Mledit, Mline, Mlstyle; *System Variables:* Cmljust, Cmlscale, Cmlstyle

---

-Mledit

-Mledit allows you to edit multiline vertices by offering options at the command line.

To Edit a Multiline at the Command Line

Command line: **-Mledit**

1. **Enter mline editing option [CC/OC/MC/CT/OT/MT/CJ/ AV/DV/CS/CA/WA]:** Enter an option.

2. **Select first mline:** Pick first multiline object.

3. **Select second mline:** Pick second multiline object.

4. **Select first mline or [Undo]:** Press ↵ to exit the command, enter **U**, or select another multiline object to edit.

Options

Undo Allows you to undo the last procedure.

CC Displays prompts to create a Closed Cross intersection.

OC Displays prompts to create an Open Cross intersection.

MC Displays prompts to create a Merged Cross intersection.

CT Displays prompts to create a Closed Tee intersection.

OT Displays prompts to create an Open Tee intersection.

MT Display prompts to create a Merged Tee intersection.

CJ Displays prompts to create a Corner Joint intersection.

AV Displays prompts to Add a Vertex to a multiline.

DV Displays prompts to Delete a Vertex from a multiline.

CS Displays prompts to Cut a Single multiline.

CA Displays prompts to Cut All multilines.

WA Displays prompts to Weld All multilines.

See Also Mledit, Mline, Mlstyle

Mline

Mline draws multiple parallel lines. Multilines consist of between 1 and 16 parallel lines, or *elements*. Each element is offset from the origin of the multiline by an amount specified in the multiline style invoked by **Mlstyle**.

To Draw a Multiline Object

Command line: **Mline, Ml**

Menu: Draw ➤ Multiline…

Draw Toolbar: ▨ Multiline

1. **Current settings: Justification = Top, Scale = 1.00, Style = STANDARD**

    Specify start point or [Justification/Scale/STyle]: Specify the first point, or select an option.

2. Continue to pick points as required to create the multiline. When you pick a third point, you are offered the option to create a closed multiline object. Enter **C** to create a closed object, or press ↵ to exit the command.

Options

Justification   Selects between Top, Zero, and Bottom. Top positions the top line of the multiline object at the pick point(s); Bottom positions the bottom line of the multiline object at the pick points; Zero uses the pick point(s) as the center line.

Scale   Enters a different scale value for the multilines. Scale controls the overall width (or separation) of the multiline elements.

Style   Selects a different multiline style from previously created styles.

Close   Creates a closed multiline by joining the last point picked to the origin point.

Undo   Undoes the previous multiline segment drawn.

See Also   Mledit, -Mline, Mlstyle, Offset

Mlstyle

Mlstyle creates named styles for multilines that specify the number of lines (from two to sixteen) and the properties of each. You may use **Mlstyle** to edit existing multiline styles.

To Create or Edit a Multiline Style

Command line: **Mlstyle**

Menu: Format ➤ Multiline Style

Toolbar: None

When the Multiline Styles dialog appears, enter the required information. The dialog displays a graphic representation of the current style and properties. As you define the new style or edit an existing style, the graphic displays the selected properties.

Options

Current   Pop-up menu for displaying and setting current multiline styles, including those stored in external reference drawings.

Name   Allows you to enter a new name for the new style or rename an existing style.

Description   Allows you to enter an optional description.

Element Properties   Displays all of the elements in the current multiline style. The Add and Delete options allow you to add or remove a line element in the style. Offset specifies the offset for line elements of the multiline. Linetype opens the Select Linetype dialog which allows you to select the element's line type. Color opens the Select Color dialog to select the element's color.

Multiline Properties The Display Joints checkbox allows you to select or deselect the display of a line at the joints of the multiline. Caps allows you to select a line or arc for each end of the multiline and also to specify an angle for the ends. Fill allows you to turn on fill for the multiline and to specify a fill Color.

Load Loads a style from an external .mln file.

Save Saves the style to the external symbol table.

Add Allows you to append a multiline style in the Name text box to the current list.

Rename Renames an existing style after it has been edited.

> **NOTE** Once a multiline style has been created, all multilines drawn after that point will have the properties of that style.

See Also Color, Linetype, Mledit, -Mledit, Mline, Offset

Model

Model switches you to the Model tab, which acts in the same manner as setting the *Tilemode* system variable to 1.

To Switch to the Model Tab

Command line: **Model**

> **NOTE** Selecting the Model tab places you in the ModelSpace environment. The equivalent procedure would require picking Tile in the status bar,

See Also Layout, Layoutwizard, Mspace, Pagesetup, Pspace, Tilemode

Move

Move displaces a single object or a set of objects.

To Move Objects

Command line: **Move, M**

Menu: Modify ➤ Move

Modify Toolbar: Move

1. Select objects: Select the objects to be moved.

2. **Specify base point or displacement:** Pick the reference or "base" point for the move.

3. **Specify second point of displacement:** Pick the distance and direction in relation to the base point, or enter the displacement value.

Alternate: Grips

If you have enabled grips for moving, the prompts for steps 1 and 2 and the Grips Options are the same as for **Mirror**, except for the following:

1. Cycle through the Grip mode commands by pressing ↵ or the spacebar or by entering **Move** or **M** a sufficient number of times until you see the following prompt:

   ```
   **MOVE**
   Specify move point or [Base point/Copy/Undo/eXit]:
   ```

2. To move the object(s) with the selected grip as the base, drag your cursor and pick the second or displacement point. To move the object(s) using a new base point, enter **B** to pick your first reference point, or enter coordinate values, and then pick the second point of displacement.

If you chose the Displacement option rather than picking a base point, you can enter the total amount of movement you want the object to make (in the X and Y direction) and press Enter twice.

AutoCAD assumes you want to move objects within the current UCS. However, you can move objects in 3D space by entering XYZ coordinates or using the Osnap overrides to pick objects in 3D space.

If you press ↵ at the Second point: prompt without entering a point value, the objects selected may be moved to a position completely off your drawing area. Use the **U** or **Undo** command to recover.

To make multiple copies of the selected object(s), follow the steps above to define your base point, then hold the Shift key while picking the first copy point (to set Copy mode on), and continue by picking additional points. (Entering **C** after selecting the base point will provide the same results.) Exit the command by pressing ↵.

Pressing the Shift key in the last step to copy the first object from its source point to a destination point will set an automatic Snap mode based on these two points. To apply Multiple Copy using the Snap mode, hold the Shift key down while copying additional objects.

See Also   Copy, Ddgrips, Grips, Mirror, Rotate, Scale, Stretch

Mslide

Mslide saves the current view as a raster image in a Slide file. (Slide files have .sld extensions.)

To Save a View as a Slide File

Command line: **Mslide**

When the *Filedia* system variable is set to 1, the Create Slide File dialog list box is displayed; when *Filedia* is set to zero, the Enter name of slide file to create <slide file name>: prompt appears. Enter a filename.

See Also   Delay, Rscript, Script, Slidelib.exe, Vslide

Mspace

Mspace lets you switch from PaperSpace to a ModelSpace viewport. This command works only when you are in Paper Space (**Tilemode** is set to 0). You move from Paper Space into Model Space via previously created viewports.

To Switch from PaperSpace to a ModelSpace Viewport

Command line: **Mspace, Ms**

> **NOTE** If the **Tilemode** system variable is set to 0 but no viewports are available in a Layout tab (Paper Space), you will receive the message. Command not allowed in Model tab.

> **NOTE** Double-clicking inside or outside a PaperSpace viewport automatically toggles **Mspace** and **Pspace** commands. Click Model in the Status Bar to toggle between Mspace and Pspace.

See Also   Layout, Layoutwizard, Model, Mview, Pagesetup, Pspace, Tilemode

Mtext

Mtext allows you to create long, complex text entries, consisting of any number of lines or paragraphs of text. Multiline or paragraph text fits within a specified width in the drawing but may run to any length.

To Create Multiline Text

Command line: **Mtext**, **Mt**, **T**

Menu: Draw ➤ Text ➤ Multiline Text...

Draw Toolbar: ![A] Multiline Text

1. **Current text style: STANDARD. Text height: 0.2000**

Specify first corner: Specify a start point for the text boundary window.

2. **Specify opposite corner or [Height/Justify/Line spacing/ Rotation/Style/Width]:** Enter an option, or drag the window to a diagonally opposite corner, and a rectangle appears to identify the location of the multiline text object. An arrow inside the rectangle indicates the direction of the paragraph's text flow.

3. The Multiline Text Editor dialog box opens for you to enter and format the multiline text.

When text entry is complete, AutoCAD inserts the text into the specified text boundary.

Options

Height Allows you to enter a specific text height for the multiline text at the Specify height <current height>: prompt.

Justification Controls the alignment and positioning of the multiline text within the text window with the Enter justification [TL/TC/TR/ ML/MC/MR/BL/BC/BR] <TL>: prompt. The two-letter options set the justification based on the combination of top, middle, or bottom and left, center, or right. For example, TL stands for "top left," and MC stands for "middle center."

Line Spacing Lets you set the spacing between lines for the multiline text object at the prompt Enter line spacing type [At least/Exactly] <current value>:. Entering **A** or **E** displays the prompt Enter line spacing factor or distance <1x>: for the results described below:

1. If you enter **A,** you can specify an absolute value or a multiple, such as 2x, to adjust each line of text based on maximum character height.

2. If you enter **E,** all text lines are spaced consistently.

Rotation Allows you to specify a rotation angle and the direction of the dragging window for the multiline text by prompting to Specify rotation angle <0>:.

Style Prompts to Enter style name or [?] <STANDARD>:, allowing you to select a different text style from the current style.

Width Allows you to specify the width only of the text-boundary window rather than both corners. If you enter a zero value, the text will not wrap but will extend horizontally until you press ↵.

Additional Options

- The Multiline Text Editor dialog contains four tabbed sections: Character, Properties, Line Spacing, and Find/Replace. Characters can be entered from the keyboard or imported from other files. The dialog background color, by default, appears the same as the graphics screen but changes to white when black text is imported or pasted.

- Text imported or pasted into AutoCAD from other Windows applications with the attribute of Auto is changed to Bylayer.

- If you highlight text and click your return or right mouse button, a cursor menu opens with options to: Undo, Cut, Copy, Paste, and Select All.

- Click Import Text... to display the Open dialog and locate the text you wish to import. Imported text is limited to 16KB and retains its original character formatting and style properties.

Character Tab   The Character tabbed section contains drop-down boxes to set controls for character formatting for text entered at the keyboard or imported into the text editor. You can edit a word or paragraph by double-clicking to select a single word or triple-clicking to select an entire paragraph. Then click the appropriate drop-down boxes to change the text's Font, Height, or Color and to display it as Bold, Italic, or Underlined, and/or Stacked or Unstacked (for fractions). Add a symbol, such as Degrees, Plus/Minus Sign, Diameter, or Nonbreaking Space, or pick Other... to select from Windows Unicode Characer Map dialog. Undo allows you to undo the previous edit.

Properties Tab   Use the Properties tab to set text Style, Width, Justification, or Rotation.

Line Spacing Tab   Use the Line Spacing tab to set the distance between lines Exactly for uniformity or At Least to adjust spacing based on maximum character size.

TIP   The drop-down boxes for Find, Replace With, Match Case, and Whole Word in the Find/Replace tabbed section will help you to search for and replace specific text strings with new text. Click the Find or Replace icons to activate an action, or press ⏎ immediately after entering your text in these edit boxes. You can use the Edit Mtext dialog to quickly set properties either for the entire object or just for selected portions. Paragraph or multiline text has more options for editing than line text. You may use underlining, overlining, and apply special fonts, color, and height to single words within a paragraph.

Find/Replace Tab   If you have created a paragraph that is too long to fit in the text window, the text will overflow in the direction specified by the arrow's direction: top-aligned text will "spill down," and bottom-aligned text will "flow up" from the specified boundary window; center-aligned text will spread both above and below the text window. Multiline text, no matter how many lines or paragraphs, forms a single object and can be moved, stretched, erased, copied, mirrored, or scaled.

TIP You can use any standard text editor to create multiline text. During installation, AutoCAD prompts you to specify a text editor.

See Also Ddedit, Dtext/Text, Mtprop, Preferences, Properties, Spell, Style; *System Variables:* Fontalt, Fontmap, Mtexted

-Mtext

-Mtext allows you to enter text without the Multiline Text Editor at the command line.

To Enter Multiline Text at the Command Line

Command line: **-Mtext**, **-T**

1. **Current text style: STANDARD Text height: 0.2000**

   Specify first corner: Pick a start point for the text boundary window.

2. **Specify opposite corner or [Height/Justify/Line spacing/ Rotation/Style/Width]:** Pick opposite diagonal corner, or enter an option.

3. **MText:** Enter desired text for the defined boundary area.

Options

Height   Specifies text height.

Justify   Specifies text alignment and positioning from available options for top, middle, or bottom.

Line spacing   Specifies adjustments or uniformity for distances between lines.

Rotation   Specifies rotation angle and direction for text.

Style   Specifies a text style.

Width   Specifies the width in lieu of corner points for text boundary.

See Also   Ddedit, Dtext/Text, Mtext, Mtprop, Properties

Mtprop

Mtprop allows you to change Mtext properties. The command opens the Mtext Properties dialog and allows you to modify the properties of paragraph text created using the **Mtext** command.

To Change Mtext Properties

Command line: **Mtprop**

1. **Select an Mtext object:** Select a section of paragraph text.

2. In the Mtext Properties dialog, modify the text properties as required.

> **NOTE** The Mtext properties that may be changed are detailed more fully in the **Mtext** command option and "Notes."

See Also Ddedit, Dtext/Text, Mtext, Mtprop, Options, Spell, Style; *System Variables:* Fontalt, Fontmap, Mtexted

Multiple

Multiple causes the next command to repeat until you cancel it.

To Repeat a Command

Command line: **Multiple**, a space, and then the command

> **NOTE** The command repeats until you press Escape. Because **Multiple** repeats only the command itself, any options, or parameters must be specified each time.

Mview

Mview creates PaperSpace viewports and controls the number, layout, and visibility of viewports. This command works in Paper Space and a Layout tab only.

To Create a PaperSpace Viewport

Command line: **Mview**, **Mv**

Menu: View ➤ Viewports ➤ 1Viewport, 2 Viewports, 3 Viewports, 4 Viewports

> **NOTE** When Tilemode is set to 0, the **View** command options selected from the menu allow you to set the number and arrangement of PaperSpace viewports.

Specify corner of viewport or [ON/OFF/Fit/Hideplot/Lock/ Object/Polygonal/Restore/2/3/4] <Fit>: Pick a point indicating one corner of the new PaperSpace or floating viewport, or enter an option. If you pick a point, you are prompted for the opposite diagonal corner. **Mview** then creates the viewport.

Options

ON/OFF   Turns the display of Model Space on or off within the chosen viewport in a Layout tab.

Hideplot   Controls hidden line removal for individual viewports at plot time. When selecting this option, enter On or Off at the prompt Hidden line removal for plotting [ON/OFF]:, and then the Select objects: prompt appears. Pick the viewport you wish to have plotted with hidden lines removed. Selecting an entity inside the viewport will not select the viewport—you must pick the edge or border.

Lock   Locks the zoom scale factor of your viewport. Enter On or Off at the prompt Viewport View Locking [ON/OFF]: to disable panning and zooming within your PaperSpace viewport, and then pick a viewport edge when prompted to Select objects:. If you attempt to edit a locked viewport, AutoCAD displays the prompt Viewport is view-locked. Switching to Paper space. Press ESC or ENTER to exit, or right-click to display shortcut menu.

Object   Allows you to create irregular shaped viewports. You can select a closed polyline, ellipse, spline, region, or circle at the prompt Select object to clip viewport: to define as your viewport edge.

Polygonal   This option is similar to Object, except it prompts first to Specify start point:, and then prompts you to Specify next point or [Arc/Close/Length/Undo]: to draw any shape as your viewport edge. If you enter an option, such as **A**, the prompt Enter an arc boundary option [Angle/CEnter/CLose/Direction/Line/Radius/Second pt/Undo/Endpoint of arc] <Endpoint>: appears with further choices to define the viewports edge.

Fit   Creates a single viewport that fills the screen in a Layout tab.

2/3/4   Lets you create two, three, or four viewports simultaneously in a Layout tab. Once you enter one of these options, different prompts appear, depending on the number of viewports requested. If you select **2**, you will be prompted to Enter viewport arrangement [Horizontal/ Vertical] <Vertical>:; if you select **3**, you will be prompted to Enter viewport arrangement [Horizontal/Vertical/Above/Below/Left/ Right] <Right>:. Then you will be prompted to Specify first corner or [Fit] <Fit>:. Pick points to indicate the location of the viewports, or select the Fit option to force the viewports to fit in the display area.

Restore Translates viewport configurations created using the **Vport** command (ModelSpace viewports) into PaperSpace viewport objects. You are prompted for the name of a viewport configuration. This option will not give you the same views that were in the ModelSpace vports at the time the vport configuration was saved.

NOTE The *Tilemode* system variable must be set to 0 to use Mview. If you are in Model Space or the Model tab when you issue Mview, you receive the message "Command not allowed unless TILEMODE is set to zero."

NOTE Grid and Snap modes, as well as layer visibility, can be set individually within each Layout tab.

TIP Viewports, like most other entities, can be moved, copied, stretched, or erased. You can hide viewport borders by changing their layer assignments and then turning off their layers. You can also align positions of objects in one viewport with those of another by using the **Mvsetup** utility. Viewport scale can be set using the XP option under the **Zoom** command.

See Also Layout, -Layout, Layoutwizard, Model, Mspace, Mvsetup, Pspace, Tilemode, Vplayer, Vports, Zoom; *System Variables:* Maxactvp, Psltscale, Psvpscale, Visretain,

Mvsetup

Mvsetup sets up the PaperSpace specifications of a drawing, including viewports, drawing scale, and sheet title block.

To Set Up a PaperSpace Viewport

Command line: **Mvsetup**

On a new drawing in the Model tab (*Tilemode* set to 1), the following prompt appears: Enable paper space?(No/Yes]<Y>:.

- If you enter **N**, you will be prompted to specify measurement Units, a Scale factor, and a Paper Height and Width. AutoCAD will then draw a bounding box and exit the command.

- If you press ⏎ to accept the default **Y**, the *Tilemode* system variable is set to 0 (Off) when switching to the Layout tab, and the following prompt appears: Align/Create/Scale viewports/Options/Title block/Undo:.

Options

Align   Aligns locations in one viewport with locations in another viewport. If you select Align (A), you will receive the following prompt: Enter an option [Align/Create/Scale viewports/Options/Title block/Undo]: Angled aligns locations by indicating an angle and distance. You are prompted to pick a base point to which others can be aligned. Next, you are prompted to pick a point in another viewport that you want aligned with the base point. You are then prompted for a distance and angle. Horizontal/Vertical Alignment aligns views either horizontally or vertically. You are prompted for a base point (the point to be aligned to) and the point to be aligned with the base point. Rotate View rotates the view in a viewport. You are prompted for a viewport and base point and then for the angle of rotation.

Create Viewports   Creates new viewports. If you select this option (**C**), you will receive the prompt Enter option [Delete objects/Create viewports/Undo] <Create>:. Delete Objects deletes existing viewport entities. <Create viewports> displays a list of options for creating viewports, as follows:

0: None   Creates no viewports.

1: Single   Creates a single viewport for which you specify the area.

2: Std. Engineering   Creates four viewports set up in quadrants. You can set up these views for top, front, right side, and isometric.

3: Array of Viewports   Creates a matrix of viewports by specifying the number of viewports in the X and Y axes. The Add/Delete option on the prompt adds or deletes options from the list. Add provides a title block for the list. Prompts specify the number of viewports and the distance between viewports in the X and Y directions for the current Layout tab.

Enter layout number to load or [Redisplay]:   Lets you view the list again.

Scale Viewports   Sets the scale between Paper Space and the viewport. For example, if your drawing in Model Space is scaled to 1/4" = 1' and your title block in Paper Space is scaled to 1" = 1", you will want the scale factor of your viewport to be 48. When you select this option (**S**), the prompt Select the viewports to scale: appears. Once you've selected more than one viewport, the prompt Set zoom scale factors for viewports Interactive/<Uniform>: appears. The Interactive option sets the scale of each selected viewport individually with a request to enter the ratio of PaperSpace units to ModelSpace units. You are prompted to Enter the number of paperspace units<current value>:, then Enter the number of modelspace units<current value>:. In the 1/4"-scale example, you would enter **1** for the PaperSpace units and **48** for the ModelSpace units.

Options   Allows you to set the preferences for the Model tab before you change your drawing. If you type **O**, you will receive the following prompt: Set Layer/Limits/Units/Xref:. Set Layer allows you to specify a layer for the title block. Limits allows you to reset the drawing limits by prompting Set drawing limits? [Yes/No] <N>:. Units allows you to specify the PaperSpace units as feet, inches, meters, or millimeters. Xref allows you to specify whether the title block is to be inserted or externally referenced.

Title Block   Produces the prompt Enter title block option [Delete objects/Origin/Undo/Insert] <Insert>:. Delete objects deletes objects from Paper Space. Origin sets a new origin point for Paper Space. <Insert title block> displays the following:

- Available paper/output sizes:
- 0: None
- ·1: ISO A4 Size (mm)
- 2: ISO A3 Size (mm)
- 3: ISO A2 Size (mm)
- 4: ISO A1 Size (mm)
- 5: ISO A0 Size (mm)
- 6: ANSI-V Size (in)
- 7: ANSI-A Size (in)
- 8: ANSI-B Size (in)
- 9: ANSI-C Size (in)
- 10: ANSI-D Size (in)
- 11: ANSI-E Size (in)
- 12: Arch/Engineering (24 × 36)
- 13: Generic D size Sheet (24 × 36in)
- Enter number of title block to load or [Add/Delete/Redisplay]:

Enter the number corresponding to the title block you want to use. Add and Delete let you add or delete a title block to or from the list. Add prompts you for a title block description for inclusion in the above list and the name of the file to be used as the title block. It allows you to specify the default usable area within the title block. Redisplay lets you view the list again.

Undo   Undoes an option without leaving the Mvsetup utility.

When adding a title block to the list in the Title Block option, you must already have a title block drawing ready and in the current path. The XP option under the **Zoom** command can also be used to set the scale of a viewport. **Mvsetup** saves the current configuration to a file called Mvsetup.dfs.

See Also   Dimscale, Layout, -Layout, Layoutwizard, Ltscale, Model, Mspace, Mview, Pspace, Zoom; *System Variables:* Psltscale, Tilemode

---

New

New lets you start a new drawing from scratch or use an existing drawing as a template for a new drawing. AutoCAD 2000 provides a Multiple Document Interface (MDI) to open multiple documents within a single session.

To Create a New Drawing

Command line: **New, Ctrl+N**

Menu: File ➤ New...

Standard Toolbar: ▢ New

1. If the *Filedia* system variable is set to 1, the Create New Drawing dialog opens to specify an option by clicking one of three buttons described under Options below. Each button displays a comment to help you understand and decide which procedure best suites your needs. The Open a Drawing button is enabled only for the start of each AutoCAD session.

   If the *Filedia* system variable is set to 0, the following command-line prompt appears instead of the dialog:

   • **Enter template file name or [. (for none)] <filename.dwt>:**
     Specify a filename containing a .dwt or .dwg extension.

Options

Open a Drawing   Use Open a Drawing to locate and open the first AutoCAD drawing in your session; otherwise, this button is disabled in the dialog. The Select a File: list box displays files opened from previous sessions under column headings: File and Path. Highlighting a filename displays an image in the adjacent preview area as well as information about the file size and when it was last modified. Clicking Browse... opens the Select File dialog, offering standard file selection features to locate a drawing file. The path you specify in the *Start in:* edit box of the AutoCAD icon's Properties dialog becomes the default.

Start from Scratch   Use the Start from Scratch button for a drawing setup that allows you to start a drawing quickly with either English or metric settings (*Measurement* and *Measureinit* variables).

Use a Template   Starts a drawing based on a template. AutoCAD has created 78 template files that you can select from, serving as prototypes; some have predefined layers, dimension styles, titleblocks, color dependent, and named plot styles and views for creating new drawings. AutoCAD stores template drawings as `.dwt` files in the `\TEMPLATE` directory. You can create your own templates by renaming the `.dwg` extension to `.dwt` and copying the file to the template directory or with the **Saveas** command, setting Save as Type to AutoCAD Drawing Template File (`.dwt`). Click Browse... to open the Select a Template file dialog and locate a `.dwt` template file from any directory or drive.

Use a Wizard   Click Use a Wizard, and choose between Quick Setup or Advance Setup. The Quick Setup Wizard contains two pages: *Units* and *Area*. The first page are similar for both Wizards and allows you to select from Decimal, Engineering, Architectural, Fractional, and Scientific units of measure. The adjacent image changes to reflect your choice of measurement. The first page in Quick Setup and the last page in Advanced Setup contains *Width* and *Length* edit boxes to help you specify the your working area. The Advanced Setup dialog box offers three additional pages: Angle, Angle Measure, and Angle Direction. Each page displays a preview window showing the results of your selection.

Angle   Pick a radio button to set an angle format for Decimal Degrees, Deg/Min/Sec, Grads, Radians, or Surveyor. Select the angle's precision from default values in the drop-down box.

Angle Measure   Pick a radio button for East, North, West, or South. Otherwise, pick Other, and enter a value to determine the direction in which AutoCAD measures angles.

Angle Directon   Set a Clockwise or Counterclockwise direction for AutoCAD to measure angles.

Finish   Exits the dialog and starts AutoCAD using the specifications selected.

Show at Startup   Toggle the Create New Drawing dialog off if you do not want it to display when you start an AutoCAD session. To toggle it on, click Show Startup dialog in the General Options section of the System tab of the Options dialog.

See Also   Exit, Open, Qsave, Quit, Save; *System Variables:* Filedia, Dwgname, Dwgprefix, Dwgtitled, Savefile, Savename

Notepad

See acad.pgp

Offset

Offset will offset only a single object. If you have multiple, sequential lines or arcs to offset, use the **Pedit** command to join them into one polyline object before performing the offset.

To Offset a Line

Command line: **Offset**, **O**

Menu: Modify ➤ Offset

Modify Toolbar: Offset

Specify offset distance or [Through] <Through>: Enter a distance value to specify a constant distance to offset, press **T** to specify an offset through-point after each object selection is made, or press ↵.

- Enter a distance value, and press ↵; you are then prompted to Select an object to offset. Pick the object to offset. At the next prompt, Specify point on side to offset:, pick the side on which you want the offset to appear. You can continue to offset objects at that distance or press ↵ to exit the command.

- Selecting Through by entering **T** prompts you to Specify through point:. Pick a point to locate the offset line.

Options

Offset Distance If you enter a value at the Distance prompt, all the offsets performed in the current command will be at that distance. The prompt will continue offsetting objects at the specified distance until you press ↵.

Through Identifies a point through which the offset object will pass after you have selected the object to offset. The prompt will continue prompting for the next point until you press ↵.

WARNING Very complex polylines may offset incorrectly or not at all. When this happens, it usually means that there is insufficient memory to process the offset or that the offset distance exceeds the command's ability to offset properly.

NOTE You cannot perform offsets on objects unless they lie in a plane parallel to the current UCS (user coordinate system). Also, if you are not viewing the current UCS in plan, you may get an erroneous result.

NOTE Window, Crossing, Fence, WPolygon, Cpolygon, and Last are not valid selections for Offset. The offset distance is stored in the system variable *Offsetdist* as the default. If the value is negative, it defaults to Through mode.

NOTE Gaps created by offsetting individual polyline segments can be controlled with the *Offsetgaptype* variable.

See Also Copy, Grips, Mline; *System Variables:* Offsetdist, Offsetgaptype

Olelinks

Olelinks allow you to update, change, and cancel existing links placed into a drawing with the **Insertobj** command.

To Update Object Links

Command line: **Olelinks**

Menu: Edit ➤ Olelinks...

Makes the required changes in the Links dialog and allows you to modify the link information.

Options

Links Provides a list of each linked object in the current drawing. If you select a linked object and right-click it, a shortcut menu opens these options: Cut, Copy, Clear, Undo, Selectable, Bring to Front, Send to Back, Properties..., and a cascading menu to Edit, Open and Convert linked document objects. The selected linked object is also identified so that you can edit it by accessing its source application or convert the object via the Convert dialog.

Source Identifies object's path, filename, and source application.

Type Lists the application name.

Automatic Click this radio button to initialize an automatic update of a linked object whenever the original object is changed.

Manual If you select the Manual radio button, you will be prompted to update the link when you open the document that contains it.

Update Now Updates any selected links from the Links list box. Right-click for the edit command in the cascading shortcut to open and modify the linked document.

Open Source Opens the application containing the source file, and highlights the object linked to the AutoCAD drawing.

Change Source   Displays the Change Source dialog, allowing you to specify a new source location or filename.

Break Link   Breaks the connection with the source object, but retains a copy of the object in your document. AutoCAD displays a dialog with the message "Breaking a link will disconnect it from its link source. Are you sure you want to break this link?"

See Also   Copyclip, Copylink, Insertobj, Olescale, Pasteclip, Pastespec

Olescale

Olescale opens the Scale OLE Object dialog, allowing you to resize the OLE object.

To Edit an Ole Object

Command line: **Olescale**

Enter information in the dialog as needed. The OLE Properties dialog appears automatically for new OLE objects when the Display Dialog when Pasting New OLD Objects box is checked.

Options

Size   Enter Height and Width in the edit boxes, or pick the Reset button to restore the object's original values.

Scale   Allows you to specify a percentage value for Height and Width. Check Lock Aspect Ratio for height or width to preserve the object's proportions.

Text Size   Select a text font and point size from the drop-down boxes, or enter a value in the adjacent edit box.

OLE Plot Quality   Allows you to choose a file type to set plot quality for the OLE object.

See Also   Olelinks; *System Variables:* Olehide, Olestartup, Olequality

Oops

Oops restores objects accidentally removed from a drawing.

To Restore an Erased Object

Command line: **Oops**

Oops retrieves all objects erased by the last **Erase** and after executing **Bmake**, **Block**, or **Wblock**.

See Also   Erase, Purge, U, Undo, Wblock

Open

Open lets you open an existing drawing.

To Open an Existing Drawing

Command line: **Open**, **Ctrl+O**

Menu: File ➤ Open...

Standard Toolbar: 📂 Open

1. The Select File dialog box contains a *Files Name* edit box to enter a filename and a list box below displaying files. Use the scroll bar to select Directories and the drop-down box to locate Drives. You can open the List Files of Type pop-up box to show .dwg, .dxf, or .dwt files in the list box.

2. A preview image is displayed in the dialog; you may preview the drawing before loading it into the drawing area.

If the *Filedia* system variable is set to 0, **Open** displays the following command-line prompt:

- **Enter name of drawing to open:** Enter the name of an existing drawing, or press a tilde (~) to display the Select File dialog.

Options

Read Only   Check this box if you wish to open a drawing in Read Only mode. Drawings that are opened in Read Only mode can be edited and saved to a new name. You may not save changes to the drawing's original name.

Select Initial View   To open a drawing to a saved view, pick from the Select Initial View dialog, and highlight a view name or the last view.

Find File   Opens the Browse/Search dialog containing Browse and Search tabbed sections, which allow you to browse or search through your drives and directories.

Search   Allows you to include search criteria, such as file creation date and time.

Preview   Displays thumbnail images of all of the drawings in a selected directory as they are selected in the file tree.

Partial Open   Opens the Partial Open dialog, allowing you to partially load layers and a saved view from a drawing saved in the current release of AutoCAD. Use the Load All and Clear All buttons to select or deselect all layer names in the Layer Geometry to Load section. Picking the Layer Name or Load Geometry column header sorts information in ascending and descending order. You can select a specific view name, either Extents or Last from the list in the View Geometry to Load section.

Index Status   The Use Spacial Index checkbox becomes available for drawing files containing a spatial or layer index.

Unload All Xref on Open   Check this box to load all external reference files when you open the drawing.

Open   Opens the drawing displaying your selections from the View Geometry to Load and Layer Geometry to Load sections.

See Also   Exit, New, Qsave, Save; *System Variables:* Dwgname, Dwg-write, Filedia, Savefile, Savename, Savetime

Options

Options allows you to set a range of variables that control AutoCAD's appearance and functioning. This command opens a series of tabbed dialog boxes to allow modification of an extensive set of controls: Files, Display, Open and Save, Output, System, User Preferences, Drafting, Selection, and Profiles.

To Set Options

Command line: **Options**, **Op**

Command line: **Preferences**, **Pr**

Command line: **Config**

Menu: Tools ➤ Options...

Menu: Tools ➤ Drafting Settings ➤ Options... button

Right-click over the drawing area or command line, and then select Options... from the shortcut menu.

Once you customize the settings in the Options dialog, click Apply to immediately see your new configurations. Pick OK to exit the dialog.

Options

Files   Use this tabbed subdialog to specify AutoCAD search paths for Support Files, Drives, Menus, Project Files (Xrefs), Help Files, Log Files, Text Editor, Dictionary, Font File Names, Print File, Spooler, Prolong Section Names, Printer Spooler Locations, Printer Support Path, Search Path for ObjectARX Applications, Automatic Save Location, Prototypes (templates), Temporary Drawing and Xref File Locations, and Texture Map Search paths.

> **Browse**   Depending upon your selection in the list, opens the Browse for Folder or Select a File dialog.

> **Add**   Adds a new search path under the selected directory.

> **Remove**   Removes selected search path or file from directory.

Move Up   Moves your directory up the search path.

Move Down   Moves your directory down the search path.

Set Current   Sets current the selected Project or Dictionary.

Display Tab   Use this tabbed subdialog box to toggle the display of scroll bars or to maximize the AutoCAD window. You can set the number of lines that appear at the command line and text window. Pick boxes open subdialog boxes that set screen colors and fonts.

Window Elements   Toggles Display Screen Menu and Display Scroll Bars in Drawing Window as well as set the number of Text Lines in Command Line Window. Click the Colors... button to set colors for drawing area, screen menu, text window, and command line, and click the Fonts... button to specify fonts for screen menu, text window, and command line.

Layout Elements   Toggles Display Layout and Model Tabs, Display Margins, Display Paper Background, Display Paper Shadow, Show Page Setup Dialog for New Layouts, and Create Viewport in New Layouts.

Display Resolution   Edit boxes for Arc and Circle Smoothness (*Viewres* variable), Segments in a Polyline Curve (*Splinesegs* variable), Rendered Object Smoothness (*Facetres* variable), and Contour Lines Per Surface (*Isolines* variable) allow you to specify a value; high values generate smoother objects but require more time to regenerate.

Display Performance   Toggles Pan and Zoom with Raster Image (*Rtdisplay* variable), Highlight Raster Image Frame Only (*Imagehlt* variable), Set True Color Raster Images and Rendering, Apply Solid Fill (*Fillmode* variable), Show Text Boundary Frame Only (*Qtextmode* variable), and Show Silhouettes in Wireframe (*Dispsilh* variable).

Crosshair Size   Specify a value in the edit box, or use the slider bar to set the cursor size. A value of 100 extends the vertical and horizontal crosshairs to the ends of the graphics screen; the default is 5 (*Cursorsize* variable).

Reference Edit Fading Intensity   Specify a value in the edit box, or use the slider bar to set the fading value for objects. Values can be set from 0 to 90; lower values display objects with less intensity. The default is 50 (*Xfadectl* variable).

Open and Save Tab   Use this tabbed subdialog box to set and specify automatic save methods. Toggles allow you to set controls for file save and open, file safety precautions, external reference files, and ARX applications.

File Save   Saves a drawing in various file formats. Checking Save a Thumbnail Preview Image saves the image that is displayed in the Preview area of the Select File dialog and stores the value in the *Rasterpreview* system variable. Enter a number for the percentage of wasted space allowed in a drawing in the *Incremental Save Percentage* edit box, and AutoCAD will determine when to perform a full save instead of increment saves. You can also use the *Isavepercent* system variable and set it to 0, making all saves perform a full save.

File Safety Precautions   Toggle allows you to set an Automatic Save and control the number of Minutes Between Saves *(Savetime variable)*. Use the *Savefilepath* system variable to stipulate location and the *Savefile* system variable to store the name of your autosave files. You can also specify the following: Create Backup Copy with Each Save, Full-Time CRC Validation, and Maintain a Log File. To specify a unique network node name, enter an extension in the *File Extension for Temporary Files* edit box. The default is .AC$.

External References (Xrefs)   Controls methods for loading external reference files. The values are stored in the *Xloadctl* system variable. Toggles allow you to set controls to Retain Changes to Xref Layers and Allow Other Users to Refedit Current Drawings.

ARX Applications   Determines appropriateness for AutoCAD to demand load third-party applications if a drawing has custom objects created in that application. Use the drop-down box to choose Demand Load ARX Apps and Proxy Images for Custom Objects. Demand load values are stored in the Demandload system variable. Checking Show Proxy Information Dialog Box toggles the display of the dialog on and off.

Output Tab   Use this tabbed subdialog to set default plot settings and style behavior, general plot options, and scripts.

Default Plot Settings for New Drawings   Select a radio buttons to Use as Default Output Device, and then choose a system printer or plot configuration file from the drop-down box, or Use Last Successful Plot Settings. You can click the Add or Configure Plotters... button to display the Windows system plotter window and select from available plotters or click the Add-A-Plotter Wizard.

General Plot Options   Picks the radio button to Keep the Layer Paper Size If Possible or Use the Plot Device Paper Size *(Paperupdate* system variable) when changing the plot device. Select a System Printer Spool Alert method and a OLE Plot Quality *(Olequality* system variable) from the drop-down boxes. Check the box if you wish to Use Ole Application when Plotting OLE Objects, or use the *Olestartup* system variable.

Default Plot Style Behavior   Picking a radio button allows you to Use Color Dependent Plot Styles or Use Named Plot Styles *(Pstylepolicy* system variable). If you are using color-dependent or named plot styles, you can select a .ctb or .stb file from the Default Plot Style Table drop-down box. You can also specify a Default Plot Style for Layer 0 and Default Plot Style for Objects or use the *Deflplstyle* and *Cplotstyle* system variables. Clicking the Add or Edit Plot Style

Tables... button displays the Plot styles system window with the Add-A-Plot-Style Table Wizard.

Scripts   Click Plot with Legacy Command Line Prompts on or off to allow workability of plot scripts from earlier releases of AutoCAD. The value is stored in the *Plotlegacy* system variable.

System Tab   Use this tabbed subdialog to set your current 3D Graphics Display, and choose the current AutoCAD pointing device as well as general and dbconnect options.

Current 3D Graphics Display   Allows you to choose a Current 3D Graphics Display system from the drop-down box. The default is *Gsheidi10*. Click Properties... to open the 3D Graphics System Configuration dialog for the selected display.

Current Pointing Device   Allows you to choose a Current Pointing Device from the drop-down box. Radio buttons become available when a digitizer is set, allowing you to Accept Input from a Digitizer Only or Digitizer and Mouse.

General Options   Toggles on or off Single-Drawing Compatibility Mode, Show Startup Dialog, Display OLE Properties Dialog, Show All Warning Messages, Beep On Error In User Input, Load Acad.lsp With Every Drawing, and Allow Long Symbol Names.

DbConnect Options   Toggles on or off Store Links Index in Drawing File and Open Tables in Read Only Mode for database connectivity.

User Preferences Tab   Use this tabbed subdialog to set Windows standard behavior conditions, controls for the AutoCAD Design Center, priorities for coordinate data entry, and object sort methods.

Windows Standard Behavior   Toggles allow you to turn on or off Windows Standard Accelerator Keys and Shortcut Menus In Drawing Area. Pick the Right-Click Customization... button to open the Right-Click Customization dialog with radio buttons that specify additional Default mode, Edit mode, and Command mode settings.

AutoCAD Design Center   Select from the drop-down box to specify Source Content Units and Target Drawing Units when units are not defined for blocks inserted into a drawing. You can use the *Insunitdefsource* and *Insunitsdeftarget* system variables to store these values.

Hyperlink   Toggles to Display Hyperlink Cursor and Shortcut Menu, and Display Hyperlink Tooltip.

Priority for Coordinate Data Entry   Specify your priority among Running Object Snap, Keyboard Entry, or Keyboard Entry Except Scripts. You can use the *Osnapcoord* system variable to store this value.

Object Sorting Method   Toggles control Object Selection, Object Snap, Redraws, Regens, Plotting, and PostScript output. Values are stored in the *Sortents* system variable.

Lineweight Settings   Click this button to open the Lineweight Settings dialog and set Lineweight options.

Drafting Tab   Use this tabbed subdialog to set AutoSnap and AutoTracking settings, AutoSnap marker size, alignment point acquisition methods, and aperture size.

AutoSnap Settings   Control the display of Object Snap Marker and Magnet geometric symbols. You can also toggle on or off Display AutoSnap Tooltip and Display AutoSnap Aperture Box features (*Apbox* variable). You can select an AutoSnap Marker Color from available colors in the drop-down box. Specifying a value of 2 enables the Autosnap tooltip.

AutoSnap Marker Size   Use the slider bar with an image tile to adjust the size of the AutoSnap marker.

AutoTrack Settings   Click the checkboxes to Display Polar Tracking Vector, Display Full-Screen Tracking Vector, and Display AutoTracking Tooltip, or depending upon the setting, use the *Trackpath* and *AutoSnap* system variables to set these controls.

Alignment Point Acquisition   Pick the radio button for *Automatic* if you wish to automatically display tracking vectors when the aperture moves over an Object Snap or Shift to Acquire, which requires pressing the Shift key to invoke this feature.

Aperture Size   Move the slider bar to visually set the Osnap box size. Aperture size is stored in the *Aperture* system variable.

Selection Tab   Use this tabbed subdialog to set controls for Selection modes, pickbox size, grips, and grips size.

Selection Modes   Toggles settings that define your method for selecting objects, including Noun/Verb Selection (*Pickfirst* variable), Use Shift to Add to Selection, Press and Drag, Implied Windowing, Object Grouping, and Associative Hatch.

Pickbox Size   Use the slider bar with an image tile to dynamically alter your pickbox size.

Grips   Toggle Enable Grips to pick objects for editing using a grip box and Enable Grips within Blocks if you wish to display one grip for the block or multiple grips for entities in the block. Use the drop-down boxes to specify Unselected Grip Color and Selected Grip Color.

Grips Size   Move the slider bar to control grip size. The image tile helps to visually display the results.

Profiles Tab   Use this tabbed subdialog box to list, set, copy, rename, describe, export, or import profiles. A profile is a user-defined Windows setup configuration.

Set Current   Sets and displays name of current profile.

Add to List...   Opens the Add Profile dialog to enter a profile name and description.

Rename...   Displays the Change Profile dialog to edit an existing profile's name and description.

Delete   Removes a profile from the list box.

Export...   Opens the Export Profile dialog box to export a profile on the same or a different computer.

Import...   Displays the Import Profile dialog to import the profile created with Export.

Reset   Restores all values to system defaults.

See Also   System variables referred to within this command.

Ortho

Ortho forces lines to be drawn in exactly perpendicular directions following the orientation of the crosshairs.

To Turn Ortho On or Off

Command line: **Ortho**, **Ctrl+O** (or **'Ortho**, to use transparently)

Click Ortho in the status bar

> **TIP** If you enter **Ortho** through the keyboard, you are prompted to turn Ortho On or OFF. Use the F8 function key or the Ctrl+O key combination to toggle between Ortho On and Ortho Off.

> **TIP** To force lines to angles other than 90 degrees, rotate the cursor using the *Snapang* system variable or by setting the Rotate option under the **Snap** command.

See Also   Snap, UCS; *System Variables:* Orthomode

Osnap

Osnap opens the Object Snap tab of the Drafting Settings, allowing you to have multiple Object Snap modes active while picking specific geometric

OSNAP

points on an object and to set the target box size for your graphic's cursor crosshairs. To override a running Osnap, enter the specific Osnap at the command line.

To Set Running Object Snap Modes

Command: **Osnap**, **Os** (or **'Osnap**, to use transparently)

Menu: Tools ➤ Drafting Settings...

Object Snap Toolbar: Object Snap Settings

Right-Click Osnap in the status bar to display the shortcut menu with options to toggle Object Snap mode On or Off or select Settings... to open the Drafting Settings dialog.

Select the desired function from the dialog.

Options

Object Snap On (F3)   Check this box or press F3 to turn running object snaps on. Object snaps are controlled by the *Osmode* system variable.

Object Snap Tracking On (F11)   Check this box or press F11 to set object-snap tracking on. Object-snap tracking is controlled by the *Autosnap* system variable. Tracking allows you to select orthogonal points relative to another point in your drawing, similar to X- and Y-point filters.

Object Snap Modes   Activating one or more pick boxes lets your pick location determine the Osnap modes applied. For example, if both the Endpoint and Midpoint boxes are checked, AutoCAD automatically selects the mode based on which point is closer to the target box. Position your cursor over the object, and then use the Tab key to cycle through checked Snap settings. Depending on the settings, when an Object Snap box is checked, an associated marker and Snap tip appears. Each mode can be overridden at the command line by entering the uppercase letters shown:

ENDpoint   Picks the end point of objects.

MIDpoint   Picks the midpoints of lines and arcs.

CENter   Picks the center of circles and arcs.

NODe   Picks a point object. (See **Ddptype**.)

QUAdrant   Picks a main point on an arc or circle.

INTersection   Picks the intersection of objects.

EXTension   Picks a point extending from temporary reference lines.

INSertion   Picks the insertion point of blocks and text.

PERpendicular   Picks the point on an object perpendicular to the last point.

TANgent   Picks a tangent point on a circle or arc.

NEArest   Picks the point on an object nearest to the cursor.

APParent Intersection   Picks the apparent intersection of two dimensionally separated lines.

PARallel   Draws a vector parallel to another object.

Select All   Toggles all Object Snap modes on.

Clear All   Toggles all Object Snap modes off.

Options...   Click this button to display the Drafting tab of the Options dialog. (See **Options**.)

See Also   Dsettings, -Osnap, Point Filters, Tracking; *System Variable:* Osmode

---

-Osnap

-Osnap sets the current default Object Snap mode, allowing you to pick specific geometric points on an object. You can have several Object Snap modes active at once if you separate their names by commas. For example, to be able to select endpoints and midpoints automatically, enter **END,MID** at the Osnap prompt. AutoCAD knows to select the correct point (MID, END, etc.) according to which point is closer to the target box. The equivalent dialog command is **Dsettings**.

To Pick Specific Geometric Points

Command line: **-Osnap**, **-Os**

Current Osnap modes: End,Mid

Enter list of object snap modes: Enter the desired default Object Snap mode(s), such as **int, endp**, or press ⏎ for None.

Options

Center (CEN)   Picks the center of circles and arcs.

Endpoint (END)   Picks the endpoint of objects.

Insertion (INS)   Picks the insertion point of blocks and text.

Intersection (INT)   Picks the intersection of objects.

Extension (EXT)   Picks a point based on an object's extended length.

Apparent Intersection (APP)   Snaps to the apparent intersection of two objects, although they may not actually intersect in 3D space.

Midpoint (MID)   Picks the midpoint of lines and arcs.

Nearest (NEA)   Picks the point on an object nearest to the cursor.

Node (NOD)   Picks a point object. (See **Point**.)

Perpendicular (PER)   Picks the point on an object perpendicular to the last point.

Quadrant (QUA)   Picks a cardinal point on an arc or circle.

Tangent (TAN)   Picks a tangent point on a circle or arc.

Parallel (PAR)   Draws parallel line when picking point on another object.

None (NON)   Disables the current default Object Snap mode. Entering **Off** or pressing ↵ at the Object snap modes: prompt does the same.

TIP You can use the Osnap overrides whenever you are prompted to select a point or object. Unlike the Osnap mode settings, the overrides are active only at the time they are issued. Enter the first three letters of the name of the override, or pick the override from the pop-up Cursor menu.

NOTE The Cursor menu is activated in different ways depending on the pointing device that you are using: If you have a two-button device, hold the Shift key down while pressing the Right button. The acad.mnu and acad.mns files supplied with AutoCAD assign these buttons to the shortcut menu. The shortcut menu lists Snap modes and point filters, and **Tracking** also allows you to open the Object Snap dialog.

See Also   Aperture, Dsettings, Osnap, Point Filters, Tracking; *System Variable:* Osmode

Pagesetup

Pagesetup contains two tabbed sections that allow you to save plot device settings and page layouts.

To Use Pagesetup

Command line: **Pagesetup**

Menu: File ➤ Page Setup...

Right-click a Layout tab, and pick Pagesetup... from the shortcut menu.

Provide information in the dialog as needed.

Options

When Show Page Setup Dialog for New Layouts is toggled on in the Display tab of the Options dialog box, the Page Setup dialog opens when you create a new Layout tab. The Layout Name section displays edit boxes for the *Layout Name* of the current tab and the *Page Setup Name* for any saved and named page setups. Click Add... to open the User Defined Page Settings dialog where you can save, rename, delete, and import layout settings.

Plot Device Tab   Pick a device from the list of available system printers and .pc3 filenames in the Name: drop-down box in the Plotter configuration section. For each selection AutoCAD also displays information for Plotter:, Where:, and Description: to identify your current choices. Click the Properties... button to open the Plotter Configuration Editor dialog to view and set controls for the current plot configurations, ports, devices, and media. The General, Ports, and Device and Document Settings tabs offer additional edit boxes, radio buttons, and pick boxes to refine and manipulate plot settings. Click Hints... to display a Help menu for device-specific information.

Plot Styles Table (pen assignments)   Contains a Name: drop-down box listing the current plot-style tables that let you choose the current drawing or layout. Click the Edit... box to open the Plot Style Table Editor for the current plot configuration file. This subdialog contains a General tab to add or modify the plot configuration Description, show File Information, toggle Apply Global Scale Factor to Non-ISO Linetypes, and enter a value in the *Scale factor* edit box. Click the Delete R14 Color Mapping Table button, and pick Yes if you wish to remove color mappings for pre-R15 drawings. Pick the Save & Close button to save your settings and exit the dialog.

> **New...**   Opens the Add-Color Dependent Plot Style Table Wizard with radio buttons to create a color-dependent plot style from scratch and to import R14 pen settings saved to a CFG, PCP, or PC2 file. (See **Plot**.)

> **Display Plot Styles**   Specifies whether the plot styles and plot style names are affiliated with objects in the drawing, allowing them to display and plot.

> **Options...**   Opens the Output tab of the Options dialog to edit controls.

Layout Settings Tab

> **Paper Size and Paper Units**   This section shows Plot Device: and Printable Area information for the current Paper Size: with defaults chosen from the drop-down list box.

> **Drawing Orientation**   This section displays an icon that changes when you specify Portrait or Landscape orientation, which you can Plot Upside-Down by clicking the checkbox. Radio buttons allow you to set the printable area (defining the X axis and Y axis direction) in inches or mm.

Plot Area   The Plot Area section contains radio buttons for selecting different area configurations: plotting your current Display screen, the drawing Extents, and Limits. You can also save a View or create a Window to define the drawing area to plot. The radio button for View allows you to retrieve saved images from the adjacent drop-down box, and Window requires you to click the Window< button and pick points from the screen.

Plot Scale   This section allows you to select a Scale from default values in the drop-down box, including Custom and Scaled to Fit. You can specify a user-defined scale using the Custom: default and entering values in inches and drawing units in the edit boxes. Click the Scale Lineweights checkbox to set Lineweight scale proportionately with plot scale.

Plot Offset   The Plot Offset section contains a checkbox to Center the Plot on the paper and edit boxes to specify the X and Y plot origins.

Plot Options   This section allows you to toggle options for Plot with Lineweights, Plot with Plot Styles, Plot PaperSpace Last, and Hide Objects.

Plot...   Select the Plot button to plot the drawing using the settings you specified.

Select Display when Creating a New Layout to open the dialog when creating a new Layout tab. The setting can be restored by selecting Create Viewport in New Layouts in the Display tab of the Options dialog.

See Also   Options, Plot, Layout, Layoutwizard, Limits, Plotstyle, Plottermanager; *System Variables:* Lwprint, Lwscale

---

Painter
*See **Matchprop***

Pan
Pan allows you to view different parts of your drawing by moving the cursor, displayed as an open hand, in any direction. Real-time pan (Rtpan) is the default option for interactive panning.

To Move Around in Your Drawing
Command line: **Pan**, **P**, **Rtpan** (or **'Pan** to use transparently)

Menu: View ➤ Pan ➤ Preset Options

Standard Toolbar: Pan Real Time

1. **Press Esc or Enter to exit, or right-click to display shortcut menu:** Enter the command and the cursor changes to a hand

cursor. Press the pick button on your pointing device to lock the cursor in its current location relative to the viewport coordinate system, and the display screen moves in the same direction as the cursor. As you drag the hand, your drawing moves around the graphics screen. To exit the command, press the Escape key or ↵.

To stop panning, release the pick button; to restart the process, press it again.

2. Right-click to display a pop-up menu for switching between Exit, Pan, Zoom, 3D Orbit, Zoom Window, Zoom Original, and Zoom Extents.

NOTE If you are using a two-button Intellimouse (or compatible) pointing device with a small wheel between the buttons, you can set Pan mode by pressing and dragging the wheel.

See Also   -Pan, Zoom, -Zoom

-Pan

-Pan moves the display of your current view to reveal parts of a drawing that are off the screen. Drawings retain the same magnification.

To See Offscreen Drawing Areas

Command line: **-Pan** (or **'-Pan** to use transparently)

Menu: View ➤ Point/Left/Right/Up/Down

1. **Specify base point or displacement:** Pick the first point of view displacement.

2. **Specify second point:** Pick the distance and direction of displacement.

You cannot use **-Pan** while viewing a drawing in perspective. Use the **Dview** command's Pan option instead.

See Also   Dview, Pan, View, -Zoom

Partiaload

Partiaload allows you to load additional selected geometry into a drawing that was open using the Partial Open... button in the Select File dialog.

To Partially Load Geometry

Command line: **Partiaload**

Menu: File ➤ Partial Load (available only for Partial Open drawings)

You are not able to unload geometry that is currently loaded into the file. Partial load states can be saved with the drawing.

Depending on how the drawing was last saved, a message box may appear indicating that the drawing was partially loaded and offering you these options: Do You Want To Fully Open or Restore Last Saved Partial Open State? or Do You Want to Specify New Partial Load Values or Restore the Last Partial Load State? Click available buttons for Fully Open, Restore, Specify, or Cancel.

Provide information as needed in the dialog.

Options

View Geometry to Load   Displays saved view names in the list box, including defaults *extents* and *current*. Click the Pick a Window icon to temporarily exit the dialog to Specify first corner: and Specify opposite corner: points for a *new view*.

Index Status   AutoCAD reports the drawings current Spacial Index and Layer Index status.

Layer Geometry to Load   Displays all layers in the drawing file. Click the checkboxes for the desired layers to load. Right-click to display a short-cut menu or pick buttons to Load All and Clear All.

See Also   Open, New, -Partiaload, Partialopen, -Partialopen

-Partiaload

-Partiaload must be used at the command line to specify and load geometry from a view, selected area, or layers.

To Partial Load Geometry at the Command Line

Command line: **-Partiaload**

Specify first corner or [View]: Lets you specify an area by picking a first point and then prompting to Specify opposite corner:.

If you type **V**, the following prompts appear:

> **Enter view to load or [?]<none>:** Specify a view name, or enter **?** for options. If you entered **?**, the prompt Enter view name(s) to list <*>: appears, with a list of available views.

> **Enter layers to load or [?]<none>:** Specify layer name(s), or enter **?** for options. If you entered **?**, the prompt Enter layers to list <*>: appears, with a list of available layers.

See Also   Open, New, Partiaload, -Partiaload, Partialopen

Partialopen

Partialopen allows you to load specific view and layer geometry for drawings saved in the current release of AutoCAD.

To Partial Open a Drawing

Command line: **Partialopen** (invokes **-Partialopen**)

Menu: File ➤ Open ➤ Partial Open... button

Select criteria from the dialog.

Options

View Geometry to Load   Lets you open a drawing to a saved view when highlighted in the list box, including defaults *extents* and *last*.

Index Status   Click the Use Spacial Index (*indexctl* variable) checkbox for drawing files containing a spatial or layer index. AutoCAD also displays the drawings current Spacial Index and Layer Index status.

Layer Geometry to Load   Toggle the checkboxes for the desired layers to load. Double-clicking the Layer name and Load Geometry column headers will sort the information in ascending or descending order. Right-click to display a shortcut menu or pick buttons to Load All and Clear All.

UnLoad All Xrefs on Open   A checkbox offers to load external reference files when the drawing opens. When opening a drawing with bound Xrefs, AutoCAD only loads the view geometry specified.

Open   Partially loads a drawing based on the geometry specified.

See Also   Open, Partiaload, -Partiaload, -Partialopen

-Partialopen

-Partialopen must be used at the command line to partially open a drawing.

To Partial Open a Drawing at the Command Line

Command line: **-Partialopen**

> **Enter name of drawing to open:** Specify a filename, or enter a tilde (~) to open the Select File dialog and locate an R15 drawing file.

> **Enter view to load or [?]<*Extents*>:** Press **[cr]** for step 3, or enter **?** to display the prompt Enter view name(s) to list <*>:. Press **[cr]** again for a list, or enter a view name.

Enter layers to load or [?]<none>: Press **[cr]** for none, enter layer names separated by commas, enter an asterisk (*) to load all layers, or enter **?** to display the prompt Enter layers to list <*>:. Press **[cr]** again for a list and repeat the command, or enter layer name(s).

Unload all Xrefs on open? [Yes/No] <N>: Press **[cr]** to load external reference files on open, or press **Y** to unload Xrefs.

See Also   Open, Partiaload, -Partiaload, Partialopen

Pasteblock

Pasteblock allows you to insert objects copied from the Clipboard into a drawing.

To Paste Objects into a Drawing

Command line: **Pasteblock**

Menu: Edit ➤ Paste as Block

Shortcut menu: Paste as Block

Terminate any active commands, or use grips to select one or more objects.

Right-click and choose Copy or Copy with Base Point, or use Ctrl+C to copy one or more objects from the display screen to the clipboard using any selection set method.

Right-click or select Paste as Block from the Edit menu to paste the object into your drawing as a block. AutoCAD controls the objects insertion point and block name.

See Also   Copy, Pasteclip, Pasteorig, Pastespec

Pasteclip

Pasteclip allows you to copy and transfer information, such as Auto-CAD objects, text, metafiles, bitmaps, and multimedia files, stored in the Clipboard into your drawing.

To Paste Objects from the Clipboard

Command line: **Pasteclip**

Menu: Edit ➤ Paste

Standard Toolbar: Paste from Clipboard

Graphic objects are inserted at the upper left corner of the drawing area. You may click them and drag them into position or resize them using grips displayed in the form of object "handles." Pasted text is inserted at the upper left corner and becomes an Mtext object. Once objects have been inserted, you can edit them in their native applications by double-clicking them in AutoCAD. The **Paste** command can also be activated by using the control key sequence Ctrl+V.

If you right-click within the drawing area when grips are displayed, the shortcut menu offers options for Cut, Copy, Copy with Base Point, Paste, Erase, Move, Copy Selection, Scale Rotate, Mtext Edit..., Deselect All, Quick Select..., Find..., and Properties.

If a grip is "hot" and you right-click, AutoCAD displays the Grips shortcut menu.

See Also   Copyclip, Copyhist, Cutclip, Hyperlink, Insert, Insertobj, Olelinks, Pastespec

Pasteorig

Pasteorig allows you to insert objects copied from the Clipboard into another drawing based on the object's original location (coordinate points) in the source drawing.

To Paste Original Objects into a Drawing

Command line: **Pasteorig**

Menu: Edit ➤ Paste to Original Coordinates

Shortcut Menu: Paste to Original Coordinates

Select objects similar to steps 1 and 2 for **Pasteblock**.

Right-click or select Paste to Original Coordinates from the Edit menu to paste the object into another drawing.

See Also   Copy, Hyperlink, Insertobj, Olelinks, Pasteblock, Pasteclip, Pastespec

Pastespec

Pastespec lets you insert objects from the Windows Clipboard, link objects to their source application, and/or convert the file format.

To Place a Linked or Embedded Object into a Drawing

Command line: **Pastespec**, **Pa**

Menu: Edit ➤ Paste Special...

When you start the **Paste Special** command, the Paste Special dialog opens, showing the following information and options: Source shows the name of the application in which the Clipboard object was created; the Paste and Paste Link radio buttons allow you select whether to simply insert the object into the drawing or to maintain a *link* with the source file (see **Insertobj**); the As list box shows the file formats you can use to paste the Clipboard object into the current drawing. As you click each object in the list box, review the description provided in the Result section.

The Display as Icon box allows you to display the source application as an icon in your drawing so that you can double-click it to retrieve the linked or imbedded information. To modify the applications associated icon, use the Change Icon... button to open the Change Icon dialog, and choose from Current, Default, and From File radio buttons in the Icon section. The dialog identifies the location, filename, and label of the icon and allows you to Browse... for a replacement.

See Also   Copyclip, Copyhist, Cutclip, Hyperlink, Insert, Insertobj, Olelinks, Olescale, Pasteblock, Pastelink, Pasteorg

Pcinwizard

Pcinwizard displays a Import PCP or PC2 Plot Settings Wizard to import existing R14 PCP and PC2 configuration file plot settings and to apply the specifications for plot area, rotation, plot offset, plot optimization, plot to file, paper size, plot scale, and pen mapping to your current model or layout tab.

To Import Plot Configuration Settings

Command line: **Pcinwizard**

Menu: Wizards ➤ Import R14 Plot Settings...

Make selections as desired, and then pick Next> to proceed through the Wizard as described in the pages below:

Introduction   Provides an overview description.

Browse File   You can enter the location of an R14 configuration file stored in your search path in the PC2 or PCP filename edit box or click the Browse... button to open the Import dialog and locate the file.

Finish   Updates the plot settings in the current Model or Layout tab. Click Page Setup... to open the Page Setup dialog, and view or edit the plot settings.

See Also   Options, Pagesetup, Psetupin

Pedit

Pedit edits 2D or 3D polylines and 3D meshes, changes the location of individual vertices in a polyline or mesh, and converts a nonpolyline object into a polyline. The editing options available depend on the type of object you select. See the following sections for information about individual **Pedit** operations.

Pedit for 2D and 3D Polylines

Pedit modifies the shape of 2D and 3D polylines. If the object you select is not a polyline, respond to the Do you want to turn it into one? <Y>: prompt with **Y**.

To Edit Polylines

Command line: **Pedit**

Menu: Modify ➤ Polyline

Modify II Toolbar: ⬚ Edit Polyline

1. **Select polyline:** Select the object you want to edit as a polyline.

   If the object selected is a 2D polyline, the following prompt appears: Enter an option [Close/Join/Width/Edit vertex/Fit/Spline/Decurve/Ltype gen Undo]:. If the object is a 3D polyline, the following prompt appears: Enter an option [Close/Edit vertex/Spline curve/Decurve/Undo]:.

   If the polyline is closed, Open appears instead of Close in the prompts above. If the object is a standard line or arc, the following prompt appears: Object selected is not a polyline. Do you want it to turn into one: <Y> Enter Y or N.

2. Depending on the option selected, additional prompts appear as described below for Pedit/Edit Vertex and Pedit for 3D Meshes.

Options

Close Joins the endpoints of a polyline. If the selected polyline is already closed, this option is replaced by Open in the prompt.

Open Deletes the last line segment in a closed polyline.

Join Joins polylines, lines, and arcs. The objects to be joined must meet exactly end-to-end.

Width Sets the width of the entire polyline.

Edit Vertex Performs various edits on polyline vertices. See the section below on **Pedit/Edit** vertex.

Fit Curve Changes a polyline made up of straight line segments into a smooth curve.

Spline Curve Changes a polyline made up of straight line segments into a spline-fit curve.

Decurve Changes a smoothed polyline into one made up of straight line segments.

Ltype Gen Causes the Linetype to continue uniformly around the vertices of the polyline when turned on.

Undo Cancels the last **Pedit** function issued.

The Spline Curve option adjusts the "pull" of the vertex points on the curve by changing the *Splinetype* system variable. The default for *Splinetype* is 6. With *Splinetype* set to 5, the pull is greater. See **System Variables** for more details.

You can view both the curve and the defining vertex points of a spline-fit curve by setting the *Splframe* system variable to 1. The *Splinesegs* system variable determines the number of line segments used to draw the curve. A higher value generates more line segments for a smoother curve but also a larger drawing file. The curve created by this process corresponds to a B-spline but is not actually a true spline curve. You may convert a spline-fit polyline into a true B-spline (NURBS) curve by using the Object option on the **Spline** command.

See Also Pedit/Edit Vertex, Pedit/3D Mesh, Pline, Setvar/Splframe, Setvar/Splinesegs, Setvar/Splinetype

Pedit/Edit Vertex

Relocates, removes, moves, or inserts vertices in a polyline. Modifies a polyline's width at a particular vertex, and alters the tangent direction of a curved polyline through a vertex.

To Edit a Polyline Vertex

Start the **Pedit** command, and then select the polyline object you want to edit.

1. **Enter an option [Close/Join/Width/Edit vertex/Fit/Spline/ Decurve/Ltype gen /Undo]:** Enter **E** for Edit vertex. An *X* appears on the first vertex of the selected polyline indicating the vertex is currently editable.

2. **Enter an option [Next/Previous/Break/Insert/Move/Regen/ Straighten/Tangent/Width]:** Enter the capitalized letter of the function to be used.

Options

Next Moves the *X* marker to the next vertex.

Previous   Moves the *X* marker to the previous vertex.

Break   Breaks a polyline from the marked vertex. Move the *X* into the position where you want the break to begin, and type **B** for Break. The prompt changes to Next/Previous/Go/eXit <N>:. Move the marker to another vertex to select the other end of the break. Once the *X* marker is in position, enter **G** to initiate the break.

Insert   Inserts a new vertex. A rubber-banding line stretches from the vertex being edited to the cursor. Enter points either using the cursor or by keying in coordinates.

Move   Relocates a vertex. A rubber-banding line stretches from the vertex being edited to the cursor. You can specify points either using the cursor or by keying in coordinates. To move a vertex, you may alternatively use the Grip editor.

Regen   Regenerates a polyline. This may be required to see effects of some edits.

Straighten   Straightens a polyline between two vertices. Move the cursor to the position where you want the straightening to begin, and enter **S**. The prompt changes to Next/Previous/Go/eXit <N>:. This allows you to move in either direction along the polyline. Once the *X* marker is in position, type **G** to straighten the polyline. This removes all vertices between the two markers and creates one segment instead.

Tangent   Attaches a tangent direction to a vertex for later use in curve fitting. A rubber-banding line stretches from the vertex to the cursor, indicating the new tangent direction. Indicate the new tangent angle by picking the direction using the cursor or by keying in an angle value. Tangent only affects curve-fitted or spline polylines.

Width   Varies the width of a polyline segment. When you have entered this function, the prompt changes to Enter starting width <current default width>:. This allows you to enter a new width for the currently marked vertex. When you have entered a value, the prompt changes to Enter ending width <last value entered>:. This allows you to enter a width for the next vertex.

eXit   Exits from vertex editing.

When you invoke the Edit Vertex option, an *X* appears on the polyline, indicating that the vertex is being edited. Press ↵ to issue the default **N** for Next Vertex, and move the *X* to the next vertex. Type **P** to reverse the direction of the *X*. When inserting a new vertex or using the Width function, pay special attention to the direction the *X* moves when you select the Next function. This is the direction along the polyline in which the new vertex or the new ending width will be inserted.

TIP You may use the Edit Vertex option to move a vertex. It is generally faster to move a vertex using the object grips. With the Grips on, click the polyline to highlight the vertices. Click the grip of the vertex you wish to move, and move it to the desired position.

NOTE If you select a 3D polyline, all the edit options except Tangent and Width are available. Also, point input accepts 3D points.

Pedit for 3D Meshes

Pedit smooths a 3D mesh or moves vertex points in the mesh.

To Edit a 3D Mesh

Start the **Pedit** command, and then select a mesh. You will be prompted to choose one of the options described below.

```
Enter an option [Edit vertex/Smooth surface/Desmooth/
Mclose/Nclose/Undo]:
```

Options

Edit Vertex Relocates vertices of a selected 3D mesh. When you select this option, you get the prompt: Current vertex (0,0) Enter an option [Next/Previous/Left/Right/Up/Down/Move/REgen/eXit]<N>:. An *X* appears on the first vertex of the mesh, marking the vertex to be moved.

Next Rapidly moves the Edit Vertex marker to the next vertex.

Previous Rapidly moves the Edit Vertex marker to the previous vertex.

Left Moves the Edit Vertex marker along the *N* direction of the mesh.

Right Moves the Edit Vertex marker along the *N* direction of the mesh opposite to the Left option.

Up Moves the Edit Vertex marker along the *M* direction of the mesh.

Down Moves the Edit Vertex marker along the *M* direction of the mesh opposite to the Up direction.

Move Moves the location of the currently marked vertex.

Regen Redisplays the mesh after a vertex has been moved.

Smooth Surface Generates a B-spline or Bezier surface based on the mesh's vertex points. The type of surface generated depends on the *Surftype* system variable.

Desmooth Returns a smoothed surface back to regular mesh.

Mclose   Closes a mesh in the *M* direction.

Nclose   Closes a mesh in the *N* direction.

Mopen   Appears when a mesh is closed to open a mesh in the *M* direction.

Nopen   Appears when a mesh is closed to open a mesh in the *N* direction.

Undo   Cancels the last Pedit option issued.

eXit   Exits the Edit Vertex option or the **Pedit** command.

You can use several system variables (see **System Variables**) to modify a 3Dmesh. To determine the type of smooth surface generated, use the *Surftype* variable with the Smooth option. A value of 5 gives you a quadratic B-spline surface; a value of 6 gives a cubic B-spline surface; and a value of 8 gives a Bezier surface. The default value for *Surftype* is 6.

The *Surfu* and *Surfv* system variables control the accuracy of the generated surface. *Surfu* controls the surface density in the *M* direction of the mesh, and *Surfv* controls density in the *N* direction. The default value for these variables is 6.

The *Splframe* system variable determines whether the control mesh of a smoothed mesh is displayed. If it is set to 0, only the smoothed mesh is displayed. If it is set to 1, only the defining mesh is displayed.

See **Bpoly** for automatically grouping lines together into a single object by picking the internal region.

See Also   Bpoly, Grips, Pline, Spline, 3Dpoly, 3Dmesh; *System Variables:* Splframe, Surftype, Surfu, Surfv

---

Pface

Pface draws a polygon mesh by first defining the vertices of the mesh and then assigning 3Dfaces to the vertex locations.

To Draw a Polygon Mesh

Command line: **Pface**

1. **Specify location for vertex 1:** Pick a point for the first vertex to be used in defining the mesh. The vertex prompt repeats after each point is selected. The vertex number increases by 1 each time you pick a point. Remember the location of each vertex; you will need to know the number for the next step. When you have finished selecting points, press **[cr]**.

2. **Face 1, Vertex 1: Specify location for vertex 2 or <define faces>:** Enter the number of the vertex from step 1 that you want to correspond to the first vertex of the first face. When you enter

a number, the Face 1, vertex 2: Enter a vertex number or [Color/Layer] <next face>: prompt appears with the vertex number increased by 1. You can define one face with as many of the points as you indicated in step 2. When you have defined the first face, press **[cr]** for the next vertex number prompt, or enter **C** for color or **L** for layer.

3. **Face 2, Vertex 1: Enter a vertex number or [Color/Layer]:** Enter the number of the vertex that you want to correspond to the first vertex of the second face. When you have finished, press **[cr]** to exit the command.

Options

-(number) Makes a face edge invisible when entered at the Face n, Vertex n: prompt. You must use a negative value for each overlapping edge.

Layer Specifies the layer for the face you are currently defining. Enter **L** or Layer at the Face n, Vertex n: Enter a vertex number or [Color/Layer]: prompt.

Color Specifies the color of the face you are currently defining. You can enter **C** or Color at the Face n, Vertex n: Enter a vertex number or [Color/Layer]: prompt.

NOTE Pface was designed for programmers who need an object type that can easily create 3D surfaces with special properties. Pfaces cannot be edited using **Pedit**. However, you can use Array, Chprop, Copy, Erase, List, Mirror, Move, Rotate, Scale, Stretch, and Explode on Pfaces. Exploding a Pface yields 3Dfaces.

See Also   Edgesurf, Revsurf, Rulesurf, 3Dmesh, Tabsurf; *System Variables:* Pfacemax

Plan

Plan displays a user coordinate system "in plan"—that is, a view perpendicular to the UCS. This allows you to create and manipulate objects in 2D more easily. **Plan** affects only the active viewport. You can set the *UCSfollow* system variable so that whenever you change to a different UCS, you get a plan view of it.

To View in Plan

Command line: **Plan**

Menu: View ➤ 3D Views ➤ Plan View ➤ Current UCS/World UCS/ Named UCS

If you are using the command line, you will see the Enter an option [Current ucs/Ucs/ World] <Current>: prompt. Enter the capitalized letter of the desired option, or press ↵ for the current UCS.

Options

[cr] Gives you a plan view of the current UCS. This is the default option.

U Gives you a plan view of a previously saved UCS. You are prompted for the name of the UCS you wish to see in plan. Enter a question mark to get a list of saved UCSs:

- **Enter name of UCS or [?]:** Enter **?** for a list or the name of your saved UCS.

- **Enter UCS name(s) to list <*>:** Press ↵ to view names.

W Gives you a plan view of the world coordinate system. This option is automatically issued when you pick PlanView (world) from the Display pull-down menu.

See Also UCS, UCSicon; *System Variable:* UCSfollow

Pline

Pline creates lines having properties such as thickness and curvature. Unlike standard lines, polylines can be grouped together to act as a single object. For example, a box you draw using a polyline will act as one object instead of four discrete lines.

To Create a Polyline

Command line: **Pline**, **Pl**

Menu: Draw ➤ Polyline

Draw Toolbar: [icon] Polyline

1. **Specify start point:** Pick the start point of the polyline.

2. **Specify next point or [Arc/Close/Halfwidth/Length/ Undo/Width]:** Enter the desired option, or pick the next point of pline.

Options

Arc Changes Pline to Arc mode. The Arc options are then listed in the prompt:

    Specify endpoint of arc or [Angle/CEnter/CLose/Direction/
    Halfwidth/Line/Radius/Second pt/Undo/Width]:

You can enter either the second point, angle, center, direction, radius, or endpoint of the arc. See the **Arc** command for the use of the Arc options.

Close Draws a line from the current polyline endpoint back to its beginning, forming a closed polyline.

Halfwidth Specifies half the polyline width at the current point. You are first prompted for the starting half width, which is half the width of the polyline at the last fixed point. Next, you are prompted for the ending half width—half the width of the polyline at the next point you pick.

Length Draws a polyline in the same direction as the last line segment drawn. You are prompted for the line-segment length. If an arc was drawn last, the direction will be tangent to the end direction of that arc.

Undo Allows you to step backward along the current string of polyline or polyarc segments.

Width Determines the whole width of the polyline. Subsequent polylines will be of this width unless you specify otherwise.

Notes To give a polyline a smooth curve shape, you must use the **Pedit** command after you create the polyline. The **Explode** command reduces a polyline to its line and arc components. Polylines with a width value lose their width once exploded. To control the uniformity of a line type that is not continuous around the vertices, set the *Plinegen* system variable to 1, or use the Ltgen option of **Pedit**.

See Also Bpoly, Explode, Offset, Pedit; *System Variables:* Plinegen, Plinewid

Plot

Plot or **Print** opens up the Plot dialog for sending your drawing to a plotter. Depending on you the tabs you choose to plot (using the Shift or Ctrl keys), tabs appear for Plot Device and Plot Settings allowing you to control the plotter pen selection and speed as well as where to preview the drawing on the plotter media. **Plot** also allows AutoCAD to reduce a scale drawing to fit on the media. Once you change any of the plotter settings, they become the default settings for the current Model or Layout tab. Several plot configurations can be saved and recalled from the dialog.

To Plot a Drawing Using the Dialog Box

Command line: **Plot**, **Ctrl+P**

Command line: **Print**

Menu: File ➤ Plot

Standard Toolbar: Plot

The Plot dialog opens to display various plotting default parameters and conditions.

> **NOTE** The **Pagesetup** command displays a dialog with settings similar to the Plot Device and Layout settings tabs.

Options

Layout Name Identifies the name of the current layout tab, or shows selected layouts if multiple tabs are chosen for plotting. If a single tab is selected, you can click Save Changes to Layout:, otherwise, this option is grayed.

Page Setup Name This section contains a drop-down box with defaults <Select plot setup to apply>, <Previous> as well as any previously saved and named page setups. Clicking the Add... button opens the User Defined Page Setups dialog:

> **New Page Setup Name** Specifying a new name in the edit box adds it to the Page Setups list box.
>
> **Page Setups** Lists page setup names and location (Model or Layout). Choosing a name from the list displays it in the *New Page Setup Name* edit box.
>
> **Rename** Clicking this button displays a box around it, allowing you to move your cursor over any character to rename an existing page setup.
>
> **Delete** Clicking this button removes the selected name from the list box.
>
> **Import...** Opens the Select File dialog to locate a .dwg, .dwt or .dxf file, and then displays the Import User defined page setup(s) dialog to select from the list.

Full Preview... Pick this button to see the drawing screen as it would appear on paper. Full Preview... displays the Zoom Real-time cursor that lets you zoom and pan for closer plot inspection by right-clicking to display a shortcut menu with these options: Exit, Plot, Pan Zoom, Zoom Window, and Zoom Original. Press the pick button and drag the cursor vertically upward to zoom closer and downward to zoom out.

Partial Preview... Pick this button to open the Partial Plot Preview dialog and view (with dashed lines), and report paper size, printable area, and effective area information. The blue area denotes the effective plot area relative to the paper size and printable area and the red arrow represents the drawings plot origin. Based on your plot specifications, a warning message, such as *Effective area too small to display,* may appear in the edit box alerting you on the results of your plot.

Options—Plot Device Tab

Use this tab to select a plot device or plot your drawings as a file, specify a plot style table, or layout(s) to plot.

Plotter Configuration Section

Name   Click the drop-down box to choose an output device or .pc3 configuration file.

Plotter   Shows the current plotter and a .pc3 plot driver filename.

Where   Shows port connection, such as LPT1 or File.

Description   Displays information about the plot device stored in the General tab of the Plotter Configuration Editor dialog.

Properties   Opens the Plotter Configuration Editor dialog with three tabs:

General   Allows you to enter a Description for display in the Plot Device tab and view Driver Information.

Ports   Radio buttons allow you to specify Plot to the Following Port, Plot to File, or Autospool (send a plot file to an assigned device for printing in the background while you continue working). Check the Show All Ports box or pick buttons Browse Network and Configure Port... for additional controls.

Device and Document Settings   Shows editable settings in a Tree View list box for the .pc3 file. Additional buttons allow you to Import... .pcp or .pc2 files, Save As... a .pc3 file, or set everything to Defaults. Click Custom Properties... to open a sub-dialog specific to the device driver.

Hints...   Displays plotting device specific information.

Plot Style Table (Pen Assignments) Section

Name   Click the drop-down box to specify a plot style table (.ctb) file.

Edit...   Opens the Plot Style Table Editor tabs as described below:

General   Shows information about the Plot Style Table File Name, Number of Styles, Path, Version, and other information. Toggles Apply Global Scale Factor for Non-ISO Linetypes to set controls for non-ISO linetypes and fill patters and specify a value in the *Scale Factor* edit box. Click the Delete R14 Color Mapping Table button to delete the color mappings for pre-2000 drawings.

Table View   Displays plot style table and settings in a spreadsheet (cell) format for the current plot style. Click the Add Style, Delete Style, or Save As... buttons to modify and save changes.

Form View   Displays same information for editing as Table View using list boxes and drop-down boxes.

Save & Close   Saves changes, and then exits the dialog.

New...   Opens the Add-Color Dependent Plot Style Table Wizard with options described below for each page. Wizard pages differ depending on whether the current drawing is color dependent or named mode.

Begin   Click Start from Scratch to create a plot style table, click Use a CFG File imported from R14 pen settings, or click Use a PCP or PC2 File that was previously saved with these file formats.

Browse File   Enter the name of an R14 configuration file in the edit box to import pen settings or locate the file using the Browse... pick button. Select from the drop-down box if your configuration file contains pen settings for multiple plotters.

File Name   Specify the name of a plot style table containing pen settings that can be imported.

Finish   Click Plot Style Table Editor... to Open the Dialog, and Edit Plot Style Settings. Checkboxes toggle on or off Use this Plot Style Table for the Current Drawing and Use this Plot Style Table for New and Pre-Tahoe Drawings. Pick Finish to exit the Wizard.

What to Plot   Radio buttons allow you to specify the Current Tab, Selected Tabs, or All Tab Layouts for plotting. Holding the Ctrl key allows you to pick multiple tabs. Selecting a single tab disables the Selected Tabs button.

Number of Copies   Pick the up/down arrows or enter a value in the edit box for the number of copies to plot. If you select multiple layouts and specify multiple copies, AutoCAD will only output one copy if you are plotting to a file or using AutoSpool.

Plot to File   Plots your drawing to a file, and enables the edit boxes to specify a File Name and Location. The Ellipsis button opens the Browse for Folder dialog to assign a destination for the plot file. The Browse the Web button opens the Browse the Web dialog to store or access Auto-CAD files on the Internet. Checking the box changes Plot to File to Plot to File (This Plot Only).

Plot Settings Section   Use this section to specify plot settings, such as plot area and scale, plot offset, and paper size.

Paper Size and Paper Units

Plot Device   Shows the name of the currently selected plot device.

Paper Size   Shows available paper sizes from the drop-down box.

Printable Area   Shows the actual area on the paper in inches or mm, depending on the radio buttons you pick.

Drawing Orientation Lets you specify an orientation by clicking Portrait or Landscape radio buttons or the Plot Upside Down checkbox. The adjacent icon verifies the plot orientation of the paper.

Plot Area Pick radio buttons Layout, Extents, Display, View, or Window to define the area of the drawing to be plotted. You can click a saved View name from the drop-down box or use the Window< button to temporarily exit the dialog and specify diagonal corner points for a new plot area.

Plot Scale

Scale Sets the scale of your plot. Plot defaults are 1:1 for a Layout tab, Scale to Fit for a Model tab, and Custom for a standard scale, which can be entered in the *Custom:* edit boxes. The list of standard scales is stored in the AutoCAD registry.

Lineweight Sets controls for Lineweight scale when plotting layouts.

Plot Offset

Center the Plot Centers your plot on the paper.

X: Inches Enter a value to set an offset for the X origin.

Y: Inches Enter a value to set an offset for the Y origin.

Plot Options Checkboxes set the following controls:

- Plot with lineweights
- Plot with plot styles
- Plot PaperSpace last
- Hide objects

See Also Options, Pagesetup, Pcinwizard, -Plot, Plotstyle, Plottermanager; *System Variables:* Lwprint, Lwscale, Plotlegacy

-Plot

-Plot allows you plot from prompts at the command line.

To Plot a Drawing at the Command Line

Command line: **-Plot**

1. **Enter a layout name <Model>:** Press **[cr]**, or specify a layout name and make it current.

2. **Enter a page setup name or press ENTER for current settings:** Press **[cr]** to apply current settings, or specify another page setup name.

3. **Enter an output device name <current>:** Press **[cr]**, or enter the name of a plot device or .pc3 file.

See Also   Options, Pagesetup, Pcinwizard, Plotstyle, Plottermanager;
System Variables: Lwprint, Lwscale, Plotlegacy

Plotstyle

Plotstyle opens the Current Plot Style dialog to assign a plot style for
new objects. The command line equivalent is **-Plotstyle**.

To Open the Plot Style Dialog
Command line: **Plotstyle**

Options

Current Plot Style   Select a plot style from the list box to set as the Current Plot Style for objects in your drawing, such as color, dithering, gray scale, pen assignments, screening, linetype, lineweight, end styles, join styles, and fill styles or use defaults Normal, Bylayer and Byblock.

Active Plot Style Table   Click the drop-down box to select a plot style table attached a Layout tab or a viewport, or pick the Editor… button to open the Plot Style Table Editor dialog to view and/or edit the plot style. AutoCAD reports if the plot style table is Attached To the Model or Layout tab. (See **Plot**.)

See Also   Options, Pagesetup, Plot, -Plotstyle, Plottermanager

-Plotstyle

-Plotstyle specifies a plot style for new objects at the command line.
The dialog equivalent is **Plotstyle**.

To Set a Plot Style
Command line: **-Plotstyle**

Current plot style is "Bylayer"

Enter an option [?/Current]: Enter **?** for a list, or enter **C** and specify a plot style at the prompt Set current plot style :.

NOTE   Depending on your current plot settings, the following AutoCAD alert message may appear at the command line: "A plot style name cannot be manually assigned when you're in color-dependent Plot Style mode. If you want more control of plot style names in this drawing, use the Convert to Named Plot Styles Wizard to convert this drawing to named Plot Style mode."

See Also   Options, Pagesetup, Plot, Plotstyle, Plottermanager

Plottermanager

Plottermanager opens Windows' Plotters application window containing icons to launch the Add-A-Plotter Wizard and Plotter Configuration Editors.

To Open the Plotters System Window

Command line: **Plottermanager**

Menu: File ➤ Plotter Manager…

Double-click the Add-a-Plotter Wizard to add and configure plotter and printers, or right-click a plotter configuration (.pc3 file) to open the Plotter Configuration Editor.

See Also   Options, Plot, Plottermanager

Point

Point creates a point object. Points can be used as unobtrusive markers that you can snap to using the Node Osnap override. You may also use the Ddptype dialog to select a point type.

To Draw a Point Object

Command line: **Point**, **Po**

Menu: Draw ➤ Point ➤ Single Point/Multiple Point

Draw Toolbar: Point

Specify a Point: Enter the point location.

Selecting Multiple Point from the menu allows you to continually pick points. Press Esc to exit the command.

Options

You can set the *Pdmode* system variable to change the appearance of points. You must set **Pdmode** before drawing points. Zero is the default setting. When **Pdmode** is changed, all existing points are updated to reflect the new setting. The setting values are as follows:

Pdmode Value	Object
0	A dot
1	Nothing
2	A cross
3	An *x*
4	A vertical line upward from the point selected

Adding 32, 64, or 96 to the values above selects a shape to draw *around* the point in addition to the figure drawn through it:

Pdmode Value	Object
32	A circle
64	A square
96	A circle inside a square

NOTE You can combine the different *Pdmode* variables to create 20 different types of points. For example, to combine a cross (2) within a circle (32), set **Pdmode** to 34 (2 + 32).

NOTE Insert points on the Defpoints layer if you do not wish to plot them.

See Also Ddptype, Divide, Measure; *System Variables:* Pdmode, Pdsize

---

Point Selection

You can enter a point by direct distance entry, object snap tracking, polar tracking, picking it with your cursor, keying in an absolute or relative coordinate value, or keying in a relative polar coordinate. You can also use modifiers called filters to align points in an X, Y, or Z axis. On the command line, whenever a point selection is required, type **.x**, **.y**, or **.z** or a combination of these modifiers (e.g., .xy).

Options

Direct Distance Entry Specify a point, move your pointing device to indicate a direction, and then enter a distance at the keyboard. Setting **Orthomode** to On makes locating vertical and horizontal points easy.

Object Snap Tracking Use object anap tracking to locate a point relative to previous or base point. Entering **tra** within a command toggles object snap tracking on.

Polar Tracking Use polar tracking with alignment paths to locate a point relative to previous or base point.

Absolute Coordinate Specifies points by giving the XYZ coordinate values, separated by commas, as follows:

Select point: 6,3,1

The X value is 6, the Y is 3, and the Z is 1. If you omit the Z value, Auto-CAD assumes the current default Z value (see the **Elev** command to set the current Z default value). Absolute coordinates use the current UCSs origin as the point of reference.

Relative Coordinates   Entered like absolute coordinates, except that an at sign (@) precedes the coordinate values, as follows:

Select point: @6,3,1

If you omit the Z value, AutoCAD assumes the current default Z value (see the **Elev** command for setting the current Z default value). Relative coordinates use the last point entered as the point of reference. To tell AutoCAD to use the last point selected, simply enter @ by itself at a point selection prompt.

Relative Polar Coordinates   Specify points by giving the distance from the last point entered, preceded by an at sign (@), the distance, and followed by a less-than sign (<) and the angle of direction, as follows:

Select point: @6<45

This entry calls for a relative distance of 6 units at a 45 degree angle from the last point entered.

Filters   Align a point along an X, Y, or Z axis by first specifying the axis on which to align, selecting an existing point on which to align, and then entering the new point's remaining coordinate values. The following example aligns a point vertically on a specific X location:

Shift+Right-click shortcut menu: Point Filters ➤ .X, .Y, .Z, .XY, .XZ, and .YZ filters

1. **Specify next point or [Undo]:** Enter .X, or select a known point to which you want to align vertically. For precision, use the Osnap overrides.

2. **(need yz):** Select a YZ coordinate. Again, you can use Osnap overrides to align to other geometries.

The acad.mnu and acad.mns files assign these buttons in the pop0 section to the shortcut menu. The shortcut menu lists Snap modes as well as Point Filters.

You can also enter **.xy**, **.yz**, or **.xz** at the prompt. For example, you can first pick an XY location and then enter a Z value for height.

NOTE   To override the current angle units, base, and direction settings (set using the transparent **'Units** command), use double or triple lesser-than signs (<).

You can enter fractional units regardless of the unit style setting. This means you can enter **5.5"** as well as **5'6"** when using the architectural format.

See Also   Filter, Osnap, Tracking, Units

Polygon

Polygon allows you to draw a regular polygon of up to 1,024 sides. To define the polygon, you can specify the outside or inside radius or the length of one side. The polygon is actually a polyline that can be exploded into its individual component lines. Use the **Pedit** command to edit a polygon's width.

To Draw a Polygon

Command line: **Polygon**, **Pol**

Menu: Draw ➤ Polygon

Draw Toolbar: ⬡ Polygon

1. **Enter number of sides <default>:** Enter the number of sides.
2. **Specify center of polygon or [Edge]:** Enter **E** to select the Edge option or pick a point to select the polygon center. If you select the default center of a polygon, the following prompts appear:

   • **Enter an option [Inscribed in circle/Circumscribed about circle] <I>:** Enter the desired option.

   • **Specify radius of circle:** Enter the radius of circle defining polygon size.

Options

Edge Determines the length of one face of the polygon. You are prompted to select the first and second endpoint of the edge. AutoCAD then draws a polygon by creating a circular array of the edge you specify.

Inscribed Forces the polygon to fit inside a circle of the specified radius; the endpoints of each line lie along the circumference.

Circumscribed Forces the polygon to fit outside a circle of the specified radius; the midpoint of each line lies tangent to the circumference.

Radius of Circle Sets the length of the defining radius of the polygon. The radius will be the distance from the center to either an endpoint or a midpoint, depending on the Inscribed/Circumscribed choice.

See Also Pedit, Pline; *System Variable:* Polysides

Preferences

See Options

Print

See **Plot**

Preview

Preview shows you a full-page view of the current drawing similar to other Windows applications. The view displayed is set in the **Plot** command, based on your current plot configuration.

To Preview Your Plot

Command line: **Preview**, **Pre**

Menu: File ➤ Plot Preview

Standard Toolbar: 🔍 Print Preview

Press Esc or Enter to exit, or right-click to display shortcut menu.

A symbol displayed as a magnifying glass with a plus and minus sign helps you zoom in and out of your preview. Right-click to display the pop-up menu, allowing you to switch between Exit, Plot, Pan, Zoom, Zoom Window, and Zoom Original. In addition to Exit, you can press the Escape key, or press **[cr]** to cancel the preview and not plot your drawing.

See Also Plot, Options

Properties

Properties opens the Properties dialog with information specific to the type of object selected. A drop-down box lists all selected objects, and two tabbed sections, Alphabetic and Categorized, contain properties that you can view or edit. There are eight properties common to all objects: Color, Layer, Linetype, Linetype Scale, Plot Style, Lineweight, Hyperlink, and Thickness.

To Open the Properties Dialog

Command line: **Properties**, **Props**

Menu: Tools ➤ Properties

Standards Toolbar: 📷 Properties

The Properties dialog can be opened by holding down Ctrl+1 (number 1 key) or right-clicking any object(s) highlighted with a "hot" grip to display a shortcut menu and then choosing Properties. Right-clicking in the dialog below the title bar opens a shortcut menu with options Allow Docking, Hide, Description, and Undo.

Double-click the status bar to "dock" it along the left side of your display area, or hold the grab bars at the top of the dialog with your pick button and drag it to the display area to "float".

Click the Quick Select icon to open the Quick Select dialog to stipulate a selection set filtering criteria using information selected from drop-down boxes. (See **Qselect**.)

Provide information in the dialog as needed.

Options

The following controls are common to the Properties dialog.

Color   Pick this cell and an arrow will appear, allowing you to pick colors from a list to change an object's color, unless you specify Bylayer or Byblock. (See **Color**.)

Layer   Pick this cell and an arrow will appear, allowing you to pick a layer from a list to change an object's layer assignment. (See **Layer** for loading layers.)

Linetype   Pick this cell and an arrow will appear, allowing you to pick linetypes from a list to change an object's Linetype, unless you specify Bylayer or Byblock. (See **Linetype** for loading Linetypes.)

Linetype Scale   Enter a value in the text box to change an object's Ltscale value. (See **Ltscale**.)

Lineweight   Pick this cell and an arrow will appear, allowing you to pick Linetypes from a list to change an object's Lineweight, unless you specify Bylayer, Byblock, or Default. (See **Lineweight** for loading Lineweights.)

Hyperlink   Pick this cell and an ellipsis button appears, allowing you to open the Insert Hyperlink dialog to attach a hyperlink to the selected object. If a description exists for the hyperlink, it will appear in the dialog; otherwise, the URL appears in the edit box. (See **Hyperlink**.)

Plotstyle   Pick this cell and an arrow will appear, allowing you to specify Normal, Bylayer, and Byblock as well as plot styles, if available, in the current plot style table. (See **Plot**, **Plotstyle**.)

Thickness   Enter a value in the text box to change an object's thickness value. (See **Thickness**, **Change**, **Chprop**, **Elev**.)

See Also   3Dface, 3D, 3Dorbit, Arc, Attdef, Bmake, Circle; *Dimensioning Commands:* Bhatch, Ellipse, Image, Leader, Line, Mesh, Minsert, Mtext, Multiline, Point, Polyline, Qselect, Ray, Region, Shape, Solid, Spline, Text, Tolerance, Trace, Viewport, Xline; *System Variables:* Cecolor, Celtscale, Celtype, Clayer, Elevation, Thickness

Propertiesclose

Propertiesclose closes the Properties window.

To Close the Properties Window

Command line: **Propertiesclose, Prclose**

See Also   Change, Chprop, Properties

Psdrag

Psdrag controls the appearance of the PostScript image as you drag it into position using the **Import/Export** command **Psin**.

To Display the PostScript Image

Command line: **Psdrag**

Enter PSIN drag mode [0/1] <0>: Enter 0 or 1, or press ↵.

Options

0   Displays only the image's bounding box and filename while the image is being dragged.

1   Displays the rendered PostScript image while the image is being dragged into place. If the *Psquality* system variable is set to 0, the Drag mode option has no effect—only the bounding box is shown.

See Also   Import/Export, Psfill, Psin; *System Variable:* Psquality

Psetupin

Psetupin lets you import user-defined page setups into a new Auto-CAD 2000 or R2000 drawing layout.

To Import a Page Setup

Command line: **Psetupin**

Displays the Select File dialog to select an AutoCAD 2000 or R2000 drawing file containing one or multiple page setup, saved with the **Pagesetup** command. Click Open to display the Import user defined page setup(s) dialog with Name and Location column headings listing the page setup name and tab (Model or Layout), then choose one or more page setup(s). You can select single or groups of names by holding the Shift key or Control key in the list box.

See Also   Pagesetup, -Psetupin

-Psetupin

-Psetupin allows you import page setups into a new drawings at the command line.

To Import Page Setups at the Command Line

Command line: **-Psetupin**

If the *Filedia* system variable is set to 0, the following prompts appear at the command line:

1. **Enter file name:** Enter name of file.

2. **Enter user defined page setup(s) to import or [?]:** Specify name of page setups, or enter **?** to display a list. If a page setup exists with the same name, the prompt `Page setup "plan view" already exists. Redefine it? [Yes/No] <N>:` appears.

   If the *Filedia* system variable is set to 1, the Select File dialog opens to locate a file and then continues to setup 2.

See Also   Pagesetup, Psetupin

Psfill

Psfill fills two-dimensional polyline outlines with any PostScript pattern defined in the `acad.psf` PostScript support file. The pattern is not visible on the screen but is output with the **Psout** command.

To Use a PostScript Fill Pattern

Command line: **Psfill**

1. **Select polyline:** Pick the two dimensional polyline outline.

2. **Enter PostScript fill pattern name (. = none) or [?] <.>:** Enter a pattern name.

Entering **?** displays the following list of available patterns: Grayscale, RGBcolor, Ailogo, Lineargray, Radialgray, Square, Waffle, Zigzag, Stars, Brick, and Specks. The prompt is then repeated with the pattern name displayed in the brackets.

   The appearance of fill patterns is controlled by a range of parameters. Depending upon the pattern you select, you will be prompted to specify the relevant parameters. AutoCAD does not display the patterns on screen, but **Psout** recognizes and exports them.

See Also   Import/Export, Psdrag, Psin/Psout

Psin/Psout

*See **Import/Export***

Pspace

Pspace lets you move from Model Space back to Paper Space in a Layout tab when you are working from Paper Space through a viewport into Model Space. Pick a Layout tab or set Tilemode to 0 before you use **Pspace**.

To Switch from a ModelSpace Viewport to PaperSpace

Command line: **Pspace**

Click Model/Paper on the status bar, or toggle **Pspace** by double-clicking in a PaperSpace viewport or any area outside the viewport.

NOTE You use Model Space in AutoCAD to do drafting and design work. Paper Space is an alternative work space that lets you arrange views of your ModelSpace drawing and scale or size them for plotting. You can create viewports in a Layout tab that are like windows into Model Space. Layers, Snap, and Grid modes can be set independently for each viewport. You can also accurately control the scale of a viewport for plotting purposes.

TIP To get into an existing PaperSpace layout in a drawing, set Tilemode to 0, or click the desired Layout tab. You can also toggle Tilemode On and Off by clicking Tile on the status bar. Your screen will go blank and the UCS icon will change to a triangle. Use the **Mview** command to set up viewports so you can display your ModelSpace drawing in Paper Space. Use the XP option under the **Zoom** command to set the scale of a viewport display. Use the Layoutwizard for easier interface and setup procedures.

TIP Viewports in Paper Space can be resized, moved, copied, and even overlapped using standard AutoCAD editing commands.

NOTE In AutoCAD 2000 you can create irregular shaped viewports with the Object or Polygonal options of the **Mview** command.

See Also   Layout, Layoutwizard, Mspace, Mview, Mvsetup, Pagesetup, Tilemode, Vplayer, Vports, Zoom/XP

Purge

Purge allows you to remove unreferenced blocks, layers, linetypes, plotstyles, dimension styles, shape files, or text styles. These objects and settings can increase the size of the drawing file, making the drawing slow to load and difficult to transport.

To Purge Elements from the Drawing File

Command line: **Purge**, **Pu**

Menu: Files ➤ Drawing Utilities ➤ Purge ➤ Preset Options

Enter type of unused objects to purge [Blocks/Dimstyles/ LAyers/LTypes/Plotstyles/SHapes/STyles/Mlinestyles/All]: Select the type of element you wish to purge.

When you select the element type, AutoCAD displays each element name of the type specified. Enter **Y** to purge the element or **N** to keep it. The All option purges all elements regardless of type.

You can purge all objects at once:

- **Enter name(s) to purge <*>:** Enter name of variable to purge.

- **Verify each name to be purged? [Yes/No] <Y>:** Enter **Y** if you wish to purge all objects or **N** for a list to selectively choose objects to purge.

The layer 0, the continuous linetype, the standard text style, UCS, views, and viewport configurations cannot be purged. Nested blocks are removed only by repetitious purging and exiting of the drawing. The **Wblock** command describes an alternative and more effective method for purging.

See Also   Layer, Linetype, Style, Wblock

Qdim

Qdim allows you to quickly dimension objects, such as circles and arcs, and is especially helpful for baseline or continued dimensioning operations.

To Dimension Quickly

Command line: **Qdim**

Menu: Dimension ➤ Qdim

Dimension Toolbar: Quick Dimension

Select geometry to dimension: Select the object(s) you wish to dimension using any object selection method.

Specify dimension line position, or [Continuous/Staggered/ Baseline/Ordinate/Radius/Diameter/datumPoint/Edit] <Continuous>: Pick a point to locate the dimension, press **[cr]** for continued dimensioning, or enter an option.

If you entered **E**, the prompt Indicate dimension point to remove, or [Add/eXit] <eXit>: appears to edit dimension strings.

Option

Staggered   Creates staggered dimensions.

Baseline   Continues a dimension string using the first extension line of the most recently inserted dimension as its first extension line.

Ordinate   Creates a dimension string based on origin points.

Radius   Adds a radius dimension to arcs or circles. Results differ depending on your selection of single or multiple objects.

Diameter   Adds a diameter dimension to arcs or circles.

Datum point   Prompts to Select new datum point: for baseline and ordinate dimensions, and then repeats options.

Edit   Selects dimension strings, then displays a prompt to pick cross points to Remove or Add them, and then repeats the prompt to "Specify dimension line position...".

See Also   Ddim, Dim, Dim1, Dimension Variables, and Dimensioning Commands

---

Qleader

Qleader lets you open the Leader Settings dialog, offering controls to draw leader lines that include text, Mtext, tolerance, block reference, or none or to copy an object.

To Draw Quick Leaders

Command line: **Qleader**

Menu: Dimension ➤ Leader

Dimension Toolbar: Quick Leader

Specify first leader point, or [Settings]<Settings>: Press **[cr]** to open the Leader Settings dialog, or specify a leader start point.

Specify next point: Specify another point.

Specify text width <0.0000>: Enter a value, or pick a point.

Enter first line of annotation text <Mtext>: Press **[cr]** to open the Multiline Text Editor dialog, or enter text. If you entered text, the prompt Enter next line of annotation text: repeats until you press Enter twice.

Select settings as appropriate in the dialog.

Options

Annotation Tab

Annotation Type　Selects a leader annotation type: Mtext opens the Multiline Text Editor dialog to enter multiline text, Copy an Object prompts to Select an object to copy:, Tolerance opens the Tolerance dialog for input of tolerance values. Block Reference displays prompts similar to the **Insert** command, and None draws the leader without an annotation.

MText Options　Offers toggles for Prompt for Width, Always Left Justify, and Frame Text when the Mtext annotation is specified.

Annotation Reuse　Offers options None, Reuse Next, and Reuse Current, allowing you to choose whether annotation is repeated when drawing the next leader lines, and then retains it as the current default.

Leader Line & Arrow Tab

Leader Line　Enables you to draw Straight or Spline leader line segments.

Number of Points　Limits the number of points you wish to pick to draw a leader line. Specifying No Limit allows endless pick points until you press Enter twice. If you enter a number or use the up/down arrows to set a Maximum value, you must specify one more than the number of leader segments you want to create.

Arrowhead　Pick a predefined Arrowhead block from a drop-down box, or apply a User Defined... block from the Select Custom Arrow Block dialog.

Angle Constraints　Sets angular controls when drawing the First Segment and Second Segment leader lines.

Attachment

Multiline Text Attachment　Attaches Text on left side and Text on right side for leader lines and multiline text annotation: Top of Top Line, Middle of Top Line, Middle of Multiline Text, Middle of Bottom Text, or Bottom of Bottom Line. Click Underline Bottom

Line if you wish to position the leader line at the last line of your text or Mtext. This tab is only available when Mtext is specified in the Annotation tab.

See Also   Ddim, Dim, Dim1, Dimension Variables, and Dimensioning Commands

Qsave

Qsave saves a named drawing quickly without asking for a filename. If saving an unnamed drawing, **Qsave** works like **Saveas**, enabling you to name the drawing before saving it.

To Save a Drawing

Command line: **Qsave**

Menu: File ➤ Save

Standard Toolbar: 🖫 Save

See Also   Save, Saveas; *System Variables:* Dwgtitled, Savename, Savetime

Qselect

Qselect allows you to stipulate a selection set based on filtering criteria using information you specify.

To Use Quick Select

Command line: **Qselect**

Menu: Tools ➤ Quick Select... 🖳 Select objects

Temporarily exits the dialog and prompts to Select objects:, allowing you to choose objects for your selection set.

Specify information in the dialog.

Options

Apply To   Click the drop-down box to specify the entire drawing or the current selection set.

Object Type   Click the drop-down box to select the object type for which the filter is applied.

Properties   Displays a list of all related searchable properties to filter, and sets available defaults in the Operations and Value boxes.

Operator   Lists the filter range which may include = Equals, <> Not Equal, > Greater Than, and < Less Than. Not all operators are available for all properties.

Value   Information in this drop-down box varies depending on the filter property being specified.

How to Apply   Radio buttons allow you to specify Include in New Selection Set or Exclude from New Selection Set. Click the checkbox if you wish to Append to Current Selection Set.

See Also   Properties

Qtext

Qtext helps reduce drawing regeneration and redraw times by making text appear as a rectangular box instead of readable text. The rectangle approximates the height and length of the text.

To Display Text as a Rectangular Box

Command line: **Qtext**

Menu: none

Enter mode [ON/OFF] <OFF>: Enter the desired option.

Click Show Text Boundary Frame Only in the Display tab of the Options dialog to set quick test mode on. You do not see the effects of **Qtext** until you issue the **Regen** command.

See Also   Dtext, Regen, Text; *System Variable:* Qtextmode

Quit

Quit exits all drawings in your AutoCAD session and allows you to save or discard changes from the last save or an unsaved drawing. AutoCAD has aliased the **Exit** command to **Quit** in the acad.pgp file.

To Exit a Drawing

Command line: **Quit**, **Exit**

Menu: File ➤ Exit

If no changes were made to the current drawing, AutoCAD exits the program. If changes were made and not saved, a dialog box opens to pick Yes, No, or Cancel. If the drawing is unnamed and you pick Yes, the

Save Drawing As dialog will open, giving you an opportunity to name the drawing.

Use **Close** to exit and save the current drawing and remain in your AutoCAD session.

See Also   Close, Qsave, Save, Saveas; *System Variable:* Dbmod

Ray

Ray creates the "semi-infinite" lines that are generally used as construction lines in a drawing. The ray extends from a selected point to infinity.

To Create a Ray

Command line: **Ray**

Draw ➤ Ray

1. **Specify start point:** Specify a start point for the ray.

2. **Specify through point:** Specify the point through which you want the ray to pass.

3. Continue to specify points to create multiple rays, if required, and then press ↵.

See Also   Line, Mline, Pline, Tracking, Xline

Recover

Recover salvages as much of a file as possible and allows AutoCAD to read the file. A drawing may become corrupted because of problems with your hard-disk drive or floppy disk. If the header information is damaged, AutoCAD will attempt to recover the file with the **Open** command.

To Recover Corrupted Files

Command line: **Recover**

Menu: File ➤ Drawing Utilities ➤ Recover...

If the *Filedia* system variable is set to 1, the Select File dialog is displayed so you can enter the drawing name that you wish to recover. Otherwise, the following command-line prompt appears:

Enter name of drawing file to recover: Enter a filename to recover or a tilde (~) to display the Select File dialog and locate the file.

A series of messages appears indicating the action AutoCAD is taking to recover the file. An AutoCAD Alert dialog opens after recovery to report whether the audit detected any errors in the recovered database. If so, the recovery is processed and reported to the screen.

See Also   Audit; *System Variable:* Auditctl

Rectangle

Rectangle allows you to draw a rectangular polyline with chamfered or filleted corners, thickness, elevation, and/or width.

To Draw a Rectangle

Command line: **Rectangle**, **Rectang**, **Rec**

Menu: Draw ➤ Rectangle

Draw Toolbar: 🔲 Rectangle

1. **Specify first corner point or [Chamfer/Elevation/Fillet/ Thickness/Width]**: Specify a point, or type one of the uppercase letters as indicated in steps 3–7.

2. **Specify other corner point:** Specify the opposing corner.

3. If you entered a **C**, you are prompted for a chamfer distance or press ↵ at the prompts: Specify first chamfer distance for rectangles <0.0000>: and Specify second chamfer distance for rectangles <0.0000>:.

4. If you entered **E**, you can Specify the elevation for rectangles <0.0000>:.

5. To Specify fillet radius for rectangles <0.0000>:, type **F**, and enter a value.

6. If you wish to Specify thickness for rectangles <0.0000>:, type **T**, and specify a thickness.

    To Specify line width for rectangles <0.0000>:, type **W**, press **[cr]**, and then enter a value.

See Also   Chamfer, Fillet, Pline, Thickness; *System Variables:* Chamfera, Chamferb, Chamferc, Chamferd, Filletrad, Plinewid, Thickness

Redefine/Undefine

Undefine suppresses any standard AutoCAD command. For example, if you load an AutoLISP **Copy** command you have written and then enter

Copy at the command prompt, you will still get the standard **Copy** command. However, if you use **Undefine** to suppress the standard **Copy** command, you can use the AutoLISP **Copy** program. **Redefine** reinstates a standard command that has been suppressed.

To Suppress or Reinstate a Standard Command

Command line: **Undefine** or **Redefine** (as appropriate)

Enter command name: Enter the command name. To enter the standard AutoCAD **Copy** command when an AutoLISP version might already be defined, precede the command with a period at the command prompt, as follows:

```
Command line: .Copy[cr]
Select objects:
```

This is the only way to use an undefined command with the AutoLISP command function.

Redo

Redo restores a command you have undone using **U** or **Undo**. **Redo** must immediately follow **Undo**. You are allowed only one **Redo** per command. If you enter a series of three **U**'s (that is, three **Undo** 1's), only the last **U** can be restored.

To Undo Your Undo

Command line: **Redo**

Menu: Edit ➤ Redo

Standard Toolbar: ⟲ Redo

Here is the most effective approach for restoring **Undo**s:

```
undo 6
```

If this undoes too much, then try **Redo**. If this undoes too much, then try **Undo 4**. Otherwise, enter **U**.

See Also U, Undo; *System Variable:* Undoctl

Redraw and Redrawall

During the drawing and editing process, an operation may cause an object to partially disappear. Often, the object was previously behind other objects that have since been removed. **Redraw** and **Redrawall** refresh the screen and restore such obscured objects. These commands also clear the screen of blips that may clutter your view.

To Redraw the Display

Command line: **Redraw**, **R/Redrawall**, **Ra** (or **'Redraw/'Redrawall** to use transparently)

Menu: View ➤ Redraw

Standard Toolbar: Redrawall

NOTE **Redraw** will act only on the currently active viewport. **Redrawall**, on the other hand, refreshes all viewports on the screen at once. These commands affect only the virtual screen, not the actual drawing database.

See Also   Regen, Regenall, Viewres

Refclose

Refclose allows you to save or discard changes to an external reference or block made during the reference editing operation.

To Save or Discard Refedits

Command line: **Refclose**

Modify menu: In-place Xref and Block Edit Save Reference Edits, or In-place Xref and Block Edit Discard Reference Edits

Toolbar: Refedit ⊞ Save back changes to reference

Toolbar: Refedit ⊠ Discard changes to reference

Enter option [Save/Discard reference changes] <Save>: Enter **[cr]** to save changes, or press **D** to abandon the **Refedit** operation and discard modifications made to external reference or block objects, and then click OK in the AutoCAD message box.

See Also   Refedit, Refset, Xref

Refedit

Refedit is intended to provide moderate editing capabililty of external references or blocks in your drawing without opening or exploding them.

To Edit an Xref or Block

Command line: **Refedit**

Modify ➤ In-place Xref and Block Edit ➤ Edit Reference

Refedit Toolbar: Edit block or Xref

1. **Select reference:** Picking a reference file or block for editing opens the Reference Edit dialog, allowing you to preview, select, and specify options for editing. Click OK to exit the dialog.

2. **Select nested objects:** Select the object(s) you wish to change, and then apply the desired editing commands to modify its properties. All objects in the drawing, including those reference objects not selected, appear "faded" (*Xfadectl* variable) to distinguish them from the actual "working set."

> **NOTE** AutoCAD displays the prompt Use REFCLOSE or the Refedit toolbar to end reference editing session.

3. Click the appropriate icon in the Refedit toolbar to edit selected objects (see **Refset**) then save changes (see **Refclose**). Objects not part of the "working set" are controlled by the 2D wireframe option of the *Shademode* system variable.

Specify and preview information in the dialog.

Options

Path identifies the location and name of the selected reference file. Click Enable Unique Layer and Symbol Names if you wish to assign the standard $#$ external reference prefix to layer and symbol names being edited. Clicking Display Attribute Definitions for Editing allows editing of attribute definitions and their associated geometry for new block insertions.

Reference Name   Lists names of external references, including nested files, that can be selected for in-place editing. Choose a file from the tree view list for editing.

Preview   Displays a preview image of the selected reference file.

Next   Allows you to cycle through and preview reference files in the image box.

See Also   Refclose, -Refedit, Refset, Xref; *System Variables*: Bindtype, Refeditname, Xedit, Xfadectl

-Refedit

-Refedit is intended for limited editing at the command line of external references or blocks in your drawing without opening or exploding.

To Edit an Xref or Block at the Command Line

Command line: -**Refedit**

1. **Select reference:** Specify external reference or block object to edit.

2. **Select nesting level [Ok /Next] <Next>:** Press **[cr]**, or enter an
   option.

Options

OK   Specifies the highlighted reference or block object for editing, and
then displays prompts as follows:

> **Select nested objects:** Select objects that you wish to edit.
>
> **Display attribute definitions [Yes/No] <No>:** Enter **Y** to dis-
> play attribute definitions for editing; otherwise, press **[cr]**.

Next   Use **Refclose** or the Refedit toolbar to end reference editing session.

See Also   Refclose, Refedit, Refset, Xref; *System Variables*: Bindtype,
Refeditname, Xedit, Xfadectl

Refset

Refset allows you to add or delete objects from a "working set" during
an **Xrefedit** operation.

To Add or Discard Objects For An Xrefedit

Command line: **Refset**

Modify menu: In-place Xref and Block Edit ➤ Add to Work set/Remove
from Work set

Toolbar: Refedit ![icon] Add objects to working set

Toolbar: Refedit ![icon] Remove objects from working set

**Transfer objects between the Refedit working set and host
drawing...**

Enter an option [Add/Remove] <Add>: Use standard selection set
methods to exchange objects between "working set" and those appearing faded in the source or "host" drawing.

Options

Add   Adds objects to the working set.

Remove   Removes objects from the working set.

See Also   Refclose, Refedit, Xref

Regen and Regenall

These two commands update the drawing editor screen to reflect the most recent changes in the drawing database.

To Regenerate the Drawing and Refresh Your View

Command line: **Regen**, **Re**, **Regenall**, or **Rea**

Menu: View ➤ Regen/Regen All

> **NOTE** If you make a global change in the drawing database and **Regenauto** is turned on, a regeneration occurs automatically. If you have **Regenauto** turned off, regeneration will not occur automatically, so changes to the drawing database are not immediately reflected in the drawing you see. If you need to see those changes, use **Regen** to update the display.

See Also   Redraw, Redrawall, Regenauto, Viewres

Regenauto

Regenauto automatically regenerates the screen display to reflect the most recent drawing changes. For complex drawings, regeneration can be very time-consuming. **Regenauto** enables you to turn off automatic regeneration. **Regenauto** is on by default.

To Control Regeneration

Command line: **Regenauto** (or **'Regenauto** to use transparently)

Enter mode [ON/OFF]<ON>: Enter On or Off as required.

Options

On   Causes the display to be automatically regenerated when required to reflect global changes in the drawing database. Your display will reflect all the most recent drawing changes.

Off Suppresses the automatic regeneration of the display. This can save time when you are editing complex drawings. When a command needs to regenerate the drawing, a prompt allows you to decide whether or not to regenerate the display.

See Also Regen; *System Variables:* Regenmode, Viewres

Region

The **Region** command allows you to create 2D enclosed areas from existing overlapping closed shapes (called *loops*). The loops can be combinations of lines, polylines, circles, arcs, ellipses, elliptical arcs, and splines. They must be closed or form closed areas.

To Create Regions

Command line: **Region**, **Reg**

Menu: Draw ➤ Region

Draw Toolbar: [icon] Region

1. **Select objects:** Select the objects you wish to combine into a region.

2. Press **[cr]** to end the command. The command line shows how many loops were detected and how many regions were created.

You can create composite regions by subtracting, combining, or finding the intersection of regions.

To Create Composite Regions

Command line: **Union**, **Subtract**, **Intersect**

1. **Select objects:** Select the regions you wish to combine into a composite region.

2. Press **[cr]** to end the command.

You may select objects in any order to unite them with the **Union** command or to find the intersection with the **Intersect** command. When you wish to subtract one region from the other, you must first select the region from which you want to subtract.

NOTE Regions may not be created from open objects that intersect to form a closed area, such as intersecting arcs or self-intersecting curves. (The related **Boundary** command allows you to create polyline boundaries from any intersecting objects.) Objects in a region must be in the same plane.

NOTE Regions are useful for calculating area properties for facilities management purposes (see the **Area** command). You can also hatch and shade regions, using the **Bhatch** or **Shade** commands, and analyze other properties.

See Also Bhatch, Boundary, -Boundary, Intersect, Shapes, Subtract, Union

Reinit

Reinit opens the Re-initialization dialog to reinitialize the Input/Output ports, digitizer, display, and acad.pgp file.

To Reinitialize Ports, Digitizer, Display, and acad.pgp File

Command line: **Reinit**

Options

I/O Port Initialization   Resets the I/O port for your digitizer and plotter.

Device & File Initialization   Reinitalizes your digitizer, display, and acad.pgp file.

NOTE If you edit your acad.pgp file with a text editor, check the PGP File box to activate those changes in your current drawing. If your cursor does not appear on the screen to permit you to select the checkboxes, you can use the *Re-init* system variable and specify the sum of several reinitialization values. For example, enter **Reinit**, and enter a value of **5** (1 = Digitizer + 4 = Digitizer reinitialization) for a digitizer analog failure. See **System Variables** for additive values.

See Also   *Express Tools:* Command Alias Editor; *System Variable:* Reinit

Rename

Rename opens the Rename dialog to change the name of a block, dimension style, layer, linetype, text style, user coordinate system, named view, or viewport configuration.

To Activate the Rename Dialog Box

Command line: **Rename**, **Ren**

Menu: Format ➤ Rename...

Select the appropriate object from the Named Objects list box.

Options

Selecting the object from the Named Objects list box registers associated names in the Items list box. Pick the item to be renamed, and it will appear in the *Old Name* edit box.

Old Name   Enter item to be renamed, or pick from Items list box. Use wildcards for renaming groups of objects with common characters. For example, hold the Shift or Ctrl key to select multiple layers (layer1, layer2, layer3), and then enter a portion of the modified name (new*) in the *Rename To* edit box.

Rename To   Enter new name of item(s) shown in the *Old Name* edit box, using wildcards for groups of objects with common characters, and then pick the *Rename To* edit box. The renamed objects will appear in the Items list box.

TIP   You can also use **Rename** to find out which objects are in use in a current drawing.

See Also   Layer, Linetype, -Rename, Style, Wildcard Characters

-Rename

-Rename renames any namable drawing element, such as a block, dim-style, layer, line type, text style, etc. The dialog equivalent command is **Rename**.

To Assign a New Object Name

Command line: -**Rename**, -**Ren**

1. **Enter object type to rename [Block/Dimstyle/LAyer/ LType/Style/Ucs/VIew/Vport]:** Enter the type of drawing element to be renamed.

2. **Enter old (object) name:** Enter old name of object.

3. **Enter new (object) name:** Enter new name of object.

See Also   -Layer, -Linetype, Rename, -Style

Render

Render uses light sources and surface settings to render a 3D model. Surfaces can be adjusted for reflectance, shininess, and smoothness. Multiple light sources can be added to the drawing to enhance the rendering, and the intensity of these light sources is adjustable. **Render** produces an image using information from a named scene, the current selection set, or the current view.

To Render a Scene, Objects, or View

Command line: **Render**, **Rr**

Menu: View ➤ Render ➤ Render (on the cascading Render menu)

Render Toolbar: Render

1. In the Render dialog, you may set the Rendering Type as required; select a Scene to Render; set Screen Palette options (shading, materials, and smoothing variables); and choose the Destination for the rendered output (Viewport, Render Window, or File).

2. Click either the Render Scene or Render Objects button.

If you choose the Render Objects button, you will be prompted to Select objects: before the rendering can begin. If no scene or selection set is specified, **Render** will use the current view. If there are no lights in the drawing, **Render** will use a standard "over the shoulder" light source with an intensity of 1.

Preset Options

The following options are available on the Render toolbar. Their command-line equivalents are shown at the command line.

Background Opens the Background dialog to define a solid, gradient, raster image or the current view as a background for renderings.

Command line: **Background**

Menu: View ➤ Render ➤ Background

Render Toolbar: Background

Hide Initiates a hide for a 3D model with hidden lines suppressed.

Command line: **Hide**

Menu: View ➤ Hide

Render Toolbar: Render

Scenes Brings up a Scenes dialog that lets you set up a scene you can later recall.

Command line: **Scene**

Menu: View ➤ Render ➤ Scene...

Render Toolbar: Scenes

Lights Brings up the Lights dialog box that lets you adjust, delete, or create a light source. You can set the intensity of the Ambient light and set the lighting drop-off to be inverse linear or inverse square.

Command line: **Light**

Menu: View ➤ Render ➤ Light...

Render Toolbar: 🔳 Scenes

Materials   Brings up a dialog that lets you create a new finish or import, delete, export, or modify an existing finish. A preview sphere gives you a sample view of what your finish looks like.

Command line: **Rmat**

Menu: View ➤ Render ➤ Materials...

Render Toolbar: 🔳 Materials

Materials Library   Brings up a dialog that shows a list of all the materials finishes available. You may select materials subsets and store them as named materials library (.mli) files.

Command line: **Matlib**

Menu: View ➤ Render ➤ Materials Library...

Render Toolbar: 🔳 Materials Library

Mapping   Prompts to Select objects:, and then Opens the Mapping dialog to assign mapping coordinates and projection Mapping dialog.

Command line: **Setuv**

Menu: View ➤ Render ➤ Mapping...

Render Toolbar: 🔳 Mapping

Fog   Displays the Fog/Depth dialog to emulate distances for objects with white (for fog), black (for traditional depth cueing), or blends of color combinations.

Command line: **Fog**

Menu: View ➤ Render ➤ Fog...

Render Toolbar: 🔳 Fog

Landscape New   Opens the Landscape New dialog to select a landscape object.

Command line: **Lsnew**

Menu: View ➤ Render ➤ Landscape New...

Render Toolbar: 🔳 Landscape New

Landscape Edit   Opens the Landscape Edit dialog to edit a landscape object.

Command line: **Lsedit**

Menu: View ➤ Render ➤ Landscape Edit...

Render Toolbar: Landscape Edit

Landscape Library Opens the Landscape Library dialog. Lets you maintain libraries of landscape objects.

Command line: **Lslib**

Menu: View ➤ Render ➤ Landscape Library...

Render Toolbar: Landscape Edit

Render Preferences Brings up the Rendering Preferences dialog that lets you set the rendering preferences for the following: Rendering Procedures defaults; Screen Palette or color-mapping techniques; Icon scale for Lights; Rendering (display) options; Render Quality and Face controls.

Command line: **Rpref**, **Rpr**

Menu: View ➤ Render ➤ Preferences...

Render Toolbar: Render Preferences

Statistics Provides information about the last scene rendered (**Stats** command).

Command line: **Stats**

Menu: View ➤ Render ➤ Statistics...

Render Toolbar: Statistics

See Also Hide; *System Variable:* Pickfirst

Rendscr

Rendscr can be used to reproduce the last rendering created with **Render**. Use the **Rendscr** command on operating systems with a nonwindowing single monitor display configured for full-screen rendering.

To Repeat Render

Command line: **Rendscr**

Loading Landscape Object module.

Initializing Render...

Initializing preferences...done.

> **NOTE** **Rendscr** causes the image to fill the entire screen. Press F2 to restore the display area or text window.

See Also Render

Replay

*See **Render***

Revolve

*See **Solid Modeling***

Resume

*See **Script***

Revsurf

Revsurf draws an extruded curved surface that is rotated about an axis, like a bell, globe, or drinking glass, as shown in Figure R.1. Before you can use **Revsurf**, you must define both the shape of the extrusion and an axis of rotation. Use arcs, lines, circles, or 2D or 3D polylines to define this shape. The axis of rotation can be a line.

FIGURE R.1: Extruded curved surface drawn by **Revsurf**

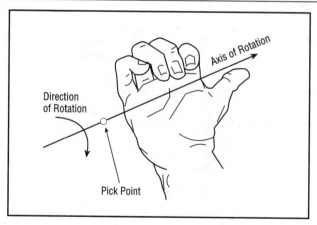

To Draw an Extruded Surface

Command line: **Revsurf**

Menu: Draw ➤ Surfaces ➤ Revolved Surface

Surfaces Toolbar: Revolved Surface

REVSURF

1. **Current wire frame density: SURFTAB1=6 SURFTAB2=6**

   Select object to revolve: Pick an arc line, circle, 2D polyline, or 3D polyline defining the shape to be swept.

2. **Select object that defines the axis of revolution:** Pick a line representing the axis of rotation.

3. **Specify starting angle <0>:** Enter the angle from the object selected as the start point of the sweep.

4. **Specify included angle (+=ccw, ~=cw) <Full circle>:** Enter the angle of the sweep.

> **NOTE** The point you pick on the object in step 3 determines the positive and negative directions of the rotation. You can use the "right-hand rule" illustrated in Figure R.2 to determine the positive direction of the rotation. Imagine placing your thumb on the axis line, pointing away from the end closest to the pick point. The rest of your fingers will point in the positive rotation direction. The rotation direction determines the *N* direction of the surface while the axis of rotation defines the *M* direction.

FIGURE R.2: Determining the positive direction of rotation

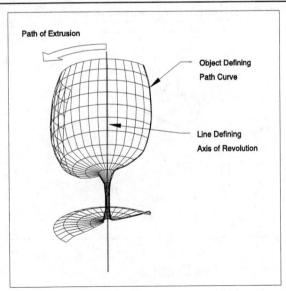

You can control the number of facets used to create the **Revsurf** by setting the *Surftab1* and *Surftab2* system variables. *Surftab1* controls the number of facets in the *M* direction, and *Surftab2* controls the facets in the *N* direction. You can set these variables through the **Setvar** command or by entering the system variable from the command prompt. Resetting a higher value in *Surftab1* or *Surftab2* will not affect already drawn surfaces.

See Also 3Dmesh, Pedit; *System Variables:* Splframe, Surftab1, Surftab2

Rfileopt

Rfileopt sets the render to file options for rendering.

To Set Render to File Options

Command line: **Rfileopt**

Arguments vary depending on the file format: .tga, .pcx, .bmp, .tif. Rfileopt arguments and color mode syntax would appear as

```
C: Rfileopt Fileformat Xres Yres A ratio
<mode-specific options>
```

A Microsoft Windows .bmp format, for example, would be specified as (c:Rfileopt "BMP" 640 480 1.0 "C8").

See Also Arx, Render

Rmat

See **Script**

Rotate

Rotate rotates an object or group of objects to a specified angle.

To Rotate Objects

Command line: **Rotate**, **Ro**

Menu: Modify ➤ Rotate

Modify Toolbar: Rotate

1. **Current positive angle in UCS**: ANGDIR=counterclockwise ANGBASE=0

   Select objects: Select as many objects as you like.

2. **Specify base point:** Pick the point about which objects are to be rotated.

3. **Specify rotation angle or [Rotation angle]:** Enter the angle of rotation, or press **R** to specify a reference angle.

Options

Reference Specifies the rotation angle in reference to the object's current angle. If you enter this option, you get these prompts:

- **Specify the reference angle <0>:** Enter the current angle of the object, or pick two points representing a base angle.

- **Specify the new angle:** Enter a new angle, or pick an angle with the cursor.

> **NOTE** **Rotate** is also a grips option. See **Mirror** for the full command sequence.

If you have enabled grips for **Rotate**, the command prompt is as follows.

```
** ROTATE **
Specify rotation angle or [Base point/Copy/Undo/
Reference/eXit]:
```

See Also Copy, Grips, Mirror, Move, Scale, Stretch

Rotate3D

Rotate3D rotates an object or group of objects about an arbitrary 3D axis.

To Rotate Objects

Command line: **Rotate3D**

Menu: Modify ➤ 3D Operation ➤ Rotate 3D

1. **Select objects:** Select as many objects as you like.

2. **Specify first point on axis or define axis by [Object/Last/ View/Xaxis/Yaxis/Zaxis/2points]:** Specify a point, or select an option.

3. **Specify rotation angle or [Reference]:** Enter the angle of rotation, or press **R** to specify a reference angle.

Options

Axis by Object   Allows you align the axis of rotation with an existing object (line, circle, arc, or 2D polyline).

Last   Uses the last axis of rotation.

View   Aligns the axis of rotation with the viewing direction of the current viewport that passes through a selected point. At the `Point on view direction axis <0,0,0>:` prompt, select a point.

X\Y\Zaxis   Aligns the axis of rotation with one of the axes (X, Y, or Z) that pass through the selected point. At the `Point on (X, Y, or Z) axis <0,0,0>:`, select a point.

2Points   Specifies two points to define the axis of rotation. At the `1st point on axis:` and `2nd point on axis:`, select two points.

See Also   Rotate

Rpref
*See **Render***

Rscript
*See **Script***

Rtpan
*See **Pan***

Rtzoom
*See **Zoom***

Rulesurf

Rulesurf generates a surface between two curves. Before you can use **Rulesurf**, you must draw two curves defining opposite ends of the desired surface (see Figure R.3). The defining curves can be points, lines, arcs, circles, 2D polylines, or 3D polylines.

FIGURE R.3: Defining the opposite ends of a surface for **Rulesurf**

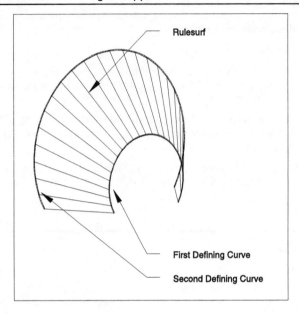

To Use Curves to Define a Surface

Command line: **Rulesurf**

Menu: Draw ➤ Surfaces ➤ Ruled Surface

Surfaces Toolbar: Ruled Surface

1. **Current wire frame density: SURFTAB1=6**

   Select first defining curve: Pick the first curve.

2. **Select second defining curve:** Pick the second curve.

> **NOTE** The location of your pick points on the defining curves affects the way the surface is generated. If you want the surface to be drawn straight between the two defining curves, pick points near the same position on each curve. If you want the surface to cross between the two defining curves in a corkscrew fashion, pick points at opposite positions on the curves.

The *Surftab1* system variable controls the number of faces used to generate the surface.

See Also Pedit; *System Variable:* Surftab1, Surftab2

Save

Save stores your currently open file to disk. Use **Save** to save changes to your drawing under the same name.

To Save Your Drawing

Command line: **Save**

If the *Filedia* system variable is set to 1 and your drawing has not yet been named, the Save Drawing As dialog opens. Enter a drawing name in the *File Name* edit box. The next time you enter Save, the Save Drawing As dialog reappears. Click the Save button to save the drawing to the same filename, or specify a new filename, directory, and/or path.

If the *Filedia* system variable is set to 0, the following command-line prompt appears: Save Drawing As <current drive\path\file name>:. Enter a new <drive><path><file name>, or press **[cr]** to accept the default current filename.

If you save the drawing into the same location with the same name, you will get another dialog telling you that a file with that name already exists and asking do you want to overwrite it. Yes overwrites the existing file; No stops the save and puts you back at the Save Drawing As dialog.

NOTE Use the **Savetime** command to set a time interval for automatically saving your drawing. The current drawing is saved to the default filename `auto.sv$`.

Options

Save   Saves the current drawing file.

Save as Type   Click the drop-down box to save your drawing in various formats: R2000, R14/LT98/LT97, R13/LT95, template (.dwt), R2000 DXF, R14/LT98/LT97 DXF, R13/LT95, or R12/LT2 DXF.

Options...   Displays Saveas Options dialog with two tabbed sections:

   Dwg Options   Contains a checkbox to Save Proxy Images of Custom Objects. Click the Index Type drop-down box for None, Layer, Special, and Spacial and Layer, or the Save All Drawings As drop-down box to save your drawing in various formats.

   DXF Options   Lets you set controls for ASCII or Binary format, toggle checkboxes to Select Objects or Save Thumbnail Preview Image, and enter a value for Decimal Places of Accuracy (0 to 16).

See Also   Options, Qsave, Saveas, Standard File Selection Dialog; *System Variables:* Savefile, Savename, Savetime

Saveas

Saveas saves an unnamed drawing with a filename or allows you to rename your drawing, making it the current drawing.

To Save an Existing Drawing as the Current Drawing

Command line: **Saveas**

Menu: File ➤ Save As...

If the *Filedia* system variable is set to 1 and your drawing has not yet been named, the Save Drawing As dialog opens. Press **[cr]** to save the drawing as the same name in the *File Name* edit box, or enter a new filename, directory, and/or path.

If the *Filedia* system variable is set to 0, the following command-line prompt appears:

1. **Current file format: AutoCAD 2000 Drawing**

Enter file format [R13(LT95)/R14(LT98/LT97)/2000/DXF/ Template] <2000>: Press **[cr]** to save the drawing in AutoCAD Release 2000 format, or enter an option.

2. **Save Drawing As <current drive\path\file name>:** Press **[cr]** to save the drawing as the same name, or enter a new <drive><path><filename>.

Options

2000   AutoCAD Release 2000 Drawing (. dwg)

DXF   AutoCAD 2000 ObjectDXF (. dxf)

R14(LT98/LT97)

AutoCAD Release 14, LT98, or LT97 Drawing (. dwg) Template   AutoCAD 2000 Drawing Template File (. dwt)

See Also   Options, Qsave, Saveas, Standard File Selection Dialog; *System Variables:* Savefile, Savename, Savetime

Saveimg

Saveimg saves a rendered image to a .bmp, .tif, or .tga file format after rendering a model to a viewport.

To Save an Image

Command line: **Saveimg**

Tools menu: Display Image ➤ Save...

Provide information as needed in each dialogs.

In Format section, click a radio button to save the image in .bmp, .tga, or .tif file format. Clicking the Options... button for .tga or .tif displays a subdialog box for with compression options for None, .rle, or PACK. The file format .rle provides run-length-encoded image compression for .tga, and PACK uses Macintosh packbits, run-length-encoded image compression) for .tif files.

The Portion section includes an Active viewport image box. You can click two diagonal points to define the lower left and upper right coordinates for the image area or enter values in the *Offset* and *Size* edit boxes. Picking points away from the extreme lower left corner (0,0) or upper right (default XY) of image selection area sets the image's Offset and Size. Click the **Reset** button to restore the default 1002×569 value.

See Also   Image, -Image, Imageadjust, Imageattach, Imageclip, Imageframe, Imagequality

Scale

Scale changes the size of objects in a drawing. You can also scale an object by reference.

To Resize Objects

Command line: **Scale**, **S**

Menu: Modify ➤ Scale

Modify Toolbar: ▣ Scale

1. **Select objects:** Pick the objects to be scaled.
2. **Specify base point:** Pick a point of reference for scaling.
3. **Specify scale factor or [Reference]:** Enter the scale factor, move the cursor to visually select new scale, or enter **R** to select the Reference option.

Options

Reference   Scales the selected objects based on a reference length and a specified new length. When using the Reference option at the Specify reference length <1>: prompt, specify a distance or scale factor. At the Specify new length: prompt, specify a new distance or scale factor. If the new length is longer than the reference length, the object(s) will be enlarged, and vice versa.

As with **Mirror** and **Stretch**, you can work with grips by selecting objects and selecting the **Scale** command. AutoCAD will display the object with grips and, after you issue the command, will show the following prompt:

```
**SCALE**
Specify scale factor or [Base point/Copy/Undo/Reference/
eXit]:
```

Except for Reference (discussed above), the options here are similar to those available when working with the **Mirror** command. You can cycle through the options shown by pressing the spacebar.

See Also   Block, Bmake, Change, Copy, Dgrips, Grips, Insert, Lengthen, Move, Properties, Rotate, Select, Stretch, Wblock

Scene
*See **Render***

Script

Script "plays back" a set of AutoCAD commands and responses recorded in a script file. Script files, like AutoCAD Shell Active DOS window batch files, are lists of commands and responses entered exactly as you would enter them while in AutoCAD.

To Invoke a Script File

Command line: **Script**, **Scr** (or **'Script** to use transparently)

Menu: Tools ➤ Run Script

If the *Filedia* system variable is set to 1, the Select Script File dialog opens. Enter a script filename in the *File Name* edit box.

If the *Filedia* system variable is set to 0, the following command-line prompt Enter script file name <current file name>: appears. Enter the script filename.

Options

Delay <milliseconds>   When included in a script file, makes AutoCAD pause for the number of milliseconds indicated.

Rscript   When included at the end of a script file, repeats the script continuously.

Resume   Restarts a script file that has been interrupted using the Backspace or Escape key.

Backspace   Interrupts the processing of a script file (you can also press Escape to do this).

NOTE You can use Script files to set up frequently used macros to save lengthy keyboard entries or to automate a presentation. Another common use for scripts is to manage layering setups. (Setting the *Expert* system variable to 1 suppresses the prompt Really want to turn the current layer off for layering scripts.)

Section

See **Solid Modeling**

Select

Select provides a variety of options for selecting objects and returns you to the command prompt once you have made your selection. The objects selected become the most recent selection in AutoCAD's memory.

To Select Objects

Command line: **Select**

Select objects: Choose an object selection method.

Options

Window/W Selects objects completely enclosed by a rectangular window by prompting for First corner: and Other corner:. Enter **W** at the Select objects: prompt, or pick two points from left to right to automatically create a window selection set.

Crossing/C Selects objects that cross through a rectangular window. Enter **C** at the Select objects: prompt, or pick two points from right to left and automatically create a crossing-window selection set.

Group/G Prompts to Enter group name:. Select all objects within a named group.

Previous/P Selects last set of objects selected for editing. You can use the Previous option to pick the objects you have picked with Select when a later command prompts you to select objects. Previous is useful when you want several commands to process the same set of objects, as in a menu macro.

Last/L Selects last object drawn or inserted.

All Selects all objects on thawed layers.

Remove/R Removes objects from the current selection of objects and displays the Remove object: prompt. Entering **A** returns to Add mode

SELECT

and restores the `Select object:` prompt. You can also hold down the Shift key and pick objects to remove them from a selection set.

Add/A   Adds objects to the current selection of objects. You will usually use this option after you have issued the **R** option. The Remove and Add modes will remain in effect only during the specific command's execution and can be interchanged as often as necessary.

Multiple/M   Picks several objects at one time before highlighting them and adding them to the current selection of objects.

Undo/U   Removes the most recently added object from the current selection of objects.

Box   Allows you to use either a crossing or a standard window, depending on the orientation of your window pick points. If you pick points from right to left, you will get a crossing window. If you pick points from left to right, you will get a standard window.

Auto/AU   Selects objects by picking them or by using a window, as you would with the Box option. After you issue the Auto option, you can pick objects individually, as usual. If no object is picked, AutoCAD assumes you want to use the Box option, and a window appears that allows you to use either a crossing or standard window to select objects.

Single/SI   Selects only the first picked object or the first group of windowed objects.

Wpolygon/WP   Selects objects that are contained within any shape you define. The shape assumes a closed polyline. There are certain restrictions. For example, you cannot include intersecting rubber-band lines, and you cannot place a vertex on an existing polygon segment.

Cpolygon/CP   Similar to WPolygon, except it selects objects that cross or enclose any shape you define. The shape assumes a closed polyline. There are certain restrictions. For example, you cannot include intersecting rubber-band lines, and you cannot place a vertex on an existing polygon segment.

Fence/F   Similar to CPolygon, except it selects intersecting or crossing objects with one or more rubber-band lines you define, including lines that intersect themselves.

NOTE   The **Select** command maintains a selection set only until you pick a different group of objects at another `Select object:` prompt. Entering the **AutoLISP** command **(setq set1 (ssget))** at the command prompt allows you to create a selection set that you can return to again and again during the course of the current editing session. Whenever you want to select this group of objects again, enter **!set1** at the `Select objects:` prompt.

See Also   Aperture, Ddselect; *System Variables:* Pickadd, Pickauto

Selecturl

Selecturl locates all objects that have URLs attached to them in a drawing.

To Select a URL

Command line: **Selecturl**

TIP Invoking **Selecturl** highlights all URL's in your current drawing.

Setvar

See System Variables

Setuv

See Render

Shade

Shade produces a quick "Z buffer" shaded view of a 3D model by removing hidden lines.

To Shade a 3D Object

Command line: **Shade, Sha**

Menu: View ➤ Shade, preset options

The *Shadedge* and *Shadedif* system variables give you some control over the way a model is shaded.

TIP You can't directly plot images that were created using **Shade**. However, you can output a shaded image to a slide using the **Mslide** command. On systems that support fewer than 256 colors, **Shade** produces an image with hidden lines removed and 3Dfaces in their original color. However, **Shade** can produce an image faster than the **Hide** command, and might be used where speed is a consideration. On systems with 256 colors or more, **Shade** produces a shaded image for which the light source and viewer location are the same.

See Also Hide, Render; *System Variables:* Shadedge, Shadedif

Shademode

Shademode allows you to set shading options in the current viewport.

To Shade Objects

Command line: **Shademode**

Enter option [2D wireframe/3D wireframe/Hidden/Flat/ Gouraud/fLat+edges/gOuraud+edges] <2D wireframe>: Press **[cr]**, or enter an option.

Options

2D Wireframe   Displays objects using lines and curves for boundaries, retaining visibility of raster and OLE objects, linetypes, and lineweights.

3D Wireframe   Displays a shaded 3D UCS icon. Objects appear similar to 2D, except raster and OLE objects; linetypes and lineweights are not visible. Shows material colors applied to objects in your drawing.

Hidden   Removes hidden lines using 3D wireframe views.

Flat Shaded   Displays objects as flat between the polygon faces.

Gouraud Shaded   Displays objects shaded with smoother edges than Flat Shaded.

Flat Shaded, Edges On   Combines Flat Shaded and Wireframe options displaying objects with exposed wireframes.

Gouraud Shaded, Edges On   Combines Gouraud Shaded and Wireframe options displaying objects with the wireframe exposed.

See Also   Render; *System Variable:* Compass

Shape

Shape allows you to insert custom shapes, such as text font characters, into your drawing. Before you use **Shape**, you must load the file containing the shape(s). Use the **Load** command to load the Select Shape file dialog box, and select and load the desired file. Shapes act like blocks, but you can't explode them or attach attributes to them.

To Insert Custom Shapes

Command line: **Shape**

1. **Enter shape name or [?]:** Enter the name of the shape or a question mark, and the prompt Enter shape(s) to list <*>: appears to list available shapes.

2. **Specify insertion point:** Pick the insertion point.

3. **Specify height <current height>:** Enter the height value, or select a height using the cursor.

4. **Specify rotation angle <0>:** Enter or visually select the angle.

NOTE Because shapes take up less file space than blocks, you may want to use shapes in drawings that do not require the features offered by blocks.

See Also Compile, Load, Wildcards; *System Variable:* Shpname

Shell/Sh

Shell and **Sh** allow you to use any command window and to run other programs with low memory requirements without exiting AutoCAD.

To Open a DOS Shell

Command line: **Shell**

OS Command: Enter a standard DOS command, or press **[cr]** to shell out to the AutoCAD Shell Active DOS window.

NOTE If you want to use external DOS commands or programs, you must, *before* starting AutoCAD, either specify or set a path to the drive and directory where the commands or programs are located. If you press ↵ at the OS Command: prompt, the DOS prompt appears, and you can enter any number of external commands. Type **Exit**, and press **[cr]** whenever you are ready to return to the AutoCAD command prompt.

Showmat

Showmat identifies an object's material type and attachment method.

To List an Object's Material Type

Command line: **Showmat**

Select object: Select the object, and then, depending on the method used to attach a material to an object, one of the following descriptions appear:

• Material <material name> is explicitly attached to the object.

• Material <material name> is attached by ACI to ACI <color number>.

- Material <material name> is attached by layer to layer <layer name>.

- Material *GLOBAL* is attached by default or by block.

See Also   Render

Sketch

Sketch allows you to draw freehand. (It actually draws short line segments end-to-end to achieve this effect.) The lines **Sketch** draws are only temporary lines that show the path of the cursor. To save the line, you must use the Record and eXit options.

To Draw Freehand

Command line: **Sketch**

1. **Record increment <default>:** Enter a value representing the distance the cursor must travel before a line segment is generated along the sketch path.

2. **Sketch. Pen eXit Quit Record Erase Connect:** Start your sketch line, or enter an option.

Options

Pen   As an alternative to the pick button on your pointing device, press **P** from the keyboard to toggle between the Pen-Up and Pen-Down modes. With the Pen-Down, the short temporary line segments are drawn as you move the cursor. With the Pen-Up, no lines are drawn.

eXit   Saves any temporary sketch lines, and then exits the **Sketch** command.

Quit   Exits the **Sketch** command without saving temporary lines.

Record   Saves temporary sketched lines during the time you are using the **Sketch** command.

Erase   Erases temporary sketched lines.

Connect   Continues from the end of a sketch line.

Period(.)   Draws a long line segment while using the **Sketch** command. With the Pen-Up, place the cursor at the location of the long line segment, and then type a period.

TIP   To draw using polylines with **Sketch** instead of standard lines, use the **Setvar** command to set the *Skpoly* system variable to 1.

The easiest way to use **Sketch** is with a digitizer equipped with a stylus. You can trace over other drawings or photographs and refine them later. The stylus gives a natural feel to your tracing.

The Record increment: prompt allows you to set the distance the cursor travels before AutoCAD places a line. The Record increment value can greatly affect the size of your drawing. If this value is too high, the sketch line segments are too apparent, and your sketched lines will appear "boxy." If the increment is set too low, your drawing file becomes quite large, and regeneration and redrawing times increase dramatically.

When AutoCAD runs out of RAM in which to store the lines being sketched, it must pause for a moment to set up a temporary file on your disk drive before it continues to store additional sketch lines in RAM. Your computer will then beep and display the message "Please raise the pen." If this occurs, press **P** to raise the pen. (You may have to press **P** twice.) When you get the message "Thank you. Lower the pen and continue," press **P** again to proceed with your sketch. Setting Record increment to a low value increases your likelihood of running out of RAM.

Turn the Snap and Ortho modes off before starting a sketch. Otherwise, the sketch lines will be forced to the snap points or drawn vertically or horizontally. The results of having the Ortho mode on may not be apparent until you zoom in on a sketch line. If you prefer, you can sketch an object and then use the **Pedit** command with the Fit option to smooth the sketch lines.

See Also   Pedit, Pline; *System Variables:* Sketchinc, Skpoly

Slice
*See **Solid Modeling***

Slidelib.exe

Slidelib.exe is an external AutoCAD program that runs independently from AutoCAD. Use it to combine several slide files into a slide library file. You use slide libraries to create icon menus and to help organize slide files.

To Build a Slide Library

At the AutoCAD Shell Active DOS window prompt, enter the following:

Slidelib slide-library-name < ascii-list ↵.

NOTE   Before you can create a slide library, you must create an ASCII file containing a list of slide-filenames to include in the library. Do not include the .sld extension in the list of names. You can give the list any name and extension. You can then issue the Slidelib program from the DOS prompt. The slidelib.exe file is located in the \Support folder.

See Also   Delay, Mslide, Script, Vslide

Snap

Snap controls the settings for the Snap mode. The Snap mode allows you to accurately place the cursor by forcing it to move in specified increments.

To Set Snap Mode

Command line: **Snap**, **Sn** (or '**Snap** to use tranparently)

Specify snap spacing or [ON/OFF/Aspect/Rotate/Style/Type] <default spacing>: Enter the desired Snap spacing, or select an option.

Options

Snap Spacing   Enters the desired Snap spacing. The Snap mode is turned on and the new Snap settings take effect.

ON   Turns on the Snap mode. Has the same effect as pressing the F9 key, Ctrl+B, or double-clicking Snap on the status bar.

OFF   Turns off the Snap mode. Has the same effect as pressing F9, Ctrl+B, or double-clicking Snap on the status bar.

Aspect   Enters a Y axis Snap spacing different from the X axis Snap spacing.

Rotate   Rotates the Snap points and the AutoCAD cursor to an angle other than 0 and 90 degrees.

Style   Choose between the standard orthogonal Snap style and an isometric Snap style.

Type   Prompts to Enter snap type [Polar/Grid] <current default>:, allowing you to specify polar or grid. You can use the Rotate option to rotate the cursor; the Ortho mode will conform to the new cursor angle. This option also allows you to specify a Snap origin, allowing you to accurately place hatch patterns. The *Snapang* system variable also lets you rotate the cursor.

NOTE   If you use the Isometric Style option, you can use the **Iso-plane** command to control the cursor orientation. Also, the **Ellipse** command allows you to draw isometric circles. You can set many of the settings in the Snap and Grid tab in the **Dsettings** dialog.

See Also   Dsettings; *System Variables:* Polaraddang, Polarang, Polarmode, Snapang, Snapbase, Snapisopair, Snapmode, Snapunit

Soldraw

See Solid Modeling

Solid

Solid creates solid-filled polygons. You determine the area by picking points in a crosswise, or "bow tie," fashion. **Solid** can be used to fill rectangular areas. Polylines or the Solid pattern in the Boundary hatch dialog are better for filling curved areas. Solids are filled only when the *Fillmode* system variable is set to On, and the view is set to Plan.

To Fill an Area

Command line: **Solid, So**

Menu: Draw ➤ Surfaces ➤ 2D Solid

Surfaces Toolbar: ▽ 2D Solid

1. **Specify first point:** Pick one corner of the area to be filled.

2. **Specify second point:** Pick the next adjacent corner of the area.

3. **Specify third point:** Pick the corner diagonal to the last point selected.

4. **Specify fourth point or <exit>:** Pick the next adjacent corner of the area, or press ↵ to create a filled triangle.

NOTE AutoCAD repeats Specify third point: and Specify fourth point: prompts to create further connected triangles and four-sided polygons as a single solid object. Continue to pick points until you have defined the area to be filled.

TIP In large drawings that contain many solids, you can reduce regeneration and redrawing times by setting the **Fill** command to Off until you are ready to plot the final drawing.

See Also Bhatch, Fill, Hatch, Pline, 3dface, Trace

Solidedit

Solidedit allows you to edit faces and edges of 3D solid objects.

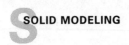

To Edit Solid Objects

Command line: **Solidedit**

Solids Editing Toolbar: 📤 Extrude Faces 📤 Move Faces 📤 Offset Faces 📤 Delete Faces 📤 Rotate Faces 📤 Taper Faces 📤 Copy Faces 📤 Color Faces 📤 Copy Edges 📤 Color Edges 📤 Imprint 📤 Clean 📤 Separate 📤 Shell 📤 Check

Solids editing automatic checking: SOLIDCHECK=1

Enter a solids editing option [Face/Edge/Body/Undo/eXit]
<eXit>: Entering an option offers additional choices to edit solid objects using one of the following selection set methods: boundary sets (picking an internal point), crossing polygon, crossing window, fence, selecting individual faces, or edges.

Options

Face Displays the prompt Enter a face editing option [Extrude/ Move/Rotate/Offset/Taper/Delete/Copy/coLor/Undo/eXit] <eXit>:, allowing you to choose a method for editing 3D solid faces.

Edge Displays the prompt Enter an edge editing option [Copy/ coLor/Undo/eXit] <eXit>:, allowing you to edit 3D solid objects.

Body Displays prompt Enter a body editing option [Imprint/ seParate solids/Shell/cLean/Check/Undo/eXit] <eXit>:, offering options to edit entire solid objects.

Undo Undoes the last editing procedure.

Exit Ends the command.

See Also Intersect, Solid Modeling, Subtract, Union; *System Variable:* Solidcheck

Solid Modeling

A full range of solid modeling commands provide an easy method to building 3D models. Besides creating basic solids (solid primitives), you can additionally create solids from 2D objects by extruding and revolving them (swept solids) and create more complex solids out of either of these by adding and subtracting volumes and calculating interferences. Solids are native AutoCAD objects, which means that they compute faster than AME objects and generally respond to standard AutoCAD commands—for example, **Chamfer**, **Fillet**, and **Scale**.

Solid objects resemble surface objects and are created in approximately the same way. The critical difference is that the solid objects have mass, which allows measurement based upon volume. It also allows edits that change the mass by addition, subtraction, and by combination with other solid objects.

TIP The **Solids** commands that create composite objects (**Union**, **Subtract**, **Intersect**) can also be used to manipulate 2D regions.

Solid Primitives

The six solid primitives—box, cone, cylinder, sphere, torus, and wedge—are basic 3D objects, which can be used to build more complex solids.

To Draw a Box

The **Box** command creates a 3D solid box.

Command line: **Box**

Menu: Draw ➢ Solids ➢ Box

Solids Toolbar: [icon] Box

1. **Specify corner of box or [CEnter] <0,0,0,>:** Pick the first corner point, enter **C** for the center point for your box, or enter a value.

2. **Specify corner or [Cube/Length]:** Pick the second corner point, enter **C** or **L**, or enter a value. See Options below.

3. **Specify height:** Provide the box height by dynamically picking two points or entering a value.

Options

Center Creates a 3D box using a specified center point.

Cube Creates a 3D box with all sides equal.

Length Allows you to enter values for Length, Width, and Height.

To Draw a Cone

Cone offers several methods for drawing a 3D solid cone. The default is to choose a center point and then pick or enter the diameter/radius and apex.

Command line: **Cone**

Menu: Draw ➢ Solids ➢ Cone

Solids Toolbar: [icon] Cone

1. **Current wire frame density: ISOLINES=4**

    Specify center point for base of cone or [Elliptical] <0,0,0>: Pick a center point, or enter **E**.

2. **Specify radius for base of cone or [Diameter]:** Provide a Diameter or Radius (or Axis endpoint for an elliptical cone by dynamically picking or entering a value).

3. **Specify height of cone or [Apex]:** Provide an apex or height by dynamically picking the point(s) or entering a value. If you pick a point, you are asked to Specify second point:.

Options

Center   Creates a cone with a circular base.

Elliptical   Creates a cone with an elliptical base.

Apex   Specifies the apex of the cone solid.

Height   Specifies the height of the cone solid.

To Draw a Cylinder

Cylinder offers several methods for drawing a 3D solid cylinder. The default is to choose a center point, and then pick or enter the diameter/radius and apex.

Command line: **Cylinder**

Draw ➤ Solids ➤ Cylinder

Solids Toolbar: Cylinder

1. **Current wire frame density: ISOLINES=4**

    Specify center point for base of cylinder or [Elliptical] <0,0,0>: Pick a center point, or enter **E**.

2. **Specify radius for base of cylinder or [Diameter]:** Provide a Diameter or <Radius> (or an Axis endpoint for an elliptical cylinder) by dynamically picking or entering a value.

3. **Specify height of cylinder or [Center of other end]:** Provide a cylinder top or height by dynamically picking the point(s) or entering a value, or enter **C**.

Options

Center   Creates a cylinder with a circular base.

Elliptical   Creates a cylinder with an elliptical base.

Center of Other End   Specifies the top end of the cylinder.

Height   Specifies the height of the cylinder.

To Draw a Sphere

Sphere creates a 3D solid sphere with its central axis parallel to the Z axis of the current UCS. The overall dimensions of the sphere can be specified using either the radius or the diameter.

Command line: **Sphere**

Menu: Solids ➤ Sphere

Solids Toolbar:  Sphere

1. **Current wire frame density: ISOLINES=4**

   Specify center of sphere <0,0,0>: Pick a center point.

2. **Diameter/<Radius> of sphere:** Provide a diameter or radius by dynamically picking or entering a value.

Options

Radius   Specifies the overall dimension of the sphere using its radius.

Diameter   Specifies the overall dimension of the sphere using its diameter. Type **D** at step 2 to use this option.

To Draw a Torus

Torus creates a 3D donut-shaped solid. The torus is defined by specifying two radius (or diameter) values, one from the center of the torus to the center of the tube and one for the actual tube. You can create a torus with no center hole (a self-intersecting torus) by specifying the radius of the tube greater than the radius of the torus.

Command line: **Torus**, **Tor**

Menu: Draw ➤ Solids ➤ Torus

Solids Toolbar:  Torus

1. **Current wire frame density: ISOLINES=4**

   Specify center of torus <0,0,0>: Pick a center point.

2. **Specify radius of torus or [Diameter]:** Provide a diameter or radius for the torus by dynamically picking or entering a value.

3. **Specify radius of tube or [Diameter]:** Provide a diameter or radius for the tube by dynamically picking or entering a value.

Options

Radius   Specifies the overall dimension of the torus or the tube using its radius.

Diameter   Specifies the overall dimension of the torus or the tube using its diameter. Type **D** at step 2 or step 3 to use this option.

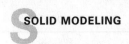

To Draw a Wedge

Wedge creates a 3D wedge-shaped solid. The base is parallel to the Z axis and the sloped face is tapered along the X axis. You may create a wedge based on the first corner point or on a specified center point.

Command line: **Wedge, We**

Menu: Draw ➤ Solids ➤ Wedge

Solids Toolbar: 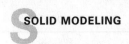 Wedge

1. **Specify first corner of wedge or [CEnter] <0,0,0>:** Specify a corner point, or type **C** and pick a center point.

2. **Specify corner or [Cube/Length]:** Pick a point for the other corner.

3. **Specify height:** Provide height by dynamically picking the point(s) or entering a value.

Options

First Corner   Creates a cylinder starting from the first corner point.

Center   Creates a wedge centered on a specified point.

Cube   Creates a cubic (equal-sided) wedge. Only one length value is required to create this type of wedge.

Length   Creates a wedge by specifying separately the length, width, and height.

To Create Swept Solids

Solid objects can also be created from 2D objects. You can draw new solids by extruding (adding height) to a 2D object along a specified path or by revolving a 2D object about an axis. For example, extruding a circle produces a cylinder, and revolving a circle about an axis produces a torus. These commands create a solid object from a common profile and are particularly useful for profiling objects that have fillets or chamfers that would otherwise be very difficult to profile.

To Create a Solid by Extruding a 2D Object

You can extrude closed objects such as circles, ellipses, closed splines and polylines, polygons, rectangles, donuts, and regions but not 3D objects, objects within a block, and polylines that self-cross, intersect, or are not closed.

Command line: **Extrude, Ext**

Menu: Draw ➤ Solids ➤ Extrude

Solids Toolbar: Extrude

1. **Current wire frame density: ISOLINES=4**

   Select Objects: Select the object(s) to extrude.

2. **Specify height of extrusion or [Path]:** Specify the height or enter **P** at the prompt Select extrusion path: and pick an object that describes the path.

3. **Specify angle of taper for extrusion <0>:** Enter a value for tapering the extruded object, if required, or press ↵.

NOTE If you wish to extrude an object that contains lines or arcs, you should first join them using the **Pedit** command to form a single polyline object or make them into a region before you extrude them. If you are extruding a polyline, it must contain at least 3 but not more than 500 vertices. If an object you have selected to extrude has width or thickness (in the case of a polyline), AutoCAD will ignore it. A thick polyline is extruded from the center of its path.

To Create a Solid by Revolving a 2D Object

Revolve works with the same kinds of objects as **Extrude**. You can revolve closed objects such as circles, ellipses, splines and polylines, polygons, rectangles, donuts, and regions but not 3D objects, objects within a block, and polylines that self-cross, intersect, or are not closed.

Command line: **Revolve**, **Rev**

Menu: Draw ➤ Solids ➤ Revolve

Solids Toolbar: 🖾 Revolve

1. **Current wire frame density: ISOLINES=4**

   Select Objects: Select the object(s) to revolve.

2. **Specify start point for axis of revolution or define axis by [Object/X (axis)/Y (axis)]:** Specify the start point and endpoint of the axis; type **X** or **Y** to specify the X axis or Y axis; or type **O**, and select an object as the axis of revolution.

3. **Specify angle of revolution <360>:** Specify the required angle of revolution, or press ↵ to accept the default (360 degrees).

To Create Composite Solids

Complex solids can be created from both Solid Primitives and Swept solids. Boolean operations can be used to create composite solids from two or more solids.

Options

Union Combines the volume of two or more solids (or regions) into one. Select the objects to join, and AutoCAD creates a single composite object. (See **Union**.)

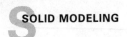

Subtract Removes the common area shared by two sets of solids (or regions). You must first select the solid(s) from which to subtract and then the solid(s) which are to be subtracted. (See **Subtract**.)

Intersect Creates a composite solid that contains only the common volume of two or more overlapping solids (or regions). It effectively joins the solids, leaving only the area where the solids intersect. (See **Intersect**.)

Interference Performs essentially the same operation as the **Intersect** command. **Interfere**, however, allows you to keep the original objects after it has created a further object based on their overlapping volumes. The original objects are kept, minus the overlapping areas. (See **Interference**.)

To Slice a Solid

Slice allows you to create a new solid or set of solids by slicing an existing solid with a plane and removing a selected side. You may choose to keep only one or both sides of the solids.

Command: **Slice**, **Sl**

Menu: Draw ➤ Solids ➤ Slice

Solids Toolbar: ▨ Slice

1. **Select objects:** Pick the required objects.

2. **Specify first point on slicing plane by [Slicing plane by [Object/Zaxis/View/XY/YZ/ZX/3points] <3points>:** Specify a point or enter an option.

3. Specify additional points at the Specify second point on plane: and Specify third point on plane: prompts.

4. **Specify a point on desired side of the plane or [keep Both sides]:** Press **[cr]** to select side to keep, or enter **B** to retain both.

> **NOTE** By default, you specify three points to define the cutting plane: the first point defines the origin of the slicing plane; the second point defines the X axis; and the third point defines the Y axis. You may also define the cutting plane using another Object, or by the current View, the Z axis, or the XY, YZ, or ZX plane.

To Create a Cross-Section of a Solid

Section allows you to create a cross-section through any solid.

Command line: **Section**, **Sec**

Menu: Draw ➤ Solids ➤ Section

Solids Toolbar: ▨ Section

1. **Select objects:** Pick the required objects.

2. Specify first point on Section plane by [Object/Zaxis/ View/XY/YZ/ZX/3points]<3points>: Specify a point, or enter an option.

3. Specify additional points at the Specify second point on plane: and Specify third point on plane: prompts.

To Convert an AME Solid Model

Ameconvert allows you to convert solid models created using the AutoDESK Advanced Modeling Extension into AutoCAD solid objects.

Command line: **Ameconvert**

Select objects: Pick the solid models you wish to convert.

> **NOTE** If the objects are not regions or solids created using AME Release 2 or 2.1, AutoCAD ignores them. Improved accuracy in the solid modeler may cause AME models to display differently, particularly filleted and chamfered objects.

To Calculate a Solid's Mass Properties

Massprop calculates and displays the mass properties of 2D and 3D objects. For solids, it provides volumetric information, such as center of gravity principal axes and moments of inertia.

Command line: **Massprop**

Menu: Tools ➤ Inquiry ➤ Mass Properties

Inquiry Toolbar: Mass Properties

1. Select objects: Pick the solid model(s) you wish to analyze. **Massprop** will display all of the properties of the object(s) on the text screen.

2. Write analysis to a file? [Yes/No] <N>: If you want the information written to a file, type **Y** and provide a filename, or press **[cr]** to return to the command prompt.

> **NOTE** The **Massprop** command can be used to list the properties of 2D regions as well as solid objects.

See Also Import/Export, Pedit, Pline, Solid, Stlout; *System Variable:* Isolines

Soldraw

Soldraw creates profiles and sections in viewports constructed exclusively from **Solview**.

SOLPROF

To Create Profiles and Sections

Command line: **Soldraw**

Menu: Draw ➤ Solids ➤ Setup ➤ Drawing

Solids Toolbar: Setup Drawing

Select viewports to draw...

Select objects: Pick one or more viewports to draw or redraw profiles and sections.

> **NOTE** AutoCAD uses visible and hidden lines that represent the silhouette and edges of solids in the viewport to create a plane perpendicular to the viewing direction. For crosshatching in sectional views, current values of the *Hpname, Hpscale,* and *Hpang* system variables are used.

Solprof

Solprof generates profile images of 3D solids in floating viewports and shows the edges and silhouettes of curved surfaces of a solid for the current view.

To Create 3DProfiles

Command: **Solprof**

Menu: Draw ➤ Solids ➤ Setup ➤ Profile

Solids Toolbar: Setup Profile

1. **Select objects:** Select object(s) in active ModelSpace viewport.

2. **Display hidden profile lines on separate layer? [Yes/No] <Y>:** Pressing **[cr]** instructs AutoCAD to create two separate unnamed profile blocks: one for visible lines and another for invisible lines. If the hidden linetype is loaded, the visible profile block is created using the Bylayer linetype and the hidden block uses the hidden linetype; otherwise, linetypes are all continuous. If you entered **N**, all profile lines are stored in a block for each solid and created as visible lines. Visible profile blocks assume the same linetype as the original solid.

3. **Project profile lines onto a plane? [Yes/No] <Y>:** Press ↵ to generate the profile lines with 2D objects. The 3D profile is projected onto a plane normal to the viewing direction, passing through the origin of the UCS. AutoCAD evaluates the 2D profile, removes lines parallel to the viewing direction, and then changes arcs and circles

viewed on edge to lines. Entering **N** creates the profile lines with 3D objects.

4. **Delete tangential edges? [Yes/No] <Y>:** Press **[cr]** to retain tangential edges, or enter **N** to have them removed.

TABLE S.1:   Layer Name and Object Types

Layer Name	Object type
Pv-viewport handle	Visible profile layer
Ph-viewport handle	Hidden profile layer

Solview

Solview uses orthographic projection with floating PaperSpace viewports to lay out multi- and sectional-view drawings of 3D solid and body objects, saving view-specific information during creation. The data collected is then used by **Soldraw** for final generation of the drawing view.

To Set Up Multi- and Sectional-Views

Command line: **Solview**

Menu: Draw ➤ Solids ➤ Setup ➤ View

Solids Toolbar: ▣ Setup View

Enter an option [Ucs/Ortho/Auxiliary/Section]: Press **[cr]**, or enter an option.

Options

UCS   Press **[cr]**, or enter a suboption at the Enter an option [Named/World/?/Current] <Current>: prompt.

Name   Lets you Enter name of UCS to restore: and then Enter view scale <1.0>: to emulate PaperSpace-scaled viewports. Prompts then appear to specify a point for the Specify view center:, to Specify first corner of viewport: and Specify opposite corner of viewport:, and then to a Enter view name:.

World   Prompts are similar to Name; the profile view created uses the XY plane of the WCS.

?   Press **[cr]**, or use wildcard combinations at the Enter UCS names to list <*>: prompt for names of existing user coordinate systems.

Current   Prompts are similar to Name; the profile view created uses the XY plane of the current UCS.

Ortho Select a viewport edge at the `Specify side of viewport to project:` prompt, and then specify information as described for Name above to generate a folded orthographic view from an existing view.

Auxiliary Specify points in the same viewport to obtain the auxiliary view's `Inclined plane's 1st point:` and `Inclined plane's 2nd point:`. Then select a point for the "side to view." A rubber-band line perpendicular to the inclined plane appears for you to pick a "view center." The next prompt sequences are the same as Name above.

Section Use the original viewport and specify two points at the `Specify first point of cutting plane:` and `Specify second point of cutting plane:` prompts to define the sectioning plane. Then define the viewing side by specifying a point on one side of the cutting plane by picking a point at the `Specify side to view from:` prompt. The remaining prompt sequences are the same as Name above.

NOTE AutoCAD appends layer names Vis, Hid, and Hat to your defined view names as shown in Table S.1.

TABLE S.2: Layer and Object Name Conventions

Layer Name	Object Type
View name-Vis	Visible lines
View name-Hid	Hidden lines
View name-Dim	Dimensions
View name-Hat	Hatch patterns (for sections)

WARNING These layer names are reserved for **Soldview**; AutoCAD automatically purges the information stored on these layers when you use **Soldraw**.

Spell

Spell checks the spelling of text in your drawing, including dimension text. You may select between several different dictionaries, which are available in different languages. You can customize any of the main dictionaries to include words that you commonly use.

To Check Spelling

Command line: **Spell**

Menu: Tools ➤ Spelling

Standard Toolbar: Spelling

1. Select the objects you want to check, or type **all** to select all text objects.

2. If a misspelled word is found, the Check Spelling dialog identifies the misspelled word.

3. Choose one of the options offered.

Options

Current Dictionary Identifies name of current dictionary.

Current Word Displays misspelled word being checked.

Suggestions List box shows replacement word.

Ignore Leaves a flagged word unchanged.

Ignore All Does not flag further instances of the word.

Change Allows you to select a word from the Suggestions list box or type in the correct spelling.

Change All Changes all instances of the flagged word without further prompting.

Add Leaves the flagged word unchanged, and adds it to a custom dictionary. This button is not selectable if you are using a standard dictionary.

Lookup Checks the spelling of a word in the Suggestions list box.

Change Dictionaries Opens the Change Dictionaries subdialog and allows you to change language-specific dictionaries during a spell check. Click the Main dictionary drop-down box for alternates. Enter a drive, directory, and dictionary name in an edit box, or use the Browse... button to replace the current custom dictionary. Use the Add or Delete buttons to append or remove custom dictionary words to the dictionary.

Custom Dictionary Enter a drive, directory, and dictionary name in an edit box, or use the Browse... button to replace the current custom dictionary. Use the Add or Delete buttons to append or remove custom dictionary words to the dictionary.

Apply & Close Accepts Current Selection, and Exits the Change Dictionaries Subdialog. Context Displays selected sentence or phrase of word being checked.

Cancel Exits the Check Spelling dialog.

TIP To create a new dictionary, select the Change Dictionaries button, and enter the new dictionary name, using `.cus` as a file extension.

See Also *System Variables:* Dctcust, Dctmain

Sphere

See **Solid Modeling**

Spline

Spline fits a smooth curve to a set of points within a defined tolerance. The particular kind of spline created by AutoCAD is a NURBS (nonuniform rational B-spline) curve. Splines can be used to produce irregularly shaped curves for mapping.

To Draw a Spline

Command line: **Spline**, **Spl**

Menu: Draw ➤ Spline

Draw Toolbar: ◠ Spline

1. **Specify first point or [Object]:** Specify a point, or enter **O** for objects to convert to splines.

2. Continue to enter points until you have defined the spline curve. After the second or next point, you will be prompted to Specify next point or [Close/Fit tolerance] <start tangent>:. Enter **C** to close the spline, **F** to change the tolerance, or continue to enter points.

3. When you have added all of the required spline segments, press ↵.

4. **Specify start tangent:** If desired, specify the tangency of the spline, or press ↵.

5. **Specify end tangent:** Pick a point, or press ↵ to terminate the spline.

Options

Object   This option allows you to convert 2D or 3D spline-fit polylines to corresponding splines. In step 2 above, type **O**, and then select the polyline objects you wish to convert. If the *Delobj* system variable is set to zero, the original polylines will be deleted.

Close   Closes the spline curve so that the last point coincides with the first point and is tangent to the joint.

Fit Tolerance   Changes the tolerance for fitting the spline curve. Tolerance defines how closely the spline fits the set of points you specify. A lower tolerance produces a closer fit to the specified points. When you adjust the tolerance, the current spline curve is redrawn so that it still fits the specified points but is adjusted per the new tolerance.

Tangent Redefines the spline start- and endpoint tangents. You may do this dynamically by picking a point, or enter **Tan** or **Perp**. Using these object snaps, you may make the spline tangent or perpendicular to existing objects. The spline is redrawn through the defined points.

> **NOTE** Once you have created a spline object, you can manipulate it easily using **Grips**. The spline retains the smoothness of the curves no matter where you position the grips.

See Also Ddgrips, Polyline, Splinedit, *System Variable:* Delobj

---

Splinedit

Splinedit allows you to edit spline objects. You can add or delete fit points and control points, remove fit points or control vertices, open or close a spline, change the fit tolerance, and edit the start and end fit point tangents.

To Edit a Spline

Command line: **Splinedit**, **Spe**

Menu: Modify ➤ Object➤ Spline

Modify II Toolbar: Edit Spline

1. **Select Spline:** Select a spline. Grips appear on the control points and also on fit data points, if they have not been purged.

2. **Enter an option [Fit data/Close/Move vertex/Refine/ rEverse/Undo]:** Enter an option, and then press **[cr]**.

Options

Fit Data Displays the prompt the `Enter a fit data option [Add/ Close/Delete/Move/Purge/Tangents/toLerance/eXit] <eXit>:` to edit the spline fit data. Fit data includes all fit points' fit tolerance and all tangents associated with the spline. If a spline has no fit data, the Fit Data option does not appear in the prompt. Type **F** to edit fit data. To add a fit point, type **A** at the next prompt, and then select an existing fit point (grip). The grips for this point and the next point are highlighted with a rubber-banding line. Enter a new point. AutoCAD interpolates the new point between the two highlighted points and refits the spline curve. To delete a fit point, type **D**, and then select the point(s) you wish to delete. The spline is redrawn to fit the remaining fit points. To move fit points to a new position, type **M** to display the `Specify new location or [Next/ Previous/Select Point/eXit/] <N>:` prompt, and then type **N** (Next) or **P** (Previous) to move sequentially along the fit points until you reach the desired point. You can also type **S** (Select Point) and pick a specific point, pick a new point, or enter a coordinate to relocate the fit point. To Purge the fit data from the drawing, type **P**. To change the start or end tangent of the spline, type **T**, and then specify a new point, or type **S** to accept the System Defaults. Type **X** to return to the main prompt.

Close   Closes an open spline and creates a smooth curve through the start/endpoint. Type **C** and select the spline to close it. A spline may have the same start- and endpoint and still be an open spline. It will, however, lack the smoothness (tangent continuity) of a closed spline.

Open   Opens a closed spline.

Move Vertex   Moves the control points on the spline. When you select this option, the start point of the spline is highlighted. Type **N** (Next) or **P** (Previous) to move sequentially along the control vertices until you reach the desired point, or type **S** (Select Point), and pick a specific vertex. Pick a new point or enter a coordinate to relocate the control point. Type **X** to return to the main prompt.

Refine   Increases the accuracy of a spline's definition. You may increase the number of points on a given portion or across the whole spline or manipulate the distance between the spline and the control points. The Add Control Point option allows you to increase the number of control points by picking them directly. The Elevate Order option allows you to increase the number of control points on the spline by a specified order of magnitude (up to 26). The Weight option allows you to assign a greater "weight" to any selected control point. Selecting a point will pull the spline more to that point.

Reverse   Reverses the direction of the spline.

Undo   Cancels the last edit performed using the Splinedit mode.

Exit   Exits the current Splinedit mode.

NOTE   A spline can lose its fit data if it is purged or refined. It may also lose its fit data if you fit the spline to a tolerance and then move its control vertices or open or close the spline.

See Also   Pedit, Pline, Spline

Standard File Selection Dialog

The same Standard File Selection features appear in many dialogs to help you locate directories and files. Some of these options are described below.

Options

Up One Level   Automatically ascends you one level of the current path tree.

Create New Folder   Makes a new folder in the current path.

List   Views filenames in a list box in columnar format.

Details   Views filenames, sizes, types, dates, and attributes in a single-column format.

Search the Web   Opens the Browse the Web dialog to view and store AutoCAD files on the Internet.

Lookin Favorites   Provides quick access to the Look In path to your system's Favorites folder.

Add to Favorites   Creates a shortcut to the selected file or folder, and appends it to your system's Favorites folder.

Preview   Displays a preview image of a file.

Find File   Opens the Browse/Search dialog, offering advanced search options.

Locate   Lets you locate a file entered in the *File Name* edit box based on paths set in Files tab of the Options dialog.

Options...   Opens the Options dialog to set controls.

See Also   Open, Options, Xref

Status

Status displays the current settings of a drawing, including the drawing limits and the status of all drawing modes. It also displays the current memory usage.

To Display Current Drawing Settings

Command line: **Status**

Menu: Tools ➤ Inquiry ➤ Status

Returns the following information:

- Model- or PaperSpace limits
- Model- or PaperSpace uses
- Display shows
- Insertion base is
- Snap resolution is
- Grid spacing is
- Current space
- Current layer
- Current color

- Current linetype
- Current plot style
- Current elevation
- Thickness
- Fill, Grid, Ortho, Qtext, Snap, Tablet
- Object Snap modes
- Free .dwg disk space
- Free physical memory
- Free swap file space

 NOTE AutoCAD uses many defaults and modes. They are all displayed using the **Status** command. All measurements are shown in the standard units specified for the drawing.

 NOTE ModelSpace limits and ModelSpace uses change to PaperSpace limits and PaperSpace uses when you are in the PaperSpace mode.

See Also Layer, Time

Stlout
*See **Import/Export***

Stretch

Stretch moves vertices of objects while maintaining the continuity of connected lines.

To Stretch an Object

Command line: **Stretch**, **S**

Menu: Modify ➤ Stretch

Modify Toolbar: [icon] Stretch

1. Select objects to stretch by crossing window or crossing polygon:

   - Enter **W** (Window) to select objects that lie entirely within a specified window. This option will move the entire object.

   - Enter **C** (Crossing window) to select objects that lie wholly or partially within a specified window.

- Enter **CP** (Crossing polygon) to select only objects that lie wholly or partly with a user-specified polygon.

2. **Select objects:** Enter **R** to remove objects from the set of selected objects, or press ↵ to confirm your selection.

3. **Specify base point or displacement:** Pick the base reference point for the stretch.

4. **Specify second point of displacement:** Pick the second point in relation to the base point, indicating the distance and direction you wish to move.

You can work with grips by selecting objects and selecting the **Stretch** command. AutoCAD will display the object with grips and, after you issue the command, will show the following prompt:

```
** STRETCH **
Specify stretch point or [Base point/Copy/Undo/eXit]:
```

You cannot stretch blocks or text. If the insertion point of a block or text is included in a crossing window, the entire block will be moved.

See Also   Copy, Ddgrips, Grips, Mirror, Move, Rotate, Scale

Style

Style and **St** both open the Text Styles dialog, allowing you to create new text styles and modify existing styles for the **Text**, **Dtext**, and **Mtext** commands. Use **-Style** to display all prompts at the command line.

To Create or Modify a Text Style

Command line: **Style**, **St** (or **'Style** to use transparently)

Menu: Format ➤ Text Style...

Options

Style Name   The Style Name section contains pick buttons to open a dialog to allow you to create New... text styles, Rename... exiting styles, and Delete unused styles. Click the list box to locate and set a text style as current.

New   Opens the New Text Style dialog. New styles appear in the *Style Name* edit box with an editable sequentially numbered default names, such as Style1, Style2, and so forth.

Rename   Opens the Rename Text Style dialog, displaying the name of the text style that appears in the pop-up list. Enter a new name.

Delete   Click the button to delete the unused style's name appearing in the list box.

Font Name   The Font Name section contains pop-up boxes to create a font name and font style, set text height or use big fonts.

> **Font Name:**   Pick a font file from the Font Name list box. The list box contains the font family name for all registered TrueType fonts and all AutoCAD compiled shape (.shx) fonts stored in the AutoCAD Fonts directory. You can define multiple styles for the same font.

> **Font Style:**   Depending on the font selected, the Font Style list box and Use Big Font checkbox ungrays. Font styles define the available font character formats, such as italic, bold, regular, light, and medium for the selected font.

> **Use Big Fonts:**   Check this box to specify an Asian language Big Font file. Fonts with the extension .shx are valid file types for creating Big Fonts.

> **Height:**   Use the *Height* edit box to set a fixed height for the style. Setting the height at 0 prompts for the text height each time you enter text using that style. A 0 height will also make changes in *dimscale* take effect on dimension text.

Effects   The Effects section has checkboxes to toggle font settings for Backwards, Upside Down, and Vertical, and edit boxes to set the text style's Width Factor and Obliquing Angle.

Preview   The Preview section contains an image tile box to view the text style. You can modify the sample text displayed by picking the box below the character preview image and editing its contents. Clicking the Preview button updates the image tile box.

Apply   Applies any text changes to the style listed in the Style Name pop-up list.

Close   Cancel is replaced by Close after a modification is made to any of the options under Style Name, and it is applied to the text style.

See Also   Change, Ddedit, Dtext, Layer, Mtext, Properties, Qtext, Rename, -Style, Text; *System Variables:* Textfill, Textqlty, Textsize, Textstyle

-Style

-Style allows you to create a text style by specifying the AutoCAD font on which it is based, its height, its width factor, and the obliquing angle. You can change a font to be backward, upside-down, or vertical. You can also use Style to modify an existing text style.

To Create a Text Style

Command line: **-Style**

1. **Enter name of text style or [?] <current style>:** Enter a style name or a question mark to display a list of styles that have been defined in the drawing. Wildcards are accepted.

2. **Existing style.**

   Specify full font name or font filename (TTF or SHX): **<txt>:** Enter a font filename, or press **[cr]** to accept the default.

3. **Specify height of text <default height>:** Enter the desired height, or press ⏎ to accept the default.

4. **Specify width factor <default width factor>:** Enter the desired width factor, or press ⏎.

5. **Specify obliquing angle <default angle>:** Enter the desired width obliquing angle, or press ⏎.

6. **Display text backwards? [Yes/No] <N>:** Enter **Y** if you want the text to read backward, or press ⏎ to accept **N**, the default.

7. **Display text upside-down? [Yes/No] <N>:** Enter **Y** if you want the text to read upside-down, or press ⏎ to accept **N**, the default.

8. **Vertical? <N>:** Enter **Y** if you want the text to read vertically, or press **[cr]** to accept **N**, the default.

Options

Text Style Name Enter either a new name to define a new style or the name of an existing style to redefine the style.

Font File Choose from several fonts, including a TrueType font or `.shx` files. In Windows you can select from a set of predefined fonts by picking Find File from the Select Font File dialog to open Browse/Search dialogs.

Height Determines a fixed height for the style being defined. A value of 0 allows you to determine text height as it is entered.

Width Factor Makes the style appear expanded or compressed.

Obliquing Angle Allows you to "italicize" the style.

Backwards Makes the style appear backward.

Upside Down Makse the style appear upside-down.

Vertical Makes the style appear vertical.

NOTE If you modify a style's font, text previously entered in that style is updated to reflect the modification. If any other style option is modified, previously entered text is not affected. Once you use the **Style** command, the style created or modified becomes the new current style.

NOTE A 0 value at the Height: prompt causes AutoCAD to prompt you for a text height whenever you use this style with the **Dtext** or **Text** commands. At the Width factor: prompt, a value of 1 generates normal text. A greater value expands the style; a smaller value compresses it. At the Obliquing angle: prompt, a value of 0 generates normal text. A greater value slants the style to the right, creating italics. A negative value slants the style to the left.

See Also   Change, Ddedit, Dtext, Qtext, Style, Text, Wildcards

StylesManager

Stylesmanager opens the Plot Styles operating system window to add plot style tables.

To Use StylesManager

Command line: **Stylesmanager**

Double-click the Add-a-Plot-Style-Table Wizard to add plot style tables or right-click on a plot style table (STB or CTB file) to initialize the Plot Style Table Editor.

See Also   Pagesetup, Plot, Plotstyle, Plottermanager, Psetupin

Subtract

Subtract allows you to remove the common area shared by two sets of solids (or regions) and create a new composite region or solid. You must first select the object(s) from which to subtract and then the object(s) that are to be subtracted.

To Subtract Solids or Regions

Command line: **Subtract**, **Su**

Menu: Modify ➤ Solids Editing ➤ Subtract

Solids Editing Toolbar: Subtract

1. **Select solids and regions to subtract from:** Click the overlapping solid(s) or region(s) that will form the basis of the new object.
2. **Select solids and regions to subtract:** Click the objects you wish to subtract.

   AutoCAD removes all of the objects selected in step 2 above.

NOTE Subtract can be used only for regions or solids. In steps 1 and 2 above, you may select both regions and solids at the same time, and you may select objects from any number of planes. Auto-CAD will group the selection set into subsets by region/solid and by plane before subtracting the common areas and creating the new object.

See Also Intersect, Subtract, Union

System Variables/Setvar

The system variables control AutoCAD's many settings. Many of the settings controlled by the system variables can be adjusted by the user. At the command prompt, type the name of the system variable you wish to manipulate.

To Adjust System Variables

Command line: **Setvar**, **Set** (or '**Setvar** to use transparently)

Menu: Tools ➤ Inquiry ➤ Set Variables

You may use the **Setvar** command to list. You can also enter **Setvar** and then the system variable.

Enter variable name or [?]: Enter the desired system variable name, a question mark for a list of variables, or the appropriate integer value or decimal value. (Values are usually numeric, but in some cases, you may also use Off and On in place of 0 and 1 values.)

Options

Table S.3 lists all of the system variables. They fall into two categories: adjustable variables and Read Only variables. Read Only system variables such as *Dwgname* cannot be directly modified by the user but are modified by AutoCAD program. Each adjustable variable has a specific set of values. The meaning of that value depends on the nature of the variable.

TABLE S.3: System Variables

Variable	Description
Acadprefix	Read Only. Displays the name(s) of the directory path or paths saved in the DOS environment variable *Acad*, using the DOS command **Set**.
Acadver	Read Only. Displays the AutoCAD version number.

TABLE S.3: System Variables (continued)

Variable	Description
Acisoutver	Controls the ACIS version of `.sat` files created using the **Acisout** command. Only supports a value of 16 for ACIS version 1.6.
Aflags	Controls the Attribute mode settings: 0 = no mode, 1 = invisible, 2 = constant, 4 = verify, 8 = preset. For more than one setting, use the sum of the desired settings. Default = 0. See **Attdef**.
Angbase	Controls the direction of the 0 angle. Can also be set with the **Units** command. Default = 0.
Angdir	Controls the positive direction of angles: 0 = counterclockwise, 1 = clockwise. Can also be set with the **Units** command. Default = 0.
Apbox	Controls the AutoSnap aperture box: 0 = not displayed, 1 = displayed. Default = 1. See **Options**.
Aperture	Controls the Osnap cursor target height in pixels. Can also be set with the **Aperture** command. Default = 0.
Area	Read Only. Displays the last area computed when invoked using **Setvar**. See **Area**, **List**, **Dblist** commands.
Attdia	Controls the attribute dialog for the **Insert** command: 0 = no dialog, 1 = dialog. Default = 1.
Attmode	Controls the Attribute Display mode: 0 = off, 1 = normal, 2 = on. Can also be set with the **Attdisp** command. Default = 1.
Attreq	Controls the prompt for attributes. 0 = no prompt or dialog for attributes. Attributes use default values. 1 = normal prompt or dialog upon attribute insertion. Can also be set with the **Units** command. Default = 1.
Auditctl	Controls the creation of Audit log (`.adt`) files. 0 = create, 1 = do not create. See **Audit**. Default = 0.
Aunits	Controls angular units: 0 = decimal degrees, 1 = degrees-minutes-seconds, 2 = grads, 3 = radians, 4 = surveyors' units. Default = 0. See **Units**.
Auprec	Controls the precision of angular units determined by decimal place. Can also be set with the **Units** command. Default = 0.
Autosnap	Controls the display of the AutoSnap marker and SnapTip, and turns the AutoSnap magnet on or off: 0 = turns off the marker, SnapTip, and magnet; 1 = turns on the marker, 2 = turns on the SnapTip, 4 = turns on the magnet, Bit values are additive, Default = 7. See **Options**.

TABLE S.3: System Variables (continued)

Variable	Description
Backz	Read Only. Displays the distance from the Dview target to the back-clipping plane. See **Dview**.
Bindtype	Controls binding method for Xrefs or editing Xrefs in-place: 0 = binding displays "xref1|one" as "xref0one"; 1 = binding similar to insert and displays "xref1|one" as "one". Default = 0. See **Xbind**, **Xref**.
Blipmode	Controls the appearance of blips: 0 = off, 1 = on. Default = 0. See **Blipmode**.
Cdate	Read Only. Displays calendar date/time read from DOS. See **Time**.
Cecolor	Displays/sets current object color. See **Color**.
Celtscale	Displays/sets current global linetype scale for objects. See **Linetype**, **Ltscale**. Default = 1.
Celtype	Displays/sets current object linetype. See **Linetype**.
Celweight	Controls an objects lineweight: -1 = Bylayer, -2 = Byblock. Value range varies from 0–200 but must be entered in millimeters. Default = -1. See **Lineweight**.
Chamfera	Displays/sets first chamfer distance. See **Chamfer**. Default = .5.
Chamferb	Displays/sets second chamfer distance. See **Chamfer**. Default = .5.
Chamferc	Displays/sets third chamfer distance. See **Chamfer**. Default = 1.
Chamferd	Displays/sets fourth chamfer distance. See **Chamfer**. Default = 0.
Chammode	Chamfer method. 0 = two distances, 1 = one distance plus angle. Default = 0. See **Chamfer**.
Circlerad	Sets a default value for circle radius. Enter 0 for no default. Default = 0. See **Circle**.
Clayer	Displays/sets current layer. See **Layer**. Default = 0.
Cmdactive	Read Only. Shows status of commands, scripts, and dialogs: 1 = ordinary command is active, 2 = ordinary and transparent commands are active, 4 = script is active, 8 = dialog is active. If more than one setting is active, the variable shows the active sum. Default = 1.
Cmddia	Controls dialog for **Plot** command for pre-R2000: 1 = use dialog, 0 = use command-line prompts. Default = 1.

TABLE S.3: System Variables (continued)

Variable	Description
Cmdecho	Used with AutoLISP to control what is displayed on the prompt line. 0 = not echoed to screen, 1 = echoed. Default = 1.
Cmdnames	Read Only. Displays in English current active command name, including transparent command.
Cmljust	Multiline object justification. 0 = top, 1 = middle, 2 = bottom. Default = 0. See **Mline**.
Cmlscale	Scales the width of a multiline object. 0 = single line, < 0 reverses line sequence. Default = 1. See **Mline**.
Cmlstyle	Displays/sets the multiline object style name. Default = standard. See **Mline**.
Compass	Controls 3D compass in current viewport: 0 = off, 1 = on. Default = 0. See **3Dorbit**.
Coords	Controls coordinate readout: 0 = coordinates are displayed only when points are picked, 1 = absolute coordinates are dynamically displayed as cursor moves, 2 = distance and angle are displayed during commands that accept relative distance input. Also controlled by the F6 function key. Default = 1.
Cprofile	Read Only. Specifies name of current profile. See **Options**.
Ctab	Current (model or layout) tab name. Default = model. See **Layout**.
Cursorsize	Sets crosshair size as percent of screen size. Default = 5. See **Options**.
Cvport	Shows/sets ID number for current viewport. Default = 2. See **Viewports**.
Date	Read Only. Displays Julian date/time. See **Time**.
Dbmod	Read Only. Identifies drawing database modification status: 0 = drawing database not modified, 1 = entity database modified, 2 = symbol table modified, 4 = database variable modified, 8 = window modified, 16 = view modified.
Dctcust	Displays/sets custom spelling dictionary (.dct). See **Spell**.
Dctmain	Displays/sets main spelling dictionary (.dct). See **Spell**.
Deflplstyle	Read Only. Stores default plot style name for new layers.
Defplstyle	Read Only. Stores default plot style name for new objects.

TABLE S.3: System Variables (continued)

Variable	Description
Delobj	Controls retention of polyline when coverting spline fit polylines to the new spline objects. 0 = delete, 1 = retain. Default = 1. See **Region**.
Demandload	Controls loading of third party applications. 0 = off, 1 = loads source application when opening with custom objects, 2 = loads source application when **Source** command is used, 3 = includes 1+2. Default = 3.
Diastat	Read Only. Dialog box exit method: 0 = via Cancel, 1 = via OK.
Dispsilh	Controls display of silhouette curves in 3D objects. 0 = on, 1 = off. Default = 0.
Distance	Read Only. Displays last distance read using **Dist**. See **Dist**.
Donutid	Sets inside diameter default value for **Donut** command. Default = .5.
Donutod	Sets outside diameter default value for **Donut** command. Default = 1.
Dragmode	Controls dragging: 0 = no dragging, 1 = on if requested, 2 = automatic drag. Deafult = 2. See **Dragmode**.
Dragp1	Controls regen-drag input sampling rate. Default = 10.
Dragp2	Controls fast-drag input sampling rate. Higher values force the display of more of the dragged image during cursor movement, and lower values display less. Default = 25.
Dwgcheck	Controls Model tab display list: 0 = save for current tab only, 1 = always saved. Default = 0. See **Dwgprops**.
Dwgcodepage	Read Only. Current drawing code page. See **Syscodepage** (System Variable).
Dwgname	Read Only. Displays drawing name. See **Status**.
Dwgprefix	Read Only. Displays drive and directory prefix or path for the current drawing file.
Dwgtitled	Read Only. Drawing name status: 0 = drawing is unnamed, 1 = drawing is named.
Edgemode	Controls definition of boundary edge for **Trim** and **Extend**. 0 = as selected, 1 = extend selected edge to apparent intersection. Default = 0.
Elevation	Controls current 3D elevation. Default = 0. See **Elev**.
Errno	Displays/sets code for errors from AutoLISP and ADS applications. Default = 0.

TABLE S.3: System Variables (continued)

Variable	Description
Expert	Controls prompts, depending on level of user's expertise. 0 issues normal prompts, 1 = suppresses the About to Regen: and Really want to turn the current layer off? prompts and the Verify Regenauto OFF setting, 2 = suppresses previous prompts plus Block already defined...Redefine it? (see **Block**, **Bmake**) and A drawing with this name already exists (see **Save**, **Wblock**), 3 = suppresses previous prompts plus Linetype warnings (see **Linetype**), 4 = suppresses previous prompts plus **UCS** and **Vports** Save warnings, 5 = suppresses previous prompts plus DIM Save and DIM Override warnings (see **Dimstyle**). Default = 0.
Explmode	Controls exploding of nonuniformly scaled blocks. 0 = explode, 1 = do not explode. Default = 1. See **Explode**.
Extmax	Read Only. Displays upper right corner coordinate of drawing extent. See **Zoom**.
Extmin	Read Only. Displays lower left corner coordinate of drawing extent. See **Zoom**.
Extnames	Controls settings for nongraphical object names (such as linetypes and layers) stored in symbol tables: 0 = applies R14 standards (max. characters is 31), 1= applies R15 standards (max. characters is 255). Default = 1. See **Options**.
Facetratio	Sets faceting aspect ratio for cylindrical and conic ACIS solids: 0 = creates an N by 1 mesh, 1 = creates an N by M mesh. Default = 0.
Facetres	Control resolution of 3D objects. Values are 0.01 to 10.0. Default = .5.
Filedia	Controls use of dialogs. 0 = off unless requested by ~ (tilde), 1 = on. Default = 0.
Fillmode	Controls fill status: 0 = off, 1 = on. Default = 1. See **Fill**.
Filletrad	Stores the current fillet radius. Default = 0.5000. See **Fillet**.
Fontalt	Defines alternate font to be used when font specified in drawing is not found. Default = simplex.shx. See **Options**.
Fontmap	Defines location of substitute fonts to be used in place of fonts defined in drawing. Default = acad.pmp. See **Options**.

TABLE S.3: System Variables (continued)

Variable	Description
Frontz	Read Only. Displays the distance from the Dview target to the front clipping plane. See **Dview**.
Fullopen	Read Only. Enables partial open of drawings enabled by AutoLISP. See **Partialopen**.
Gridmode	Controls grid: 0 = off, 1 = on. Default = 0. See **Grid**.
Gridunit	Controls grid spacing. Default = 0.5000,0.5000. See **Grid**.
Gripblock	Sets the appearance of grips in blocks: 0 = grip appears at block insertion only (default value), 1 = grips assigned to all entities within blocks. Default = 1. See **Options**.
Gripcolor	Sets color for nonselected grips. Default = 5. See **Options**.
Griphot	Sets color for selected grip. Default = 1. See **Options**.
Grips	Displays grips for **Stretch**, **Move**, **Rotate**, **Scale**, and **Mirror**: 0 = grips off, 1 = grips on. Default = 1. See **Grips**.
Gripsize	Sets grip box size. Default = 3. See **Grips**, **Options**.
Handles	Read Only. Displays Handles status.
Hideprecision	Controls hide and shade precision: 0 = single (less memory), 1 = double. Default = 0. See **Hide**, **Shade**.
Highlight	Controls object-selection ghosting: 0 = no ghosting, 1 = ghosting. Default = 1.
Hpang	Sets default hatch pattern angle. Default = 0. See **Bhatch**, **Hatch**.
Hpbound	Sets object type created by **Hatch** and **Boundary**. 0 = region, 1 = polyline. Default = 1.
Hpdouble	Sets default double hatch for user-defined pattern: 0 = single hatch, 1 = double hatch. Default = 1. See **Bhatch**, **Hatch**.
Hpname	Sets default hatch pattern name and style. Default = ANSI31. See **Bhatch**, **Hatch**.
Hpscale	Sets default hatch pattern scale. Default = 1. See **Bhatch**, **Hatch**.
Hpspace	Sets default line spacing for user-defined hatch pattern. Default = 1. See **Bhatch**, **Hatch**.
Hyperlinkbase	Defines path for hyperlinks. Dot (.) = current drawing path. See **Hyperlink**.

TABLE S.3: System Variables (continued)

Variable	Description
Imagehlt	Controls raster-image highlighting: 0 = frame, 1 = entire raster image. Default = 0. See **Options**.
Indexctl	Controls layer and spatial indexes in drawing files: 0 = no indexes created; 1 = layer index created; 2 = spatial index created; 4 = layer and spatial indexes created. Default = 0. See **Partiaload**.
Inetlocation	Stores the Internet location used by the **Browser** command. Default value: www.autodesk.com/acaduser.
Insunitsdefsource	Sets value for source content units. Range limits are 0–20. See **Options**, **Units**.
Insunitsdeftarget	Sets target drawing units. Range limits are 0–20. See **Options**, **Units**.
Insunits	Stores value of drawing units for block insertions. Limits range from 0 to 20. Default = 1. See **Options**.
Isavebak	Improves speed of incremental saves: 0 = no .bak is created (even for a full save), 1 = created .bak. Default = 1. See **Options**, **Status**.
Isavepercent	Controls tolerance for wasted space in a drawing file. Values = 0 to 100. Default = 50. See **Options**.
Insbase	Controls insertion base point of current drawing. Default = 0,0,0. See **Base**.
Insname	Default block name for **Insert** command.
Isolines	Sets number of lines displayed per surface on solids. Values = 0 to 2047. Default = 4. See **Options**.
Lastangle	Read Only. Displays the end angle of last arc or poly arc.
Lastpoint	Displays coordinates of last point entered. Same point referenced by at sign (**@**). Default = 0,0,0.
Lastprompt	Read Only. Stores the last command line entry.
Lenslength	Read Only. Displays the current lens focal length used during the **Dview** command Zoom option.
Limcheck	Controls limit checking: 0 = no checking, 1 = checking. Default = 0. See **Limits**.
Limmax	Stores the coordinate of drawing's upper right limit. Default = 12, 9. See **Limits**.
Limmin	Stores the coordinate of drawing's lower left limit. Default = 0,0. See **Limits**.

TABLE S.3: System Variables (continued)

Variable	Description
Lispinit	Controls loading of AutoLISP-defined functions and variables: 0 = saved in AutoCAD session, from drawing to drawing; 1 = saved in current drawing only. Default = 0. See **Options**.
Locale	Read Only. Displays ISO language code of the version of AutoCAD.
Logfilemode	Sets log file on and off; 0 = file not created, 1 = file is created. Default = 0.
Logfilename	Read Only. Saves path for the log file.
Logfilepath	Stores drawings log file path in a session. Dot (.) = none
Loginname	Read Only. Displays user's login name set during configuration.
Ltscale	Global line type scale factor. Default = 1. See **Psltscale**, **Celtscale**.
Lunits	Controls unit styles: 1 = scientific, 2 = decimal, 3 = engineering, 4 = architectural, 5 = fractional. Default = 2. See **Units**.
Luprec	Stores unit accuracy by decimal place or size of denominator. Default = 4. See **Units**.
Lwdisplay	Controls lineweight display: 0 = not displayed (Off), 1 = displayed. Default = Off. See **Lineweights**.
Lwunits	Controls lineweight units: 0 = not displayed (Off), 1 = displayed. Default = Off. See **Lineweights**.
Maxactvp	Number of viewports to regenerate at one time. Range limits are 2–64. Default = 48.
Maxobjmem	Controls object pager, specifying allotment of virtual memory, and begins paging to disk into the object pager's swap files. Default = 0 (Off).
Maxsort	Sets the maximum number of symbols or filenames to be sorted by any listing command. Default = 200.
Mbuttonpan	Controls behavior of third button or wheel on pointing device: 0 = stored in AutoCAD menu (.mnu) file, 1 = panning enabled. Default = 1.
Measureinit	Sets initial drawing units: 0 = English, 1 = Metric. Default = 1. See **New**.
Measurement	Sets drawing units as English or metric for hatch patterns and linetypes for existing drawings. 0 = English, 1 = Metric. Default = 0.

TABLE S.3: System Variables (continued)

Variable	Description
Menuctl	Controls swapping of the screen menus whenever a command is entered: 0 = doesn't switch, 1 = switches. Default = 0.
Menuecho	Controls the display of commands and prompts issued from the menu. A value of 1 suppresses display of commands entered from menu (can be toggled on or off with Ctrl+P), 2 suppresses display of commands and command prompts when command is issued from AutoLISP macro, 3 is a combination of options 1 and 2, 4 disables Ctrl+P menu echo toggle, 8 enables the printing of all input and output strings to the screen for debugging Diesel macros. Default = 3.
Menuname	Read Only. Stores the current menu filename. See **Menu**.
Mirrtext	Controls text mirroring: 0 = no text mirroring, 1 = text mirroring. Default = 1. See **Text**.
Modemacro	Allows display of text or special strings like current drawing name, time, date, or specials modes at the status line. See Diesel macro language in AutoCAD Customization manual. Dot (.) = none.
Mtexted	Name of program for text editing. See **Ddedit**, **Mtext**.
Nomutt	Message display (muttering): 0 = displayed, 1 = not displayed. Default = 0.
Offsetdist	Offset default distance. Negative value = offset through point. Default = -1. See **Offset**.
Offsetgaptype	Controls gap for offset polylines: 0 = extends seg-ments, 1 = use filleted arc segment (arc radius deter-mined by size of the gap based on offset distance), 2= use chamfered line segment. Default = 0. See **Offset**.
Olehide	Controls display of OLE objects: 0 = all objects visible, 1 = visible in Paper Space only, 2= visible in Model Space only, 3 = objects not visible. Default = 0. See **Insertobj**, **Olelinks**.
Olequality	Determines quality level for embedded OLE objects: 0 = line art (e.g. spreadsheets), 1 = text (e.g., word-processed documents), 2 = graphics (e.g., pie chart), 3 = photographic, 4 = high photographic quality. Default = 1. See **Insertobj**, **Olelinks**.
Olestartup	Controls loading of OLE source application when plot-ting: 0 = not loaded, 1 = loaded. Default = 0. See **Insertobj**, **Olelinks**.

TABLE S.3: System Variables (continued)

Variable	Description
Orthomode	Controls the Ortho mode: 0 = off, 1 = on. Default = 0. See **Ortho**.
Osmode	Sets the current default Osnap mode: 0 = none, 1 = endpoint, 2 = midpoint, 4 = center, 8 = node, 16 = quadrant, 32 = intersection, 64 = insert, 128 = perpendicular, 256 = tangent, 512 = nearest, 1024 = quick, 1028 = appint. If more than one mode is required, enter the sum of those modes. Default = 0. See **Osnap**.
Osnapcoord	Controls entry of coordinates at command line: 0 = running Object Snap settings override keyboard coordinate entry, 1 = keyboard entry overrides Object Snap settings, 2 = keyboard entry overrides Object Snap settings except in scripts. Default = 2. See **Options**.
Paperupdate	Controls display of warning dialog for Layout plotting: 0 = enabled if paper size not supported by output current device plotter, 1 = paper size set by configured paper size of plotter configuration file. Default = 0. See **Layout**.
Pdmode	Sets the display style for point object. Default = 0. See **Ddptype**, **Pdsize**, **Point**.
Pdsize	Controls the display size of the point object. Default = 0. See **Ddptype**, **Pdmode**, **Point**.
Pellipse	Controls the type of ellipse created with the ellipse command. 0 = true ellipse, 1 = polyline ellipse. Default = 0. See **Ellipse**.
Perimeter	Read Only. Displays the perimeter value currently being read by Area, List, or Dblist. See **Area**, **List**, and **Dblist**.
Pfacevmax	Read Only. Defines maximum number of vertices for mesh entity faces.
Pickadd	Controls ability to add or remove entities from a selection set using the Shift key. 0 = disabled, 1 = enabled. Default = 1. See **Select**.
Pickauto	Controls automatic windowing for `Select objects:` prompt: 0 = disabled, 1 = enabled. Default = 1. See **Options**.
Pickbox	Sets object selection target height in screen pixels. Default = 3. See **Options**.
Pickdrag	Controls how a selection window is drawn: 0 = click mouse at each corner, 1 = click mouse at one corner, hold mouse down while dragging, and then release at other corner. Default = 0. See **Options**.

TABLE S.3: System Variables (continued)

Variable	Description
Pickfirst	Lets you select first, and then use an edit/inquiry command: 0 = disabled, 1 = enabled. Default = 1. See **Options**.
Pickstyle	Sets group and associative hatch selection. 0 = none, 1 = group, 2 = associative hatch, 3 = group and associative hatch. Default = 1. See **Group**, **Options**.
Platform	Read Only. Message indicating platform in use for current AutoCAD version, such as Microsoft Windows NT 4 (x86).
Plinegen	Controls linetype pattern to adjust its appearance between vertices. 0 = linetype displays dash at vertices, 1 = linetype continuous around vertices. Default = 0. See **Pline**.
Plinetype	Sets 2D polylines optimization: 0 = not converted, old-format used; 1 = not converted, pline is optimized; 2 = older drawings converted and optimizes polylines. Default = 2. See **Pline**.
Plinewid	Default polyline width. Default = 0.
Plotid	Absolute (maintains pre-R2000 compatibility).
Plotlegacy	Controls compatibility of pre-R2000 scripts: 0 = plot scripts ignored, 1 = AutoCAD assigns plot style name per object color. Default = 0. See **Plot**.
Plotrotmode	Sets plot orientation. 0 = corner with icon aligns with paper at lower left for 0, top left for 90, top right for 180, and lower right for 270; 1 = aligns lower-left corner of effective plotting area with lower-left corner of paper; 2 = similar to 0 except X and Y origin offsets are calculated relative to rotated origin position. Default = 2.
Plotter	Absolute (maintains pre-R2000 compatibility).
Plquiet	Controls dialogs and nonfatal errors for batch plotting and scripts: 0 = displays dialogs and errors, 1 = not displayed. Default = 0. See **Batchplt**.
Polaraddang	Allows you to add a maximum of 10 user-defined polar snap angles (maximum of 25 characters, separated with semicolons (;)). Dot (.) = none. See **Dsettings**.
Polarang	Sets increment of polar angles. Default = 90. See **Dsettings**.
Polardist	Sets Snap increment when Snapstyl = 1 (Polar Snap). Default = 0.

TABLE S.3: System Variables (continued)

Variable	Description
Polarmode	Controls settings for autotracking: 0 = orthogonal alignment behavior (additional angles not applied), 1 = absolute (measures polar angles based on current UCS), 2 = relative (measures polar angles from selected object), 4 = applies polar settings to object snap tracking, 8 = turns on Polar tracking. Default = 1.
Polysides	**Polygon** command's default for number of sides; can be 3 to 1024. Default = 4.
Popups	Read Only. Displays the availability of the Advanced User Interface based on the display driver. 0 = not available, 1 = available.
Product	Read-Only. Displays product name.
Program	Read-Only. Displays program name.
Projectname	Assigns project name to drawing for search path of Xref and images.
Projmode	Sets projection mode for **Trim/Extend**. 0 = True 3D (no projection), 1 = XY plane of the current UCS, 2 = Current view plane. Dot (.) = none.
Proxygraphics	Controls images of proxy objects in drawing: 0 = displays bounding box, image not saved; 1 = image saved. Default = 1. See **Options**.
Proxynotice	Sets proxy notification: 0 = no proxy warning; 1= proxy warning displayed. Default = 1. See **Options**.
Proxyshow	Controls proxy objects: 0 =not displayed, 1 = graphic images displayed, 2 = bounding box displayed. Default = 1. See **Options**.
Psltscale	Sets linetype scale for Paper Space: 0 = regular linetype scaling, 1 = adjust all linetypes to use the current ltscale, including Xrefs, viewed from Paper Space. Default = 1.
Psprolog	Assigns a name for the prologue section in file acad.psf for **Psout** command. Dot (.) = none.
Psquality	Sets rendering quality PostScript image when imported into a drawing: 0 = disabled, >0 displays PostScript paths as outlines, >0 sets pixels per drawing unit. Default = 75. See **Render**.
Pstylemode	Read Only. Displays current drawings color dependent or named plot style mode: 0 = color dependent plot style table used, 1 = named plot style tables used. See **Plot**.

TABLE S.3: System Variables (continued)

Variable	Description
Pstylepolicy	Determines association of an object's color property with its plot style name when creating a new drawing: 0 = associated, 1 = not associated. Default = 1. See **Deflpstyle**, **Defpstyle** (variables).
Psvpscale	Controls view scale factor for all newly created viewports. 0 = scale to fit. See **Viewports**, **Vports**.
Pucsbase	Store UCS name for origin and orientation of orthographic UCS setting in Paper Space. Default = none.
Qtextmode	Controls the Quicktext mode: 0 = off, 1 = on. See **Qtext**. Default = 0.
Rasterpreview	Controls BMP preview images: 0 = off, 1 = on. Default = 1. See **Options**.
Refeditname	Read Only. Determines state of reference editing operation: 0 = not active, 1 = active.
Regenmode	Controls the Regenauto mode: 0 = off, 1 = on. See **Regenauto**. Default = 1.
Re-init	Resets I/O ports: 1 = digitizer input/output port; 4 = digitizer; 16 = `acad.pgp` file. Values are additive. Default = 0. See **Reinit**.
Rtdisplay	Controls display of raster images while performing a real-time pan and zoom: 0 = display image, 1 = display outline. Default = 1.
Savefile	Read Only. Displays current auto-save filename. See **Options**.
Savefilepath	Sets path for automatic saves. See **Options**.
Savename	Read Only. Filename assigned to the currently saved file.
Savetime	Automatic-save time interval: 0 = disabled. Default = 120 (minutes). See **Options**.
Screenboxes	Read Only. Number of boxes displayed on screen menu of graphics area.
Screenmode	Read Only. Controls graphics/text screens: 0 = text screen, 1 = graphics mode, 2 = dual screen. Values are additive.
Screensize	Read Only. Reads the size of the graphics screen in pixels.
Sdi	Sets method for single or multiple-document interface: 0 = enabled, 1 = disabled, 2 = disabled by an application that does not support multiple drawings, 3 = disabled by user and an application that does not support multiple drawings. Default = 0.

TABLE S.3:   System Variables (continued)

Variable	Description
Shadedge	Sets shading parameters: 0 = faces shaded, edges not highlighted; 1 = faces shaded with edges drawn using background color; 2 = faces unfilled with edges in entity color; 3 = faces in entity color, edges with background color. Default = 3.
Shadedif	Sets the ratio (in percent) of diffuse reflective light to ambient light. Default = 70. See **Render**.
Shortcutmenu	Controls display of shortcut menu modes: 0 = restores pre-R14 behavior by disabling Default, Edit, and Command mode shortcut menus; 1= enables default mode, 2 = enables edit mode; 4 = enables command mode whenever a command is active; 8= enables Command mode only when command options are available from the command line. Values are additive. Default = 11.
Shpname	Stores default shape name. Dot (.) = none.
Sketchinc	Sets the sketch record increment. Default = .1 See **Sketch**.
Skpoly	Controls whether the **Sketch** command uses regular lines or connected lines in a polyline. 0 = lines, 1 = polyline. Default = 1.
Snapang	Controls snap and grid angle. Default = 0. See **Snap**.
Snapbase	Controls snap, grid, and hatch pattern origin. Default = 0,0. See **Snap**.
Snapisopair	Controls isometric plane: 0 = left, 1 = top, 2 = right. Default = 0. See **Snap**.
Snapmode	Controls snap toggle: 0 = off, 1 = on. Default = 0. See **Snap**.
Snapstyl	Controls snap style: 0 = standard, 1 = isometric. Default = 0. See **Snap**.
Snaptype	Controls snap type: 0 = grid or standard, 1 = polar. Default = 0. See **Osnap**.
Snapunit	Sets snap spacing given in X and Y values. Default = .5, .5. See **Snap**.
Solidcheck	Controls solid validation: 0 = off, 1 = on. Default = 1.
Sortents	Controls entity sorting order: 0 = disabled, 1 = object selection, 2 = object snap, 4 = redraws, 8 = Mslide slide creation, 16 = regens, 32 = plotting, 64 = PostScript output. Values are additive. Default = 96.

TABLE S.3: System Variables (continued)

Variable	Description
Splframe	Controls the display of spline vertices, surface-fit 3D meshes, and invisible edges of 3Dfaces. 0 = no display of Spline vertices of invisible 3dface edges. Displays only defining mesh or surface-fit mesh. 1 = display of Spline vertices or invisible 3dface edges. Displays only surface-fit mesh. Default = 0.
Splinesegs	Controls the number of line segments used for each spline patch. Default = 8.
Splinetype	Controls the type of curved line generated by the **Pedit Spline** command. 5 = quadratic B-spline, 6 = cubic B-spline. Default = 8.
Surftab1	Controls the number of mesh control points for the **Rulesurf** and **Tabsurf** commands and the number of mesh points in the *M* direction for the **Revsurf** and **Edgesurf** commands. Default = 6.
Surftab2	Controls the number of mesh control points in the *N* direction for the **Revsurf** and **Edgesurf** commands. Default = 6.
Surftype	Controls the type of surface fitting generated by the **Pedit Smooth** command. 5 = quadratic B-spline, 6 = cubic B-spline, and 8 = Bezier surface. Default = 6.
Surfu	Controls the accuracy of the smoothed surface models in the *M* direction. Default = 6. See **Pedit**.
Surfv	Controls the accuracy of the smoothed surface models in the *N* direction. Default = 6. See **Pedit**.
Syscodepage	Read Only. Indicates system code page of acad.xmx file.
Tabmode	Sets tablet mode: 0 = disabled, 1 = enabled. Default = 0.
Target	Read Only. Displays the coordinate of the target point used in the **Dview** command.
Tdcreate	Read Only. Displays time and date of drawing creation. See **Time**.
Tdindwg	Read Only. Displays total editing time. See **Time**.
Tdupdate	Read Only. Displays time and date of last save. See **Time**.
Tdusrtimer	Read Only. Displays user-elapsed time. See **Time**.
Tempprefix	Read Only. Displays the name of the directory where temporary AutoCAD files are saved. See **Options**.

TABLE S.3: System Variables (continued)

Variable	Description
Texteval	Controls whether prompts for text and attribute input to commands are taken literally or as AutoLISP expressions. 0 = literal, 1 = text you input with left parens and exclamation points will be interpreted as AutoLISP expression. **Dtext** takes all input literally, regardless of this setting. Default = 0.
Textfill	Controls the display of TrueType fonts. 0 = outline, 1 = filled. Default = 1.
Textqlty	Controls the resolution of TrueType fonts. Values are 0 to 100. Default = 50.
Textsize	Controls default text height except for styles with an assigned fixed height. See **Dtext**, **Style**. Default = .2.
Textstyle	Sets the current text style. Default = Standard. See **Style**.
Thickness	Controls 3D thickness of objects being drawn. Default = 0. See **Elev**.
Tilemode	Toggle between Model tab and last Layout tab (Paper Space and Model Space): 0 = activates last active layout tab (Paper Space), 1 = activates Model tab . Default = 1.
Tooltips	Controls the display of ToolTips (Windows only). 0 = off, 1 = on. Default = 1.
Tracewid	Sets default trace width. Default = .05). See **Trace**.
Trackpath	Controls autotracking path methods: 0 = full screen, 1 = displayed between the Alignment point and From point to cursor location, 2 = disables polar tracking path, 3= disables polar or object snap tracking paths. Default = 0. See **Osnap**.
Treedepth	Lets you set a four-digit integer coding that ultimately affects AutoCAD's quickness for searching a database to execute commands. Changing the value of this variable forces a drawing regeneration regardless of **Regenauto** setting. Default = 3020.
Treemax	Limits memory (RAM) usage during regen operations. Default = 10000000.
Trimmode	Controls whether corner lines are trimmed during **Chamfer** and **Fillet** commands. 0 = no trim, 1 = trim. Default = 1.
Tspacefac	Stores value for multiline text line spacing distance. Default = 1.

TABLE S.3: System Variables (continued)

Variable	Description
Tspacetype	Controls type of line spacing used in multiline text: 0 = at least (based on tallest character), 1 = exactly. Default = 1.
Tstackalign	Determines vertical alignment of stacked text: 0 = bottom, 1 = center, 2 = top. Default = 1
Tstacksize	Controls percentage of stacked text fraction height relative to current text height. Range values are 1 to 127. Default = 70.
UCSaxisang	Controls default angle when rotating UCS around one of its axes using the X, Y, or Z options of the **UCS** command. Default = 90.
UCSbase	Stores name of UCS that defines the origin and orientation of orthographic UCS settings. Default = world.
UCSfollow	Controls whether changing the current UCS automatically displays the plan view of the new current UCS. 0 = displayed view does not change, 1 = automatic display of new current UCS in plan. Default = 0.
UCSicon	Controls UCS icon display: 0 = off, 1 = on, 2 = at origin and off, 3 = at origin and displayed when origin is visible. Accessed using **Setvar**. Default = 3.
UCSname	Read Only. Displays the name of the current UCS. See **UCS**.
UCSorg	Read Only. Displays the current UCS origin point. See **UCS**.
UCSortho	Controls orthographic UCS setting based on orthographic view: 0 = no change when orthographic view is restored, 1 = setting automatically restored when orthographic view is restored. Default = 1. See **UCS**.
UCSview	Determines if current UCS is saved with a named view: 0 = not saved, 1 = saved. Default = 1.
UCSvp	Controls UCS in active viewports: 0 = unlocked (reflects the UCS of the current viewport), 1 = locked (UCS stored in viewport and is independent of UCS of current viewport). Default = 1.
UCSxdir	Read Only. Displays the X direction of the current UCS. See **UCS**.
UCSydir	Read Only. Displays the Y direction of the current UCS. See **UCS**.

TABLE S.3: System Variables (continued)

Variable	Description
Undoctl	Read Only. Displays state of **Undo**: 1 = set if **Undo** enabled, 2 = set for one undo, 4 = set if Auto-group mode enabled, 8 = set if group currently active.
Undomarks	Read Only. Displays the number of undo's by Mark and Back options placed in the current drawing.
Unitmode	Sets how fractional, feet-and-inches, and surveyors' angles are displayed on the status line. 0 = normal (e.g., 1'– 6$\frac{1}{2}$"). 1 = same as input format (e.g., 1'– 6– $\frac{1}{2}$").
Useri1-5	Five variables for storing integers for custom applications. Default = 0.
Userr1-5	Five variables for storing real numbers for custom applications. Default = 0.
Users1-5	Five variables for storing text strings for custom applications. Dot (.) = none.
Viewctr	Read Only. Displays the current UCS coordinates of the center of the current viewport.
Viewdir	Read Only. Displays the view direction of the current view port. This also describes the camera point as a 3D offset from the TArget point.
Viewmode	Read-only. Controls view mode for current viewport: 1 = perspective on, 2 = front clipping plane on, 4 = back clipping plane on, 8 = UCS follow mode on, 16 = front clipping plane not at eye level.
Viewsize	Read Only. Displays the height of the current view in drawing units.
Viewtwist	Read Only. Displays the view twist angle for the current viewport. See **Dview**.
Visretain	Stores Xref freeze/thaw, on/off, color and linetype layer settings. 0 = Xref layer settings are as defined in the Xref drawing itself. 1 = Xref layer settings are controlled and stored by the current drawing. One Xref may be called into multiple drawings with different layer settings, if *Visretain* is set in the calling drawing, the Xrefs will conform to each of the called layer definitions. Default = 1.
Vsmax	Read Only. Displays the 3D coordinate of the upper right corner of the current viewport's virtual screen relative to the current UCS.

TABLE S.3: System Variables (continued)

Variable	Description
Vsmin	Read Only. Displays the 3D coordinate of the lower left corner of the current viewport's virtual screen relative to the current UCS.
Wmfbkgnd	Sets background and border of the output Windows metafile resulting from the **Wmfout** command: 0 = transparent (no background, no borders), 1 = matches AutoCAD current background color with reverse border color. Default = 0 (Off).
Worlducs	Read Only. Displays the status of the world coordinate system. 0 = WCS is not current, 1 = WCS is current. See **UCS**.
Worldview	Controls whether point input to the **Dview** and **Vpoint** commands is relative to the WCS or the current UCS. 0 = commands use the current UCS to interpret point value input, 1 = commands use WCS to interpret point value input. Default = 1.
Writestat	Read Only. Displays drawings write and Read Only status: 0 = writing not allowed, 1 = writing allowed.
Xclipframe	Sets controls for visibility of Xref clipping boundaries: 0= not visible, 1 = visible. Default = 0.
Xedit	Controls Xref in-place editing when referenced by another user: 0 = not allowed, 1 = allowed. Default = 1. See **Refedit**.
Xfadectl	Sets Xref fading intensity: 0% = minimum, 90% = maximum. Default = 50.
Xloadctl	Toggles Xref demand loading and controls whether it opens the original drawing or a copy: 0 = off, entire drawing is loaded; 1 = on, reference file is kept open; 2 = on, a copy of the reference file is opened. Default = 1.
Xloadpath	Creates path for storing temporary copies of demand-loaded Xref files. Default = C:\temp.
Xrefctl	Controls creation of external .xlg files: 0 = not written, 1 = written. Default = 0.
Zoomfactor	Controls speed of Intellimouse wheel. Higher value cause greater incremental change for each mouse-wheel forward/backward movement. Range limits are: 3–100.

Syswindows

Syswindows allows you to arrange (tile or cascade) the AutoCAD windows or arrange the window icons. It works in AutoCAD in the same way as the Window menu in the Windows Program Manager works.

To Arrange AutoCAD Windows

Command line: **Syswindows**

Enter an option [Cascade/tile Horizontal/tile Vertical/ Arrange icons]: Select an option.

Options

Cascade   Overlaps the windows with visible title bars.

Tile Horizontal   Arranges the windows horizontally, in nonoverlapping tiles.

Tile Vertical   Arranges the windows vertically, in nonoverlapping tiles.

Arrange Icons   Arranges the window icons.

Tablet

Tablet is useful only if you have a digitizing tablet. Use it to set up your tablet for accurate tracing.

To Set Up a Tablet

Command line: **Tablet**

Menu: Tools ➤ Tablet ➤ On/Off/Calibrate/Configure

1. **Enter an option [ON/OFF/CAL/CFG]:** Enter an option. If you do not have a digitizing tablet, you will get the message "Your pointing device cannot be used as a tablet."

Options

ON/OFF   Toggles the Calibrated mode on or off. When on, you cannot access the screen menus. Use the F4 key to toggle On/Off. Alternatively, you may set the *Tabmode* system variable: 0 = Off, 1 = On. Pressing Ctrl+T on some systems turns Tablet mode On and Off.

CAL   Calibrates a tablet so distances on the tablet correspond to actual distances in your drawing. The calibration is effective only for the space (Paper/Model Space) in which it is performed. After calibrating the tablet, set the transformation to Orthogonal, Affine, or Projective, depending on the drawing dimensions and the digitizing requirements.

CFG Configure your digitizing tablet for a tablet menu like the one provided by AutoCAD.

Orthogonal Requires two calibration points to set translation, uniform scaling, and rotation. Appropriate for dimensionally accurate paper drawings and paper drawings in which the portion to be digitized is long and narrow, and points are confined to single lines.

Affine Useful when specifying arbitrary linear transformation in two dimensions consisting of translation, independent X and Y scaling, rotation, and skewing with three calibration points. Applicable when horizontal dimensions in a paper drawing are exaggerated with respect to vertical dimensions, and lines that are supposed to be parallel actually are parallel.

Projective Sets a transformation representing a perspective projection of one plane in space onto another plane with four calibration points. Adjusts parallel lines that appear to converge.

See Also Options (Systems tab), Sketch, Trace; *System Variable:* Tabmode

Tabsurf

Tabsurf draws a surface by extruding a curve in a straight line, as shown in Figure T.1. Before using **Tabsurf**, you must draw a curve defining the extruded shape and a line defining the direction of the extrusion (the direction vector).

FIGURE T.1: A curve extruded in a straight line.

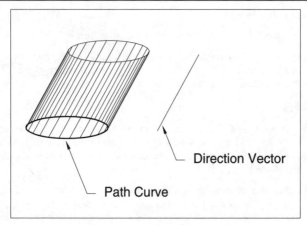

Direction Vector

Path Curve

To Straighten a Curved Surface

Command line: **Tabsurf**

Menu: Draw ➤ Surfaces ➤ Tabulated Surface

Surfaces Toolbar: 🔳 Tabulated Surface

1. **Select object for path curve:** Pick a curve defining the surface shape.

2. **Select object for direction vector:** Pick a line defining the direction of the extrusion.

The point at which you pick the direction vector at the `Select object for direction vector:` prompt determines the direction of the extrusion. The endpoint nearest the pick point is the base of the direction vector, and the other end indicates the direction of the extrusion.

You can draw the curve with a line, arc, circle, 2D polyline, or 3D polyline. The direction vector can be a 3D line. **Tabsurf** has an effect similar to changing the thickness of an object, but extrusions using **Tabsurf** are not limited to the Z axis. The *Surftab1* system variable will affect the number of facets used to form the surface.

See Also   Edgesurf, Revsurf, Rulesurf; *System Variable:* Surftab1

Text
*See **Dtext***

Textscr

Textscr opens the AutoCAD Text Window as a separate window on top of the drawing window.

To Switch to the Text Screen

Command line: **Textscr**

See Also   Graphscr

3D

3D creates basic 3D surface objects. You may select from a predefined set of 3D shapes: box, cone, dish, dome, mesh, pyramid, sphere, torus, or wedge. The objects initially display as wire-frame objects, although they are actually faceted surfaces. You may use **Hide**, **Shade**, or **Render** on them to simulate solid objects. At the command line, you can enter **3D** and choose an option: Box, Cone, Dish, Dome, Mesh, Pyramid, Sphere, Torus, or Wedge.

NOTE If you enter **box** at the command prompt, you get a 3D solid.

To Create a Simple 3D Surface Object

Command line: **3D**

Menu: Draw ➤ Surfaces ➤ 3D Surfaces

Surfaces Toolbar: Box Cone Dish Dome
3Dmesh Pyramid Sphere Torus Wedge

1. **Enter an option [Box/Cone/Dish/DOme/Mesh/Pyramid/ Sphere/Torus/Wedge]:** Select a 3D surface. When you select 3D Surfaces... from the menu, the 3D Objects icon menu displays the predefined surface objects for selection.

TIP The simple Mesh option is available from the icon menu.

2. Depending on the 3D surface chosen, you will be prompted for Diameter, Radius, Height, etc.

3. **Enter number of segments <current value>:** Enter the number of facets desired on the surface. This prompt appears only for curved surface objects, not for flat-sided objects such as a box or pyramid. For dish, dome, and sphere, you will be prompted for both latitudinal and longitudinal segments; for torus, you will be prompted for segments around tube circumference and segments around torus circumference.

NOTE Surface objects fall somewhere between wire frame models and solid objects. They initially display as wire frames but can be shaded or rendered to appear as solid objects. Unlike solids, they provide no information about physical properties (such as mass, weight, or center of gravity), cannot be combined into more complex shapes, and cannot be used to calculate interferences.

See Also   Hide, Render, Shade, Solid Modeling, 3Dmesh

3Darray

3Darray creates copies of an object or group of objects in 3D and is similar to the **Array** command.

To Create Object Arrays

Command line: **3Darray**, **3A**

Menu: Modify ➤ 3D Operation ➤ 3D Array

1. **Select objects:** Pick objects to array.

2. **Enter the type of array [Rectangular/Polar] <R>:** Enter desired array type. If you enter **R**, you are given the following series of prompts:

   Enter the number of rows (---) <1>: Enter the number of rows.

   Enter the number of columns (|||) <1>: Enter the number of columns.

   Enter the number of levels (...) <1>: Enter the number of levels.

   Specify the distance between columns (|||): Enter the numeric distance between columns.

   If you enter **P** for the Polar option at the Enter the type of array [Rectangular/Polar] <R>: prompt, you are asked for the following information:

   Specify center point of array: Pick a center point for the polar array.

   Enter the number of items in the array: Enter number of items in the array, including the originally selected objects.

   Specify the angle to fill (+=ccw,-=cw) <360>: Enter the angle the array is to occupy. Use a negative value to indicate a clockwise array.

   Rotate arrayed objects? [Yes/No] <Y>: Enter **N** if the arrayed objects are to maintain their current orientation or **Y** to rotate objects.

   Specify center point of array: Pick a center point or enter an XYZ coordinate value for the polar array.

   Specify second point on axis of rotation: Specify a point or enter an XYZ coordinate value for the other end of the array axis.

Options

*See **Array***

See Also   Array, Copy, Divide, Group, Measure, Minsert, Multiple, Select, Snap/Rotate; *System Variable:* Grips

3Dclip

3Dclip opens the Adjust Clipping Planes window with objects rotated at a 90-degreee angle from the current 3Dorbit view, allowing you to dynamically set clipping planes.

To Adjust Clipping Planes

Command line: **3Dclip**

3Dorbit Shortcut Menu: More ➤ Adjust Clipping Planes

3Dorbit Toolbar: ▨ 3D Adjust Clip Plane

Choose options using the icon buttons in the Adjust Clipping Planes window, or right-click to select from the shortcut menu. Commands are active if they appear with a check mark in the shortcut menu or display recessed in the floating AutoCAD window. Depending on the icon you select, one or two horizontal bars allow you to adjust the clipping plane by holding down the pick button and dragging an icon.

Options

Adjust Front Clipping   Adjusts the front clipping plane by dragging the bottom line.

Adjust Back Clipping   Adjusts the back clipping plane by dragging the top line.

Create Slice   Creates a slice by moving the back and front clipping planes at the same time.

Front Clipping On   Toggles the front clipping plane on or off.

Back Clipping On   Toggles the back clipping plane on or off.

Click the "X" box at the upper right corner, or use the right-click menu to close the window and return to the display screen. You can rotate the view in 3Dorbit by holding down the pick button and adjusting the view through circular clipping plane guides. Use the right-click shortcut menu to display additional menu and submenu commands.

See Also   Shademode, Solid Modeling, 3D, 3Dcorbit, 3Ddistance, 3Dorbit, 3Dpan, 3Dswivel, 3Dzoom

3Dcorbit

3Dcorbit initializes the **3Dorbit** command, allowing you to continually change the appearance of objects displayed in the 3D viewing window.

To Start 3Dcorbit

Command line: **3Dcorbit**

3D Orbit Toolbar: 3D Continuous Orbit

3D Orbit Shortcut Menu: More ➤ Continuous Orbit

3Dcorbit displays the cursor as a sphere encircled with two arrows. Click and drag the continuous orbit if you wish to change its direction.

See Also   Shademode, Solid Modeling, 3D, 3Dclip, 3Ddistance, 3Dorbit, 3Dpan, 3Dswivel, 3Dzoom

---

3Ddistance

3Ddistance allows you to adjust the zoom distance of 3D objects.

To Set Orbit Distance

Command line: **3Ddistance**

3D Orbit Toolbar: 3D Adjust Distance

3Ddistance displays a cursor with a line and an arrow pointing up and down, allowing you to dynamically zoom in closer to or farther away from your 3D objects.

See Also   Shademode, Solid Modeling, 3D, 3Dclip, 3Dcorbit, 3Dorbit, 3Dpan, 3Dswivel, 3Dzoom

---

3Dface

3Dface draws a 3D face in 3D space. 3D faces are surfaces defined by four points in space picked in circular fashion. Although they appear transparent, 3D faces are treated as opaque when you remove hidden lines from a drawing. After the first face is defined, you are prompted for additional third and fourth points, which allow the addition of adjoining 3D faces.

To Draw a 3D Face

Command line: **3Dface**

Menu: Draw ➤ Surfaces ➤ 3D Surfaces

Surfaces Toolbar: 3D Face

1. **Specify first point or [Invisible]:** Select the first corner, or enter **I**.

2. **Specify second point or [Invisible]:** Select the second corner, or enter **I**.

3. **Specify third point or [Invisible] <exit>:** Select the third corner, enter **I**, or press **[cr]** to end the command.

4. **Specify fourth point or [Invisible] <create three-sided face>:** Select the fourth corner, enter **I,** or press **[cr]** to create a three-sided face.

5. **Specify third point or [Invisible] <exit>:** Continue to pick pairs of points defining more faces, enter **I**, or press **[cr]** to end the command.

Entering **Invisible** or **I** at the first point of an edge repeats the prompt while making that edge of the 3D face invisible.

NOTE The Invisible option hides the joint line between joined 3D faces. Make invisible edges visible by setting the *Splframe* system variable to a nonzero value. See **Setvar** for more on *Splframe*.

NOTE The **Edge** command can also be used to change the visibility of 3D faces. All meshes are composed of 3D faces. If you explode a 3D mesh, each facet of the mesh will be a 3D face.

See Also   Edge, Solid Modeling; *System Variables:* Pfacevmax, Splframe

3Dmesh

3Dmesh draws a 3D surface mesh using coordinate values you specify. **3Dmesh** can be used when drawing 3D models of a topography or performing finite element analysis. **3Dmesh** is designed for programmers who want control over each node of a mesh. You may also use **3Dmesh** along with scripts and LISP routines to automate the process.

To Draw a Rectangular Mesh

Command line: **3Dmesh**

Menu: Draw ➤ Surfaces ➤ 3Dmesh

Surfaces Toolbar: 3Dmesh

1. **Enter size of mesh in M direction:** Enter the number of vertices in the *M* direction (2 to 256).

2. **Enter size of mesh in N direction:** Enter the number of vertices in the *N* direction (2 to 256).

3. **Specify location for vertex (0,0):** Enter the XYZ coordinate value for the first vertex in the mesh.

4. **Specify location for vertex (0,1):** Enter the XYZ coordinate value for the next vertex in the *N* direction of the mesh.

5. **Specify location for vertex (0,2):** Continue to enter XYZ coordinate values for the vertices.

TIP To use **3Dmesh** to generate a topographical model, arrange your XYZ coordinate values in a rectangular array, roughly as they would appear in the plan. Fill any blanks in the array with dummy or neutral coordinate values. Start the **3Dmesh** command, and use the number of columns for the mesh *M* size and the number of rows for the *N* size. At the prompts, enter the coordinate values row by row, starting at the lower left corner of your array and reading from left to right. Include any dummy values. **3Dmesh** creates a polygon mesh that is open in both directions (*M* and *N*).

See Also Mface, Pedit, Pface, Solid Modeling; *System Variables:* Surftype, Surfu, Surfv

3Dorbit

3Dorbit allows you to change the display of 3D objects you select by clicking and dragging your cursor.

To View 3D Objects

Command line: **3Dorbit**, **3Do**

Menu: View ➤ 3D Orbit

3D Orbit Toolbar: 3D Orbit

If your UCS icon is on, a 3D UCS graphic icon appears, allowing you to drag and adjust views using an arcball (large circle segmented with four equally spaced smaller circles).

Activating **3Dorbit** allows the target of the view to remain stationary while you are moving the camera location or point of view. The center of the arcball becomes the target point.

See Also Shademode, Solid Modeling, 3D, 3Dclip, 3Dcorbit, 3Ddistance, 3Dpan, 3Dswivel, 3Dzoom

3Dpan

3Dpan starts the **3Dorbit** command and then allows you to dynamically drag your view horizontally and vertically.

To Pan Objects in a 3D View

Command line: **3Dpan**

3D Orbit Toolbar: 3D Pan

Options

3D Pan   Allows you to move around your drawing by holding down your cursor and dragging with the icon that appears as an open hand.

See Also   Shademode, Solid Modeling, 3D, 3Dclip 3Dcorbit, 3Ddistance, 3Dorbit, 3Dswivel, 3Dzoom

3Dpoly

3Dpoly draws a polyline in 3D space using XYZ coordinates or Object Snap points. 3D polylines are like standard polylines, except that you can't give them a width or use arc segments. Also, you cannot use the **Pedit** command's Fit Curve option with **3Dpoly**. To create a smooth curve using 3D polylines, use the Pedit Spline option. This creates a Spline fit curve. To convert this into a true spline, use the **Spline** commands Object option.

To Draw a 3D Polyline

Command line: **3Dpoly**

Menu: Draw ➤ 3D Polyline

1. **Specify start point of polyline:** Enter the beginning point.

2. **Specify endpoint of line or [Undo]:** Enter the next point of the line.

3. **Specify endpoint of line or [Close/Undo]:** Continue to pick points for additional line segments, or press ↵ to end the command.

Options

Close   Connects the first point with the last point in a series of line segments.

Undo   Moves back one line segment in a series of line segments.

See Also   Pedit, Pline, Spline

3Dswivel

3Dswivel begins the **3Dorbit** command and allows you to twist your view.

To Swivel a 3D View

Command line: **3Dswivel**

3D Orbit Toolbar: 3D Swivel

3Dswivel operates similar to turning a camera on a tripod, allowing you to adjust the target of your view. The cursor resembles a camera encircled partially by an arc with arrows at both ends.

See Also   3D, 3Dclip, 3Dcorbit, 3Ddistance, 3Dorbit, 3Dpan, 3Dswivel, 3Dzoom

3Dzoom

3Dzoom allows you to zoom into a 3D view.

To Zoom with 3Dzoom

Command line: **3Dzoom**

3D Orbit Toolbar: 3D Zoom

Use **3Dzoom** to magnify your 3D view similar to a camera's zoom lens without changing the camera's position.

See Also   Shademode, Solid Modeling, 3D, 3Dclip, 3Dcorbit, 3Ddistance, 3Dorbit, 3Dpan, 3Dswivel

Thickness

Thickness allows you to extrude a 2D object into a 3D object in a direction perpendicular to the plane in which it was drawn.

To Set Thickness

Command line: **Thickness**, **Th**

Enter new value for THICKNESS <0.0000>: Enter a value.

See Also   Elevation, Extrude; *System Variable:* Setvar/Thickness

Tilemode

Tilemode allows you to toggle between Model tab (Model Space) and a Layout tab (Paper Space) in AutoCAD. The Model tab is where you do basic design and drafting. You can create and manipulate different views of your model for plotting in any Layout tab. When Tilemode is On (= 1), you are working in the Model tab, and the ModelSpace UCS icon is visible in the lower left corner. When Tilemode is Off (= 0), you are in a Layout tab, and the triangular PaperSpace icon is visible in the lower left corner.

While you are in a Layout tab (Tilemode = 0), you may create *floating viewports* of the objects drawn in your Model tab using **Mview** or right-clicking a Layout tab and choosing options (New layout, From template…) from the shortcut menu, and then switch to *floating ModelSpace* (Tilemode still = 0) to edit the views. AutoCAD automatically displays the Page Setup dialog to arrange views for your plotted drawing and control plot settings each time you choose a Layout tab in a drawing session unless you have disabled this feature in the Options dialog.

To Switch between Model and Layout Tabs

Command line: **Tilemode**, **Ti**, **Tm**

Enter new value for TILEMODE <1>: Enter 0 for the last active Layout tab and 1 to switch back to the Model tab.

Tilemode moves you from a Model tab (Model Space) to the last-activated Layout tab (Paper Space), and it can also be used to switch from floating Model Space back into Paper Space in a Layout tab. So it activates both the **Tilemode** toggle and starts the **Pspace** command.

You can use the status bar to turn on Paper Space. Click the Model button. The button changes to Paper.

See Also   Layout, Layoutwizard, Mspace, Mvsetup, Pagesetup, Pspace

Time

Time keeps track of the time you spend on a drawing. The time is displayed in military format, using the 24-hour count.

To Display Drawing-Time Data

Command line: **Time** (or **'Time** to use transparently)

Menu: Tools Inquiry ➤ Time

1. **Enter option [Display/ON/OFF/Reset]:** Enter date and time.
2. Times for this drawing:

   Created   Displays date and time.

   Last updated   Displays date and time.

   Total editing time   Displays days and time.

   Elapsed time   Displays days and time.

   Display/On/Off/Reset   Enter an option.

Options

Display   Redisplays time information.

On   Turns elapsed timer on.

Off   Turns elapsed timer off.

Reset   Resets elapsed timer to 0.

See Also   *System Variables:* Tdcreate, Tdindwg, Tdupdate, Tdusrtimer

Tolerance

Tolerance allows you to specify maximum allowable variations of form, profile, orientation, location, or runout from those that are defined by the geometry shown in the drawing. These geometric tolerances define the maximum variations on the specified dimensions that will still allow the drawn object to function and to fit as required. AutoCAD positions the specified tolerances on the drawing in a feature control frame.

To Add Geometric Tolerances to Object Dimensions

Command line: **Tolerance, Tol**

Menu: Dimension ➤ Tolerance…

Dimension Toolbar: Tolerance

1. When the Geometric Tolerance dialog opens, enter the relevant tolerance information for the feature selected. In addition to the tolerance value, you may add a diameter symbol and supplementary datums and symbols pertaining to material conditions and projected tolerances. Edit boxes are available to enter *Height* and *Datum Identifier*. Clicking the Projected Tolerance Zone places a symbol in the field.

2. Depending on text field (box) you pick, the Symbols dialog or Material Condition dialog appears, allowing you to select the desired feature control symbol. Choose OK when you have entered all of the required information.

3. **Enter tolerance location:** Pick the point at which the tolerance information is to be located. The symbol(s) selected, surrounded by a standard frame, will appear at the selected location.

Options

Feature Control Symbols   The Symbols dialog provides an icon menu of the geometric feature symbols: the first three symbols pertain to *Location* (position, concentricity, and symmetry); the next three symbols to *Orientation* (parallelism, perpendicularity, and angularity); the next three symbols to *Form* (flatness, roundness, and straightness); the next two symbols for *Profile* (surface profile and line profile); and the final two symbols pertain to *Runout* (circular runout and total runout). When you select a feature symbol, AutoCAD closes the Symbols dialog and inserts the symbol into the Sym text box in the Geometric Tolerance subdialog.

Tolerance 1/Tolerance 2 You may enter up to two tolerance values for the object dimension. The tolerance Value specifies the amount by which the dimensions of the built object may deviate from the dimensions indicated on the drawing. Two additional modifiers may be added to value. You may optionally insert a diameter symbol (if appropriate) before the value by clicking the Dia box. You may also add material condition information; clicking the MC box opens the Material Condition subdialog and allows you to specify maximum material condition (symbol M), least material condition (symbol L), or regardless of feature size (symbol S). Material conditions apply to features that can vary in size.

Datum 1/2/3 You may add up to three optional datum reference letters (*A, B, C*) after the tolerance values. Each datum represents a point, axis, or plane from which you can measure and verify dimensions. Usually these are three mutually perpendicular planes called the Datum Reference Frame. Each datum may be followed by a material condition modifier symbol (*M, L,* or *S*) as described immediately above.

Height/Projected Tolerance Zone You may define projected tolerances in additional to positional tolerances to increase accuracy. Specify a Height value. This value specifies the minimum projected tolerance zone. Selecting the Projected Tolerance Zone box will add the projected tolerance symbol (*P*) after the height value.

Datum Identifier Specifies a datum-identifying symbol. This identifier consists of a reference letter.

NOTE AutoCAD inserts all of the tolerance information and symbols into a feature control frame. A feature control frame will at minimum contain two elements: the symbol of the geometric characteristic being defined and the tolerance value. The tolerance value field will additionally contain all modifiers and datum references selected. The projected tolerance height and *P* symbol (if any) are inserted in a frame below the feature control frame, and the datum identifier is placed in a frame below these frames.

TIP Feature control frames are a single AutoCAD object, and you may copy, move, stretch, scale, and rotate them. You may use **Osnap** and **Grips**, and you may edit them using **Ddedit**.

Feature control frame characteristics are controlled by the dimension variables as follows: color (*Dimclre*); text color (*Dimclrt*); text gap (*Dimgap*); size of text (*Dimtxt*); and text style (*Dimtxsty*).

See Also Ddedit, Dimensioning Commands; *Dimension Variables:* Dimclre, Dimclrt, Dimgap, Dimtxt, Dimtxsty

Toolbar

Toolbar opens the Toolbar dialog showing a list of standard toolbars
with frequently used commands grouped for easy access. You may display multiple toolbars on the screen at once, and you may hide them
when you are not using them. The Toolbars dialog allows you to create
new toolbars, delete toolbars, customize the supplied toolbars by adding
or removing commands to meet your current needs, and modify properties on toolbars.

Toolbars may be either *docked* or *floating*. If a toolbar is docked, it locks
into position along the top, bottom, or sides of the screen. A floating
toolbar can be moved around with your pointing device and may overlap other toolbars.

To Display a Toolbar

Command line: **Toolbar**, **To**, or **Tbconfig**

Menu: View ➤ Toolbars...

Toolbar: Right-click any icon in any toolbar to display the shortcut
menu, and then pick Customize....

When the Toolbars dialog appears, check the box adjacent to a toolbar
name to display it, or select an option. You may reposition a toolbar by
dragging it across the screen. To close it, click on the "X" at the upper
right corner.

If you wish to "dock" a floating toolbar, drag it by holding your pick
button over the title bar to a dock location at the top, bottom, or sides
of the screen, and release the pick button. To "float" a docked toolbar,
you can either pick the "field" or edge of the toolbar or hold your pointing device over the raised double grab bars along the left edge, drag it to
your display screen, and then release the button.

Some toolbars have *flyouts,* or nested toolbars (identified by a black
arrow in the lower right corner) that contain more tool icons. For example, the Inquiry flyout on the standard toolbar contains tools for Distance, Area, Mass Properties, List, and Locate Point. For specific tasks,
you may wish to display the Inquiry toolbar itself on your screen rather
than access it repeatedly via the standard toolbar. To activate an icon's
command in a flyout, hold your pick button down while dragging your
cursor across the toolbar's icons, and then release the button when you
reach the appropriate choice. When selected from a flyout, icons appear
recessed; otherwise, they are raised in a 3D appearance.

Each tool icon on a toolbar has a Tooltip that serves as a label. When
you pass your pointing device slowly across the icon, the Tooltip
appears and a line of help text is displayed on the status bar.

The position of tools on a flyout customizes itself based upon your usage. The flyout tool most recently used moves to the first position for easier access.

All of the toolbars are flexible and can be customized extensively to meet your specific needs.

Options

Toolbars   The Toolbars list box displays all available toolbars, both hidden and shown. Click the box for the toolbar to display and it immediately appears on the graphics screen. Highlight the toolbar whose properties you wish to customize, delete, or modify.

Close   Exits the Toolbar dialog and implements any changes that you have made.

New   Opens the New Toolbar subdialog. Enter a toolbar name for the new toolbar. This is the name that will appear above the tools on the toolbar. In the Menu Group drop-down box, select the menu group associated with the new toolbar. The list box contains all menus currently loaded, including the ACAD standard menu and any others you may have created and loaded (see **Menuload**). The internal AutoCAD name, or alias, of a toolbar consists of the toolbar name prefixed by the menu group name—for example, ACAD.*CUSTOM*. When you choose OK, an empty toolbar will appear on your drawing area. You should now use the Customize option to add tools to the toolbar.

Delete   Use this option to delete any toolbar. You may create temporary toolbars and then delete them when you no longer need them.

Customize   Opens the Customize Toolbars subdialog. The new or existing toolbar(s) that you wish to modify must be visible on your screen. To delete a tool from the displayed toolbar, simply drag it off the toolbar. To add a new tool to a displayed toolbar, select the relevant tool category from the Categories drop-down box. When you select a category (for example, Solids or Attributes), all of the tool icons for that category appear in the Categories box. Click any tools that you want, and drag them to the onscreen toolbar that you are customizing. You may also move and copy tools from one displayed toolbar to another. To move a tool from another toolbar, drag the tool to the new toolbar. To copy a tool from another toolbar, press the Ctrl key as you drag the tool to the new toolbar. During all of the above operations, the displayed toolbar resizes itself as tools are added or deleted. Choose the Close button to save the toolbar changes. Use the Customize category to add an empty icon to a toolbar, and then right-click your mouse button over the icon to display the Button Properties toolbar for editing it.

Properties   Opens the Toolbar Properties subdialog, and allows you to change the toolbar name or help string and identify that particular toolbar's alias.

Large Buttons   Changes the icons on the toolbars from the standard 16(vert.)×16(horiz.) pixels to 32(vert.)×32(horiz.) pixels.

Show Tooltips   Turns on or off the display of the tool name each time a pointing device passes over any tool icon. It is controlled by the system variable *Tooltips*.

Open the Toolbars dialog, and then right-click a tool icon to open the Button Properties dialog for that tool. You may change the name, command, and tool icon associated with that tool. If you click a flyout toolbar icon while the Toolbars dialog box is displayed, the Flyout Properties dialog will open. You may change the flyout name, toolbar, and icon.

You can edit the .mns file with an ASCII text editor and any changes made to toolbars are saved to the associated compiled menu (.mnc) file.

NOTE   If you wish to create new toolbars, creating your own custom menu (.mns) file is recommended.

If you have used **Menuload** to load the acetwain.mns menu file, then the Menu Group pop-up box will display the Express toolbar.

See Also   -Toolbar; *System Variable:* Tooltips

-Toolbar

-Toolbar is used at the command line to display, hide, relocate, or dock a toolbar.

To Use the Toolbar Command

Command line: -**Toolbar**

1. **Enter toolbar name or [ALL] :** Enter the full alias for the toolbar, and press ↵.

2. **Enter an option [Show/Hide/Left/Right/Top/Bottom/Float] <current>:** Enter an option, or press ↵.

Options

All   Type All to activate this option. Choose Hide or Show all toolbars. If you choose Show, every toolbar, both top level and lower level, will display on your screen. If you choose Hide, every toolbar, including your default toolbars, will close.

Show   Displays the named toolbar.

Hide   Closes the named toolbar.

Left/Right/Top/Bottom   Docks the named toolbar at the left, right, top, or bottom of the screen. The Enter new position (horizontal,vertical) <0,0>: prompt sets the position of the toolbar relative to an existing docked toolbar.

Float   Changes the named toolbar from docked to floating. The Enter new position (screen coordinates) <0,0>: prompt sets the position of the floating toolbar in XY coordinates. The Enter number of rows for toolbar <1>: prompt allows you to define the number of rows in the toolbar.

See Also   Toolbar; *System Variables:* Tooltips

Torus
See **3D**

Trace

Trace can be used where a thick line is desired. Alternatively, you can accomplish the same thing using the **Pline** command. If you draw a series of Trace line segments, the corners are automatically joined to form a sharp corner.

To Draw a Thick Line
Command line: **Trace**

1. **Specify trace width <default width>:** Enter the desired width.

2. **Specify next M point:** Pick the start point for the trace.

3. **Specify next point:** Pick the next point.

As with the **Line** command, you can continue to pick points to draw a series of connected line segments. Trace lines appear only after the next point is selected.

NOTE If you draw a series of Trace line segments, the corners are automatically joined to form a sharp corner. For this reason, traces do not have an Undo option, and the starting and ending segments will not join and bevel properly. To make traces bevel properly for the start and end segments, begin the trace not on the desired corner/endpoint but at any point midway on the desired first segment, and then make the end segment complete the actual first segment.

See Also   Fill; *System Variable:* Tracewid

Tracking

Tracking helps to locate points based on a reference point in your drawing. Use **Track**, **Tra**, or **Tk** to initialize tracking during execution of a command. The shortcut menu tracking command operates differently when entered at the command line.

To Start Tracking

Command line: (*command*) **Tracking**, **Track**, **Tra**, **Tk**, **Shift+Right-Click** and choose temporary trackpoint

Object Snap Toolbar: Tracking

Clicking Otrack on the status bar or pressing F11 opens the Object Snap tab of the Drafting Settings dialog, allowing you to check Object Snap Tracking (F11) and toggle tracking on.

To draw a circle centered within a rectangle, you could set tracking on to locate the rectangles vertical and horizontal midpoints and use these as reference points. For example, enter the **Circle** command and then use the middle button or hold the Shift key and right-click your mouse button to display the shortcut menu and select Temporary Track Point. Open the cursor menu for the midpoint option, pick a line (perhaps the vertical line) on the rectangle, repeat the procedures, and then pick the opposite (the horizontal line), and the circle's center point will start at the center of the rectangle. When selected from the shortcut menu, tracking ends after the first point is selected.

The following describes the command sequence if you enter tracking (**track**, **tra**, or **tk**) at the command line:

1. **Specify center point for circle or [3P/2P/Ttr (tan tan radius)]:** Press Shift+Right-Click to choose temporary track point, **tk**, **track**, or **tra** to begin tracking operation.

2. **First tracking point:** Press the middle button, or use the Shift key, and right-click the mouse button, and then select midpoint of a vertical line of the rectangle.

3. **Next point (Press Enter to end tracking):** Drag your cursor toward the center of the rectangle (stretching the "rubber band–like" line), and then extend it to the midpoint of the horizontal line, right-click the mouse button, and select midpoint a horizontal line of the rectangle.

4. **Next point (Press Enter to end tracking):** Press [cr].

5. **Diameter/<Radius>:** Specify radius, or enter **D** for the diameter of circle.

See Also   Dsettings

Transparency

Transparency allows you to set background pixels in an image as transparent or opaque so that graphics on the screen shows through those pixels.

To Set an Image's Transparency

Command line: **Transparency**

Menu: Modify ➤ Object ➤ Image ➤ Transparency

Reference Toolbar: Image Transparency

1. **Select image(s):** Select an image to set its transparency.

2. **Enter transparency mode [ON/OFF] <OFF>:** Enter On or Off.

> **TIP** **Transparency** is available for both bitonal and nonbitonal (Alpha RGB or gray-scale) images and is determined on a per-object basis.

Transparent Commands

The transparent commands can be used while AutoCAD is still executing another command. Control is transferred temporarily to the transparent command until it is completed or until you terminate it by pressing Escape. Not all commands can be used transparently.

To Use a Command while Another Is Executing

Type an apostrophe preceding the command name. (This only works for commands that are identified as transparent commands throughout this book.)

Treestat

Treestat displays data regarding the drawing's current spatial index, allowing you to improve drawing efficiency via the *Treedepth* system variable. Information is provided separately for Model Space and Paper Space.

To View the Tree

Command line: **Treestat**

The number of nodes being reported is shown in the ModelSpace branch and PaperSpace branch. Each node requires approximately 80 bytes of memory. Setting the *Treedepth* system variable to a large number increases disk swapping, negating the performance benefits of the spatial index. The objective is to have fewer objects per node to take advantage of spatial indexing, the optimum number being dependent on the amount of memory your computer has. The more memory you have, the more you can take advantage of spatial indexing. The use of *Treedepth* and *Treestat* is best suited to large drawings in order to optimize performance.

AutoCAD indexes objects in a region by recording their positions in space. The result is called a spatial index.

See Also   *System Variable:* Treedepth

Trim

Trim shortens an object to meet another object or objects. One or more objects may also be trimmed to a point of *implied* intersection—that is, to the point at which they *would* intersect with the cutting edge if the cutting edge were extended out. Additionally, objects may be trimmed to the current UCS plane or along the current view direction—that is, to an apparent intersection in the current view. These options are controlled by the system variables *Projmode* and *Edgemode*.

To Trim an Object

Command line: **Trim, Tr**

Menu: Modify ➤ Trim

Modify Toolbar: ⊁ Trim

1. **Current settings: Projection = UCS Edge = None**

   Select cutting edges...

   Select objects: Press **[cr]** to select all objects as a cutting edge or choose object(s) that define the cutting edge(s) at which you want to trim other objects.

2. **Select object to trim or [Project/Edge/Undo]:** Pick the objects you want to trim, one at a time or using the Fence Selection Set option, or select an option:

   - If you type **P**, you will be prompted Enter a projection option [None/Ucs/View] <Ucs>:.

   - If you type **E**, you will be prompted Enter an implied edge extension mode [Extend/No extend] <No extend>:.

Options

Project   Specifies the Projection mode for AutoCAD to use when trimming objects: None specifies that only objects that actually intersect the cutting edge will be trimmed, UCS specifies projection onto the XY plane of the current UCS, View trims all selected objects which intersect with the cutting edge in the current view. The system variable *Projmode* settings control the projection mode.

Edge   Allows cutting edges to be extended to the point where they *would* intersect with an option. You may select either Extend or No Extend (system variable *Edgemode* settings 1 and 0). If you choose No Extend, only objects that *actually* intersect the cutting edge will be trimmed.

NOTE   Objects that may be trimmed include arcs, circles, elliptical arcs, lines, open 2D and 3D polylines, rays, and splines. These same objects may be selected as cutting edges. Regions, floating viewports, text, and Xlines may also be used to define cutting edges.

TIP   At the Select cutting edge: prompt, you can pick several objects that intersect the objects you want to trim. Once you've selected the cutting edges, press ⏎ and the Select object to trim: prompt appears, allowing you to pick the sides of the objects to trim. You cannot trim objects within blocks or use blocks as cutting edges.

See Also   Break, Change, Extend; *Express Tools:* Extrim; *System Variables:* Edgemode, Projmode

U

U reverses the most recent command. You can undo as many commands as you have issued during any given editing session. The **Undo** command can also be activated by using the control-key sequence Ctrl+Z.

To Reverse a Command

Command line: **U**

Menu: Edit ➤ Undo

Standard Toolbar: Undo

The Auto, End, and Control options under the **Undo** command affect the results of the **U** command. **U** is essentially the **Undo** command with 1 as the parameter.

See Also   Oops, Redo, Undo

UCS

UCS, the user coordinate system, is a tool for creating and editing 3D drawings. A UCS can be described as a plane in 3D space on which you can draw. Using the **UCS** command, you can create and shift between as many UCSs as you like. It determines the orientation in which 2D objects are drawn and the direction in which objects are extruded.

To Modify a UCS

Command line: **UCS**

Menu: Tools ➤ UCS ➤ Preset Options

UCS Toolbar: ⬚ UCS ⬚ Display UCS Dialog ⬚ UCS Previous ⬚ World UCS ⬚ Object UCS ⬚ Face UCS ⬚ View UCS ⬚ Origin UCS ⬚ Z Axis Vector UCS ⬚ 3 Point UCS ⬚ X Axis Rotate UCS ⬚ Y Axis Rotate UCS ⬚ Z Axis Rotate UCS ⬚ Apply UCS UCS II Toolbar: ⬚ Display UCS Dialog ⬚ Move UCS Origin

| ● World ▼ | (Orthographic drop-down box) |

Current UCS name: *WORLD*

Enter an option [New/Move/orthoGraphic/Prev/Restore/ Save/Del/Apply/?/World]

<World>: Enter or select an option.

Options

New Displays prompt Specify origin of new UCS or [ZAxis/ 3point/OBject/Face/View/X/Y/Z] <0,0,0>:. Press **[cr]** to define a new origin point, or enter an option.

Zaxis Determines the direction of the Z-coordinate axis. You are prompted for an origin for the UCS and for a point along the Z axis of the UCS.

3point Defines a UCS by selecting three points: the origin, a point along the positive direction of the X axis, and a point along the positive direction of the Y axis.

Object Defines a UCS based on the orientation of an object. Objects not eligible for selection include a 3D solid, 3D polyline, 3D mesh, viewport, Mline, region, spline, ellipse, ray, Xline, leader, and Mtext.

Face Uses the Face of a Solid Object that You Choose to Align UCS.

View Defines a UCS parallel to your current view. The origin of the current UCS will be used as the origin of the new UCS.

X/Y/Z   Defines a UCS by rotating the current UCS about its X, Y, or Z axis.

Move   Displays the prompt `Specify new origin point or [Zdepth]` `<0,0,0>:`, allowing you to change the UCS's origin, or enter **Z** to move the UCS along the Z axis.

Orthographic   Displays the prompt `Enter an option [Top/Bottom/` `Front/BAck/Left/Right]<Top>:`, allowing you to specify preset UCS positions.

Apply   Displays the prompt `Pick viewport to apply current UCS or` `[All]<current>:`, allowing you to select specific viewports or to choose all viewports.

Prev   Places you in the previously defined UCS. Restores up to 10 previous coordinate systems in a Model and a Layout tab.

Restore   Restores a saved UCS. Displays the prompt `Enter name of UCS` `to restore or [?]:`, restoring a saved UCS. Entering **?** lists all saved UCS names or allows you to enter a name using wildcards when the prompt `UCS name(s) to list <*>:` appears.

Save   Saves a UCS for later recall by prompting `Enter name to save` `current UCS or [?]:`.

Del   Deletes a previously saved UCS. Enter the UCS name at the prompt `Enter UCS name(s) to delete <none>:`.

?   Displays a list of currently saved UCSs. You can use wildcard filter lists to search for specific UCS names.

World   Returns you to the world coordinate system.

> **NOTE**   The world coordinate system, or WCS, is the base from which all other UCSs are defined. The WCS is the default coordinate system when you open a new file. The *UCSfollow* system variable automatically shifts your drawing into the appropriate plan view whenever the UCS is moved. If you use the Objects option, the way the selected object was created affects the orientation of the UCS. Table U.1 correlates selected objects with UCS orientation.

TABLE U.1:   UCS Orientation Based on Objects

Object Type	UCS Orientation
Arc	The center of the arc establishes the UCS origin. The X axis of the UCS passes through one of the endpoints nearest to the picked point on the arc.
Circle	The center of the circle establishes the UCS origin. The X axis of the UCS passes through the pick point on the circle.

TABLE U.1:   UCS Orientation Based on Objects (continued)

Object Type	UCS Orientation
Dimension	The midpoint of the dimension text establishes the UCS origin. The X axis of the UCS is parallel to the X axis that was active when the dimension was drawn.
Line	The endpoint nearest the pick point establishes the origin of the UCS, and the XZ plane of the UCS contains the line.
Point	The point location establishes the UCS origin. The UCS orientation is arbitrary.
2D Polyline	The starting point of the polyline establishes the UCS origin. The X axis is determined by the direction from the first point to the next vertex.
Solid	The first point of the solid establishes the origin of the UCS. The second point of the solid establishes the X axis.
Trace	The direction of the trace establishes the X axis of the UCS, with the beginning point setting the origin.
3Dface	The first point of the 3Dface establishes the origin. The first and second points establish the X axis. The plane defined by the face determines the orientation of the UCS.
Shapes, Text, Blocks, Attributes, and Attribute Definitions	The insertion point establishes the origin of the UCS. The object's rotation angle establishes the X axis; the object has a rotation angle of zero in the new UCS.

See Also   Dview, Elev, Plan, Rename, UCSicon, Vpoint, Wildcard Characters; *System Variables:* UCSfollow, UCSicon, UCSname, UCSorg, UCSxdir, UCSydir, Vsmax, Vsmin, Worlducs, Thickness

UCSicon

UCSicon controls the display and location of the UCS icon. The UCS icon tells you the orientation of the current UCS. It displays an L-shaped graphic symbol showing the positive X and Y directions. The icon displays a *W* when WCS is the current default coordinate system. If the current UCS plane is perpendicular to your current view, the UCS icon displays a broken pencil to indicate that you will have difficulty drawing in the current view. The UCS icon changes to a cube when you are displaying a perspective view. When you are in Paper Space, it turns into a triangle.

To Modify the UCS Icon

Command line: **UCSicon**

Menu: View ➤ Display ➤ UCS Icon ➤ On/Origin

Enter an option [ON/OFF/All/Noorigin/ORigin] <ON>: Press **[cr]**, or enter an option.

Options

ON   Turns the UCS icon on.

OFF   Turns the UCS icon off.

All   Forces the UCSicon settings to take effect in all viewports if you have more than one viewport. Otherwise, the settings will affect only the active viewport.

No Origin   Places the UCS icon in the lower left corner of the drawing area, regardless of the current UCS's origin location.

Origin   Places the UCS icon at the origin of the current UCS. If the origin is off the screen, the UCS icon will appear in the lower left corner of the drawing area.

NOTE   Instead of selecting the Origin option as shown above, achieve the same effect by selecting View ➤ Display ➤ UCS Icon ➤ Origin. The UCS icon will always move automatically with the origin, unless the origin is not within the drawing view window.

See Also   UCS, UCSman, Viewports; *System Variables:* UCSicon

UCSman

UCSman opens the UCS dialog to help you manage user coordinate systems.

To Open the UCS Dialog

Command line: **UCSman**

Specify information in the dialog as needed.

Options

Named UCS Tab   Contains a list of UCSs, including World and Previous, defined in the current drawing. Click Set Current to set the specified user coordinate system current, or pick Details for more detailed information, including options to select a UCS from the *Relative To* drop-down box.

Orthographic UCS   Shows current UCS in list box and allows you to select a new UCS and make it current. You can also click the same buttons or the drop-down box as described in the Named UCS tab.

Settings   The UCS icon settings section toggles controls On, Display at UCS Origin Point and Apply to All Active Viewports.

The UCS icon settings section contains checkboxes to Save UCS with Viewport and Update View to Plan when UCS Is Changed.

See Also   UCS, UCSicon; *System Variables:* UCSbase, UCSfollow

Undefine
*See **Redefine***

Undo

Undo allows you to undo parts of your editing session. This can be useful if you accidentally execute a command that destroys part of your drawing. **Undo** also allows you to control how much of a drawing is undone.

To Reverse Commands
Command line: **Undo**

Menu: Edit ➤ Undo

Standard Toolbar: ⟲ Undo

Enter the number of operations to undo or [Auto/Control/ BEgin/End/Mark/Back]: Enter an option to use or the number of commands to undo.

Options

Auto   Makes AutoCAD view menu macros as a single command. If Auto is set On, the effect of macros issued from a menu will be undone regardless of the number of commands the macro contains.

Control   Turns off the Undo feature to save disk space, or limits the Undo feature to single commands. You are prompted for All, None, or One. All fully enables the Undo feature, None disables Undo, and One restricts the Undo feature to a single command at a time.

Begin, End   Begin marks the beginning of a sequence of operations. All edits after that point become part of the same group. End terminates the group. This allows you to mark a group of commands to be undone together.

Mark, Back Allows you to experiment safely with a drawing by first marking a point in your editing session to which you can return. Once a mark has been issued, you can proceed with your experimental drawing addition. Then, you can use Back to undo all the commands back to the place that Mark was issued.

> **NOTE** Many commands offer an Undo option. The Undo option under a main command will act more like the **U** command and will not offer the options described here.

See Also U

Union

Union creates a composite object by combining the total area or volume of two or more regions or solids.

To Combine Regions or Solids

Command line: **Union**, **Uni**

Menu: Solids Editing ➤ Union

Solids Editing Toolbar: Union

Select objects: Click the overlapping solids or regions that you want to combine.

> **NOTE** **Union** can be used only for regions or solids. You may select both regions and solids at the same time, and you may select objects from any number of planes. AutoCAD will group the selection set into subsets by region/solid and by plane (in the case of regions) before combining them.

See Also Intersect, Region, Solid Modeling, Subtract

Units

Units opens the Units Control dialog to set up the drawing's units of measure, angle measurement and direction, and precision. Use **Units** to display all the prompts at the command line.

To Display the Units Dialog Box

Command line: **Units**, **Un** (or **'Units**, to use transparently)

Menu: Format ➤ Units...

Provide information as needed in the dialog(s).

Options

Length   Provides drop-down box for setting Type for units of measure: Scientific, Decimal, Engineering, Architectural, and Fractional.

Angle   Provides drop-down box to set Type for angle measurement: Decimal Degrees, Deg/Min/Sec, Grads, Radians, and Surveyor.

Precision   Provides drop-down box to select Precision for length (measurement) and angles.

Direction...   Opens the Direction Control subdialog with radio buttons to indicate the direction of angles: East, North, West, and South indicate the location for 0. Another button enables a pick button and *Angle* edit box. Click the checkbox for clockwise and counterclockwise direction of positive and negative angles. Pick the drop-down box When Inserting Blocks into This Drawing, Scale Them To: to set the unit of measure for any blocks inserted from the DesignCenter.

See Also   -Units; *System Variables:* Angbase, Angdir, Aunits, Auprec, Insunits, Insunitsdefsource, Insunitsdeftarget, Lunits, Luprec, Unitmode

-Units

-Units sets AutoCAD to the unit format appropriate to the drawing. For example, if you are drawing an architectural floor plan, you can set up AutoCAD to accept and display distances using feet, inches, and fractional inches. You can also set up AutoCAD to accept and display angles as degrees, minutes, and seconds of an arc rather than the default decimal degrees. The dialog equivalent of this command is **Units**. The Units format also appears as a tab in the Setup dialog for both Quick and Advanced setups.

To Change Drawing Units

Command line: **-Units**, **-Un** (or **'-Units** to use transparently)

1. **Report formats: Enter choice, 1 to 5 <2>:** Enter the number corresponding to the desired unit system, as described below. With the exception of the Engineering and Architectural modes, you can use these modes with any basic unit of measurement.

2. **Enter number of digits to the right of decimal point (0 to 8):<4>:** Enter a number to specify the degree of precision.

3. **System of angle measure: Enter choice, 1 to 5 <1>:** Enter the number corresponding to the desired angle measure system.

4. **Enter number of fractional places for display of angle (0 to 8) <0>:** Enter a number to specify the degree of precision.

5. **Enter direction for angle <0> <0>:** Enter the desired angle for the 0 degree direction.

6. **Measure angles clockwise? [Yes/No] <N>:** Enter **Y** if you want angles measured clockwise; otherwise, press **[cr]**.

Options

System of Units   Sets format of units that AutoCAD will accept as input:

Report Format	Example
1. Scientific	1.5500E+01
2. Decimal	15.5
3. Engineering	1'-3.50"
4. Architectural	1'3 1/2"
5. Fractional	15 1/2

System of Angle Measure   Sets format of angle measurement AutoCAD will accept as input:

Measurement Format	Example
1. Decimal	45.0000
2. Degrees/minutes/seconds	45d0'0"
3. Grads	50.0000g
4. Radians	0.7854r
5. Surveyor's units	N 45d0'0"E

Direction for Single 0   Sets direction for the 0 angle:

East	3 o'clock = 0
North	12 o'clock = 90
West	9 o'clock = 180
South	6 o'clock = 270

NOTE   You can set decimal or fractional input regardless of the unit format being used. This means you can enter 5.5' as well as 5'6" when using the Architectural format. Decimal mode is perfect for metric units as well as decimal English units.

See Also   Mvsetup, Units; *System Variables:* Aflags, Angbase, Angdir, Aunits, Auprec, Insunits, Isnunitsdetsource, Isunitsdettarget, Lunits, Luprec, Unitmode

Vbaide

Vbaide opens the Visual Basic Editor, allowing you to edit code, forms, and references for any loaded global VBA project or to embed multiple VBA projects in an open drawing.

To Open the Visual Basic Editor

Command line: **Vbaide**, **Alt+F11**

Menu: Tools ➤ Macro ➤ Visual Basic Editor

The Visual Basic Editor provides you with the capability to debug and run projects from the Visual Basic Editor.

See Also   Vbaload, Vbaman, Vbarun, Vbastmt, Vbaunload

Vbaload

Vbaload allows you to load a global VBA project into your current AutoCAD drawing session.

To Load a VBA Project

Command line: **Vbaload**

Menu: Tools ➤ Macro ➤ Load Project

If *Filedia* is set to 0, the prompt Open VBA Project <Project.dvb>: appears at the command line. If *Filedia* is set to 1, the Open VBA Project dialog appears with standard file selection features allowing you to specify a name in the *File Name* edit box and locate folders in the list box. Clicking the checkbox lets you Open Visual Basic Editor after the specified project is loaded.

   Sample projects can be loaded from the \Sample\Vba folder. You can load several VBA projects in an AutoCAD session. If you wish to load or unload embedded VBA projects, you must open the drawing containing that project.

See Also   Vbaide, Vbaman, Vbarun, Vbastmt, Vbaunload

Vbaman

Vbaman loads, unloads, saves, creates, embeds, and extracts VBA projects.

To Open the VBA Manager

Command line: **Vbaman**

Menu: Tools ➤ Macro ➤ VBA manager

Enter information in the dialog.

Options

Drawing   Clicking the drop-down box in this section selects a drawing to make active from among all open drawings in your current AutoCAD session. You can select from names displayed in the *Embedded Project:* edit box. Drawings without an embedded project are disabled and display "none."

Extract Extracts the embedded project into a global project file. If the project has not been saved, the prompt Do you want to export VBA project before removing it? appears. Click Yes to open the File Save dialog to enter a drive, folder, and filename, No to extract the project with a temporary filename, or Cancel to rescind the operation and return to the VBA Manager dialog.

Projects Lists of all the VBA projects available in the current AutoCAD session.

Embed Embeds a project into the selected drawing.

New Creates a new project with the default name "Global," appended with a sequentially incremented number.

Save As… Opens the Save As dialog, specifying a .dvb filename and location to save a global project.

Load Opens the Open dialog, specifying an existing project to load into your current AutoCAD session.

Unload Unloads a saved global project or displays the prompt Save changes to your current VBA project? if your project has not been previously saved.

Macros Opens the Macros dialog to execute a VBA macro.

See Also Vbaload, Vbaman, Vbarun, Vbastmt, Vbaunload

Vbarun

Vbarun opens the Macros dialog, allowing you to create, run, edit, or delete a VBA macro.

To Run a VBA Macro

Command line: **Vbarun**

Entering a name in the *Macro Name* edit box or selecting from the list box lets you run, edit, delete, or create a VBA macro. The Description box allows you to add or edit information about your macro and saves it when you choose another option in the dialog.

Specify information in the dialog as needed.

Options

Run Executes the selected macro.

Close Exits the dialog.

Help   Provides access to the AutoCAD Help file.

Step Into   Opens the Visual Basic Editor to run the macro, and stops at the first executable line of code.

Edit   Displays the selected macro for editing in the Visual Basic Editor.

Create   Opens the Select Project subdialog to Select a Project or Drawing for Macro, allowing you to create a macro with the name you entered in the *Macro Name* edit box and then open the Visual Basic Editor to write the macro code.

Delete   Displays the message "Do you want to delete macro (macro name)?" and allows you to click Yes to remove it or No to cancel the procedure.

VBA Manager   Opens the VBA Manager dialog.

Options...   Opens the VBA Options dialog to toggle checkboxes Enable Auto Embedding, Allow Break on Errors, and Enable Macro Virus Protection.

Macros In: Click the drop-down box to Specify All Active Drawings and Projects, All Active Drawings, All Active Projects, any individual drawing currently open in AutoCAD, or any individual project currently loaded in AutoCAD.

See Also   Vbaide, Vbaload, Vbaman, Vbastmt, Vbaunload

-Vbarun

-Vbarun allows you to run a macro at the command line.

To Run a VBA Macro at the Command line

Command line: **-Vbarun**

Macro name: Enter name of macro.

See Also   Vbaide, Vbaload, Vbaman, Vbastmt, Vbaunload

Vbastmt

Vbastmt lets you run a VBA code or statement from the command line. A Visual Basic statement consists of keywords, operators, constants, and expressions.

To Run a VBA Statement at the Command Line

Command line: **Vbastmt**

Statement: Specify the VBA statement you wish to run. Any return value from the statement is simply discarded.

See Also   Vbaide, Vbaload, Vbaman, Vbarun, Vbaunload

Vbaunload

Vbaunload allows you to unload a global VBA project.

To Unload a VBA Project

Command line: **Vbaunload**

Unload VBA Project: Enter the name of a global VBA project to unload. The active global project is unloaded if no name is specified.

See Also   Vbaide, Vbaload, Vbaman, Vbarun, Vbastmt

View

View opens the View dialog to make, delete, rename, and restore views. The equivalent command-line prompt is **-View**.

To Invoke the View Dialog

Command line: **View**, **V**

Menu: View ➤ Named Views...

Standard Toolbar: ⬚ View Flyout

View Toolbar: ⬚ Named Views

Provide information as needed in the dialogs.

Options

Named Views Tab   The Current View name is identified at the top of the list box ofr both tabs.

Current View List Box   Displays Name, Location, UCS, and Perspective, which can be sorted by clicking their column heading. You can select a view name and then right-click for shortcut menu options to Set Current, Rename, Delete, and Details. The current view name is marked by an arrow along the left side and displays information about its Model or Layout location, the UCS name (if saved with the view), and whether the view was saved in perspective or clipped.

Set Current   Click Set Current to restore a view name.

New...   ⬚ Define View Window

Opens the New View subdialog for saving a new view. Option buttons allow you to save the Current Display as a view or to Define Window. Assign a *New Name* in the edit box, and then use the Define View Window icon to temporarily exit dialog for creating the view. Pick the OK button to exit. The UCS Settings section contains a checkbox to Save UCS with View and a *UCS Name* drop-down box.

Delete   Right-click in the list box to open the shortcut menu, and pick Delete to remove a view name from the list box.

Rename   Right-click in the list box to open the shortcut menu, and choose Rename to rename a view.

Details   Opens the View Details subdialog, specifying Area, Target, Direction, Clipping, and Perspective data on the highlighted view. The *Relative To:* drop-down box, which appears in both tabs, allows you to choose the orientation of the orthographic view based on coordinate systems saved in the current drawing (*UCSbase* variable).

Orthographic & Isometric Views   Lets you choose a predefined orthographic and isometric view. Click Set Current to restore the view, or double-click a name in the Current View: list box. Click to toggle Restore Orthographic UCS with View (*UCSortho* variable).

See Also   Mspace, Pspace; *System Variable:* Tilemode

-View

View allows you to save views of your drawing. Instead of using the **Zoom** command to zoom in and out of your drawing, you can save views of the areas you need to edit and then recall them using the Restore option of the **View** command. The corresponding dialog box command is **View**.

To Save Views of Your Drawing

Command Line: -**View**

Enter an option [?/Orthographic/Delete/Restore/Save/Ucs/ Window]: Enter an option.

Options

?   Lists all currently saved views. Wildcards filter lists are accepted.

Orthographic   Displays the prompt Enter an option [Top/Bottom/ Front/BAck/Left/Right]<Top>: to restore preset orthographic view.

Delete   Displays the prompt Enter view name(s) to delete: for deleting a view from the drawing database.

Restore   Displays the prompt Enter view name to restore: for restoring a view name to the screen.

Save   Saves the current view. You are prompted to Enter view name to save:.

UCS   Displays Save current UCS with named views?[Yes/No]<Yes>:. Enter **Y** or **N**. If you enter **Y**, you can save the current UCS and elevation settings with your view name.

Window Displays prompt Enter view name to save:, for saving a view defined by a window. Enter a view name and then Specify first corner: and Specify opposite corner: to window the area to be saved as a view.

View will save 3D orthographic projection views, perspective views, and PaperSpace or ModelSpace views in Model and Layout tabs. **View** does not save hidden-line views or shaded views.

See Also   Open, View

Viewports
See Vports

Viewres

Viewres controls whether AutoCAD's virtual screen feature is used and how accurately AutoCAD displays lines, arcs, and circles.

To Invoke Fast Zoom Mode

Command line: **Viewres**

Do you want fast zooms? <Y>: Enter **Y** or **N**. If you respond with **Y**, the following prompt appears: Enter circle zoom percent (1-20000) <100>:. Enter a value from 1 to 20,000, or press **[cr]** to accept the default.

Options

Yes Sets up a large virtual screen within which zooms, pans, and view/restores occur at redraw speeds. You are prompted for a circle zoom percent (based on the current zoom magnification). This value determines how accurately circles and noncontinuous lines are shown.

No Turns off the virtual screen. All zooms, pans, and view/restores will cause a regeneration.

The circle zoom percent value also affects the speed of redraws and regenerations. A high value slows down redraws and regenerations; a low value speeds them up. Differences in redraw speeds are barely noticeable unless you have a very large drawing.

Use a high percent value for circle zoom to display smooth circles and arcs and to accurately show noncontinuous lines. A low value causes arcs and circles to appear as a series of line segments when viewed up close. Noncontinuous lines, however, may appear continuous. This does not mean that prints or plots of your drawings will be less accurate; only the display is affected.

The default value for the circle zoom percent is 100, but at this value, dashed or hidden lines might appear continuous, depending on the

Ltscale settings and how far you are zoomed into the drawing. A value of 2000 or higher reduces or eliminates this problem with little sacrifice of speed.

A low circle zoom value causes object endpoints, intersections, and tangents to appear inaccurately placed when you edit a close-up view of circles and arcs. Often, this results from the segmented appearance of arcs and circles and does not necessarily mean the object placement is inaccurate. It may also be hard to distinguish between polygons and circles. Settings the circle zoom percent to a high value also reduces or eliminates these problems.

The drawing limits affect redraw speed when the virtual screen feature is turned on. If the limits are set to an area much greater than the actual drawing, redraws are slowed down.

To force the virtual screen to contain a specific area, set your limits to the area you want, set the limit's checking feature to On, and issue a **Zoom/All** command. The virtual screen will conform to these limits until another **Regen** is issued or until you pan or zoom outside of the area set by the limits.

See Also   Limits, Redraw, Regen, Regenauto

Vpclip

Vpclip allows you to clip a viewport in a Layout tab, so objects are displayed within any boundary shape that you draw.

To Clip a Floating Viewport

Command line: **Vpclip**

Select viewport to clip: Pick the viewport you wish to clip.

Select clipping object or [Polygonal] <Polygonal>: Select an object defining the clipping boundary, or press **[cr]** to display the prompts:

- Specify start point: Select a point.

- Specify next point or [Arc/Close/Length/Undo]: Continue selecting points or enter an option to create a closed boundary. (See **Pline** for options.)

Options

Object   Selects closed polylines, circles, ellipses, closed splines, or regions defining the clipping boundary.

Polygonal   Chooses pick points with prompts similar to the **Pline** command to create a clipping boundary.

See Also   Pline, Vports

Vplayer

Vplayer controls the visibility of layers for each individual viewport and allows display of different types of information in each viewport, even though the views are of the same drawing. You can use **Vplayer** in conjunction with overlapping viewports to create clipped views.

To Modify Viewport Layer Visibility

Command line: **Vplayer**

Enter an option [?/Freeze/Thaw/Reset/Newfrz/Vpvisdflt]:
Enter the desired option.

Options

? Displays the names of layers that are frozen in a given viewport. You are prompted to select a viewport. If you are in Model Space, AutoCAD temporarily switches to Paper Space during your selection.

Freeze Lets you specify the name of layers you want to freeze in selected viewports. You are first prompted for the names of Layer(s) to Freeze <>: and then All/Select/<Current>: appears for the viewport(s) in which to freeze them.

Thaw Thaws layers in specific viewports. You are prompted for the layer names to thaw and then the viewports in which the layers are to be thawed.

Reset Restores the default visibility setting for layers in a given viewport. See the Vpvisdflt option for information on default visibility.

Newfrz Creates a new layer that is automatically frozen. You can then turn this new layer on for each viewport individually.

Vpvisdflt Presets the visibility of layers for new viewports to be created using **Mview**, **Vports**, or **Pagesetup** by prompting:

- Layer name(s) to change default viewport visibility <>: Enter layer name.

- Change default viewport visibility to Frozen/<Thawed>: Enter an option.

NOTE All options that prompt you for layer names allow use of wildcard characters to set multiple layer names. You can also use comma delimiters for lists of layers with dissimilar names.

See Also Layer, -Layer, Mview, Mvsetup, Pagesetup, Pspace, Vports; *System Variables:* Tilemode, Visretain

Vp

*See **Ddvpoint***

Vpoint

Vpoint selects an orthographic, 3D view of your drawing.

To Set a Viewing Point

Command line: **Vpoint**

Menu: View ➤ 3D Views ➤ Vpoint

View Toobar: 🔲 Top View 🔲 Bottom View 🔲 Left View
🔲 Right View 🔲 Front View 🔲 Back View 🔲 SW Isometric View
🔲 SE Isometric View 🔲 NE Isometric View 🔲 NW Isometric View

1. **Current view direction:** VIEWDIR=-1.0000,-1.0000,1.0000.

2. **Specify a view point or [Rotate] <display compass and tripod>:** Enter a coordinate value, or enter **R** for the Rotate option, or press **[cr]** to set the view with the compass and axes tripod.

Options

Rotate Specifies a view in terms of angles in the XY plane and from the X axis. You are first prompted to enter an angle in the XY plane from the X axis. Next, you are prompted to enter an angle from the XY plane.

View Point Specifies your viewpoint location by entering an XYZ coordinate value.

[cr]/Tripod Select visually a view by using the compass and axes tripod.

There are three methods for selecting a view: Enter a value in XYZ coordinates that represents your viewpoint. For example, entering 1,1,-1 will give you the same view as entering 4,4,-4.

Use the Rotate option to specify a viewpoint as horizontal and vertical angles in relation to the last point selected. Use the **ID** command to establish the view target point (the last point selected) before you start **Vpoint**.

Press **[cr]** at the Vpoint prompt, and visually select a viewpoint, using the compass and axes tripod. To select a view, move your pointing device until the tripod indicates the desired X-, Y-, and Z-axis orientation. A cross on the compass indicates your location in plan. For example, placing the cross in the lower left quadrant of the compass places your viewpoint below and to the left of your drawing. Your view elevation is indicated by the distance of the cross from the compass center. The closer the cross is to the center, the higher the elevation. The circle inside the compass indicates a 0 elevation. If the cross falls outside of this circle, your view elevation becomes a minus value, and your view will be from below your drawing.

-Vports

-**Vports** displays multiple tiled and floating viewports of your drawing at one time.

To Display Multiple Viewports

Command line: -**Vports**

If you are in a Model tab, the prompts are:

**Enter an option [Save/Restore/Delete/Join/SIngle/?/2/3/4]
<3>:** Enter the desired option, or press [**cr**] for the Enter a config-
uration option [Horizontal/Vertical/Above/Below/Left/Right]
<Right>: default prompt. If you are in a Layout tab, prompts are the
same as the **Mview** command.

Options

Save   Saves the current viewport arrangement.

Restore   Restores a previously saved viewport arrangement.

Delete   Deletes a previously saved viewport arrangement.

Join   Joins two adjacent viewports of the same size to make one larger viewport.

Single   Changes the display to a single viewport.

?   Displays a list of saved viewport arrangements along with each view-port's coordinate location.

2   Splits the display to show two viewports. You are prompted for a hor-izontal or vertical split.

3   Changes the display to show three viewports.

4   Changes the display to show four equal viewports.

Layout   Each viewport can contain any type of view you like. For example, you can display a perspective view in one viewport and a plan view of the same drawing in another viewport.

You can only work in one viewport at a time. To change active view-ports, pick any point inside the desired viewport. The border around the selected viewport will thicken to show that it is active. The standard cur-sor appears only in the active viewport. (When you move the cursor into an inactive viewport, it changes into an arrow.) Any edits made in one viewport are immediately reflected in the other viewports.

Each viewport has its own virtual display within which you can pan and zoom at redraw speeds. For this reason, the **Regen** and **Redraw** commands affect only the active viewport. To regenerate or redraw all the viewports at once, use the **Regenall** and **Redrawall** commands.

NOTE Tiled vports are helpful when working with 3D objects. If you attempt to plot while your screen is arranged in tiled viewports, you will only be plotting the view displayed in the active viewport.

See Also Mview, Redraw, Regen, Vports; *System Variables:* Cvports, Maxactvp, Viewctr, Viewdir, Viewtwist, Vsmax, Vsmin, Viewres

Vslide

Vslide displays raster image slide files in the current viewport. Slides are individual files with the extension .sld. You many combine slide files into a slide library by using the extension .slb.

To Display Slide Files

Command line: **Vslide**

Enter name of slide file to view <current file name>: Enter the name of the slide file to be displayed. If *Filedia* is set to 1, the Select Slide File box will appear to specify a drive, path, and filename.

To View a Slide from a Slide Library

Slide file <current file name>: Enter the slide library name followed by the slide's name in parentheses, as in library-name(slide-file-name).

See Also Mslide, Script, Slidelib.exe

Wblock

Wblock opens the Write Block dialog to let you create a new file from a portion of the current file or from a block of the current file.

To Write a Block to Disk

Command line: **Wblock**, **W**

Specify information in the dialog as needed.

Options

Block   Select existing blocks from a drop-down box, and write them to your disk as a drawing file.

Entire Drawing   Write the entire drawing to your disk as a block, purging all unused blocks, layers, linetypes, dimension styles, and text styles. This option is similar to entering an asterisk (*) at the Enter name of existing block or [= (block=output file)/* (whole drawing)] <define new drawing>: prompt.

Objects   Enables the Base point and Objects sections to pick an insertion point and select objects in your drawing.

Base Point

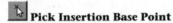 **Pick Insertion Base Point**

Temporarily exits the dialog to pick a point in your drawing.

X/Y/Z   Specify XYZ coordinate values in edit boxes.

Objects

 **Select Objects**

Temporarily exits the dialog to pick objects in your drawing.

Select Objects

Opens the Quick Select subdialog, allowing you to specify a filter when choosing objects in your drawing. See **Quick Select.**

Retain   Retains the original entities after creating the block; otherwise, they are deleted.

Convert to Block   Creates a block of selected objects in the current drawing and also writes it to your disk.

Delete from Drawing   Writes the entities to your disk, and removes the original object(s) from your drawing.

Destination

File Name   Enter a name for the block in the edit box.

Location   Clicking the drop-down box or picking the ellipsis to open the Browse for Folder subdialog allows you to specify a drive and folder name.

Insert Units   Specifies a unit of measure that will be used for files when inserted as a block into your drawing (*Insunits* variable).

See Also   Block, Bmake, Insert, -Wblock

-Wblock

-Wblock lets you create a new file from objects in your current file or a block of the drawing. The equivalent dialog command is **Wblock**.

To Write a Block to Disk

Command line: **Wblock**, **W**

If the *Filedia* variable is set to 1, the Create Drawing File dialog opens for you to enter information in edit boxes and locate folders for the new drawing file.

If the *Filedia* variable is set to 0, the prompt Enter name of output file: appears, allowing you to enter the filename, directory, and drive letter for the new drawing file. Entering a tilde (~) at this prompt opens the Create Drawing File dialog.

Enter name of existing block or [= (block=output file)/* (whole drawing)] <define new drawing>: Enter the block name, press **[cr]** to create a block or enter an option.

The block or set of objects will be written to your disk as a drawing file.

To write a portion of the current drawing view to a file, press **[cr]** and you will receive the following two prompts:

- Specify insertion base point: Enter a coordinate, or pick a point.

- Select objects: Select objects using the standard AutoCAD selection options.

The objects you select are written to your disk as a drawing file. The point you select at the Specify insertion base point: prompt becomes the origin of the written file.

Options

= (block=output file)   If you are exporting a block from your drawing and you want the filename to be the same as the block name, enter an equals sign (=) at the **Enter name of existing block** prompt, or enter the same block name again. If you enter the name of an existing file at the File name: prompt, you receive the prompt <drive><path><file name> already exits. Do you want to replace it?. You can replace the filename or return to the command prompt to restart **-Wblock**.

* (whole drawing)   Entering an asterisk (*) at the **Enter name of existing block** prompt writes the entire current file to disk, stripping it of all unused blocks, layers, linetypes, dimension styles, and text styles. This can reduce a file's size and access time. (See **Purge**.)

Objects are placed in the Model tab (Model Space) of the output file unless the asterisk is used. In that case, objects are placed in the space they are in. Also whatever layer is set current at the time of the **-Wblock** will be the current layer in the new file.

See Also   Base, Bmake, Insert, Wblock; *System Variables*: Expert, Handles, Insbase

Wedge
*See **Solid Modeling***

Wildcard Characters

Wildcard Characters allow you to list filenames by using a filter to include or exclude files according to similarities in their names. AutoCAD wildcard characters are extensions of the standard DOS wildcard characters. Here are the wildcard characters you can use:

Character	Description
#	Matches any number. For example, **C#D** selects all names that begin with C, end with D, and have a single-digit number between.
@	Matches any alphabetical character. For example, **C@D** selects any name that begins with C, ends with D, and has a single alphabetical character between.
. (period)	Matches any character not numeric or alphabetical. For example, **C.D** might select the name C-D.
* (asterisk)	Matches any string of characters. For example, ***CD** selects all names of any length that end with CD.
? (question mark)	Matches any single character. For example, **C?D** selects all names of three characters that begin with C and end with D.
~ (tilde)	Matches anything but the set of characters that follow. For example, **~CD** selects all names that do *not* include CD.
[ ] (brackets)	Typing any set of characters between two brackets matches any one of the characters enclosed in brackets. For example, **[CD]X** selects the names CX and DX but not CDX. Brackets can be used in conjunction with other wildcard characters. For example, you could use **[~CD]X** to find all names except CX and DX.

Character	Description
- (hyphen)	Lets you specify a range of characters when used within brackets. For example, **[C-F]X** selects the names CX, DX, EX, and FX.
` (single quote)	Forces the character that follows to be read literally. (The reverse quote is the character that is located to the left of the 1 key on most keyboards.) For example, ` selects the name *CD, instead of all names that end in CD.

Wmfin
*See **Import/Export***

Wmfopts
*See **Import/Export***

Wmfout
*See **Import/Export***

Xattach

Xattach attaches an external reference to the current drawing. When first invoked, it displays the Select Reference File dialog, and then displays the External Reference dialog. Subsequent attachments only display the External Reference dialog, which contains insertion options similar to the **Image** and **Xref** commands.

To Attach an Xref File

Command line: **Xattach**, **Xa**

Menu: Insert ➤ External Reference

Reference Toolbar: 🔲 External Reference Attach

Xattach can be used to quickly insert an Xref file into the drawing; otherwise, select the **Xref** command, and click the Attach... button to display the same External Reference dialog. Depending on which boxes are unchecked, prompts appear at the command line. (See **-Xref**.)

Options

Name Displays names of attached Xref files by clicking the drop-down box. Clicking Browse... opens the Select Reference File dialog to search using standard selection set dialog methods.

Reference Type Identifies whether Xref is an attachment or overlay. Path information is displayed above the Reference Type section.

Retain Path Checkbox indicating Xref path is saved in the drawing database or saved in the database without a path.

Parameters Specifies insertion point, XYZ scale factors and rotation angle.

See Also Image, -Image, Xbind, -Xbind, Xref, -Xref

Xbind

Xbind opens the Xbind dialog to import a block, dimension style, layer, linetype, or text style from an external reference (Xref).

To Bind Symbols Using a Dialog

Command line: **Xbind**, **Xb**

Menu: Modify ➤ Object ➤ External Reference ➤ Bind...

Reference Toolbar: [icon] External Reference Bind

Opens the Xbind dialog to graphically assist you in selecting a block, dimension style, layer, linetype, or text style to bind into your drawing.

Options

Xrefs Depending on the icon you select, the list box displays Xref files in your drawing.in a Tree View format. Highlight and then double-click an Xref filename to display named objects: Block, Dimstyle, Layer, Linetype, and Textstyle. Double-click an object, such as Layer, to expand the branches and display specific Xref layer names to bind. The layer names will appear in the Xref-*filename|blockname* format. If you highlight a layer and click Add->, the definition is transferred into the Definitions to Bind list box.

Definitions to Bind A list box displaying the name of the item to import into your drawing. If you wish to remove a selected item or definition, highlight it, and click the <-Remove button.

See Also -Xbind, Xref

-Xbind

-Xbind imports a block, dimension style, layer, linetype, or text style from an external reference (Xref). The equivalent dialog command is **Xbind**.

To Bind Symbols into Your Drawing

Command line: **-Xbind**

1. **Enter symbol type to bind [Block/Dimstyle/LAyer/LType/Style]:** Enter the desired option.

2. You are then prompted for the name of the item to import. Enter a single name, a list of names separated by commas, or use wildcard characters to specify a range of names.

> **NOTE** Named variables from an Xref file must be prefixed with their source filename. Be sure to include the full Xref filename, including the vertical bar symbol (|), for example, Xref-*filename| blockname*. When you use **-Xbind** to import the named block, its name will change to Xref-*filename*0*blockname* to reflect its source file. If a block of the same name already exists, the 0 is replaced with a 1, as in Xref-*filename*1*blockname*.

See Also Xattach, Xbind, Xref

Xclip

Xclip allows you to create a user-defined clipping boundary, consisting of planar straight-line segments, for one or more external reference files or blocks. You can also set front or back clipping planes.

To Create a Clipping Boundary

Command line: **Xclip**, **Xc**

Menu: Modify ➤ Object ➤ External Reference

Toolbar: External Reference Clip

1. **Select objects:** Select one or more Xrefs or blocks to clip.

2. **Enter clipping option [ON/OFF/Clipdepth/Delete/generate Polyline/New boundary] <New>:** Press **[cr]**, or specify an option. If you pressed **[cr]** at the Delete old boundary(s)? [Yes/No]<Yes>: prompt, another prompt appears Specify clipping boundary: [Select polyline/Polygonal/Rectangular] <Rectangular>:, offering you additional choices: enter **S** to select

an existing polyline, **P** to draw a new polygonal shape, or accept the default **R** to draw a rectangle.

3. If you pressed **[cr]** to create a new boundary using **P** or **R**, the external reference file is clipped to the boundary edge, and then the polyline disappears. To restore the polyline, reissue the command, and type **P** or **Polyline** for the Generate Polyline option.

Options

Polygonal   Pick a point at the Specify first point: prompt, and then continue to select or adjust points at the Specify next point or [Undo]: prompt to define the clipping boundary.

Rectangular   Specify two corner points to create a rectangular boundary.

ON   Displays the clipped portion of the Xref or block.

OFF   Restores the entire Xref or block that was clipped.

Clip Depth   Displays prompts Specify front clip point or [Distance/ Remove]: and Specify back clip point or [Distance/Remove]: to set front and back clipping planes on an Xref or block preventing objects outside the clip-depth range from being displayed. Use the Remove option to delete the clip-depth specifications.

Delete   Removes the clipping boundary on one or more selected Xrefs or blocks.

Generate Polyline   Recreates the polyline, using the current layer, linetype, and color settings that define the edge of the clipping boundary. You can edit the polyline with **Pedit** or **Grips**. If you wish to use this new polyline as the new boundary edge, then reissue the **Xclip** command, and enter **S** as descibed in item 3 above.

> **NOTE**   If you can use the Spline option of the **Pline** command to create a smooth curved clipping boundary, the fit curve or arc options are decurved prior to being used as a clip boundary.

See Also   Xclipframe; *Express Tools:* Clipit

Xclipframe

Xclipframe sets the visibility of Xref clipping boundaries On or Off.

To Display an Xref's Clipping Boundary

Command line: **Xclipframe**

Menu: Modify ➤ Object ➤ External Reference ➤ Frame

Reference Toolbar: ⬛ External Reference Clip Frame

Enter new value for XCLIPFRAME <0>: Enter a value of 0 to turn the clipping boundary Off and 1 to make it visible. The Clipping Boundary is a block in the drawing that has the name of the Xref.

See Also   Xclip, Xref

Xline

Xline allows you to create construction lines anywhere in 3D space. By default, **Xline** creates an infinite line based on two input points. The first point specified—the root—becomes the "midpoint" of the infinite line. You may specify the **Xline**'s orientation in a variety of ways.

To Draw a Construction Line

Command line: **Xline**, **Xl**

Menu: Draw ➤ Construction line

Draw Toolbar: ![icon] Construction line

1. **Specify a point or [Hor/Ver/Ang/Bisect/Offset]:** Pick a first point (the Xline "root" or midpoint) or select an option.

2. **Specify through point:** Pick a second point or enter coordinates to orient the Xline. Continue to pick additional through points as required to create additional construction lines radiating from the midpoint.

Options

Hor/Ver   Draws a construction line parallel to the X axis (Hor) or Y axis (Ver). You need only pick a single point to define Xlines of this type. Continue picking through points to create as many parallel construction lines as are required.

Ang   Draws an Xline at a specified angle to the X axis by either entering an angle value or by dynamically picking two points. Continue picking through points to create as many parallel construction lines as are required.

Bisect   Creates a construction line that bisects a specified angle. First, pick the angle vertex point, and then point to mark the lines of the angle.

Offset   Draws a construction line parallel to a selected line object (including plines) at a specified offset. First, specify the offset by picking two points or entering a numeric value. Then, select a line object and pick a point to indicate the side on which to offset the construction line.

NOTE   Xlines are ignored by commands that display the drawing extents.

See Also   Line, Mline, Ray

Xplode

Xplode lets you explode multiple compound objects and blocks, including nonuniformly scaled objects. You may also control and change the color, layer, and linetype, either of individual objects or of all of the objects globally.

To Explode Compound Objects

Command line: **Xplode**

1. **Select objects to XPlode.**

   Select objects: Use an object selection method to pick all of the objects you wish to explode. (AutoCAD will show how many were selected and how many are valid compound objects.)

2. **Enter an option [All/Color/LAyer/LType/Inherit from parent block/Explode] <Explode>:** Press **[cr]** to explode all of the selected objects without changing any of their characteristics. Type in an option **A/C/LA/LT/I/E** if you wish to change all or any of the selected object's characteristics.

Options

Global/Individual   If you chose the default global option in step 2, Xplode will apply your choices to all objects in a single pass. If you chose the **I** option in step 2, **Xplode** will cycle through each of the selected objects one at a time.

All   If you select this option, **Xplode** will prompt you through all of the other options in turn, allowing you to select or enter new values.

Color   Allows you to specify any of the standard colors or to choose color Bylayer or Byblock. The prompt Enter new color for exploded objects [Red/Yellow/Green/Cyan/Blue/Magenta/White/BYLAYER/BYBLOCK] <BYLAYER>: lists the options.

Ltype   Specifies a new linetype at the prompt Enter new linetype name for exploded objects <BYLAYER>:.

Layer   Enter new layer name for exploded objects <0>: Enter a new layer name, or press **[cr]** to explode the block into the current layer.

Inherit from Block   Explodes properties of object (color, linetype, lineweight, and layer) based on to that of the exploded object if the component objects' color, linetype, and lineweight are Byblock and object is drawn on layer 0.

Explode   Returns a block, polyline, assocative dimension, body, multi-line, polyface, polygon, mesh, region, group, 3D mesh, or solid to their original component objects.

See Also   Block, Explode, Wblock, Xbind, Xref

Xref

Xref helps to manage how you attach, detach, reload, unload, bind, and locate external drawing files in your current drawing.

To Manage Insertion of Xref Files

Command line: **Xref**, **Xr**

Reference Toolbar: 🔲 External Reference

Draw Toolbar: 🔲 Insert Block Flyout

🔲 External Reference

Insert Toolbar: 🔲 External Reference

Xref opens the Xref Manager dialog, similar to the **Image** command, to manage your Xref files. Select the desired function from the dialog box.

Options

List View Click the List View box, or press the F3 function key to display external reference files in a columnar format with headings as described below. Based on their function, the six drag division headings sort information in ascending and descending order.

> **Reference Name** Names of Xref files in block definition symbol table.
>
> **Status** Identifies whether an Xref file is loaded, unloaded, unreferenced, not found, unresolved, orphaned, or marked for unloading or reloading.
>
> **Size** Shows the size of the Xref file.
>
> **Type** Specifies whether Xref file is an overlay or attachment.
>
> **Date** Displays last modified date of Xref file. If Xref is unloaded, not found, or unresolved, this field is empty.
>
> **Saved Path** Shows you the saved path for Xref file but does not update the path if the Xref file may actually have been relocated.
>
> **Tree View(F4)** Displays the Xref files in a Tree View format with branches identifying subdirectories. The *Xref Found At* edit box below shows you its full path. You can also press the F4 key to display the Tree View.
>
> **List View(F3)** Displays the Xref files in a List View format with details for division headings as described above.

Attach Displays the Select Reference File dialog executed with the **Xattach** command. (See **Xattach**).

Detach   Detaches one or more highlighted external reference files from your drawing. You can only detach those Xref files that are directly attached or overlaid in your drawing. It does not detach nested Xrefs.

Reload   Reloads Xref files that have been unloaded.

Unload   Unloads, but does not remove, Xref files. Unloading prevents the display and regeneration of the Xref to improve editing and drawing performance.

Bind   Displays the Bind Xrefs dialog to Bind or Insert an Xref file. Bind will insert the Xref file as a permanent object using the *blockname-$#$symbolname* syntax. Insert is similar to the **Insert** command where an object assumes the current properties defined in the drawing. For example, if a layer named Wall in the Xref file was defined with the color yellow and your drawing contains a Wall layer with the color green, the inserted Xref would assume the color green.

See Also   Xattach, Xbind, Xref

-Xref

-Xref lets you attach and detach, list and reload, or bind external drawing files to your current drawing file. You may also overlay external files over your current drawing to check the consistency or relationship between the drawings. Xrefs should be regarded as Read Only files for reference purposes only.

To Import an External File

Command Line: **-Xref**, **-Xr**

Enter an option [?/Bind/Detach/Path/Unload/Reload/ Overlay/Attach]: Enter the desired option.

Options

?   Displays a list of cross-referenced files in your current drawing. The name of the file as well as its location on your storage device is shown. You can filter the Xref'd filenames by using wildcard characters.

Bind   Causes a cross-referenced file to become a part of the current file. Once Bind is used, the Xref file becomes an ordinary block in the current file, and AutoCAD replaces the pipe character (|) with a number (usually 0) between two dollar signs ($$).

Detach   Detaches a cross-referenced file, so it is no longer referenced to the current file.

Enter Xref name(s) to detach: Enter name or names separated with commas or wildcard.

Path Specifies a new DOS path for a cross-referenced file. This is useful if you have moved a cross-referenced file to another drive or directory. You are prompted Edit Xref name(s) to edit path:. Enter the name of an Xref file, and AutoCAD responds with the Old Path: <drive> <path><filename> prompt.

Enter new path: Enter new path.

Reload Reloads a cross-referenced file without exiting and reentering the current file. This option is useful if you are in a network environment and you know that someone has just finished updating a file you are using as a cross-reference. A temporary lock is created if the drawing you are editing is externally referenced during an Xref Reload operation and, if it encounters an error while reloading, ends the **Xref** command undoing the entire reload sequence.

Enter Xref name(s) to reload: Enter name or names separated with commas or wildcard.

Attach Attaches another drawing file as a cross-reference. If *Filedia* is set to 1, the Select Reference File dialog opens to identify the filename, path, and drive letter, and then you are requested for an insertion point, scale factor(s), and rotation angle for the cross-reference. If *Filedia* is set to 0, you are prompted at the command line to Enter name of file to attach:.

Specify insertion point or [Scale/X/Y/Z/Rotate/PScale/ PX/PY/PZ/PRotate]: Specify an insertion point for the Xref file, or enter an option. (See **-Insert**.)

Enter X scale factor, specify opposite corner, or [Corner/ XYZ] <1>: Enter a new value, or press **[cr]**.

Enter Y scale factor <use X scale factor>: Enter a new value, or press **[cr]**.

Specify rotation angle <0>: Pick a rotation angle dynamically, or enter a value.

Overlay Overlays another drawing file as a cross-reference for comparison purposes. It operates in a similar way to the Attach option by opening the Select file to overlay dialog. You are prompted, in the same way, for a filename, notified if the file exists, and then requested for an insertion point, scale factor(s), and rotation angle for the cross-reference. However, overlay cross-references cannot be nested; that is, if you reference a drawing with an overlaid cross-reference, the overlaid cross-reference will not be referenced into your drawing. The overlay option allows multiple users to access the same drawing without circularity of Xrefs.

Xref files act like blocks; they cannot be edited from the file they are attached to. The difference between blocks and Xref'd files is that Xref'd files do not become part of the current file's database. Instead, the current file "points" to the Xref'd file. The next time the current file is opened, the Xref's file is also opened and automatically attached. This has two advantages. First, because the Xref'd file does not become part of the current file, the current file size remains small. Second, since the Xref'd file stays independent, any changes made to it are automatically reflected in the current file whenever it is reopened.

In most of the options, you can enter a single name, long filenames containing spaces, a list of names separated by commas, or a name containing wildcard characters. Named variables from the Xref'd files will have the filename as a prefix. For example, a layer called "wall" in an Xref'd file called "house" will have the name House|wall in the current file.

AutoCAD keeps a log of Xref activity in an ASCII file. This file has the same root name as your current drawing file and has the extension .xlg. You can delete this file with no effect on your drawing. It can be set by checking Maintain a Log File in the General tabbed section of the Preferences dialog box.

See Also   Block, Bmake, Insert, Properties, Wblock, Xbind, -Xbind, Xref; *System Variables*: Indexctl, Projectname, Visretain, Xloadctl, Xloadpath, Xrefctl

---

Zoom

Zoom controls the display of your drawing dynamically in real time.

To Use Zoom

Command line: **Zoom**, **Z** (or **'Zoom** to use transparently)

Menu: View ➤ Zoom ➤ Realtime/Previous/Window/Dynamic/ Scale/In/Out/All/Extents

Zoom Toolbar: 🔍 Zoom Window   🔍 Zoom Dynamic
🔍 Zoom Scale   🔍 Zoom Center   🔍 Zoom In   🔍 Zoom Out
🔍 Zoom All   🔍 Zoom Extents

Specify corner of window, enter a scale factor (nX or nXP), or [All/Center/Dynamic/Extents/Previous/Scale/Window]
<real time>: Press Esc or Enter to exit, or right-click to activate pop-up menu. Press ↵ for real time Zoom, or enter the desired option.

Options

In/Out   The Zoom In and Zoom Out icon tools on the Zoom toolbar or the Zoom flyout on the Standard toolbar allow you to zoom in and out by a predefined scale factor. Zoom In doubles the size of the drawing display; Zoom Out shrinks the display to half of the current size so that you can view double the drawing area.

Realtime   Displays a magnifying glass with a plus and minus sign for real-time pan and zoom. Combines **Rtzoom** and **Rtpan** into a single command allowing you to switch between pan and zoom. Right-clicking your mouse displays a cursor menu to alternate among Pan, Zoom, Zoom Window, Zoom Previous, Zoom Extents options or the **Exit the Zoom** command.

All   Displays the area of the drawing defined by the drawing's limits or extents, whichever are greater (see **Limits**).

Center   Displays a view based on a selected point. You are first prompted for a center point for your view and then for a magnification or height. A value followed by an *x* is read as a magnification factor; a lone value is read as the desired height in the display's drawing units.

Dynamic   Displays the virtual screen, and allows you to use a view box to select a view. The drawing extents, current view, and the current virtual screen area are indicated as a solid white box, a dotted green box, and red corner marks, respectively. You can pan, enlarge, or shrink the view by moving the view box to a new location, adjusting its size, or both. When the view box appears, press the pick button to adjust the view box size, and then pick again to restore the *x* in the view box. Press Enter to set the new view.

Extents   Displays a view of the entire drawing centered on the screen.

Previous   Displays the last view created by a **Zoom**, **Pan**, or **View** command.

Window   Enlarges a rectangular area of a drawing, based on a defined window.

Scale(X)   Expands or shrinks the drawing display. If an *x* follows the scale factor, it will be in relation to the current view. If no *x* is used, the scale factor will be in relation to the area defined by the limits of the drawing. A value of .5*x* displays a view half the size of the current view.

Scale (XP)   Sets a viewport's scale in relation to the PaperSpace scale. For example, if you have set up a title block in Paper Space at a scale of 1″=1″, and your full-scale ModelSpace drawing is to be at a final plot scale of 1/4″–1′, you can enter **1/48xp** at the Zoom prompt to set the viewport at the appropriate scale for Paper Space. You must be in floating Model Space to use this option.

NOTE **Zoom** can be used transparently as long as the Viewres Fast Zoom option is on. **Zoom** cannot be used transparently while viewing a drawing in perspective. Use the **Dview** command's Zoom option instead. **Zoom** cannot be used transparently in Paper Space.

See Also   Limits, Mspace, Mvsetup, Pspace, Redraw, Regen, Regenauto; *System Variables*: Viewres, Viewsize

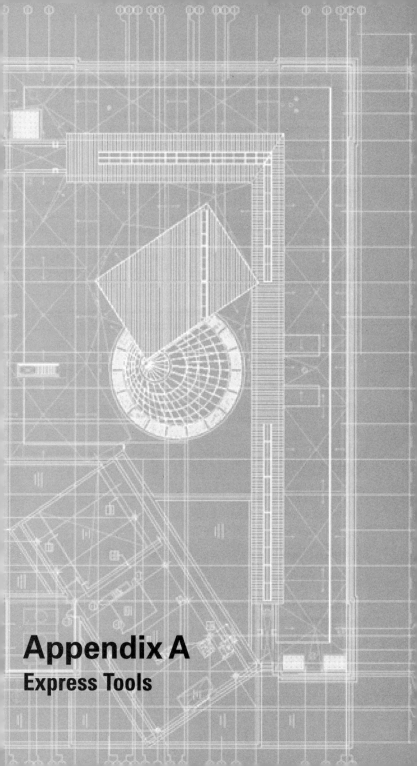

Appendix A
Express Tools

AutoCAD Express Tools

The Layer, Block, Text, and Standard Bonus toolbars offer routines with expanded capabilities of some AutoCAD commands. They have been contributed from various sources, including Autodesk programmers. Some Express Tools commands can only be entered at the command line; others can be selected from the Express pull-down menu or a toolbar.

Select the Full Installation option, or pick the Custom button, and check Express Tools in the Components list box in the Custom Components dialog to install the Express commands. The commands are stored in the Express subdirectory in your default ACAD 2000 directory. Commands described in this section of the book are intended to provide you with a brief overview of their application. Additional AutoCAD Express Tools commands in volumes are available for purchase from Autodesk: tel. 800/964-6432; Web http://www.autodesk.com/expresstools.

Aliasedit

Opens a dialog to edit the acad.pgp file and to create shortcut keys for DOS and AutoCAD commands.

Command line: **Aliasedit**

Express Menu: Tools ➤ Command Alias Editor...

See Also   Reinit

Arctext

Aligns text along an arc.

Command line: **Arctext**, **Atext**

Express Menu: Text ➤ Arc Aligned Text

Express Text Tools Toolbar Arc Aligned Text

See Also   Arc, Divide, Dtext, Measure, Mtext, Text

Bcount

Reports the number of occurences of each block in selected objects or an entire drawing.

Command line: **Bcount**

See Also   Block, Bmake, Wblock

Bextend

Extends entities to nested blocks or Xrefs.

Command line: **Bextend**

Express Menu: Blocks ➤ Extend to Block Entities

Express Block Tools: Extend to Block Entities

See Also　Extend, Fillet, Trim; *Express Tools:* Btrim

Block?

Returns a list of block objects.

Command line: **Block?**

See Also　Block, Bmake, Wblock

Browser

Opens Web browser to Autodesk Express Tools Web sites.

Command line: **Browser**

Express Menu: Web Links ➤ Express Tools Web Site (www.autodesk.com/
expresstools)

Express Menu: Web Links ➤ Express Tools Newsgroup (news://adesknews
.autodesk.com/autodesk.expresstools)

Btrim

Trim entities using nested blocks or Xrefs.

Command line: **Btrim**

Express Menu: Blocks ➤ Trim to Block Entities

Express Block Tools Toolbar Trim to Block Entities

See Also　-Block, Bmake, Trim, Wblock; *Express Tools:* Bextend

Burst

Converts attributes to text entities.

Command line: **Burst**

Express Menu: Blocks ➤ Explode Attributes to Text

Express Block Tools Toolbar Explode Attributes to Text

See Also　Attdef, Ddattdef, Dtext, Explode; *Express Tools:* Gatte

Clipit

Curved clipping of block or Xref with arc, circle, and polyline.

Command line: **Clipit**

Express Menu: Modify ➤ Extended Clip

Express Block Tools Toolbar [icon] Extended Clip

See Also   *Express Tools:* Wipeout

Dimex

Uses a dialog with options to export saved dimension styles to an external file.

Command line: **Dimex**

Express Menu: Dimension ➤ Dimstyle Export...

See Also   Ddim; *Express Tools:* Dimin

Dimin

Uses a dialog to import dimension styles saved as a .dim file into the current drawing.

Command line: **Dimin**

Express Menu: Dimension ➤ Dimstyle Import...

See Also   Ddim; *Express Tools:* Dimen

Expressmenu

Loads the Express Tools menu.

Command line: **Expressmenu**

See Also   Menu, Menuload, Menuunload

Expresstools

Loads the Express Tools library, appends the search path to your profile, and adds the Express menu to the menu bar.

Command line: **Expresstools**

See Also   Menu, Menuload, Menuunload, Profile

Extrim

Allows multiple trimming for a polyline, line, circle, arc, ellipse, text, Mtext, and attribute definition objects.

Command line: **Extrim**

Express Menu: Modify ➤ Cookie Cutter Trim

Express Standard Toolbar Toolbar 🔲 Extended Trim

See Also   Extend, Trim; *Express Tools:* Bextend, Btrim

Fullscreen

Maximizes the AutoCAD display screen removing the title and menu bars.

Command line: **Fullscreen**

Express Menu: Tools ➤ Full Screen AutoCAD

See Also   Fullscreenoff, Fullscreenon, Fullscreenoptions; *System Variables:* Acet-fscreen-status, Acet-fscreen-toggle

Fullscreenoff

Toggles off Fullscreen mode.

Command line: **Fullscreenoff**

See Also   Fullscreen, Fullscreenon, Fullscreenoptions; *System Variables:* Acet-fscreen-off

Fullscreenon

Toggles on Fullscreen mode to maximize the AutoCAD display screen.

Command line: **Fullscreenon**

See Also   Fullscreen, Fullscreenoff, Fullscreenoptions; *System Variable:* Acet-fscreen-on

Fullscreenoptions

Displays dialog to show status bar for Fullscreen mode.

Command line: **Fullscreenoptions**

See Also   Fullscreen, Fullscreenoff, Fullscreenon; *System Variable:* Acet-fscreen-options

Gatte

Edits attribute block values globally.

Command line: **Gatte**

Express Menu: Blocks ➤ Global Attribute Edit

Express Block Tools Toolbar ⬚ Global Attribute Edit

See Also   Attedit, -Attedit; *Express Tools:* Burst

Getsel

Collects objects to form a selection set.

Command line: **Getsel**

Express Menu: Selection Tools ➤ Get Selection Set

See Also   *Express Tools:* Sstools

Julian

Converts AutoCAD Julian dates/calendar dates.

Command line: **Julian**

Laycur

Changes layer of selected object(s) to current layer.

Command line: **Laycur**

Express Menu: Layers ➤ Change to Current Layer

Express Layer Tools Toolbar ⬚ Change to Current Layer

See Also   Ai_molc, Layer, -Layer, Properties

Laydel

Deletes and purges objects and their assigned layers.

Command line: **Laydel**

Express Menu: Layers ➤ Layer Delete

See Also   Dellayer, Layer, -Layer, Linetype, -Linetype, Purge, Rename, Style

Layfrz

Select object(s) to freeze their layer(s).

Command line: **Layfrz**

Express Menu: Layers ➤ Layer Freeze

Express Layer Tools Toolbar Freeze Object's Layer

See Also   Layer, -Layer, Properties

Layiso

Select object(s) to only display or isolate their layer

Command line: **Layiso**

Express Menu: Layers ➤ Layer Isolate

Express Layer Tools Toolbar Isolate Object's Layer

See Also   Layer, -Layer, Properties

Laylck

Select object(s) to lock their layer.

Command line: **Laylck**

Express Menu: Layers ➤ Layer Lock

Express Layer Tools Toolbar Lock Object's Layer

See Also   Layer, -Layer, Properties

Laymch

Matches layer of selected object.

Command line: **Laymch**

Express Menu: Layers ➤ Layer Match

Express Layer Tools Toolbar Match Object's Layer

See Also   Layer, -Layer, Matchprop, Painter

Laymrg

Reassigns selected objects to a different layer, and then purges original layer(s).

Command line: **Laymrg**

Express Menu: Layers ➤ Layer Merge

See Also   Layer, -Layer

Layoff

Select object(s) to turn off their layer(s).

Command line: **Layoff**

Express Menu: Layers ➤ Layer Off

Express Layer Tools Toolbar 💡 Turn Object's Layer Off

See Also   Layer, -Layer, Properties

Layon

Turns on all layers.

Command line: **Layon**

Express Menu: Layers ➤ Turn All Layers On

See Also   Layer, -Layer, Properties

Laythw

Thaws all layers.

Command line: **Laythw**

Express Menu: Layers ➤ Thaw All Layers

See Also   Layer, -Layer, Properties

Layulk

Select object(s) to unlock their layer(s).

Command line: **Layulk**

Express Menu: Layers ➤ Layer Unlock

Express Layer Tools Toolbar 🔓 Unlock Object's Layer

See Also Layer, -Layer

Lman/-Lman

Helps you to save and restore layer configurations based on various options into "layer states" in your drawing from a dialog or command line. Exports and imports saved settings from a .lay file. You can also edit, delete, and rename layer configurations.

Command line: **Lman**, **-Lman**

Express Menu: Layers ➤ Layer Manager...

Express Layer Tools Toolbar 🗾 Layer Manager

See Also Layer, -Layer, Script

Lsp

Displays AutoLISP commands at the prompt: **?**, **Commands**, **Functions**, **Variables**, and **Load**.

Command line: **Lsp**

See Also AutoLISP

Mkltype

Creates custom linetypes using selected object(s) in drawing.

Command line: **Mkltype**

Express Menu: Tools ➤ Make Linetype

See Also Layer, -Layer, Linetype, -Linetype

Mkshape

Creates custom shape definitions using selected object(s) in drawing.

Command line: **Mkshape**

Express Menu: Tools ➤ Make Shape

See Also   Load

Mocoro

Combines **Move**, **Copy**, **Rotate**, and **Scale** into a single command.

Command line: **Mocoro**

Express Menu: Modify ➤ Move Copy Rotate

Express Standard Toolbar ▨ Move Copy Rotate

See Also   Copy, Grips, Move, Rotate, Scale

Mpedit

Edits multiple polylines.

Command line: **Mpedit**

Express Menu: Modify ➤ Multiple Pedit

Express Standard Toolbar ▨ Multiple Pedit

See Also   Pedit, Pline

Mstretch

Allows multiple selection windows for stretching objects in one operation.

Command line: **Mstretch**

Express Menu: Modify ➤ Multiple Entity Stretch

Express Standard Toolbar ▨ Multiple Entity Stretch

See Also   Change, Extend, Grips, Lengthen, Stretch, Trim

Ncopy

Makes copies of objects nested in Xref or block objects.

Command line: **Ncopy**

Express Menu: Blocks ➤ Copy Nested Entities

Express Block Tools ⬚ Copy Nested Entities

See Also   Bmake, Copy, Wblock, Xlist, Xref

Pack

Copies files associated with a drawing to specified directory; useful for Xref exchanges.

Command line: **Pack**

Express Menu: Tools ➤ Pack 'n Go...

Express Standard Toolbar ⬚ Pack 'n Go

See Also   Xref

Pljoin

Joins nonintersecting multiple polylines using a single selection set.

Command line: **Pljoin**

Express Menu: Modify ➤ Polyline Join

See Also   Pedit, Pline

Qlattach

Attaches a leader line to selected Mtext, tolerance, or block reference objects.

Command line: **Qlattach**

Express Menu: Dimension ➤ Leader Tools ➤ Attach Leader to Annotation

See Also   Ddim, Leader, Qleader; *Express Tools:* Qlattachset, Qldetattachset

Qlattachset

Automatically attaches leader lines to selected Mtext, tolerance, or block reference objects.

Command line: **Qlattachset**

Express Menu: Dimension ➤ Leader Tools ➤ Global Attach Leader to Annotation

See Also Ddim, Leader, Qleader; *Express Tools:* Qlattach, Qldetattachset

Qldeattachset

Detaches leader line(s) from selected Mtext, tolerance, or block reference object.

Command line: **Qldeattachset**

Express Menu: Dimension ➤ Leader Tools ➤ Detach Leaders from Annotation

See Also Ddim, Leader, Mtext, Qleader; *Express Tools:* Qlattach, Qlattachset

Redir

Executes hard-coded path search and replace options for Xrefs, images, shapes, styles, and Rtext.

Command line: **Redir**

Express Menu: Tools ➤ Path Substitution

See Also *Express Tools:* Redirmode

Redirmode

Displays dialog to set mode type for **Redir** command: Styles, Xrefs, Images, and Rtext.

Command line: **Redirmode**

See Also *Express Tools:* Redir

Rtedit

Text editor for Rtext objects.

Command line: **Rtedit**

See Also Rtext, Rtextapp

Rtext

Imports ASCII test files and diesel expressions into drawing as text or Mtext objects.

Command line: **Rtext**

Express Menu: Text ➤ Remote Text

See Also Dtext, Text, Mtext, Rtedit, Rtextapp

Rtextapp

Allows you to specify a text editor for **Rtedit**.

Command line: **Rtextapp**

See Also Rtedit, Rtext

Revcloud

Offers options to display arcs, and then draws arc segmented revision clouds on current layer by dragging cursor and forming a closed shape.

Command line: **Revcloud**

Express Menu: Draw ➤ Revision Cloud

Express Standard Toolbar Revision Cloud

See Also Arc

Showurls

Opens a dialog listing all URLs in current drawing and provides options to display, find, replace, or edit them.

Command line: **Showurls**

Express Menu: Tools ➤ Showurls

Express Standard Toolbar Show URLs

See Also Hyperlink, -Hyperlink, Hyperlinkoptions

Sstools

Invoke with an editing command to exclude selected drawing objects.

Command line: **Sstools**

Express Menu: Selection Tools ➤ 'exw (for window exclusion)

Express Menu: Selection Tools ➤ 'exc (for crossing window exclusion)

Express Menu: Selection Tools ➤ 'exp (for previous exclusion)

Express Menu: Selection Tools ➤ 'exf (for fence exclusion)

Express Menu: Selection Tools ➤ 'exwp (for window polygon exclusion)

Express Menu: Selection Tools ➤ 'excp (for crossing window exclusion)

See Also *Express Tools:* Getsel

Ssx

Creates a previous selection set.

Command line: **Ssx**

Superhatch

Opens a dialog with options to create a hatch pattern using an image, block, Xref, or wipeout object.

Command line: **Superhatch**

Express Menu: Draw ➤ Super Hatch...

Express Standard Toolbar Super Hatch

See Also Bhatch, -Bhatch, Boundary, -Boundary, Hatch, -Hatch

Textfit

Expands or shrinks text object(s) based on the text's base point.

Command line: **Textfit**

Express Menu: Text ➤ Text Fit

Express Text Tools 🔤 Text Fit

See Also   Change, Properties; *Express Tools:* Textmask, Textunmask

Textmask

Hides entities behind a text or Mtext object with an option to set the offset distance.

Command line: **Textmask**

Express Menu: Text ➤ Text Mask

Toolbar: Express Text Tools

Tooltip: 🔤 Text Mask

See Also   Dtext, Text; *Express Tools:* Textfit, Textunmask

Textunmask

Removes the mask created using **Textmask** for text and Mtext objects.

Command line: **Textunmask**

Express Menu: Text ➤ Unmask Text

See Also   Dtext, Text, Xclip; *Express Tools:* Textfit, Textmask

Tframes

Toggles on and off image and wipeout frames.

Command line: **Tframes**

See Also   Dtimage; *Express Tools:* Wipeout

Ttc2ttf

Converts TTC TrueType font files to TTF files.

Command line: **Ttc2ttf**

Txt2mtxt

Changes selected text to Mtext.

Command line: **Txt2mtxt**

Express Menu: Text ➤ Convert Text to Mtext

See Also   Dtext, Mtext, Text; *Express Tools:* Burst, Txtexp

---

Txtexp

Changes text and Mtext to lines and/or arcs, allowing their elevation and thickness to be edited.

Command line: **Txtexp**

Express Menu: Text ➤ Explode Text

Express Tools Text [ABCD] Explode Text

See Also   Dtext, Mtext, Text; *Express Tools:* Burst

Wipeout

Hides entities defined by a polyline for display and plotting. Wipeouts in Paper Space used for objects in Model Space are ignored during plotting.

Command line: **Wipeout**

Express Menu: Draw ➤ Wipeout

Express Standard Toolbar [ABCD] Wipeout

See Also   Xclip

Xdata

Specifies.an application name to attach extended entity data (Xdata) to selected object(s).

Command line: **Xdata**

Express Menu: Tools ➤ Xdata Attachment

See Also   Dblist; *Express Tools;* Xdlist, Xlist

Xdlist

When an application name is specified, it displays the Xdata associated with an object.

Command line: **Xdlist**

Express Menu: Tools ➤ List Entity Xdata

See Also   Dblist; *Express Tools:* Xdata,Xlist

Xlist/-Xlist

Displays dialog with entity information nested in external references or blocks.

Command line: **Xlist**, **-Xlist**

Express Menu: Tools ➤ List Xref/Block Entities

Express Block Tools 🗐 List Xref/Block Entities

See Also   *Express Tools:* Xdata, Xdlist

Xpath

Opens dialog offering options to redefine Xref paths for one or more drawings.

Command line: **Xpath**

Express Menu: Tools ➤ Edit Xref Paths

See Also   Xattach, Xref

Index

Note: Throughout this index *italics* page numbers refer to figures; **bold** page numbers refer to primary discussions of the topic.

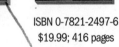